THE DUEL
IN EUROPEAN HISTORY

THE DUEL
IN EUROPEAN HISTORY

Honour and the Reign of Aristocracy

V. G. KIERNAN

OXFORD UNIVERSITY PRESS

1989

Oxford University Press, Walton Street, Oxford OX2 6DP

Oxford New York Toronto
Delhi Bombay Calcutta Madras Karachi
Petaling Jaya Singapore Hong Kong Tokyo
Nairobi Dar es Salaam Cape Town
Melbourne Auckland

and associated companies in
Berlin Ibadan

Oxford is a trade mark of Oxford University Press

First published 1986 by Oxford University Press
First issued as an Oxford University Press Paperback 1989

British Library Cataloguing in Publication Data
Kiernan, V.G.
The duel in European history: honour
and the reign of aristocracy
1. Dueling—Europe—History
I. Title
394´.8´094 CR4595.E85
ISBN 0–19–285128–4

Library of Congress Cataloging in Publication Data
Kiernan, V.G. (Victor Gordon), 1913–
The duel in European History: honour and the reign
of aristocracy/V.G. Kiernan.
p. cm.
Bibliography: p.   Includes index.
1. Dueling—Europe—History.   2. Dueling in literature.
3. Aristocracy—Europe—History.   I. Title.
CR4595.E85K54   1989   394´.8´094—dc19   87–28196
ISBN 0–19–285128–4

Printed in Great Britain by
Richard Clay Ltd.
Bungay, Suffolk

TO HEATHER

PREFACE

THE story of duelling has a fascination of its own; it takes on a deeper significance when looked at in its social, evolutionary setting. As a badge of rank, the privilege of duelling was a not unimportant item, down to the beginning of this century, in the panoply of Europe's dominant classes; it was an assertion of their pre-eminence. All corporate claims to superiority and exclusive rights have an unnatural character, and a malign influence on the claimants and on society as a whole; a fact more easily recognized when they are put forward by castes, nations, races, than by classes, in whose case they are too often admitted without question. From the delusive rationality of the medieval trial by combat, the invoking of divine judgement, duelling descended in later times to a complete, scarcely disguised, unreason. It could not be otherwise with an institution cherished by minorities with no rational title to the place they held, in societies distorted and out of joint.

In 1789 the cry for Liberty, Equality, and Fraternity was an outburst from the depths of a social consciousness still haunted by dreams of a golden age long gone by, when mankind, simple and unspoiled, lived in amity. Its echoes were stifled before long, though never entirely silenced. In our day versions of élitism, arguments from sociology or genetics or other cupboards to prove the naturalness and inevitability of the subjection of the many to the few, are still aggressively alive. A study of the long ascendancy of aristocracy may be granted some practical and topical, as well as historical, bearing.

Anyone engaged on a lengthy study must often stand in need of help. My first debt, older than this study itself, is to the writer whose manifold descriptions and discussions of duelling first fired my interest in the subject, Walter Scott. I have devoted a chapter to his thinking about it, a tribute warranted by his place in British literature, his European fame, and his anxious preoccupation with the duel, as a hereditary curse of his class and his civilization. Scott's concern with it is an expression of his more serious side as a novelist, seldom adequately recognized. No other writer had more to say about it, or wrote of it more earnestly.

My second debt is to my wife, for encouragement all through the writing of this book and for valuable aid in the search for materials, especially those relating to her native Canada. Assistance from many others on a miscellany of points is acknowledged in footnotes. I must mention here two allies in particular: my brother, who has been my guide to the Sagas, and Dr Brian Smith, County Archivist of Shetland, indefatigable in giving me the benefit of his rare knowledge of his native region of Scotland, and of his wide historical and literary reading.

V.G.K.

Stow,
February 1987

CONTENTS

ILLUSTRATIONS

I

The Problem of the Duel

Few things, in this so surprising world, strike me with more surprise. Two little visual Spectra of men, hovering with insecure enough cohesion in the midst of the UNFATHOMABLE, and to dissolve therein, at any rate, very soon,—make pause at the distance of twelve paces asunder; whirl round; and, simultaneously by the cunningest mechanism, explode one another into Dissolution; and off-hand become Air, and Non-extant!

Carlyle, *Sartor Resartus* (1838), Bk. II, chap. 8.

THE institution that so astonished Carlyle had a complex history, with roots stretching far down into a manifold past. Primitive man took his revenges as he could, but often in modes prescribed and restricted by custom; the duel was an equally ritualized encounter, but often both less rational and more dangerous. An ancestral form can be found in the Scandinavia of the Vikings and sagas; the barbarian invasions of western Europe brought old Nordic or Germanic customs into inter-action with other elements. Trial by ordeal was widespread, if not ubiquitous, in olden times and might take some of the same forms in Vedic India as in Dark Age Europe; in a feudal Europe ruled by military standards of conduct the ordeal could turn into something much more exceptional, trial by combat. This was inspired by belief, readily cherished by the stronger or luckier, that the outcome was overruled by Providence. It was only gradually that the duel of later times came to be completely secularized, and winning or losing were seen to bear no relation to divine or any other justice.

Trial by battle between members of the knightly class could run on into the jousting of later medieval Europe, single fights that might take place on their own or under the auspices of the tournament. It was in the Frankish lands of north-western Europe that full-blown ideas of chivalry found their outlet in the tourney and in crusading. They blended with the consciousness of a dominant people, or the dominant class it gave birth to, bestriding the stage and posturing before its conquered subjects. In modern times Poland was to be known for the chivalric follies of a nobility which boasted itself a different race from the serfs whose backs it lived on. Between the ordeal by combat, intended to determine right or wrong, and the joust, an exhibition of courage and prowess, the spirit of the modern duel would waver, but with its leaning more and more towards the latter.

Its affiliation was always and everywhere with social groups occupying a pre-eminent and privileged position, or inspired by the striving towards such a position that has become, if not a component of human nature, at least a perennial feature of social behaviour. Man's strongest 'springs of action', beyond the physical and elementary, seem to have been desire for inclusion in a group with some special title to respect, and for a place of influence within it. In 'civilized' or class-divided times this is an impulse that easily turns into desire for power, ability to extort rather than to earn, to be feared rather than respected. Primitive man wants to be looked up to by women, and to exploit their labour; this duality has run through history; pursuit of superior status has kept pace with accumulation of wealth. In all heroic times, as they may be called, men in Highland huts or baronial castles have fixed their ambitions on renown, prominence, display, and have valued themselves on their places in a hierarchy of military cast.

If power and wealth have gone hand in hand, they have wished to claim kinship also with virtue, or merit, of a kind proper to their station. An Athenian gentleman was known honorifically as *kalos kai agathos,* 'fine (physically or morally) and good'; Cicero's friends, the oligarchs of the Roman republic, were the *optimi,* or *optimates,* 'the best men'. 'Aristocracy', the rule of the finest, came into medieval literature through translations of Aristotle, and by the seventeenth century could be used to denote a highest class; in the next century 'aristocrat' followed.

Some dominant groups, or ruling classes as Marx would call them, have seen it as their duty to set a norm for the masses to emulate so far as they are capable. This may be said particularly of the mandarins with their Confucian outlook and time-honoured maxim that 'As the wind blows, the grass will bend'. Others have adopted standards of conduct from which the masses have been excluded, as in Europe they were from duelling. An ascendancy which instead of growing up within a society has been superimposed on it from outside, as was the case to a considerable extent through a great part of European history, is likelier to belong to the second pattern. This goes too with the contrast between the moral principles of Confucianism, or Islam, intended for all, and those of official Christianity, designed chiefly for the lower orders, including women.

What has come to be called 'élitist' thinking has found a congenial soil in all class societies. The entire ordering of the universe, an English writer declared in 1662, proves that some elements must stand higher than others; nobility and gentry are naturally entitled to elevation to high posts.[1] In 1857 a Spanish conservative laid down that the dull-witted masses should always be subject to the enlightened minority, just as matter is inferior to spirit.[2] 'Élitism', however, only curdled into a distinct political theory when Europe came to be haunted by the spectre turned loose by Karl Marx, and philosophers had to be found to conjure it away. Ruling classes had to be legitimated, presented as permanently necessary to society instead of obstacles to be swept from the path of progress. Pareto's vast treatise on sociology has been called 'a gargantuan retort to Marx', a polemic whose over-ambitious purpose prevented it from being the useful supplement to Marxism it might have been.[3]

With class conflict astir there could be little prospect of the masses docilely following any wholesome example set to them. In élitist theory the upper class admits individuals from below, as useful recruits, but stands always apart from the many-headed beast, controlling it by force or manipulation more than by persuasion. Mosca, the first systematizer, thought in typical conservative style of human nature as full of 'wicked instincts': really this was the theologians' original sin over again.[4] 'Man is always the same, even in little things, through the ages.'[5]

Writers of this school shifted the emphasis from economic to political relations, from class struggle to political management; Mosca called his élite 'the political class'. He and Pareto, both Italians, in a country lacking an authentic aristocracy, were more free than many others to look round for alternatives; but whereas Mosca made a serious, often instructive, effort to learn from world history, Pareto ignored the past, and all questions of origins. Another mark of Mosca's superiority shows in his far less indulgent approach to Fascism. But all élitist theory can be seen as a preparation for fascist rule, a pessimistic abandonment of bourgeois thinking in its heyday. A class confidently in power, or coming close to it, can convince itself that its prosperity will benefit all. Even feudalism, with its ally the Church and their proclaimed ideal of chivalry, could savour the flattering belief. By the late nineteenth century its successors could do so no longer.

Instead Pareto relied on coercion to maintain the social equilibrium. Mosca came less willingly to the 'grave and terrible conclusion' that wars have to be fought now and then, to justify the standing armies which alone can keep society from degenerating.[6] Ruling classes of

[1] Peacham, I, 13.
[2] Andrés Borrego, *Lo que ha sido, lo que es, y lo que puede ser el Partido Conservador* (Madrid, 1857), 50–1.
[3] Pareto, Editor's Introd., 77–8.
[4] S. Hook, in Meisel (ed.), 137.
[5] Mosca, 85.
[6] Ibid. 242–3.

military origin, as most of Europe's have been, are always predisposed to think the same. Mosca rejected their claim to the military virtues as a birthright, but he thought them likely to be more long-lived than mere plutocracies; Venetian merchant-princes, he pointed out, commanded armies and fleets.[7] Such classes did preserve a spirit akin to military discipline and *esprit de corps*; the duel was one of its guardians.

Weber's concept of classes or social strata forms a valuable caveat for Marxists, though it need not be deemed irreconcilable with their tenets. He stresses that the homogeneity of all such sections of society is 'highly relative and variable'. It is not determined solely by property or income.[8] Officers, or students, do not all have the same amount of money to spend, but they share a common status, 'because they adhere to the same mode of life in all relevant respects'.[9] There is some overstatement here; and as regards what Marx thought of as 'classes', as distinct from Weber's 'status groups', their leading ranks can be defined well enough in terms of property and power; but they regularly attract to themselves satellites, less well endowed groups that have some affinity, real or fancied, with them. It is the higher that benefit from the linkage. As examples we may think of the upper and lower nobility of modern Europe, and the high finance and humble shopkeeping of today. And just as Marx pointed out that the dominant class of a nation shapes much of the ideology accepted by the rest, so within a class the thinking of the top group is accepted at the subsidiary levels.

In this country G. D. H. Cole was critical of the Marxist doctrine of 'ruling classes', but found the 'élite' substitute wavering and uncertain. He pointed out that English had no equivalent term of its own, and the borrowed French term—earlier used of 'high society'—retained an awkward foreign flavour.[10] Englishmen with no debt to Marx may have been helped by their traditional reverence for the peerage to take the existence of a ruling class for granted, just as their empire made them believe in ruling races. Another English sociologist, Bottomore, agrees with Gramsci that Mosca's ideas were puzzlingly indistinct, and while critical of some aspects of Marx's identification of power with property he concludes that some social structures have corresponded closely enough with Marx's model. In particular he applies this to the feudal state in Europe: 'the nobility of the *ancien régime* does come close to the ideal type of a ruling class'.[11]

What protects an ascendancy, what thoughts, habits, culture, lend

---

[7] Ibid. 64, 246.
[8] Weber, ed. Eldridge, 87.
[9] Ibid. 91.
[10] Cole, 102–4.
[11] Bottomore, 26–9.

a ruling class cohesion and nourish its inner life, is a question on which neither Marx nor his élitist opponents shed much light. Its bedrock is economic power, but in order to pose impressively to itself and the world it must have both an ideology, however jejune or flimsy, and self-imposed standards of behaviour. This applies in a special way to the exceptional case of a ruling class that is also a governing class. Usually administration has been delegated, to a monarchy or a bureaucracy. Republican Rome with its city-state origin and land-owning patricians is one grand exception; another is western Europe in feudal times, which in many ways long outlasted the Middle Ages. Feudal rule could only be dispersed, uncentralized; it had all the stronger need of customs and convictions to keep it intact.

Among these, the duel is an institution little noticed by writers on aristocracy and élitism, but deserving close scrutiny. It came naturally to Weber's mind when he was arguing that within the same social group, and even by the same individual, contradictory 'systems of order' may be recognized. He chose the instance of a duellist, who acts on a code of honour, but by keeping his act secret, or by surrendering after it to the police, takes account also of the law which forbids it.[12] Pareto held that 'violence has supreme human value in and by itself'. He might have been talking of the duel when he declared that 'A human being who is afraid to return blow for blow ... places himself by this attitude at the mercy of his enemy'.[13] At all events such a mode of thinking derived easily enough from a society whose ruling groups indulged so often in wars, and privately in duels; the same can be said of the cult of senseless bellicosity that Nietzsche lapsed into in his later years.

There is another aspect of élitism to which the duel can easily be related. Pareto laid much emphasis on the irrational, and on the false reasonings designed to cover it. He was not desirous of sweeping it away: on the contrary he held that the running of public affairs cannot be based in any exclusive way on rational decisions. Ritual, a non-logical factor, has an appreciable part in maintaining the tone of society.[14] Any doctrine of aristocracy must itself contain much of the irrational. It may prescribe that our laws should be made for us by hereditary legislators, a notion on a par with the Eastern credulity which reveres the remote descendants of a holy man. A streak even of insanity can hardly be denied a place as one component of the human make-up, an unreason reaching its collective climax in war, and in individual conduct exhibiting itself as forcibly in the duel as anywhere

[12] Weber, ed. Parsons, 114–15.
[13] Meisel (ed.), Introd., 32, 34.
[14] T. Parsons, in Meisel (ed.), 87.

else. Fascism has been the culmination of a widespread willingness in the past hundred years to accept and welcome all this, to denigrate reason and exalt instinct.

More soberly an Edinburgh reviewer of 1813 met the Benthamite argument of utility by counterposing 'prudence' with 'sensibility', idealism, enthusiasm. Passions are intermittent, he wrote, while prudent self-interest works so steadily that economics has acquired 'the character of an exact science'. It is necessary for national well-being, but we must look elsewhere for what makes social life worth living, creates culture, inspires heroism. 'A coarse and brutish selfishness is the natural vice of the great majority of men'; sentiment, generous emotion, are far rarer, but they have the grand, incalculable vitality of a thunderstorm.[15] In the Edinburgh of 1813 duelling was still very much in vogue, and could claim a full share of both the venturous rashness and the superb destructiveness that a storm may symbolize.

It was amidst the chronic warfare of the sixteenth and seventeenth centuries that the modern duel took shape. During that time of transition from medieval to modern, State power and the reign of law were being established by absolutist monarchy; but aristocracy, its half-brother, survived in altered guise, a permanent anachronism, and often canker, in the life of Europe. Private warfare between baronial families or factions was suppressed with difficulty; in France in the second half of the sixteenth century, with religious combustibles added, it flared up into civil war. Madrid in the next century was still disturbed by brawling among noblemen and their retinues; in disorderly Poland much later still enemies with their followers or fellow-clansmen carried on mass raids like the one described in Mickiewicz's epic poem *Pan Tadeusz*. Compared with these manifestations of the unruly aristocratic temper, the duel can be viewed as an advance towards a more limited trespass on law and order. It can be viewed too as a more decent reprisal than assassination, the poisoning of opponents for instance so much a matter of use and wont in the Italy of the Borgias.

Duelling was first formulated and elaborated in Italy; it was quickly taken up in France, whose soldiers saw so many campaigns in Italy, and from there by stages it spread over Europe. Its name, *duello*, came from the archaic Latin *duellum*, war, used in medieval times for judicial combats and seemingly misunderstood to mean conflict between two men. In French and then English it became 'duel'; Shakespeare speaks of a 'duellist'. Both by law and by religion the practice was often heavily frowned on, if also often winked at, the more readily as it gradually took on a more refined character. An elaborate etiquette was upheld

[15] Anon., review of Mme de Stael, *De l'Allemagne*, *Edinburgh Review* (Oct. 1813), 151–3.

by 'seconds', when these ceased to take part in the fray alongside of their principals. Informally tolerated, it was most at home in the more progressive countries, where aristocratic values were defending themselves under pressure from a more modern and encroaching social order. Eighteenth-century enlightenment threatened to undermine it, yet even after the French Revolution's thunderous condemnation of everything feudal or aristocratical, the ensuing twenty years of European war seemed to revive and reinvigorate it, as though with the smell of fresh blood. It lingered on in Britain to near the middle of the nineteenth century, on the continent until the deluge of the Great War made bloodshed over petty private grudges meaningless. Meanwhile it had been carried overseas, especially to the Americas, by the expansion of Europe.

What has been remembered of the duel has been mostly of an anecdotal kind. It may be surmised that a good many of the countless stories connected with it lost nothing in the telling and retelling; some have a decidedly novelistic flavour. Encounters frequently involved personalities in the public eye, or had some special feature, dramatic or bizarre, that ensured their being often recalled. Jarnac's feat in 1547 of putting La Chastaigneraye out of action by hamstringing him with two cunning strokes may be not easy to visualize, but it passed into the French language: the *coup de Jarnac* came to stand for any tricky mode of attack. In 1643 there was vast excitement in Paris over a fight on the Place Royale between descendants of two protagonists of the Wars of Religion, a Coligny, who was wounded and defeated, and a Duc de Guise. Londoners were titillated in a different way when Wilkes the demagogue and Lord Talbot, who complained of having been libelled, discharged their horse-pistols at eight yards, and managed to miss each other. In 1861, when the duel was verging towards its decline, two spirited Frenchmen helped to reduce it to absurdity by fighting with swords over a point of musical criticism.[16]

Duels have real importance at times in political or civic life. In January 1668 London was all agog at news of a fight between the leading figure in Charles II's cabal, the Duke of Buckingham, and the Earl of Shrewsbury, whose wife was Buckingham's mistress; the ill-used husband was mortally wounded. 'This will make the world think that the King hath good councillors about him', Pepys wrote in his diary, 'when the Duke of Buckingham, the greatest man about him, is a fellow of no more sobriety than to fight about a whore.'[17] Britain's burgeoning empire in India was shaken by a duel in 1780, during the second war with Mysore, between its first Governor-General, Warren Hastings,

---

[16] Steinmetz, ii. 174.
[17] Pepys, 17–18 Jan. 1667/8.

and his rancorous opponent in the council, Sir Philip Francis. Hastings'
bullet was the better winged of the two, but he was, as Macaulay said
in the famous essay on him, jeopardizing the whole British position in
Asia, which without him might have collapsed at that critical juncture,
as British power in the American colonies was doing.

Americans won their independence without shaking off all the social
or moral trammels of their colonial history. In 1804 their Vice-President, Colonel Burr, shot and mortally wounded Alexander Hamilton,
the nation's most eminent citizen and one of its founding fathers, on a
ledge across the Hudson River from New York; it was a coign where
other men of mettle found a conveniently private meeting-place. In
September 1809 Britain's foreign secretary and later premier Canning
had an encounter on Putney Heath with the bungling war minister
Castlereagh, who was resentful of his colleague's efforts to jockey him
out of the cabinet. An undisclosed factor may have been that the storm-
tossed remnants of the expeditionary army sent to Spain under Sir John
Moore had been straggling back to Britain and stirring much public
sympathy; Lady Castlereagh accused Canning of proposing to her
indignant husband a scheme for putting the blame for its defeat on the
dead Moore, and making him the scapegoat.[18] Canning was wounded
at the second shot, both resigned, a new government had to be formed.
Meanwhile Napoleon's forces were pushing down from northern into
southern Spain, and Austria, Britain's other ally, was reeling under the
hammer-blow of Wagram. A century later, only a few years before the
First World War, the government of the most powerful country in
Europe was jeopardized by an issue of duelling in the German army.

Duelling was a significant strand in the tangled web of European
history, not a mere excrescence. There was no time when it lacked
critics. In the late sixteenth century the outstanding French writer on
the subject, Brantôme, quoted with disapproval some objectors who
proposed that enemies instead of being allowed to fight should each be
made to drink half of a cup of poison, or be turned loose in a cellar
carpeted with razors.[19] More serious threats to duelling were official
bans. Yet it proved tenacious enough to survive centuries of thunders
of the law and lightnings of the Church. It intertwined itself with
politics, and love, and with social habits like drinking and gambling.
As any such prominent institution is apt to do, it entered into a
wide variety of metaphorical turns of speech. In military parlance an
'artillery duel' became a common phrase. Trelawney, the acquaintance
of Shelley and Byron, in a self-dramatizing style typical of him looked
back on a boyhood fight with a raven as 'the first and most fearful duel

[18] Sir John Moore, ii. 394–5.
[19] Brantôme, 166.

I ever had'.[20] Carlyle wrote of Burns's hard lot as an illustration of 'material Fate matched against man's Free-will; matched in bitterest though obscure duel'.[21]

The vast majority of recorded duels survive only as fossil memories; all the heat and passion that filled them has evaporated without trace. Boswell is a rare case of a man in danger of having to fight who set down his tormented feelings from hour to hour, so that we can know intimately how he felt and what he thought. For the most part, in search of such revelations we cannot do better than turn to the many imaginative writers who have tried to conjure up the sensations that duellists of many different sorts, and their friends and enemies, may be supposed to have experienced. The duel lent itself admirably to the requirements of literature, and its fictional value is still being tapped today. For the relationship between literature and life it offers a rewarding case-study. What serious writers or artists have made of it is often more meaningful than the actual fights, most of them vulgarly trivial, some disgustingly brutal. Their ways of looking at it offer much in the way of insight into the manners, the social or moral atmosphere, the self-picturing of the upper classes.

Among the older novelists Smollett is a prominent example. In *Humphry Clinker* (1771) we first see Squire Bramble preventing his nephew Jery from fighting, and later the nephew trying to dissuade his uncle from sending a challenge: the squire is a sensible man of sedate years, who thinks Jery 'as hot and hasty as a Welch mountaineer', yet— as Jery tells a confidant—he is 'one of those who will sacrifice both life and fortune, rather than leave what they conceive to be the least speck or blemish upon their honour or reputation'.[22] Too often 'reputation' meant nothing better than to be known as ready at all times to resent injury or insult with sword or pistol. We see Sir Mulberry Hawk, of *Nicholas Nickleby*, at night after the races carousing with his amiable dupe Lord Frederick Verisopht, who has begun to be stung into resenting his mentor's domineering. At a low gaming-house a dispute breaks out between them, and the tipsy disciple strikes Hawk, who, mad with rage, insists on an immediate fight. They post off with their seconds to a riverside meadow, by 'the avenue of trees which leads from Petersham to Ham House'. Lord Frederick's sensations on his last journey, his disordered brain 'one unintelligible and senseless whirl', make a fine piece of writing, Dickens's imagination stirred to its deepest. The antagonists fire together, and the young man drops dead.[23]

[20] E. J. Trelawney, *The Adventures of a Younger Son* (1831), chap. 2.
[21] 'Burns', in *Scottish Miscellanies*, 22.
[22] *Humphry Clinker*, 11–13, 268 ff.
[23] *Nicholas Nickleby*, chap. 50.

A recent novel by Gore Vidal has narrated afresh the story of Burr and Hamilton. Science fiction has carried duelling to other planets or galaxies. In one ingenious tale a device has been invented to let Adam's pugnacious descendants out there work off their animosities without harm to themselves or others, a 'dream machine' that allows a man to 'engulf himself in a world of his own making'. In a fantasy landscape two men stalk each other, each at once hunter and hunted, until one falls, when both return, tranquillized, to their normal existence.[24]

Europe was a chosen home of the theatre, and the duel, itself strongly theatrical in character, was well adapted to the dramatist's needs, ranging from Mercutio and the tragical down to Bob Acres and the ludicrous. Principals and seconds were actors, carefully conning the parts laid out for them, each word and gesture, ideally at least, carefully calculated for effect. The duel indeed, like the pulpit and the rostrum, must have owed much to the theatre. Man is an imitative creature. It has often been noticed how the cinema, reflecting life with greater or lesser distortion, helps in turn to mould attitudes; how, for instance, young men caught up in wars like that of Vietnam have modelled themselves on their favourite Hollywood heroes. Fiction and stage could induct young men of social strata rising towards gentility, amid the unceasing convection currents of European history, into the patterns of behaviour that their new status would require of them.

Elizabethan drama belonged to an era of exceptionally rapid social change, in the double sense of movement of individuals from one class to another, and of altering mentalities of classes themselves. Single combats abound in its wild medley of situations more or less realistic and beings less or more human. Shakespeare led the way, as in so many other directions, with his Romeo and Tybalt, or his fencing-match between Laertes and Hamlet, a disguised duel so far as Laertes' intentions are concerned. Corneille made use of the theme more deliberately; the duel was in fact a salient one of seventeenth-century French drama. Inevitably it was not long in finding its way into opera, when this took wing. The fatal encounter in *Eugene Onegin* is only the most famous example, and the aria Tchaikovsky gives to Lensky, under the shadow of coming death, breathes a spirit as deeply tragic as the extinction of the light-hearted Mercutio. Like the tragic hero, the duellist was often forced into and destroyed by a collision he had not sought, under the pressure of an unthinking world and its deaf laws.

Duelling riveted the attention of a long line of thinkers. Brantôme brushed aside religious cavilling as 'all right for monks and hermits',[25] but the purpose of his discussion of the duel was to give it a higher,

[24] Bova, 26.
[25] Brantôme, 138.

more chivalrous character. More often than not Europe's judgement was hesitant or contradictory. Shakespeare could see the absurdity of Honour and its heroics as clearly as Falstaff; but his heroes were not free to act on the same logic, and turn their backs on battlefield or duelling-ground. Romeo must avenge his friend, killed fighting pointlessly on his behalf, at whatever risk to himself or his love-quest. Early in the seventeenth century the scholar, jurist, and historian Selden wrote a book on the old trial by combat; he was inclined to think that in some circumstances there is not 'any other measure of justice left upon earth but arms'.[26]

That great moralist Johnson so often seemed willing to find justification for the duel, that Boswell felt obliged to caution his readers against taking any of the sage's dicta on it as 'his serious and deliberate opinion'. Boswell went on to reflect that 'from the prevalent notions of honour, a gentleman who receives a challenge is reduced to a dreadful alternative'.[27] Carlyle, reviewing Boswell on Johnson, was contemptuous of any admiration paid to mindless defiance of death. 'Considered as Duellist, what a poor figure does the fiercest Irish Whiskerando make in comparison with any English Game-cock, such as you may buy for fifteenpence!'[28] Yet in his never-completed work on seventeenth-century England he narrated several duels in detail, and felt constrained to pay tribute to the dauntless resolution they displayed; very much as Hazlitt applauded his pugilist the 'Gas-man', still unyielding after dozens of bare-knuckle rounds had left him a bloody wreck.[29] Scott's young hero Lovel, goaded by the reckless Highlander Captain M'Intyre into taking up a challenge, was a proved soldier, and 'as brave as most men; but none can internally regard such a crisis as now approached, without deep feelings of awe and uncertainty'. He could avoid death or blood-guilt by a single word, but that word would leave him 'a mean dis-honoured poltroon' in the eyes of all, his beloved Miss Wardour among them. Yet when M'Intyre lay at his feet bleeding and remorseful, and Lovel's second urged him to flee—'to stay here is mere madness'—he could only ejaculate 'It was worse madness to have come hither.'[30]

It is more surprising to find Marx and his friend Engels gravely discussing questions of honour and its demands. Both came from the middle classes, and settled in relatively pacific England. They came, however, from a less advanced Germany. Though he might not have passed muster there as a gentleman born, Marx married into an

[26] Selden, *Table Talk*, 62.
[27] Boswell, *Johnson*, iii. 245 n. (1783).
[28] 'Boswell's Life of Johnson', in *English Essays*, 53.
[29] Hazlitt, *Works*, ed. P. P. Howe, xvii (London, 1933), 72 ff.
[30] *The Antiquary*, chap. 20.

ennobled family related to the ducal line of Argyle. Fencing remained his favourite exercise down to his early years in London. He had indulged in student duelling during his time at Bonn, and seems to have had one serious 'meeting'; his attitude to the duel has been called 'curiously ambivalent'.[31]

All human living-together has generated frictions and tensions, a permanent social stock of irritability, often manifesting itself with astonishing brutality when it gets a chance to break out. Every society has needed licensed channels for the overflow of destructive impulses. The Roman arena, the bullfight, cock-fighting, mass sacrifices of animals to Kali, the goddess of destruction, must all have served as purgatives. Dominant classes in particular have always been riddled by internal feuds, which at an ordinary level are useful for keeping their muscles in trim, but at times have run wild and verged on the suicidal, as in the proscription-lists of the late republican oligarchy in Rome, or the baronial conflicts of the late Middle Ages. Duelling reduced such feuds to symbolic proportions, confined them to individuals, and required only a limited number of victims.

Like all combat, the duel leaves us to ask whether human nature is innately violent. But the individual is always conditioned by his social environment, and the duel is an object-lesson in aggression aroused by social incitements, as well as in aggressiveness brought under social regulation. Some masochistic relish for self-punishment may be at work; in martial peoples the fighting instinct often seems to turn inward on itself. Spartan boys whipped themselves, while Roman tourists looked on; British public schoolboys of the empire era submitted as stoically to fagging and flogging. In all prostrations before creed, country, or class, there may lurk an atavistic feeling from the primitive dawn of religion, whispering of blood sacrifice as the demand of tyrannical gods. The duellist risking death to prove his allegiance to a code of honour may be only one special case of a general phenomenon, or malady.

Disputes and hostilities over women have been part of the life of many of the simplest as well as some of the most advanced peoples. Most quarrels in aboriginal Australia belonged to this category; women changed hands so frequently there that its domestic life has been compared to 'an endless French comedy'.[32] But nowhere in the 'civilized' world apart from Europe were women of rank sufficiently emancipated, and entitled to consideration, to influence a custom like duelling. At tournaments it was the bright eyes of ladies, in Milton's phrase, that rained influence and adjudged the prize; in later times they were a usually unseen but always acutely felt audience. How the

[31] Raddatz, 15–16.
[32] Coon, 291.

status of women, of the upper classes chiefly, affected the quality of European militarism is a large subject; the duel affords an opportunity to observe it in a more confined sphere.

Each sex, as well as class, views itself in the mirror of its opposite. As in more pacific walks of life, women could help to bring out the best or worst in man, protectiveness or crude truculence. Bjarni the saga chieftain was reluctant to attack Thorstein, who had killed a dependant of his, but who had a blind father to support; it was his wife's taunts that at length stung him into going out alone to challenge Thorstein.[33] Don Quixote wanted to fight all and sundry to make them acknowledge the charms of his Dulcinea. More laudably a knight-errant professed the defence of hapless dames as one of his prime duties. More realistic, and proof of Shakespeare's belief in the rightness at times of a resort to the sword, is Benedick's challenge to Claudio, after Beatrice's appeal to him—one of the most poignant moments in all Shakespeare—to punish the slandering and death of her cousin. Even Jane Austen, who after all had naval brothers, felt obliged to invent a bloodless duel, when her jilted heroine had a family friend in the army, staid and sensible though he might be, and sigh though the heroine's sister might over the 'fancied necessity'.[34]

Women's respect for physical courage has meant appreciation of a quality they have not been encouraged to cultivate in any like degree; it must have been linked also, through a sense of their need for protection, with an admiration of power, instinctive in the weaker and, even in Europe, very subordinate sex. 'No woman will ever forgive a coward', a character in a Lever novel reflects as he plans to insult the man he hates in the presence of ladies.[35] We seldom hear of protests by wives, never of any concerted effort by women to put an end to the duel. Those of the class addicted to it must have grown up thinking of it as an inescapable duty of their men-folk, like going to the wars, or like childbirth in their own case.

The duel was rooted in, and spread out from, regions of western Europe which were also the hearth and home of a peculiar form of feudal organization. From this arose a protracted ascendancy of aristocratic classes, military by vocation or at least never forgetful of a sword-bearing ancestry, and cherishing or concocting coats of arms full of menacing hands gripping deadly weapons, plumed helmets, rampant beasts, some of them as mythical as some of the ancestors. War came to be invested with a mystic value scarcely known elsewhere; something analogous shows in the duellist's concept of 'satisfaction'. An injured

---

[33] Phillpotts, 202.
[34] *Sense and Sensibility* (1811), chap. 31.
[35] Lever, *A Rent in a Cloud*, chap. 6.

individual was 'satisfied' by being allowed to fight, irrespective of his chances of winning. It must be granted that Italian vendettas and hired bravoes were a good deal more rational as a method of retaliation. Horace tells us of the risks an amorous interloper ran in the Rome of his time; a Roman husband would have judged it lunacy to offer a trespasser an opportunity to do him further damage, with a sword.

'Satisfaction' implied that the supreme injury a man could suffer was the imputation of cowardice, if he failed to show his resentment directly and personally, by resort to arms. In warlike Europe the over-valuation of physical courage grew steadily. 'Coward' and 'cowardice' are words that go back to the thirteenth century, and can be traced to the Latin *cauda*, tail: surely the same association of ideas as in the expression 'to turn tail', or run away. A kindred image, the 'white feather', derived from an idea that cocks with white feathers made poor fighters. Yet despite the excess to which such thinking was pushed, the fact of physical courage as a constituent of moral and intellectual courage, though no substitute for them, could not be overlooked by thinkers. It must underlie Shakespeare's high esteem for the martial virtues. Milton peopled his heaven with angelic warriors. Adam Smith lamented an inevitable decline of warlike spirit in societies softened by civilization; 'a coward, a man incapable either of defending or of revenging himself, evidently wants one of the most essential parts of the character of a man'.[36]

As an institution central for very many years to the philosophy or conventions of élite classes in most of Europe, the duel can be expected to shed light on the nature of a 'class', its psychology and evolution. Over most of the world's more sophisticated regions warfare came to be left as a rule to professional groups, who were welcome to claim a monopoly of hardihood. Feudal China was very early reorganized on a bureaucratic basis; in India the warrior caste of Kshatriyas was relegated to the background by the Brahmins, and its place only partially taken by the newer Rajputs. In the European case, on the contrary, readiness to fight was the badge of the entire élite of nobility or 'gentlefolk'. In terms like 'gentleman', 'gentilhomme', and their cognates, there survives the first meaning of 'gentle': noble, generous, from *gens*, signifying good family descent. Readiness to draw the sword enshrined contempt or defiance of death, for plebeian mortals the king of terrors. It was a standing reminder of the title under which blue blood kept its place. Every superior class, even the most secure, holds over its members the menace of forfeiture of status if they deviate from its prescriptions. Even a Brahmin can lose caste. In Europe, unlike Asia, the property and legal rights of a man of position were safe, but he could only too easily lose his respectable place among his peers.

[36] *The Wealth of Nations* (London 1776; 'World's Classics' edn., London, 1904–8), ii. 423.

Liability to the ordeal of the duel was a burden imposed on itself by the élite as the gage of its right to be considered a higher order. There were times and places where it was a further duty to perform military service and set an example of self-exposure on the battlefield; later on (until the nineteenth century) conscription was limited to the commoners who provided the armies' rank and file, while the duel stood out as a symbolic or moral imperative for their betters. All claims to collective superiority, or exclusive virtue, partake of the sin of hubris, and seem to demand some penalty, some conspicuous mortification, to render them credible in the eyes of the multitude; a compulsion that an instinct of self-torment, if this is indeed part of man's make-up, must render easier. Rajput queens submitted to suttee, and to immolation *en masse* when the enemy was within the gates; often it seems willingly, or with assumed willingness, because their high rank and dignity were bound up with readiness to renounce life when deprived of the submissive respect due to them. Humbler Hindu widows could be tutored to emulate their example. Confucian precepts too could make it incumbent on a virtuous woman to follow her husband to the grave, or sacrifice herself for her parents.[37]

By the ritual of the duel, private resentments were lifted above the merely personal level of revenge; the combatant's honour merged into that of the class to which both he and his antagonist belonged, and to which they were making a joint obeisance. It was this corporate honour that all its members were bound to uphold. Refusing to seek safety by retreating from the sanctions of his code, the duellist epitomized the determination of his class not, under any threat, to abdicate its leading position. Europe was the home also, more than any other region, of 'sport', or hunting, another aristocratic excitement and mode of self-display. In modern England, with no quarry more formidable than a fox, its stalkers had to show their nerve by taking hazardous leaps over fences or ditches; to balk at the challenge of a five-barred gate was only less demeaning than to refuse a challenge to a fight. When elephants tigers became available, hunting could take the form of a contest between lone pursuer and savage beast, with an evident likeness to the duel.

To shirk a duel rendered an individual no longer worthy of membership of his class, and at the same time compromised the reputation and stability of that class. Aristocracy took its stand, when in search of justification, on the community's need for 'leadership', and for protection by an élite dedicated to the cult of Mars. Gentlemen were not to reason why, when called out to fight at daybreak, any more than

[37] M. Elvin, 'Female Virtue and the State in China', in *Past and Present,* 104 (1984).

when called to the colours, however questionable the rights of any particular war might be. A similar note is struck in the Gita when the ancient Indian hero Arjuna is urged on by his divine charioteer, although the battle in prospect is against men whom he has no wish to harm, with the argument that if the Kshatriyas turn away from their vocation of fighting, the dividing-lines of caste will be blurred and all society will fall into confusion.

The duel's irrationality, a symptom of social atavism, did not of itself imply decadence or insignificance. An old class's struggle for survival might indeed generate both energy and talent for manœuvre. How its prestige could be helped by the spectacle of its members seeking one another's lives, oftener than not in defiance of law, may not seem obvious. But men's habitual judgements have been more impressionable than logical, and if duelling did nothing to making a ruling class liked, it might well make it feared for boldness and arrogance. Moreover some underlying sentiments of the duel could be shared by others, outside the boundaries of heraldry. 'Notions of honour ... percolated far down the social order—certainly far beyond the lowest reaches of the nobility'; every corporation or profession in old Europe had its own.[38]

Aristocracy was nowhere so closely sealed off within its charmed circle as an Indian caste. New blood was always filtering in, or waiting for entry. Two entities evolving over a long epoch in close proximity or symbiosis with each other, like nobility and bourgeoisie in Europe, would develop an ambivalent relationship compounded of hate or contempt and respect or admiration. Duelling was one of the things round which such uneasily fluctuating feelings could gather and crystallize. It has been observed how great a debt nineteenth-century Russian literature owed to the stimulating tension in Russian minds between native and foreign, Slavophil and westernizing, ideas. Something like this can be said equally of the tension between antithetical but interacting classes, and can help to explain how the duel came to mean so much to European literature.

With a potent admixture of snobbery, acceptance of the standards of conduct epitomized in the code of honour could help to incorporate middle-class candidates, native or immigrant, in an old aristocracy, or in later times to promote a partnership. It could form one aspect of what has been called the 'invention of tradition', the adjustments by which the *novus homo,* the newcomer to 'good society', is induced to identify himself with its way of thinking and behaving. German student duelling has been pointed to as an instance of how rising new élites can be assimilated into 'pre-bourgeois ruling groups or authorities'; English

[38] Powis, 11–12.

public-school life, with its fisticuffs, supplies another, less sanguinary example.[39] At the same time, in each case, an upper-middle class was finding means, in a nineteenth century of indistinct social limits, to mark itself off from those below.[40]

It is part of what makes man human that he should be capable of a conviction, or at any rate of being impressed by it in others, that life is not worth living at any price. He needs the assurance—illusory it may be—of an impregnable inner self that the outer world cannot tamper with; the *pundonor,* the point of honour, is its boundary-stone. Yet conscience, the dictate of duty, is itself moulded by the world around. A 'person' was originally a mask, then an actor; personality began as a social construct, what we are to others rather than to ourselves. 'Honour' has always a twofold nature, external as well as internal. The word has sometimes stood for the tangible rewards bestowed by society on those who obey its rules: the *cursus honorum,* or sequence of offices to which a public man in Rome was elected, or the 'honour', or fief, bestowed by the crown on a high feudal vassal in England. Taking the abstraction *honour* in its outward sense, of the pressure brought to bear on an individual to behave in a certain fashion, it has very often been no more than a matter of 'saving face', as the Chinese put it.

What society wills may be a mandate from the past, no longer in harmony with men's maturing ethical sense. It is always warped by society's class divisions, which dislocate its standards of conduct, detach them from any all-embracing moral concepts, and overload them with prejudices and interests of a minority. Yet however much distortion the idea of honour suffered from its feudal origins, it could permeate the social whole, as may be seen from common turns of speech like 'word of honour', 'on my honour', 'honour bright', often glibly conventional, but not without true meaning. Honour led soldiers and duellists to quickly forgotten graves, but in other garb it led martyrs to graves sacred to the causes they stood for. 'Set honour in one eye and death in the other': Shakespeare's high-souled Roman conspirator is an illustration of what the oligarchic outlook had to contribute to the progress of all Europeans, as well as to the qualities that enabled Europe to subjugate the world.

Tributaries from the same hilltop may flow into valleys far apart, and feed opposite streams. The irrational has had an immense part in the thwarting of men's better social purposes; yet men have not always been wrong in admiring the recklessly adventurous, like the 'madmen' of Muslim tradition who sacrifice all for love or an ideal. A commentator

---

[39] E. Hobsbawm, in Hobsbawm and T. Ranger (edd.), *The Invention of Tradition* (Cambridge, 1983), 10.
[40] Ibid. 291.

on the Cuban revolution spoke of how Castro found a response in the 'feudal strain in Cuban character', among the most impoverished country-dwellers, 'the mystic bonds of a fellowship of sacrifice' that could carry them out of their cramping daily lives into 'exhilarating dangers, and the taste of nobility'.[41] The duel is a salient instance of how intricately entangled has been mankind's moral history, and by what devious channels its recognition of higher things than personal survival or advantage has evolved.

[41] J. P. Morray, 'Cuba and Communism', in *Monthly Review* (July–Aug. 1961), 24.

2

Ancient and Primitive Analogies

> We set out on our return to Rome by the same way ... nor made we any stay save at Albano, to view the celebrated place and sepulchre of the famous Duelists who decided the ancient quarrel between their imperious neighbours with the loss of their lives. These brothers, the Horatii and Curiatii, lye buried neere the highway, under two ancient pyramids of stone, now somewhat decay'd and overgrowne with rubbish.
>
> Evelyn, *Diary*, February 1645.

FOLKLORISTS have been ferreting out duel motifs in fairy-tales and folk literature. Among some of the materially most backward tribes of South America have been found elaborate codes of honour, heroism, noble revenge, with a heaven awaiting the brave. Early man suffered from chronic food shortages, lack of all physical comforts; by conjuring up the thrills of adventure, love, myth, he could compensate for the poverty and monotony of his existence. He had a brain as potent, though untutored, as any of his descendants; he may have had to spin fantasies in order to give it employment, and fill up the vacancies of life, as a substitute for mental activity yet to come.

Out of this arose the 'mighty opposites' whose collisions remain an enthralling spectacle to this day. Gilgamesh and Enkidu, king and wild man of the desert in the Mesopotamian epic, began their friendship with a wrestling encounter, won by Gilgamesh.[1] In the Finnish epic, the *Kalevala*, a long duelling episode is preceded and followed by contests in spell-weaving;[2] an atmosphere of magic suffuses the whole poem. Most of the twelve labours of Hercules might be called a series of duels with strange beasts or prodigies. Mankind was struggling for its share of earth's living-space, and in folk fancy its animal competitors might easily swell to such dimensions. In the Anglo-Saxon epic the hero Beowulf's sternest contests are with creatures like the water-monster Grendel, and its hideous mother, and in the end he is mortally injured while finishing off a dragon. Hrungir the Nordic ogre laid a wager with Odin as to which had the swifter horse. They galloped into the abode

---

[1] G. S. Kirk, *Myth* (Cambridge, 1970), 136.
[2] *Kalevala. The Land of Heroes*, trans. W. F. Kirby (London, 1936), vol. ii, Runo 27.

of the gods, where Thor grew angry to see an intruder drinking; Hrungir challenged him, and a complicated bout ended in the ogre's death.[3]

Man was at odds with an alien world surrounding him, but men, and human groups, were also at odds with one another. There have been needs and instincts drawing them together, but others pushing them apart, as can be seen in any children's playground. Every Corsican valley had its leading families, always hating one another though able to combine at moments against intruders. In India each village, it has been said, is likely to house two men, who may be of the same family, tirelessly jockeying for the top position.[4] But animosities have not habitually been translated into violent action, among human beings any more than among the animals whom they must have observed and sometimes conceivably may have imitated. An animal seldom kills another of the same species; their fights are often more bark than bite, with what has been called a stylized, 'tournament-like', procedure.[5] Peoples as deeply addicted to warlike activity as some tribes of North America, or Amazonia, seem to have been exceptional, whether quarrels between individuals or clans are in question. In the management of private disputes a desire to economize blood, and avoid social disruption, has often been visible. Fighting has been restricted by convention, as it was in the European duel of later times.

In simple communities the 'set fight' or 'duel', Hobhouse wrote, generally takes place 'under prescribed conditions': it could be deadly, but might take a quite mild form. 'The public or the chief may look on, and act as judges.'[6] Among the Nuer people of the Nile valley men of the same village or band were only allowed wooden clubs as weapons, though men from distant localities, even if they belonged to the same tribe, could fight to the death. As an alternative, graded compensation for injury could be paid.[7] In the Andaman islands resentments were seldom bloodthirsty. Two men might shoot arrows towards each other, wide of the mark,[8] like a pair of European duellists firing in the air. By contrast, quarrels between members of different bands of the Ona people in the Andamans were more businesslike, and wounds or deaths were frequent. A challenger stood naked, dodging and moving forward, while his opponent shot six arrows at him; then, if he were not *hors de combat*, he had the same chance. 'To retreat during this ordeal was a great disgrace.'[9]

[3] Davidson, 41.

[4] R. Jeffrey, *What's Happening to India* (London, 1986), 120–1.

[5] D. Barash, *The Whisperings Within* (1979; Harmondsworth, 1981), 182–3.

[6] Hobhouse, 95. Many examples will be found in Feest's illustrated work on tribal warfare; see e.g. 12, 15, 20, 28, 30.

[7] Lewis, 322.

[8] Coon, 274.

[9] Ibid. 280.

'Duels' among Bushmen collected at a water-hole were likely to begin with 'vociferous verbal battles' and conclude with a ceremony of reconciliation.[10] Australian natives could boast something not very different from a formal duel; most fighting among them seems, however, to have been make-believe. When men squabbled their friends kept them separated until tempers cooled, and a standardized combat, which might take place between women as well as men, ended without rancour.[11] It was when clansmen were uprooted and jumbled together by the white man that frictions might multiply, with graver consequences. Mrs Bates, who for sixteen years ran a camp for strays and remnants, saw much of this. 'Thigh-spearing and duelling were frequent.' She permitted some duels, under her own supervision, because a slight wound was likely to be followed by harmony, whereas tactless interference could lead to smouldering bitterness and worse harm.[12]

Up and down the world various means were found of dispensing with force altogether and diverting animosities into less noxious channels. Commenting on the modest style of living of King Alcinoos and his household in Homer, Kautsky remarked that 'Prince Odysseus does not challenge his rival to a duel, but to a competition in mowing and plowing'.[13] Anthropologists have bestowed the title of 'duel' on a wide range of non-violent contests: rhyming exchanges of wit between Turkish boys, for instance, and the widespread practice of resorting to poetic or musical contests, exercises in mutual abuse instead of blows. 'Banjo duels' took place among some hill-billies in America. Frictions may arise between settlements of Eskimos passing the winter in long-houses, but within each of these 'there is a strong moral compulsion to settle disagreements peaceably', by means of 'a "song-duel", a battle of words, the outcome of which is judged by public opinion'.[14] Once it is over the rivals are expected to be good friends. If Eskimo tempers are too far ruffled, custom among many groups provides for forms of 'regulated combat—wrestling, buffeting, and butting'.[15] 'Flyting', or exchange of gibes (the term survives in Scotland), was part of Scandinavian life too. There is a scurrilous dialogue in one of the legends between the hero Helgi with his friend Atli and a giantess, who keeps it up too long, until daybreak turns her to stone.[16]

Occasionally the European mind has had some inkling that duels

[10] Ibid. 286–7.
[11] D. Lockwood, '*I, the Aborigine* (London, 1963), 142–3; Montagu, 179.
[12] Bates, 215; cf. J. Dewey and J. H. Tufts, *Ethics* (New York, 1908), 63.
[13] Karl Kautsky, *Foundations of Christianity* (London, 1925), 52.
[14] Lewis, 155; cf. Hobhouse, 96 ff.
[15] E. A. Hoebel, 'Song Duels among the Eskimo', in Bohannan, 255, 259.
[16] Phillpotts, 77.

between nations might be conducted on quieter lines. While Tolstoy was serving at Sevastopol during the Crimean War, a fellow-officer, Prince Urusov, 'the best Russian chess-player of his day', suggested to their unresponsive commander that the British might be challenged to a chess match to decide who should occupy a line of trenches that had been bloodily changing hands.[17] In older times collective conflict tended to fall under the same kind of restraints as individual discord. An aboriginal fight in northern Australia in the 1880s started, after long preludings, with three men from each party duelling in pairs, and little harm done; a mêlée ensued, but even this was subject to rules.[18] An observer in New Guinea witnessed a battle consisting of half an hour of confrontation between warriors with blackened faces, feathers, and huge spears, shouting curses, and at dusk withdrawing.[19] Among the Dani people of New Guinea there was chronic fighting, and virile courage was so highly esteemed that a skulker was expected to lose his physical powers, even his eyesight.[20] Despite this philosophy of *Pugno, ergo sum,* losses were very light. Red Indian braves sometimes carried a stick to tap an opponent with during a battle: this 'coup' earned as much applause as a blow with a weapon.

Casualty lists could be further shortened by battles being left to chosen representatives. It became customary in many lands for champions to meet single-handed before an onset, or as a substitute for a general scrimmage. David and Goliath were often thought of in later days as prototype duellists. Dramatic situations dear to the bards could emerge, as in the Germanic *Hildebrandslied* and many legends from other areas where the antagonists turn out to be father and son.[21] A flesh-and-blood warrior, Tamerlane, was faithful to time-honoured tradition when, even in middle age, he would ride out in front of his army and summon the enemy leader to meet him hand to hand.[22] Humbler parallels abound. Among the Maoris, before the white man and his firearms, hostilities were small-scale and desultory, and the issue might be settled by a challenge and single combat, conducted with some degree of chivalry even if tricks like throwing sand in an opponent's eyes were resorted to at times.[23] It was much the same among the Zulus, before Shaka the 'Zulu Napoleon' organized his military machine and put an end to the sporadic sort of 'reluctant warfare' they had been accustomed to.[24]

[17] Maude, i. 121.
[18] Coon, 289–90; cf. Harris, 42–3.
[19] R. T. Hitt, *Cannibal Valley* (London, 1969), 25.
[20] Ibid. 118.
[21] Jackson, 37.
[22] Jack Chen, *The Sinkiang Story* (New York, 1977), 114.
[23] A. P. Vayda, 'Maori Warfare', in Bohannan, 359, 370–1.
[24] Kunene, xv–xvi.

Chosen groups of paladins, instead of single stalwarts, might be allowed to decide the fortunes of the day. The story of the Horatii and Curiatii enshrines a custom of 'representative fighting' among the early Latins, and Herodotus preserves Greek parallels coming down to the sixth century BC.[25] Hard training at running, jumping, fencing, fitted the Chuckchee warrior of Siberia for 'the type of combat he was called upon to fight, the mass duel and the duel of champions'.[26] Arrangements for an encounter with limited forces might be made beforehand: thus, among Malays, clan frictions were sometimes settled by duels, or by battles at agreed times and places. Similar 'duelling battles' took place between small Zulu tribes in their amateur days, with few losses.[27] In 1830 when the Zulu army in its prime came face to face with Mzilikaze's Matabeles, before the clash 'the *izimbongi*, or praise-singers, on both sides started chanting, and the champion warriors rushed out to engage their opponents in single combat'.[28]

Among Highlanders too there was something of a habit of hostilities being entrusted to picked groups, or even to one pair of swordsmen if the ground made it hard for the rest to take up positions. Scott made good use of the match between two sets of thirty fighting-men, from hostile clans, at Perth in 1396, in the presence of King Robert III.[29] Only ten men survived. It was very much like a group-duel, as Scott noted, and the trusted adviser whom each chief had with him when they met before the fray was a kind of second.

On the whole, primitive man appears irascible, but not over-vindictive. To brutalize him further, nature had to be reinforced by social advances, division into higher and lower classes as well as into kinships, and all the consequences that such division would give rise to. The process was early marked by a more inveterate pursuit of the blood feud, as a hereditary duty of revenge. This became as much a part of a clan's collective furnishings as its ownership of land or reverence for ancestors.[30] It could arise at a very precocious stage of development, as among the warlike Blackfoot Indians with whom every killing had to be avenged by a relative, 'even though that relative might know for a certainty that he would be killed in the effort.'[31]

Even in ostensibly pacific China a character in a medieval play can talk of the carrying on of a vendetta as a half-sacred duty of the

[25] Hobhouse, 235.

[26] H. H. Turney-High, *Primitive War* (Columbia, S. Carolina, 1949), 80.

[27] K. F. Otterbein, 'The Evolution of Zulu Warfare', in Bohannan, 354.

[28] P. Becker, *The Rise and Conquests of Mzilikaze* (Harmondsworth, 1979), 157–8.

[29] *The Fair Maid of Perth*, chap. 34.

[30] R. Fox, *Kinship and Marriage* (Harmondsworth, 1967), 52.

[31] *Long Lance: The Autobiography of a Blackfoot Indian Chief* (London, 1976), 62 (apocryphal, but probably well-informed).

lineage.[32] When religions of the more militant sort arose they put a sharper edge on all human malevolences. In many areas of the Muslim world feuding flourished luxuriantly. One of the French officer Ferrier's most lurid impressions of the Afghanistan he travelled through, at daily risk of his life, was the ferocity of its blood feuds; another traveller found that in one part of the country a man might have to stay shut up for years in his stronghold, leaving his wife to manage his affairs.[33]

Addiction to organized violence, growing as a morbid accompaniment of man's progress in destructiveness as well as in some better things, showed also in the training of men and animals to fight each other, or of men to fight animals, or one another, for display. Cockfighting had many homes, and cocks were bred for pugnacity, into demons as insatiable as any human beings. Fights between stallions were avidly watched by Vikings, and by their women.[34] Such cases suggest a latent love of spectacles or fantasies of bloodshed, only waiting for the right environment to awaken it; but often at least it is easy to recognize here an index of social degeneration. Court fiestas in the kingdom of Oudh, that feeble offspring of the senile Mogul empire, consisted largely of mauls between all kinds of creatures from leopards and rhinoceroses down to partridges. An Englishman writing about the kingdom of Oudh shortly before its extinction in 1856 gave the title 'Duello' to the chapters of his book devoted to this subject.[35] Martial's *Liber Spectaculorum* details, along with animal fights, a bout between rival gladiators that clearly had some quality of a duel.[36] Aztec religion was permeated by cosmic conflict between light and dark, heat and cold, south and north, and their deities. 'Gladiatorial combats, often to the death, expressed this idea in ritual.'[37] Others took place between Aztec warriors and their captives, before the latter were sacrificed and, if Marvin Harris is right, eaten.[38] In all these duels any lack of zest in one of the combatants was disgraceful. In the Scottish Highlands a cock that did not show fight was stoned to death,[39] as a man anywhere refusing a challenge was ostracized. In the bullring when the bull showed insufficient ardour the crowd yelled for the *luna*, the crescent-

[32] Liu Jung-en (trans.), *Six Yüan Plays* (Harmondsworth, 1972), 21.

[33] J. P. Ferrier, *Caravan Journeys and Wanderings* (London, 1857; Karachi, 1976), 432 ff.; cf. Sir A. Burnes, *Cabool* (London, 1841; Lahore, 1961), 114, and Richard Curzon on a feud between two districts in Egypt, and annual raidings, in *Visits to Monasteries in the Levant* (London, 1865; London, 1916), 168–9.

[34] M. W. Williams, *Social Scandinavia in the Viking Age* (New York, 1920), 330.

[35] W. Knighton, *The Private Life of an Eastern King* (London, 1855; Oxford, 1921), chaps. 10, 11.

[36] *Selected Epigrams of Martial*, ed. H. M. Stephenson (London, 1903), pp. ix, xi, xxix, 171, 175.

[37] G. C. Vaillant, *The Aztecs of Mexico* (Harmondsworth, 1950), 175.

[38] Harris, 111.

[39] I. F. Grant, *Highland Folk Ways* (London, 1975), 343.

shaped knife used for hamstringing, and the unlucky beast was dragged off to the shambles.

Despite many lingering common features, from Greek and Roman times if not much earlier Europe was diverging from the rest of the world. It was an integral part of this bifurcation that the duel as a distinctive institution was to be specifically European. It was the prerogative of a certain kind of hereditary aristocracy, born in warfare, a class such as outside Europe had only an occasional, fitful growth. In Japan, next of kin in so many ways to feudal Europe, some analogies can be traced. Most bizarre was 'a strange sort of duel' cited by Durkheim in his study of suicide, between two men vying in skilful performance of hara-kiri, a death favourably regarded if not insisted on, in appropriate cases, by public opinion.[40] Parallels have been noted between chivalric ideas engendered by the aristocracies of medieval Europe and old Iran,[41] where Firdausi's epic perpetuated the memory of doughty deeds of bygone kings and cavaliers. Rajputs too as a warrior nobility cherished heroic ideals, and a man whose honour was wounded 'never failed to challenge the offender to a duel'.[42] It may be conjectured that Rajput influence helped to give single combat its vogue in the medieval Hindu kingdom of Vijayanagar in south-central India, always at war with the expansionist Muslims and requiring a warlike spirit equal to theirs.

Heroic manners of the sort that in Europe pointed the way towards the modern duel may have been smothered in Persia, and clipped in India, by Muslim conquest. Islam, though a creed of the sword, fostered an ideology of equality and fraternity, overlaid by the sole form of government known to it, military despotism. Later Iran had no regular duel; men, and it seems even women, might challenge opponents to a wrestling match. Similarly in India, where the medieval sultanate of Delhi tried to suppress all private fighting, competitions in physical endurance and skill took the place of duelling. Wrestling was a favourite diversion of high and low, in which even rulers might take part.[43] Indo-Muslim nobles, however lavishly rewarded, were only *ministeriales*, servants of the state, whereas Rajput chiefs were noble by right of birth and an ancestry stretching back to the sun or the moon. Brantôme knew that the Turks of his day laughed at Christendom's duelling antics. At his uncle La Chastaigneraye's famous encounter with Jarnac, he tells us, many foreign envoys were to be seen in the fashionable audience, including the ambassador of Suleiman the Magnificent, who

[40] Durkheim, 222.
[41] J. S. Critchley, *Feudalism* (London, 1978), 40.
[42] K. M. Ashraf, *Life and Conditions of the People of Hindustan* (Delhi, 1959), 187.
[43] Ibid. 187–8.

was astonished at the king allowing a fight between two of his favourites. Turkish honour, Brantôme concluded, lay in service to the ruler alone: Europeans were better off, being free to engage in either national or personal causes.[44]

A Homeric battle is really a set of grapplings of man with man, a good deal resembling duels; Hector's overthrow by Achilles is very much a duel to the death between two heroes, though they are alone, without seconds or witnesses, and Achilles receives unfair help from Athene. Before it begins the Trojan proposes an honourable pledge that the victor shall hand over his opponent's corpse to his countrymen. Achilles refuses. After all its preliminaries the fight itself is brief, and one must say amateurish.[45] Rubens's sketch of the death of Hector is more impressive. Virgil's Aeneas, invading Italy, settles accounts with the native prince Turnus by the long-drawn single combat, with the gods as well as the rival armies looking on, which ends the poem—as Antony in Virgil's day would have liked to fight it out with Octavian.

Graeco-Roman culture shows no direct forerunner of the modern duel, but it bequeathed to later times elements that were to enter into their make-up, and helped to fashion the social psychology on which duelling could feed. Well-born self-esteem, vigilant regard to conduct in the public eye, the training of youth in martial exercises, the vogue of competitive sports, wrestling and boxing as well as running and charioteering—all had a formative influence on later Europe. Roman history and literature were to be its schoolroom pabulum. Stoical readiness to undergo ordeals was a virtue needed by the duellist, along with the preference of death to dishonour. Shakespeare, and 'noble' Europe at large, were deeply impressed by the 'high Roman fashion' of suicide when life could not be clung to without degradation. Christendom had a 'canon 'gainst self-slaughter' which kept it from eulogizing suicide, as it deterred Hamlet from committing it; but to hazard life in a duel was often next door to a self-inflicted death. It was from classical antiquity that the hypnotic idea of *glory* reached later Europe, however coloured on the way by religious additions. A young man 'who would form his mind to glory', the Corsican hero General Paoli told Boswell, must read Plutarch and Livy rather than any modern writings.[46]

In Spain, and among the Celts and Germans, the Romans found species of duelling practised. A great part of Europe was at one time

[44] Brantôme, 150–1.

[45] *Iliad*, Bk. 22, ll. 245 ff.

[46] *Boswell on the Grand Tour: Italy, Corsica, and France 1765–1766*, ed. F. Brady and F. A. Pottle (London, 1955), 191.

or another Celtic, and some lingerings of the Celtic warrior spirit can be glimpsed in medieval feudal culture, above all in the romanticism of chivalry. This drew heavily on Celtic myth and legend, suffused with the ethos of an early feudalism inspired by the ideal of personal fealty, which could blossom only in a society still rooted in clan life. Norman or Anglo-Norman soldiers of fortune who settled in Ireland or the Highlands inherited the place of an older clan chieftainship, very different from the essentially contractual, legalistic relationship between lord and vassal in mature Franco-Norman feudalism. It was not this, but an older, indefeasible duty of the follower to his chief, a devotion without legal bounds, that could be elevated into fidelity to a code of honour linking all members of a divinely appointed ruling class.

The Mabinogion, for whose sake Tennyson learned Welsh, was compiled in the eleventh century from much older materials. It abounds in single fights. In one story the gallant Peredur is assailed by numerous opponents, who chivalrously attack him one by one.[47] With them, as with the modern duellist, the guiding motive is not desire for victory, but flaunting of personal bravery. An old Irish poem, which may have taken shape about AD 800 as 'The Story of Mac Da Tho's Pig', contains a scene of warriors feasting. It resembles, Nora Chadwick points out, what Diodorus Siculus tells us of the Celts of his time, feasting on vast joints of meat cooked in cauldrons: 'some of the company often fall into an altercation and challenge one another to single combat—they make nothing of death'.[48]

In the Irish epic about the great cattle-raid and the war it brought on between Connacht and Ulster, an aristocratic society not unlike Homer's is portrayed, where warriors fight from two-horse chariots, or on foot. Here too there are rules of fair play, and a man does not expect to have to take on more than one opponent at a time. The most truly heroic episode of a narrative clogged by far too much bardic rigmarole and a plethora of improbable magic, is the duel between Cuchulainn the Ulster champion and Ferdia, the only warrior capable of standing against him. They have learned the arts of war together, and been brothers in arms; each begs the other to remember their old friendship, and not let the conflict part them, and after each successive day's fighting, at a river crossing, they embrace and share their food and medicines and curative spells, until at last Ferdia falls and Cuchulainn is carried away covered with wounds.[49]

---

[47] *The Mabinogion,* trans. G. Jones and T. Jones (London, 1978), 197 ff.; cf. 6, 60, 161–3, 172–3.
[48] Nora Chadwick, *The Celts* (Harmondsworth, 1970), 231.
[49] *The Tain,* trans. T. Kinsella: *the Irish Epic Tain Bo Cuailnge* (Oxford, 1970), 170 ff.

A hand-to-hand fight on the battlefield is described in a poem, 'The Tryst after Death', where the ghost of a war-band leader addresses the woman whose love he won, and whom he carried off, pursued by her angry lord. Their two forces grappled, and the chiefs came face to face:

> We fell by each other,—though it was senseless, it was the encounter of two heroes.[50]

A thousand Irish years later we come on a Mayday mummers' play, English in origin but Irish in spirit, like an echo from the Celtic twilight, where St Patrick falls foul of St George, calls him out in doggerel verse, and inflicts punishment for an insult.[51] Irishmen and Highlanders in modern times had a reputation of ungovernable fondness for duelling.

Part of the Germanic hero's code was a calm defiance of fate, even if what was at stake was 'the maintenance of external reputation rather than internal honour'.[52] Accidental misfortunes were compounded by the duties of revenge imposed on them by their station. Hence many of the tragic threads running through the Eddic poems, as has been observed, with hero or heroine so often caught in a fatal dilemma, between two choices, each destructive.[53] The latter-day duellist, compelled against his will and conscience to take the field, was the heir to a dark curse with its beginnings in the blood-stained cradle of aristocracy.

Unlike the ingenuous folk of more equal societies, the man of blue blood, whose warrant was the sword, could not allow an affront or injury to end in a mere token fight or exchange of abuse. Helgi of the nocturnal 'flyting' perished from a mortal wound after being challenged by a prince. Scandinavia was a simple democracy in course of being feudalized by the rise of the Viking war-leaders, and then of monarchy; its far-flung contacts with Europe, and even Asia, were reflected in the wild jumble of exotic personages and places that throng the sagas. Here too trials of individual strength on the battlefield were a feature of all the epic tales; in an Icelandic saga there is one such between the hero, hoping by it to win a princess and a kingdom, and Soti, champion of King Menelaus of Tartary; soon after this he is pitted against one of King Eirik of Russia's henchmen.[54]

Ordeal by battle was common to all the Germanic peoples, and

---

[50] Kuno Meyer, *Selections from Ancient Irish Poetry* (London, 1928), 9–14. For a European style painting of a Red Indian chief's death in battle see M. L. Benham, *Paul Kane* (Don Mills, Ont., 1977), 49.

[51] Gailey, 60.

[52] Jackson, 28.

[53] Phillpotts, 90–2.

[54] *Göngu-Hrolf's Saga,* trans. H. Pálsson and P. Edwards (Edinburgh, 1980), 166 ff.

served as touchstone of honour, or as settlement of legal disputes. In Scandinavia it had varied forms; the most murderous was the 'girdle-duel', in which the combatants were strapped together and fought with knives to the death. It may have found its way into Saxon or Danish England; the circle of greensward between Penrith and Ullswater known as 'King Arthur's Round Table' has been thought a venue for such encounters. The classic form was the *holm-ganga*, 'island-going', withdrawal by the parties to a spot on an islet. Such episodes are numerous in the sagas, though only one of them contains a detailed account of the procedure. A small square would be marked out with strips of hide or cloth, three furrows along the sides, and at each corner a hazel-post. Each combatant had an assistant who protected him with a shield, and blows were delivered by turns. A wounded man could pay compensation and withdraw; to be forced out of the square was an ignominious admission of defeat.[55] 'Ritual or sacrificial practices' may have played a part, but rather to ward off magical tricks than with any faith in 'divine intervention'.[56] There seems, however, to have been some linkage of ideas between justice and the god of battle; in Iceland this 'official sword-duel' was held close by the meeting-place of the *Thing*, or law-declaring assembly.[57]

A memorial of the custom may be the name 'Battle *Pund*' (pound, enclosure) still given to a circular plot on a small island in the Shetlands.[58] Iceland in its early days was the Wild West of the Scandinavian world. It suffered from a plague of berserkers, lawless freebooters who might prey on a neighbourhood, compelling a farmer for instance to face them sword in hand or to surrender his wife. One ruffian in a scene of an Icelandic saga set in Norway was Ljot the Pale, a vagrant from Sweden who amassed wealth by this kind of duelling. 'He had slain many worthy landowners, whom he had first challenged to wager of battle for their lands and heritages.' A defeated challenger had to ransom himself, or if he were killed his whole property was forfeit. The hero Egil, a historical personage whose grave is still shown in Iceland, undertook to defend a family with a daughter in danger from Ljot. On the island of Vors, where the matter was brought to the test, Ljot was found in a fit of the celebrated berserk fury (often one may guess histrionic), bellowing and biting his shield. Egil was not one

---

[55] P. Foote and D. M. Wilson, *The Viking Achievement* (London, 1970), 380–1; *The Saga of Gisli*, trans. G. Johnston (Toronto, 1963), 66–7. In this story a man buys himself off after losing a leg, and goes about thereafter on a wooden leg.

[56] Foote and Wilson, 379.

[57] Davidson, 58.

[58] Information from Brian Smith, County Archivist of Shetland.

to be scared, and before long Ljot was a dying man, with one leg cut off.[59]

The story of St Patrick and St George at cut and thrust is outdone by one told triumphantly by an Icelandic pagan woman to a missionary—'that Thór had challenged Christ to a duel, and that Christ had not dared to fight'.[60]

[59] *The Story of Egil Skallagrimsson*, trans. W. C. Green (London, 1893), chap. 67.
[60] G. Turville-Petre, *The Heroic Age of Scandinavia* (London, 1951), 85.

3

Europe of the Knights

First of all, knights were created to uphold and defend Christianity. They should not return evil for evil, but rather humbly forgive their enemies. A knight's first duty is to protect the Church, which would be lost without him. We read in the Scriptures that no man dared to ride a horse until knights were created and armed to chastise the wicked.

Joanot Martorell, *Tirant lo Blanc* (1490), XXXIII.

WITH the 'barbarian invasions' which submerged the Roman West, a complex interweaving of old and new into a novel pattern took place; a pattern with scarcely any close parallels in history, the specific European version of feudalism. One determining factor was that the subjugated population had a higher culture than its new masters, who absorbed fragments of it and adopted, however half-heartedly, what had become the official religion of the vanished empire. To maintain their power they had always to stand before their subjects in shining armour; between this and Christianity there was to be a perennial disharmony.

Nobles began as retainers of the men who held sway; they gained before long hereditary possession of the fiefs they were rewarded with, but the code of knighthood which they eventually embraced continued in ideal guise the principles of duty and loyalty, combined with independent self-respect. They kept the privileges and spirit of freemen, when the masses were being reduced to serfdom. Military service was their obligation, instead of the less honourable burden of taxpaying: the terms *miles* or soldier, and knight, were interchangeable. This status, as Pirenne said, 'naturally generalised among them certain mental and moral attitudes', which would later take on more refined outlines.[1] They were borrowing the idea of nobility from those above them; reciprocally, they were carrying upward with them the idea of knighthood, until by 1200 royalty itself was proud to share the accolade.[2] Despite great inequalities among the free, their freedom was a badge

---

[1] Pirenne, 157, 160.
[2] G. Duby, 'The Diffusion of Cultural Patterns in Feudal Society', *Past and Present*, 39 (1968), 7.

to be cherished by all alike, and an ideal which could in time be linked with the Roman republican virtue of liberty.

Every social order suffers from its own specific discords. Feudal Europe was a competitive and rapacious world, and its enmities were frequently embittered by the prevalence of the blood feud; this, inherited from a more primitive past, persisted throughout its history and in some areas long outlived it. Such tenacity might seem to denote firm family solidarity; perhaps it was oftener a turning outward of the animosities always accumulating within a family or kindred, much as nationalism has turned the rancours of class division against others. 'The Middle Ages ... lived under the sign of private vengeance', and regarded this as 'the most sacred of duties', often extending from individuals to their kin.[3] Compensation might be paid as in ancient times, to buy off revengers, but acceptance of it might seem basely mercenary. Feudalism was a system of man-to-man relationships; at every level it was vital to retain the respect of those below as well as above, and this could most effectively be done by a bold response to every challenge.

'In the tales chanted by the minstrels, the nobility found the echo of their passions, elevated to epic grandeur.'[4] In the choir of Naumburg cathedral stand a dozen thirteenth-century statues of benefactors; old tradition reads into two of them a long-forgotten feud, for they are drawing their swords, one hiding his sword-hand in his dress as if to restrain himself.[5] A quarrel at a wedding feast in 1464 between the Extremaduran families of Solis and Monroy led to years of blood-letting over much of southern Spain.[6] In England alone, after the Conquest, did private revenge come under a firm ban. Too much feuding among the Normans might have perilously weakened their sway over the Saxon masses. There was sharp disparity here with Scotland, where it was far longer 'Ere humane statute purged the gentle weal'. The blood feud ran on, drawing its vitality from both Gaelic and Anglo-Saxon past; crime and justice were viewed in much the same light in Highlands and Lowlands.[7]

Enmity between great families inevitably involved their retainers or vassals as well as kindred, and turned into a species of private warfare, which was indeed for long a cherished feudal right. It was the same at bottom as that claimed by the latter-day duellist, of putting himself above the law whenever honour, or pride, called for blood. Attempts

[3] Bloch, i. 125–6.
[4] Ibid. 127.
[5] Information from Prof. H. H. Höhne, of the University of Rostock.
[6] Powis, 59.
[7] Wormald, 60–3.

sponsored by the Church to restrain this lawlessness by a 'Truce' or 'Peace' of God bore little fruit. In the Holy Roman Empire the Golden Bull of 1356 confirmed the right of warfare among the territorial princes who were throwing off any central control. Three days' notice was to be given, a proviso with some likeness to the formalities prefacing a duel.

Reprisals and counter-reprisals would drift down from the nobility, through its lower ranks, and help to keep habits of violence alive among common people. Commoners have often imitated their betters as a way of asserting some degree of equality with them, more than from admiration. Breton peasants in the early nineteenth century, Balzac tells us, were still wearing a broad hat, formerly the ornament of noble heads only, which their ancestors had been proud of acquiring a right to wear.[8] Plebeian versions of organized brawling might be carried on for generations by neighbouring villages. A chapbook story of 1632, 'The Pinder of Wakefield', tells of a high-spirited band of young fellows who were wont to pick quarrels with others of like mettle, and had a midsummer-day encounter with a band from Halifax and Kendal, with cudgels, quarterstaffs, and pitchforks, followed more amicably by football and wrestling.[9]

As an alternative or corrective to unlicensed, unlimited scrimmaging, there was the judicial combat, or trial by battle. Its antecedents can be looked for in the *holmganga* and its cognates in Germanic custom. Old Swedish law allowed an aggrieved person to settle scores on the highway, and there was a similar Danish custom; a Burgundian edict of 501 gave formal recognition. In some areas women could take on men, with suitable handicapping. As trial by combat grew up its defects were soon being noticed, and some checks were provided by the Lombard laws of 713–35.[10]

Combat could arise from an ordinary trial; feudal convention permitted a defendant to accuse one of his judges, who in a seigneurial court would be his peers, of 'false judgement', and offer to fight him. Not all of them would relish the thought of having to uphold their verdict in this style; they might dodge the risk by delivering it collectively. It was from the term *calumnia*, for false accusation, that the fourteenth-century word 'challenge' was derived. Rules of trial by combat were being codified, ceremonial was growing. There was a *champ clos*, like the enclosure marked out for combatants in old Scandinavia;

[8] Balzac, *Les Chouans* (1830), chap. 21.
[9] B. Capp, 'English Youth Groups and *The Pinder of Wakefield*', *Past and Present*, 76 (1977), 129–30.
[10] J.B. Bury, *The Invasion of Europe by the Barbarians* (London, 1928), chap. 15; cf. Selden, *The Duello*, 60 ff.

proceedings were public, with representatives present of both Church and secular authority. The challenger threw down a gauntlet, and had originally it seems the choice of weapons, later transferred to the other party. Defeat entailed punishment, which might be death, since the infallible justice of Heaven had been invoked. A substitute champion was allowable, for a woman, an ecclesiastic, or an old man. When the old Fulcher de Waldegrave, who had come to England with the Conqueror, was summoned to trial, his elder son declined to take his place; a younger son fought and won, and was rewarded by the legacy of his father's estate, whereupon his brother hanged himself out of mortification.[11]

Heavenly justice being open to all, individuals of any rank could claim the right to ordeal by battle, though in practice it became increasingly a prerogative of the upper classes, accustomed to the use of their weapons. Fights between plebeians did take place, and no doubt afforded their betters much amusement. At Valenciennes in 1455 two townsmen fought in the market-place with wooden clubs, before the Duke of Burgundy and a large gathering; the loser was promptly executed. In Shakespeare's *Henry VI* the encounter between Horner and Peter has sunk to a mock-heroic level.

Trial by combat had a wide vogue. It found its way into adventure stories like that of the Cid, who appealed to King Alfonso at Toledo against ill-treatment of his two daughters by their husbands. Each of the miscreants was ordered to face one of the Cid's best warriors, who proved more than a match for them. Saxon England was exceptional among the Germanic nations in not adopting the custom; it was brought in by the Conquest. When Godefroy Baynard accused the Comte d'Eu of conspiracy against William Rufus they were brought together at Salisbury, before the royal court; the count paid for his defeat by being castrated and blinded.[12] On the Shetland island of Papa Stour tradition long preserved the memory of a duel about 1200 between two men, one of them 'Lord Terwil', who must have been Thorval Thoresson, chamberlain to the duke Hakon Magnusson, later king of Norway. This affair seems to show a clear descent from old Scandinavian practice, and the enclosure where it took place may have been also the 'Thingstead' or meeting-place of the assembly.[13]

Froissart narrates a *cause célèbre* of 1387 that brought spectators flocking to Paris from far and wide. It was alleged by the attractive young wife of Jean de Carogne that, in her husband's absence on pilgrimage, their neighbour Jacques le Gris requested her to show him

[11] E. Searle, 'Merchet in Medieval England', *Past and Present*, 82 (1979), 34.
[12] Baldick, 18.
[13] Information from Brian Smith, Lerwick.

round their castle. When they reached the dungeon he bolted the door, and raped her. She kept quiet until her husband came home, and then told him. The case went before the Parlement, which after a year-long failure to decide it ordered a combat. It took place before a large crowd, with the king and many noblemen present. The lady was observed to pray fervently for Jean's success, as well she might, for if defeated he would be hanged and she burned. They charged on horseback, then fought on foot until Jean was wounded, Jacques killed. A reward to the victor and a post in the royal household rounded off this happy ending.[14] We must hope that the lady's story was true.

A detailed record survives from James I's day, early in the next century, of how 'Combats for life' were conducted in Scotland, under the supervision of the Great Constable. If treason were in question the loser was dragged off to execution. 'If the combat wer only for tryall of virtew or honour', he merely forfeited his weapons and armour.[15] A Border ballad tells of a folk-tale queen on whom a rejected lover cast suspicion of adultery. A bold champion was with difficulty found to defend her against the charge, and the penalty of burning. He and the traducer entered the lists:

> They then advanced to fight the duel
> With swords of temper'd steel,

and the villain was slain.[16]

In July 1453 a London chronicler made mention in his dog-Latin of a fight at Smithfield between an Irishman and an Englishman who accused him of treason; it ended in a draw.[17] Trial by battle might help a citizen to maintain the port of a gentleman even while carrying on an urban vocation. Hervey Dunning, who may have been the first mayor of Cambridge, but owned land and had landed relatives, 'claimed the rank of knight and twice demanded wagers of battle in suits concerning landed property.'[18]

At the other end of Europe, Muscovy was evolving a form of judicial combat of its own. As reported by sixteenth-century travellers, a man accused of robbery or murder could ask for it: he and the plaintiff could each employ substitutes, and choose their own weapons, with bow or gun excluded. Professionals were ready to take anyone's place for money; they wore cumbrous armour, and gave one another bribes,

---

[14] Sir John Froissart, *Chronicles of England, France, Spain* (London, 1849), vol. ii, chap. 46.

[15] *Miscellany of the Spalding Club*, vol. ii (Aberdeen, 1842), sect. xiv (381–90).

[16] 'Sir Hugh le Blond', in *Border Ballads*, ed. Beattie, 150 ff.

[17] *John Benet's Chronicle* (1400–62), ed. G. L. Harriss (London, 1972), 210.

[18] A. B. Hibbert, 'The Origins of the Medieval Town Patriciate', in P. Abrams and E. A. Wrigley (edd.), *Towns in Societies* (Cambridge, 1978), 100. On procedures of trial by battle in England cf. Selden, *The Duello*, 69 ff.

methods which ensured their being the losers when they came up against foreigners.[19]

Ecclesiastical views on trial by ordeal, and by combat in particular, shifted as time went on. Pope Nicholas I gave his sanction to trial by battle in 858. Certain saints came to be credited with a special interest in it. In the porch of the eleventh-century romanesque church of San Zeno at Verona the lower reliefs depict scenes of hunting or fighting. In one of them, two armoured cavaliers are meeting in full career, spear to spear, their horses nose to nose with forefeet in the air. Perhaps we are seeing a trial by battle, possibly one that really took place in fair Verona, long before the first Montagu or Capulet lorded it there. But already before the close of the ninth century the Church was having second thoughts. It was always in principle, though seldom in its long history with any consistency, opposed to bloodshed. When combatants were made to deny use of magic charms—as they often were in early modern duelling too—some lack of trust in Providence peeped out. 'This is indeed the judgment of God', solemnly declares the Grand Master after the Templar's unexpected collapse and death, when he has only the wound-enfeebled Ivanhoe to deal with. Seldom can the outcome have been accepted so unquestioningly. When Dr Johnson was at Edinburgh in 1773 he told Boswell that 'the ancient trial by duel' did not appear to him 'so absurd as is generally supposed'; but it came to be realized, he had to concede, that 'he who was in the right had not a better chance than he who was in the wrong'.[20]

During the twelfth century norms of Roman law were percolating into the schools, and helping to discredit such clumsy old procedures. Trial by ordeal or battle was uncongenial to the cities that were growing up. 'The rational townsman detested the superstitions of the barbarian and the warrior.'[21] Roman justice made use of torture, if only of slaves, and during the twelfth century there was an increasing preference for judicial torture over ordeal as a means of ascertaining facts.[22] This implies a turning away from divine to human arbitrament; the administering classes were growing more self-reliant, more confident of their ability to unravel problems instead of leaving them to God, or chance.

In 1215 the fourth Lateran Council prohibited priests from having anything to do with ordeals. Most of these disappeared quickly, but

---

[19] S. von Herberstein, *Description of Moscow and Muscovy 1557*, ed. B. Picard (London, 1969), 51; H. von Staden, *The Land and Government of Muscovy*, ed. T. Esper (Stanford, 1967), 15–16; H. C. Lee, 'The Wager of Battle', in Bohannan, 248.

[20] Boswell, *Hebrides*, Introd. As Voet said (p. 60), many must have abandoned their cases rather than risk defeat by a brawnier antagonist.

[21] C. D. Darlington, *The Evolution of Man and Society* (London, 1969), 420.

[22] See the article 'Torture', by J. Williams, in vol. 27 of the *Encyclopaedia Britannica* (Cambridge, 1911).

trial by battle kept up a rearguard action in spite of ecclesiastical censures. Governments too were coming to prefer legal proceedings under their own direction. Curiously, in view of its turbulent past, Iceland led the way: in 1011 fights were banned by the *Allthing* or general assembly, which had lately adopted an adequate legal framework for coping with disputes. In England the reforms of Henry II provided for trial by grand assize, or jury, as an alternative. In France Saint Louis rejected a demand for trial by battle from a lawless nobleman charged with arbitrary hangings, because it would favour the strong against the weak.[23] Trial by battle was curtailed by Philip the Fair in 1303, and dwindled away until the Jarnac–La Chastaigneraye affair in 1547 could be looked back on as the last fully regular case in French history.

Trial by combat offered a substitute for private revenges; the tournament provided a formalized version of anarchic feudal scrapping. All military élites face opposite risks: some of their members cannot stop fighting, others—far more, probably—lapse too readily into sloth. Medieval campaigning involved burdensome armour and many other discomforts. Feudal obligation to serve only extended to a limited part of a year, and with warfare expanding professional forces had increasingly to be drawn on. Nobility was in danger of being supplanted, and losing the martial character which its social ascendancy required that it should retain, at least in appearance or repute. It kept up its warlike trappings, and by displaying prowess in the tournament a minority of bolder spirits kept them from rusting away too far, while martial ardour was restrained from running wild. Emulation was fanned by pageantry and the presence of applauding spectators, including women.

As a training exercise for practical warfare, on the other hand, the tournament must have been worse than useless. It reduced tactics to the sort of mass charges by iron-clad horsemen that proved so futile at Agincourt. Feudal military training always suffered from being 'excessively individualistic, even anarchic', lacking any such mode of fighting in close order that Spartans, for example, excelled in. 'The knight was never really melted into the soldier; he always stood out.'[24] He had begun as a simple man at arms, but social elevation spoiled him, and as holder of a fief he had become financially independent. Wherever warfare is well developed, battlefield habits will influence attitudes to private combat; the self-willed knight, not the well-drilled Greek or Roman, was the ancestor of the duellist.

[23] B. W. Tuchman, *The Calamitous 14th Century* (New York, 1979), 65–6. On trial by combat in France cf. Massi, pt. 1.
[24] Brinton, 181; cf. 183.

Tourneying had its distant origins in old pagan mimic battles. It grew up in France, as a mêlée at first hardly distinguishable from a real set-to, and long continued to be a 'ferocious and thoroughly dangerous affair', with only the loosest of rules. Sixty or eighty knights lost their lives in one knockabout in 1240.[25] Sometimes deadly disputes were being settled, as at Darmstadt in 1403 between bands of Franconian and Hessian knights who accused each other of highway robbery, when twenty-six of them lost their lives.'[26] Only by slow degrees did the conduct of the tourney become more formal and ceremonious.

The difference between a feudal and a slave society is epitomized in the contrast between the tournament, where noblemen clashed, and the amphitheatre with its wild beasts and gladiators. Both furnished diversions, opportunities for gaping and gossip, and no doubt for wagers on one stalwart or another. It must have been an attraction of the tournament to many groundlings that they might have the pleasure of seeing a gentleman unhorsed or battered. But a spectacle like the one depicted by Scott in *Ivanhoe* would be entertainment for both high and low, and might do something to soften plebeian resentments against lordly oppressors, as fox-hunting has done in the English countryside. It would seem that nobility stood higher in popular regard than might be expected: tales of knightly adventure circulated widely, sundry saints were dubbed knights.[27] In such contexts it is always well to recall that the bourgeois who dreamed of becoming a nobleman had an understudy in the craftsman who dreamed of becoming an alderman, and whose day-dreams might take more exotic shapes. A ballad went on being sung into the eighteenth century about a London prentice who took part in a tournament and ended by marrying the king's daughter.[28] But the clashing swords and thundering hooves would also serve, like a military parade in our own time, to impress and awe the watchers by their theatrical display of the armed strength of the ruling class.

Knights might fight in honour of their ladies' charms, as duellists might in defence of their wives' reputations. Women had not been absent from the Roman circus, as we can learn from some of Martial's epigrams; familiarity with the mimic warfare of the tourney must have helped to give those of the upper classes an appreciative interest in war. Each severally would be flattered by having a champion carrying her 'favour' and getting the better of competitors devoted to rival beauties. Yet it may be suspected that collectively they, like the plebeian

---

[25] Keen, 87; cf. Léon Gautier, *Chivalry* (Paris, 1884; London, 1965), 268–9, 272 ff.; Bloch, ii. 304; R. Barbar, 159 ff.

[26] Max von Boehn, *Modes and Manners* (English edn., New York, 1971), i. 289–90.

[27] Burke, 157–8.

[28] Ibid. 41.

onlookers, sometimes had a secret gratification in the sight of men belabouring one another. Women too were an inferior species, on whom their lords and masters by this parade of strength were impressing the lesson of their inferiority. Ladies had plenty of flattery bestowed on them, but as Huizinga says little true understanding or sympathy.[29] Here is another current of feeling that may have persisted into later feeling about duelling.

Occasionally a woman would have sufficient independence of mind to dismiss the whole vainglorious charade. There is one such in the late medieval novel *Tirant lo Blanc*, about the martial and amatory exploits of a Breton knight, the former chiefly against Saracens anywhere from England to north Africa and Byzantium. When Earl William insists on his son going to the wars betimes, because warfare is best learned in youth, his wife inveighs against 'this art of chivalry', as something 'cursed, sorrowful, and useless'.[30]

Tourneying might be mixed up with jealousies of feudal factions, as happened at times in thirteenth-century England; some official measures against it were the consequence.[31] They were most efficacious in England, where 'the wisest sovereigns frowned upon these frolics',[32] Henry II for one. Saint Louis was another crowned head who disapproved. The Church was more uncompromisingly hostile. Death in a tournament was put on a par with suicide, and in Saint Bernard's view ensured immediate relegation to hell. As Clement V made clear at the Council of Vienne in 1312–13, what Rome wanted was to divert warlike energy into renewed wrestling with the heathen. Between Christendom and Islam there was always, in actuality or in prospect, what might be called a duel between two continents, two civilizations. Yet despite all papal denunciations the institution could not be eliminated, proof as Bloch said of 'how deep was the need that it satisfied' within feudal society.[33]

A refining process is observable, one feature being a growing taste by the fourteenth century for the joust, or single combat, an outgrowth from the mêlée. An obvious cause was that it gave more scope for the individual to distinguish himself. Individual consciousness was enlarging itself, as in Europe it has always, if irregularly, been doing, It could find a simple outlet in the lists, with a young cavalier galloping full-tilt (as we still say) with lance in rest, under the sparkling eye of his mistress. As a spectacle also it would have great appeal; the two

[29] Huizinga, 128.
[30] Martorell, 24–5.
[31] R. Barber, 183–5.
[32] Bloch, ii. 305.
[33] Ibid.

jousting figures on horseback above the astronomical clock face of Wells Cathedral may be a reminder of this. It could be either an exhibition of skill, with what were termed *armes courtoises*, such as a blunted sword, or an occasion for working off personal enmities, with sharp edge or point, the *armes à outrance*. 'Come, Fate, into the lists', cries Macbeth, 'and champion me to the utterance' (challenge me *à outrance*, to the death). In this mood the joust could have a close resemblance to the judicial duel, whose terminology, it has been pointed out, it shared.[34]

An offshoot of the joust was the *pas d'armes*, a single combat independent of any official management, though quickly developing conventions and elaborations of its own, 'a near-obsession with ritual gesture'.[35] Everything in the feudal world shows this leaning towards overblown parade, which was to culminate in the magnificent courts and pageants and costumes of the sixteenth- and seventeenth-century monarchies. The *pas d'armes* was a martial exercise, but served also to feed hunger for glory. A knight fired by ambition lived on applause and admiration. In the Romances his prime concern must be pursuit of distinction, and a challenge should never be rejected.[36] Rather he should go out of his way to confront others. He might pledge himself to bar a certain spot against all comers; a river-crossing was a natural choice, familiar to heroes of the fabulous past like Cuchulainn, or those of Mallory's tales, or Tennyson's Idylls. An illuminated manuscript composed in the fifteenth century for René of Anjou, king of Sicily, is an allegory of love; one of its pictures shows a traveller, a knight on horseback led by Melancholy, having to hew his way across a wooden bridge in the teeth of an opponent in black armour representing trouble.[37]

The *pas d'armes* differed from the duel of later days in having no motive but fame, but the difference was not always great, since many duels had no cause or purpose beyond giving proof of courage. This unreasoning pugnacity was carried furthest in the duel between man and bull, perhaps of Moorish origin but taken up by Spanish cavaliers with lances. Only in Spain's time of decay, the later seventeenth century, was it abandoned to the plebeian professional, on foot, as the poor man's ladder to fame and fortune.

All the diverse forms of single combat contributed to the 'duel of honour' that was coming to the front in the later Middle Ages, and was the direct ancestor of the modern duel. Like trial by combat or the joust, it required official sanction, and took place under regulation. In

[34] M. Vale, *War and Chivalry* (London, 1981), 76.
[35] Keen, 201 ff.
[36] R. Barber, 130–1.
[37] *Le Cueur d'Amours Espris*, ed. F. Unterkircher (New York, 1975).

England Edward III set up a court of honour to supervise it; Nicholas Upton extolled it in the early fifteenth century as a test of manhood.[38] Encounters were gravest when property or smarting 'honour' was at stake, and after a fight *à outrance* the winner was entitled to kill his opponent, or leave him to be shamefully put an end to by those watching. Here the axioms of the trial by battle, where defeat proved guilt, may be seen shading into those of a military élite, for which surrender proved a man unworthy of knightly rank, and of life itself. Anyone thus confessing cowardice was a 'recreant'—'an odious term' as Bracton the thirteenth-century jurist called it, which was later to stigmatize the renegade or apostate. In all this was the strange mixture of brutality and formality pervading feudal behaviour, one element expressing the unbridled passions of the individual, the other the *esprit de corps* of the class; together they, like the courtesies observed in war, reflected the unnaturalness of the whole feudal structure.

As nationalism dawned on Europe, it could serve to inspire duels of honour which had no personal animus, and could find room for magnanimity. Near the end of the fourteenth century, when a number of jousts were taking place between English and Scottish knights in the aftermath of their countries' long wars, Sir David Lindsay, later first earl of Crawfurd, and Lord Wells crossed swords on a crowded London Bridge, each in arms to assert his country's superior valour. The Scot won, and handed over his captive to the queen, who thanked him and set Lord Wells free.[39] About the same time a duel was fought in Italy, with a cardinal's sanction, between two Florentines and two Bretons, from the same motive.[40] In such episodes the duel was taking on one more aspect that was to accompany it through all its later career. Men fought not for private reasons alone: personal and collective honour might intertwine.

A parallel phenomenon was the ideology of Chivalry, which the Church, hostile to fighting in other ways, could willingly endorse, for instance by its share in the ceremony of induction to knighthood, with the *benedictio ensis* or blessing of the sword.[41] A conception of knighthood as 'the bulwark of society against disorder runs right through the manuals on the subject'.[42] It could gild the self-image of the upper classes; those who live at the expense of others have always wanted to pose as their protectors, and the cant of 'service' is much older than our own smooth-spoken century. In the Indian epic, the *Ramayana*, the

[38] Baldick, 27; M. James, 6.
[39] Charles Mills, *The History of Chivalry* (London, 1825), i. 287–9.
[40] Steinmetz, i. 24.
[41] H. O. Taylor, *The Mediaeval Mind*, 4th edn. (London, 1927), i. 544–5.
[42] R. Barber, 40.

Kshatriyas or warriors were depicted as bearing arms in order to relieve distress and misery,[43] a good example of the kind of complacent self-delusion that any dominant group is liable to fall into. In Europe the cult of nobility, with battle as its chief activity, placed a vision of Honour above desire for material gain. Something has always to be done to lend substance to such notions. Duelling was to take on very much of this function; the ideology of chivalry, in essence a cloak for power and privilege, helped to prepare the way. It was strongest in northern France, and French speech and literature were everywhere current as the accompaniment of good breeding.[44] Yet the fifteenth century in France, so prolific in high-flown romances, was a gross and licentious one, and a time also when aristocracy was suffering rude shocks and tradesmen were rising in the scale.

Knight-errant fantasy could offer a refuge from these unpleasant realities. Always a severe critic of medieval attitudinizing, Huizinga speaks of 'the continual illusion of a high and heroic life', the 'fine make-believe of heroism and love'.[45] When men in command of such sword-ruled societies turn from workaday business to the realm of imagination, they may find it hard to distinguish fact from dream; alienation from the common herd blinds them to the light of common day. Yet the star-neighbouring pinnacles of the Gothic cathedrals were no less real than the dungeons or brothels. Aristocracy in Europe, in many changing guises, was to have a very long life, and a class cannot survive for very long without some of its members having genuine convictions, and virtues such as feudalism possessed in its standards of personal honour, self-respect, loyalty. A thirteenth-century book of chivalry by Raymond Lull could become two hundred years later, in the translation printed by Caxton in the 1480s, 'the textbook of honour' of English readers.[46]

It was in imaginative literature that the chivalric ideals could shine most alluringly. The *pas d'armes* could be dressed up by courtly writers as knight errantry, part of a life dedicated to exploits of an improving sort, rescuing of maidens in distress or ridding the world of malefactors. All this could easily take wing and soar into the quelling of ogres or sorcerers that Don Quixote supposed himself to be engaged in. It was easy also to associate such stirring activities with those of men fighting for the Cross in strange lands, as Milton was to portray them, defying Saracens in hand-to-hand combat on the stricken field.[47]

[43] B. Khan, *The Concept of Dharma in Valmiki Ramayana* (Delhi, 1965), 159–60. He cites a speech of Rama: 'the Ksatriya carries arms in order that the word "distressed" may not exist'.

[44] Pirenne, 249–50.

[45] Huizinga, 80, 83.

[46] M. James, 2, 10.

[47] *Paradise Lost*, i. 763–5.

Western Europe's still living store of Celtic myth and marvel supplied a great deal that could nourish the fantasia of chivalry. French romancers drew from the outset on the deep dark well of Breton legend, and Arthurian tales blended with echoes of Charlemagne. Malory naturalized all this in fifteenth-century England, with Welsh legend to help him. It shares with Irish (and Indian) mythology a kaleidoscope of charm, pathos, romance, and violence, hyperbole, childlike absurdity, very different from the stark realism characteristic of Nordic or Greek epic at their best. Yet a work of fiction like *Tirant lo Blanc* is not without its more down-to-earth moments. Its Valencian author Joanot Martorell himself took part in feats of derring-do, and spent some time at the English court. 'Iberian knights actually did set out to perform deeds in places as far apart as England and Bohemia.'[48]

Moreover the romance writers can be given credit for trying to lend civilizing touches, a more humane feeling, to the rude world they lived in. Martorell's hero spares the hapless Thomas, whom he has defeated in single fight. In the story of King Florus an ordeal by battle, between Sir Robert and Sir Raoul, who has filched his land and traduced his lady, is detailed blow by blow, until the villain has to beg for mercy: the victor then intercedes for him, and the king lets him off with banishment.[49] Chaucer tells how Duke Theseus of Athens generously took up the cause of some ladies of rank, widowed by the usurping king Creon of Thebes, and hastened there with his army to attack Creon, killing him with his own hand. When Theseus held a tournament he laid restrictions on the weapons to be used, so as to prevent waste of noble blood, and ordained that the losers were not to be killed. The freemasonry of knighthood could be extended even to Saracens, just as modern duelling extended its privileges to gentlemen of all nations. Some of Martorell's Moslems are no less *preux chevaliers* than their Christian antagonists, and share the same criteria of honour.

Here again women must be remembered; they were the greediest devourers of romances of chivalry, to make up for the boorishness of most of their flesh-and-blood husbands or lovers. If not confined to harems, like their Asian sisters, ladies were in other ways closely enough mewed up in their castles, through whose narrow windows the landscape which they could only fantasize, not comprehend, might indeed appear as a dream-world. For them love and war went hand in hand. Aucassin was as doughty a fighter as he was a devoted lover of his Nicolette.

In war knightly buffetings still had their place. Trial by combat had an analogy, and divine judgement another sphere of activity, in the

[48] A. MacKay, *Spain in the Middle Ages* (London, 1977), 208.
[49] *Aucassin and Nicolette and other Mediaeval Romances*, trans. E. Mason (London, 1910), 144 ff.

single fights that took place within battles. These abounded in the *chansons de geste*, early medieval poems chiefly about Charlemagne and his companions. These paladins, engaging Moorish champions, were clearly entitled to the favour of heaven; subsequently the crusades revived the aura of single-handed encounters with the paynim. In the first part of *Tirant lo Blanc* an ambitious young Saracen, ruler of Canary, invades England and overruns the country, killing and pillaging, before challenging its king to single combat. Too old and weak to take the field, the king abdicates in favour of a venerable hermit, the disguised Earl William of Warwick, lately home from the crusades. He and the aggressor meet on horseback; William of course wins, and carries away the unbeliever's head on his lance.

In a somewhat less fanciful legend, an Earl Guy of Warwick returned in 960 from pilgrimage to the Holy Land to find the Danes besieging Winchester, and to overpower the Danish champion who volunteered to settle the issue by single combat.[50] It came into fashion from the thirteenth century for commanders to throw out challenges, more for show than with any expectation of their invitations being taken up. Trials of skill between individual warriors of lesser degree, or groups, were not uncommon. Froissart tells of thirty Frenchmen belonging to a force in Brittany in 1351 taking on an equal number from a mixed enemy corps. In 1503 a Frenchman and a Spaniard, Bayard and Sotomayor, crossed swords in view of their two armies in south Italy.

A fable survived from the crusades of Richard Cœur de Lion fighting Saladin, and a still older one of Charlemagne, with timely aid from the archangel Gabriel, getting the better of a Saracen chief. Later monarchs surprisingly often manifested a desire to emulate their example nearer home, and went through the motions of being eager to get to grips with each other. Somehow some impediment always prevented them. They too were enveloped in the pomp and circumstance of war, the corporate day-dream of knightly glory, however sordid the true motives of their sparrings might be. In 1283 Pedro III of Aragon offered to take on Charles of Anjou, singly or with a hundred followers each, the stake to be the rich prize of Sicily. The pope intervened and forbade a contest, perhaps a piece of collusion to save them from having to do any more than play to the gallery. Wars grew steadily bigger and costlier, and kings may have felt some need to soften the resentment of their hard-pressed subjects by pretending to want to take all the risk on themselves. In 1340 Edward III challenged Philip of France; his grandson Richard II copied his fearless gesture. At Bannockburn Robert Bruce is said to have fought an English knight in earnest.

---

[50] Basnage, 41; on such combats cf. Selden, *The Duello*, 59.

A fifteenth-century duke of Saxony was still on his deathbed 'vowing a duel to the death with the Grand Turk'.[51] What rulers were really beginning to do was to take part in tournaments, in the later Middle Ages mellowing into a colourful masque which monarchies building up their power could use for self-advertisement and self-glorification. As an appendage to court festivities it became a preserve of the higher nobility. There could still be hazards. Henri II lost his life in 1559 when Montmorency's lance penetrated his helmet. It has been suggested that Henry VIII incurred head injuries from jousting, and it is not hard to suppose that he and many others suffered something like the punch-drunk boxer's condition. In 1612 even the unwarlike James I was to be seen tilting; a reminder of how firmly the so-called 'new monarchies' had one foot planted in the feudal past.

[51] Warner, 178.

4

Emergence of the Modern Duel

In our encounters either a man settles a difference at once in a
blaze of glory, or he dies leaving a fine reputation, because he had
the courage and resolution to venture on a fight; and if the fortune
of the sword did not smile on him, still it is a great thing to have
made the attempt. As they say in Latin, *In rebus arduis tentare satis
est.*

Brantôme, *Mémoires ... touschant les duels*, 142.

WHAT Brantôme, who died in 1614, has to say of duelling down to
about the middle of the sixteenth century relates to the formal duel of
honour of the late Middle Ages. This hybrid of joust and trial by combat,
conducted in a *champs clos* under official supervision, belonged mainly
to a time when the feudal order was decaying, an era as Huizinga
said of exhausted ideas, of shallow thinking and trivial writing, very
noticeable in chroniclers like Froissart.[1] Politically the fifteenth century
saw the disruption of the old feudal order in various countries, England
and Spain among them, by civil strife, akin to the duel in being inspired
chiefly by jealousies within the feudal nobility. A new field of gravity
to hold a swarm of unstable atoms together was offered by the nation-
state, but the patriotic mystique could not mature quickly. More
tangible as a bond of union was the class, at least for the higher classes
with a consciousness firmly rooted in the past.

Brantôme saw much that was amiss in the way the old-style duelling
was carried on. Its formalities left much room for subterfuges to dodge
a challenge; an injured party might have to go to heavy expense, in
posting up *manifestes* as a means of compelling his enemy to come
forward, and then furnishing the armoury of weapons he was entitled
to demand.[2] Brantôme shows no regret at this old stilted system being
brought to an end, as in his opinion it indisputably was, by the Council
of Trent's ban. This illustrious General Council was overhauling Catholic faith and morals, and preparing the ground for the Counter-
Reformation. Its ruling, unlike many earlier papal pronouncements
against tourney or joust, had to be accepted as binding by all Catholic

---

[1] Huizinga, 238.
[2] Brantôme, 51–2, 61. At Paris in 1608 Marc de la Beraudière depicted the old style in his
painting 'Le Combat de Seul à Seul en Camp Close'.

secular authorities, to the extent at least that they would withdraw from any active patronage of duelling.

Many of their subjects, like Brantôme himself—very much an old soldier—were far from willing to do so. Instead of petering out the duel transformed itself into something more informal, flexible, and speedy, needing few of the old tortuous arrangements. It must of course be supposed that swords had been drawn often enough before without any publicity, as was now coming to be accepted practice under the name, first appearing at Naples, of *combatere a la mazza*; the origin of the phrase Brantôme was unable to discover.[3] The new duelling, which could be resorted to in a quarrel of any kind, however trifling, was a private, man-to-man affair; another landmark in the rise of individualism, even if self-assertion of this kind was always entangled in the constraints of class.

Weaponry too was being simplified, and defensive armour discarded; this enabled a fight to be won and lost expeditiously, before any interference could take place. There was an accompanying shift in warfare, away from heavily armoured cavalry to infantry tactics, with firearms of growing importance. The modern duellist stood nearly always on his own two feet. An objection noted by Brantôme was that whereas hitherto things were managed publicly, before 'tout un petit monde' of spectators, now men fought in out-of-the-way spots, with few or none to watch or admire.[4] But within the same 'little world' report would quickly spread; and as Ségur observed during the Russian campaign of 1812, a soldier can be roused to brave deeds by the notice of a handful of comrades, men whose hearts beat with the same pulse.[5]

Brantôme recognized Italian military men as the founders of the new mode, and as the best versed in its principles; Spaniards too were proficient, though somewhat less so; by the late sixteenth century France had taken the lead.[6] Italians served in numbers in the Spanish and other armies, as well as in their own principalities. Italy was well qualified also to provide a technical literature, of treatises both on duelling skills, especially the art of fencing, and on the code of honour which governed the art of giving and taking offence in a polished, gentlemanly style. It was the most fertile breeding-ground of lawyers and legalism; partly because it was also the earliest home of an urban mixture of mercantile and aristocratic, each component having to adjust itself to a changing society. Higher-class boundaries being blurred, status had to be upheld by attention to externals. Niceties of

[3] Ibid. 70–1.
[4] Ibid. 144.
[5] Comte Philippe de Ségur, *La Campagne de Russie* (1824; 'Nelson' edn., Paris, n.d.).
[6] Brantôme, 131.

social behaviour were given an importance now scarcely comprehensible. Reasons or pretexts for fighting proliferated and grew more
and more complex; in the eyes of critics, more and more absurd. There
was a patent streak of silliness in the whole business, which Shakespeare
was only one of many writers to make fun of.

In principle allegiance was to that lodestar of Italian humanism,
virtú: 'manliness', or the ideal of 'manly and courageous action', with
overtones strongly aristocratic; 'vitality to the point of aggression,
activity to the point of hyper-individualism'.[7] Andrea Alciato, born in
1492, a lawyer whose works found readers all over Europe, was one of
the first to compile a regular code to define the circumstances in which
a gentleman ought to feel a duel incumbent on him. Girolamo Muzio's
treatise *Il duello*, published at Venice in 1550, became the best-known
of all. Like all synthetic ideas produced by complex social situations,
Honour as presented by such theorists had multiple starting-points.
Aristotle might have been surprised to find himself one of its godfathers,
often called on for testimony by the Italians. Often it is true he was
turned to by those who recommended arbitration, and some writers
favoured resort to law in preference to combat.[8] Lawyers of course had
a professional bias towards litigation; when they prescribed arms, legal
instinct made their rules as intricately arcane as pen and ink could
compass, and wrapped them up in a rigmarole vocabulary. A practical
point amid the hair-splitting was that by insult or aggression a man
could be compelled to challenge his assailant, and thus give him the
choice of weapons. The two gravest transgressions were a blow, and an
accusation of lying. Either implied treatment as an inferior: a nobleman
is above any need to tell falsehoods. Sir Walter Ralegh was not an
apologist of the duel, but in his poem 'The Lie' each stanza, denouncing
one social plague and its carriers after another, ends with the refrain
'give them all the lie'—even though as he writes towards the close,

> to give the lie
> Deserves no less than stabbing.

A charge of mendacity might be direct or indirect (anything up to
thirty-two species could be reckoned), and the reply might be a 'retort
courteous' or any one of a graduated ruder series.

A personal sense of honour could be, in a time of turmoil, men's
refuge from 'the moral disarray of their world';[9] but for all except a
thoughtful few it was little but an enslavement to the prejudices of a
class. Montaigne saw no haven in 'these lawes of honour, which so often

[7] F. I. Polak, *The Image of the Future* (Leiden, 1961), i. 208.
[8] Bryson, 2, 43–4, 73, 80.
[9] Council, 29.

shock and trouble those of reason'.[10] The code was a bastard substitute for a genuine morality. Any class likes to feel, however hazily, that it has an ethic of its own, by which its members can be touched to fine issues. In Europe this craving was heightened by Christianity, but in the case of the sword-bearing classes in a very contradictory way, since their social posture and outlook were incompatible with Christian teaching, or could only be reconciled with it by fictions like those of medieval chivalry. Gentlemanly honour was blossoming amid the whirlwinds of Reformation and Counter-Reformation, and was singularly little touched by them. To its devotees religion was something for the common herd; what counted for them was status, the world's opinion. Their virtue continued to be mainly exterior, as in earlier times (if not later) a lady's 'reputation' was—so that Isolde could indulge in adultery and talk of safeguarding her honour.[11]

Rules of honour aped in minuteness the casuistry of the churchmen, and might press on a man as harshly as any Christian austerity. He could be ruined by bad luck, Samuel Butler observed,

> And mere punctilio of chance.[12]

The fantastical pedantries of 'punctilio' suggest that, from lack of national life, or other cause, the Italian intellect was running to seed. It had been giving western Europe a Renaissance, but with a by-product of rubbish that could be just as infectious. Swarms of idle gentry, in France most of all, with no more serious occupations than hunting, gambling, drinking, wenching, had plenty of time to kill; duelling could lend a pinch of spice to the monotony, and, because of its risks, a touch of elevation.

It cannot be thought that the average rustical squireen or court peacock troubled his head overmuch about the finesses of the manuals; but the code of honour as it passed into general circulation amounted to a lay morality for the gentleman. Printing-presses groaned under their load of theology; a bulky parallel literature detailed the habits of witches; at the same time science, political theory, the arts, were flourishing as never before. Altogether there was an outpouring of ideas, an incongruous mixture of old and new, dross and gold, retrogression and progress, such as no epoch of world history had known. Europe was on the move, tumultuously, towards an unguessed goal, while the other continents, comparatively speaking, sat still.

There was no 'true aristocracy' in post-medieval France, Burckhardt

---

[10] Montaigne, Bk. 2, chap. 27.
[11] Jackson, 82.
[12] *The Poems of Samuel Butler*, ed. R. Bell (London, n.d.), iii. 164.

could declare.[13] A true aristocracy is far from easy to define, and sixteenth-century conceptions of it were in many ways loose and elastic. A title was one warrant, an estate might be a better one. All Spanish Basques claimed noble status. Men were acutely conscious of a confusion of ranks, old families sinking out of sight and upstarts taking their place. Conservative resentment of these mutations had a spokesman in Shakespeare's Prince of Aragon, with his lament over the many who have been buried in 'the chaff and ruin of the times', and his characteristic assumption that the 'merit' which should entitle men to distinction belongs to 'the true seed of honour', to the exclusion of all 'low peasantry'.[14] Europe was floundering through its contorted passage from medieval to modern; politically the transition was from the older feudalism of dispersed authority to stronger, centralizing monarchy, destined to last much longer in France than in England, in Germany than in France. Submitting to its sovereignty, the nobility retained and might even enlarge its rights and its social ascendancy, keeping the bourgeoisie in second place. Paying few or no direct taxes itself, as the major landowning class it shared with the government tax-collector the shearing of the peasant fleece. Monarchy and aristocracy, however apparently at odds at times, remained inseparable associates.

Privilege without responsibility was now the happy lot of the man of blue blood, on condition that he had enough land, or other source of income, to keep him afloat. Aristocracy had many grades, and it was those higher up, with influence at court and access to the many good things in its bestowal, who benefited most from the new dispensation. Landowners might have more real power over their tenants than the king had; in either case it was a power far more for ill than for good. But many of the minor nobles, who in England passed for no more than gentry, were finding themselves left out, with scanty rents, seldom any qualifications except for fighting, and facing intense competition for posts in the new standing armies. They were debarred or self-excluded, though never completely, from trade, as an ignoble occupation; ignoble because a man of sixteen quarterings ought to be able to live at free quarters, on the public if not on his own property. Nobility's essence is power, best displayed by living well without working, being able to command the labour of others. Those of modest rank suffered chronic insecurity, faced with the prospect of decline into the plebeian mass, the fate of unluckier families all through feudal times but now hanging over them far more generally. This, and the dependence of so many of them or their portionless younger sons on what bread their swords could win, must have helped to keep their sword-hands itching and

---

[13] J. Burckhardt, *Judgements on History and Historians*, trans. H. Zohn (London, 1959), 187.
[14] *Merchant of Venice*, Act II, sc. ix.

their readiness to quarrel keen. Each individual eliminated in a duel meant better chances for others.

As a class the lesser nobility was able to blackmail governments into doing a good deal for it, especially by expanding their armies at the expense of the peasants who did most of the paying; its more intelligent families learned to diversify their resources, by entering professions or the ballooning bureaucracies. It had time to find ways of preserving its identity and its pretensions, and in this the code of honour and its sanction, the duel, had a crucial part to play. In France the gentry has been called the hardest-hit of all classes: long-drawn wars in Italy supplied relief, but also inflated men's notions of how expensively a gentleman ought to live,[15] as the crusades and the taste of oriental luxuries had done long before. In Catalonia banditry was endemic; its social bases are unclear,[16] but nobles were often implicated, as they were in other regions like Galicia or Naples. Much later, in respectable England, a squire might be in league with smugglers.

Psychologically as well as materially it was a time of stress, as the crumbling of the old feudal structure and its ties and loyalties left the individual in danger of isolation. How acutely this was felt is shown by the hold of clientage, a ghost of the old order lingering on the stage. Reliance on highly placed patrons could help some, but painful gaps were left. Everywhere in sixteenth- and seventeenth-century Europe there were strained relations, taking many forms, sometimes religious, between higher and lower grades, which could hinder united defence of common interests. Ruling classes, always stratified, will be weakened by jealousies or grudges between higher and lower when they come to have too little to maintain cohesion. An ideology or sentiment is required to bind the élite together against internal divisions as well as against inferior classes. It is probable that every aristocracy, however well drilled in most respects, preserves something of the old Polish *szlachta's* irresponsible individualism, along with a conviction that any man of blue blood is as good as any other; if this goes unchecked it will leave men at the top isolated, and the élite leaderless.

Chivalry had supplied a kind of common language, fantastical but well enough in key with the climate of medieval thinking. Now western Europe was entering an age of greater realism, where cannon roared louder than any heraldic lions, and the earth went round the sun. No utilitarian compact could make brothers of the ducal owner of far-spreading estates and the out-at-elbows squireen, or allow the whole heterogeneous nobility to move forward on new lines, as the times required; but a substitute could be found. If early modern Europe saw,

---

[15] J. R. Major, *The Estates General of 1560* (Princeton, 1951), 17.
[16] Pierre Vilar, *La Catalogne dans l'Espagne moderne* (Paris, 1962), i. 621 ff.

broadly speaking, one of aristocracy's repeated recoveries from spells of weakness or dislocation, part of the reason must be sought in its ability to find a new or refurbished ethos, a pattern of conduct respected by all its ramifying branches. Thanks to this it could feel as one great family, animated by sentiments which raised it above the common level of mankind. Duelling and its code of honour met the need admirably. It came to form a powerful link between all noble ranks, and 'strengthen their sense of belonging to a single privileged class'.[17] Without this there would have been danger of the less well-endowed ranks drifting into subversive outbreaks, as they did in the 'Knights' War' in Germany in 1520. Monarchy, where it was rising in strength, could be a common rallying point; the higher nobles, so long restive under its control, by continuing to claim the right of duelling made a symbolic show of still not having surrendered their independent spirit. (Grandees of Spain did so also by insisting on their right to keep their hats on in the royal presence.) Without their sponsorship of it, the lower cadres might have been less eager to carry it on.

It may have been prized most of all by the younger sons or free-lances who were hard put to it to keep their foothold in society; just as they were keenest to expose themselves to the risks of war, for the sake of its possible windfalls, while wealthy grandees preferred their comfortable mansions. But blue blood was indivisible, and if poor nobles insisted on bandying challenges, magnates could not with dignity evade them. From this point of view the duel was the sign and seal of a mystic equality between higher and lower, a fraternal bond uniting the whole multifarious class. It was, in short, a leveller, even though in practice a peer would oftenest be embroiled with one of his own kind, a squire with another of the squires he consorted with. A duke ought to accept a challenge from a simple gentleman, Selden argued, because by treating him improperly the duke brought himself down to the same level. Selden did not ask whether a swineherd might urge the same point against a landowner, but he did go on to draw a parallel (in private talk) with a right of subjects to challenge their sovereign, if he infringed the unwritten contract between them.[18]

It may have occurred to rulers that others might reach this undesirable conclusion; and their own social if not always political affiliation was with the grandees. A royal embargo prevented the Comte de Soissons, a prince of the blood, from taking the field with a gentleman who was paying attentions to the same lady: the count showed splendid generosity, in Brantôme's view, by consenting to a meeting with one so far beneath him, for whom it would have been, living or dying, 'the

[17] Demeter, 119.
[18] Selden, *Table Talk*, 61–2.

summit of his glory'.[19] Queen Elizabeth banned Philip Sidney from court in 1579 for presuming, as a simple knight, to want to fight the Earl of Oxford, and their duel was vetoed by the Council; clearly it was felt that 'social revolution' was going too far.[20] It continued, nevertheless; in England it was aided by the presence of a large stratum of wealthy landowners below the limited peerage, but the achievement of a social parity may be given some credit for the fact that when political revolution came the diverse landed strata on the Parliamentary side were able to hold together, even though incompetent peers had to be elbowed out of the leadership.

Duelling provided a warrant of aristocratic breeding, increasingly threatened with submergence. It preserved to the entire class a military character, a certificate of legitimate descent from the nobility of the sword of feudal times, and of its title to officer the new mass armies. Duelling was in itself an assertion of superior right, a claim to immunity from the law such as a ruling class is always likely to seek in one field or another: it is for the common herd to submit to parchment trammels and shackles. For the man of noble birth it was all the more natural to put himself above the law because he, as seigneur, had been in command of justice in his own domain. On a reduced scale he was so still, in France down to 1789, in England as a JP far longer.

The duel was a vestigial survival of the early feudal right of private warfare. Paradoxically, the noble class announced and confirmed its solidarity by insisting on the privilege—or liability—of its members to exchange blows with one another. A class, particularly a dominant one, combines unity against outsiders with internal jealousies. Inner tensions coexist with, and indeed help to sustain, the bonds holding together any group; love and hate go together, as so often within the family. Class consciousness is always most alive in élites, but penalties as well as prerogatives are needed to keep it intact. A gentleman had to be ready to fight within his own degree, as well as against its enemies.

These enemies often took the form of mutinous peasants; a different menace came from the higher bourgeoisie. It was very seldom that the merchant showed any wish to sweep away the nobleman. On the contrary, attainment of noble status was for centuries the grand object of middle-class ambition. The individual pines for social transformation, elevation, for himself and his heirs, long before his *class* envisages any similar collective advancement. To acquire the trappings of nobility was the recognized badge of success for the man of the counting-house, marking him as an exceptionally gifted member of his kind. It may be said that the rudiments of all social categories can be found lurking in

---

[19] Brantôme, 216.
[20] C. Morris, *Political Thought in England, Tyndale to Hooker* (London, 1953), 63.

every individual's make-up, if in varying ratios; environment brings out one set of traits at the expense of others, and moulds a standard type within which these traits are dominant. Hence the so frequent readiness of individuals to make the jump from one orbit to another, knocking out of it, often enough, someone else.

Rewards that men have sought have been to a remarkable degree non-material, merely honorific, titles and medals and ribbons. Thirst for them can be seen as a lingering on of a primeval hankering for distinction within any small group, such as the right to wear an extra feather might confer on a Red Indian brave. In latter-day terms this easily took the form of vulgar snobbery. But material advantages also could accrue to noble status, and it was partly because governments did not want too many to slip through their tax net that investigations of claims to it became 'a regular feature of life in early modern Europe'.[21] Aristocracy could have yet other attractions, of a superior kind: qualities of self-respect and independence, confident ability to look the world in the face, and a courage which more refined spirits could transmute into moral values. Of all this the sword and the duel were the most obtrusive decorations, with the prestige of descent from remote ages.

On its side an élite class, even when sensible enough to abstain from closing its doors to newcomers, never wants to open them too wide, and erects obstacles against a press of entrants. Governments had only too many motives for granting ennoblement; the fountain of honour played with obliging readiness, more or less as though in response to a coin in a slot. Blue blood had to fear excessive dilution. It could seek to multiply rules of ancestry; an immense proliferation of heraldic detail was going on in the sixteenth and seventeenth centuries. A self-made man could ennoble himself, but he could not (as in China) ennoble his grandparents. Purchase of a landed estate was the high road to gentility, and might as in France carry a title with it, but it might also bring feudal liability to military service, or a tax in lieu of this.

Obligation to fight duels was in a way a continuation of this condition of tenure. As an acid test of the self-made gentleman it might be no bad means of reminding him of the change in his position, the compulsions of *noblesse oblige* he was subjecting himself to. It was in its way a not unsuitable punishment for the desertion of the Third Estate that endless generations of self-seekers were guilty of. In another way it could serve as a rite of initiation, helping to ensure the assimilation of aspirants into their new class, as public-school bullying would one day do in England, by denaturing the ingenuous youth of the prosperous middle class, and so turning away a threatening rival of the old order.

[21] Powis, 15.

Not all land-buyers would want to adopt the landed way of life, among them the hazards of hunting, and still more those of the honour code. A good many must have remained modestly and comfortably in town, treating their estate as an investment only. A more spirited parvenu, or more likely a son and heir, might feel impelled to claim his new rank by submitting to its most crucial test. In 1675 a Yorkshireman named George Aislabie, with a lately acquired estate and coat of arms, was 'stung into a duel by a trivial slur on his gentility', and killed; had he been patient until the Revolution of 1688 he would have found landed wealth, however come by, weightier in most men's eyes than a pedigree.[22] One may wonder how many impoverished scions of old families relieved their feelings by picking quarrels with *bourgeois gentilhommes*. Pirenne pointed out how aristocracy was rescued from decay in later medieval times by an influx of new blood, especially of commoners ennobled for services to the crown.[23] But this meant that weaker members of the nobility, and even some of the stronger, were in danger of being pushed into the background. Upstart lawyers were especially obnoxious. In any dispute over property, law would favour the rich, the sword the strong and active. A nobleman petitioning Louis XIII against the ban on duels argued that a man of his blood ought not to have to entrust his honour to 'menial lawyers'[24]—or his purse to such bloodsuckers, he might have added.

Montaigne was no enthusiast for duelling, but he could sympathize with noblemen aggrieved at the rise of 'a fourth estate of Lawyers, breath-sellers, and pettifoggers', so much in control of legislation that its principles and those of the noble code were in conflict; with the result that a man who pocketed an injury would be 'degraded of honour and nobilitie', while if he revenged it he was liable to capital punishment.[25]

While so many townsmen removed to country estates, many gentlemen were removing to the towns, a phenomenon very noticeable in France. They might have been ousted by bourgeois buyers, or might be on bad terms with the peasantry, or feel they could live more cheaply in town, with less display to keep up; or they might be growing bored with country life, and seduced by the amenities of theatre, tavern, gambling-house. It behoved them all the more to advertise their rank by wearing a sword, and being ready to draw it against any opponent worthy of it. Disgruntled men of birth could grumble, look down superciliously on the citizenry, or 'Cits' as London courtiers termed

[22] Ripon Civic Society, *Ripon: Some Aspects of its History* (Clapham, Yorks., 1972), 72.
[23] Pirenne, 396–7.
[24] Steinmetz, i. 158.
[25] Montaigne, Bk. 1, chap. 22.

them; they might try to make free with their wives, and if possible with their money too, like Falstaff. They could mark themselves off from the parvenu by refusing 'satisfaction' for an insult, if he was angry enough to demand it.

After the late sixteenth century French nobles made more of a point of declining to fight plebeians. This may be one cause of burghers sometimes getting gentlemen to fight duels for them, presumably by offering cash or other inducements. In older days there had been, as in Muscovy, professional swordsmen to take the place of men reluctant to undergo trial by combat in person. An early edict of Louis XIV forbade this employment of gentlemen.[26] It was derogatory to the whole class; and for any man well born but hard up it must have been a sad come-down to have to hire his blade to a fat moneygrubber, instead of to his sovereign.

Rankling in the minds of all the poorer grades of gentry would be fear of derogation, loss of all that made up the complex image of the gentleman and his status; a loss as painful as exclusion from his caste to a Hindu. An individual's 'honour', or 'reputation', was quite as important to him as Iago declared, and it was easily blighted by any failure to defend it. Readiness to fight was a peremptory duty. It had, besides, a utilitarian value in a jostling time, most of all among needy seekers of army commissions, but higher up as well. A courtier, wrote Castiglione in his manual of court life, must be skilled with weapons, beginning with 'those weapons commonly used among gentlemen', because, to say nothing of war, he might at any time be drawn into a quarrel.[27] We may contrast the sophisticated Italian with the blunt French nobles of the old school described by Montaigne, who scorned tricks of fencing and fought in order to show courage, not cleverness.[28] Physical hardihood could be exalted as an ancestral virtue coming down from manlier times, and too likely to be overlaid by modern foppery.

The bearded soldier in Shakespeare's seven ages of man is 'sudden and quick in quarrel'. A superfluity of minor nobles, holding life cheap, their own or anyone else's, might well come to think of duelling as an opportunity to exhibit the spirit and the proficiency required in an officer. In feudal times the élite had liked to claim a monopoly of courage, but some credit had to be allowed to stalwarts like the English bowmen, and now battles were becoming longer and grimmer, demand-

---

[26] Bennetton, 79.

[27] Castiglione, 61; cf. Leguina, 12 ff., and, on sometimes deplorable methods, 10–11. Spaniards carried their habits to the Americas; there were at one time four fencing-schools in Potosí (ibid. 17–18).

[28] Montaigne, Bk. 2, chap. 27.

ing courage from all. Officers must be known to possess it in a superior degree, and the duel, where the individual had to stand alone, served admirably to demonstrate it. To be well-born, again, meant an innate ability and right to command—or, as bowdlerized in later days, to 'lead'; but with the condition attached that to be fit to command others a man must be able to display complete self-command, whatever the situation. Apart from this, duelling kept open a chance for the individual to shine and stand out. War offered this less and less; the individual was being obliterated by gunpowder and infantry columns, tedious marches and sieges, with disease, that hateful guerrilla foe, dogging every army's heels. Shakespeare with his nostalgically unreal embroidery of war could still see dashing young soldiers like Claudio performing the feats of a lion.[29] Montaigne was more realistic when he asked 'How many notable particular actions are buried in the throng of a battell', amid which the faint-hearted could skulk equally unnoticed.[30] In a duel a would-be hero with a strong right arm could feel that he was the centre of things.

Armies met another need of the gentleman-soldier by giving him a new home or family, animated by ties of allegiance not unlike those of the feudal order, most evidently in early modern days when a regiment was raised and led by a nobleman. Uniforms, coming into use from the seventeenth century, served to infuse a sense of brotherhood and loyal attachment; at the same time they were an external manifestation of the code of conduct that both sustained and oppressed their wearers. They surrounded a human being uncertain of his place in the world with a throng of mirror images of himself, so that instead of feeling isolated he could deem himself a model of just what he ought to be.

But the mature regiment, with a permanent existence and *esprit de corps*, was a slow growth, and in the mean time duelling habits might have a disruptive influence, especially in an army on campaign. A case of two senior officers falling out occurred when Edward Norris, serving in the Netherlands in the 1570s with the Earl of Leicester's forces, in support of the revolt against Spain, challenged a German general, Count Hohenlohe, in Dutch service.[31] Brantôme reports discussions as to whether a commander on active service could accept a challenge, and cites instances.[32] At the siege of Juliers in the Netherlands in 1610 Sir Hatton Cheek, leading a storming party, gave offence to Sir Thomas Dutton by the brusque tone of his orders. Dutton resigned, returned to England, and complained. A challenge was the retort, and they met

---

[29] *Much Ado about Nothing*, Act I, sc. i.
[30] Montaigne, Bk. 2, chap. 16: 'Glory'.
[31] Tex, i. 104.
[32] Brantôme, 171.

on the Calais sands on a winter morning, with rapier and dagger. When the seconds withdrew from 'the measured fate-circle', in Carlyle's words, each made a deadly onset with both weapons: Dutton was wounded, Cheek killed.[33]

Leicester's regulations for his army forbade anyone to fight an officer senior to him, or to engage in quarrels in camp or in a garrison town. These were points frequently emphasized in military codes of that era.[34] Captain Thomas Stukeley, a character taken from life, in George Peele's play *The Battle of Alcazar* (1594), while serving in Ireland challenges the governor, an old *bête noire* of his, who reminds him of military law and of the folly of bickering in face of the enemy. Officers moreover who set a bad example might be imitated by other ranks, and lines of demarcation might in some ways be less clear in early modern armies than they became later on. There were duels in the English garrison at Tangier in 1683, and they were not confined to officers.[35] It was another theme of debate in Brantôme's time whether a soldier could be allowed to fight an officer; one view was that a man who had served with credit for two years was entitled to call out an officer he had a grievance against, even if it was his own captain. Italians, Brantôme says, were more liberal in this matter than Spaniards or, at an earlier date, Frenchmen.[36] In Louis XIV's army officers and soldiers were two separate communities, but the gap between junior officers and *bas officiers* or NCOs was narrower than might be expected.[37]

How captivating was the chivalric concept of the man standing forth alone to face his fate, like a knight errant, or as religion saw the soul facing its Maker, can be gleaned from the convention which was still kept up of kings proposing to fight one another, and spare bloodshed. A duel between those arch-enemies Charles V of Spain and Francis I of France was more than once mooted, but came to nothing. Many years later, near the end of the Peninsular War, the British captured documents about the proposals in the baggage-train of King Joseph Bonaparte; they suggest the quaint thought that Joseph was toying with the idea of a duel with the Prince Regent. Wellington sent them to Principal Robertson of Edinburgh university, an authority on Charles V.[38] In 1611 Charles IX of Sweden, old and ailing, early in the Kalmar War with Denmark challenged Christian IV to end it by

[33] 'Two Hundred and Fifty Years Ago', 137.

[34] G. G. Langsam, *Martial Books and Tudor Verse* (New York, 1951), 68–9.

[35] Leask and McCance, 36.

[36] Brantôme, 160–1. In the Venetian forces it was accepted that military service conferred nobility (Molmenti, 72 n. 1).

[37] A. Corvisier, *Louvois* (Paris, 1983), 97.

[38] Earl of Stanhope, *Conversations with the Duke of Wellington 1831–1851* (1886; London, 1938), 100.

single combat, 'according to the old custom of the Goths', with only helmet and sword. Christian scornfully declined.[39]

It was only on the stage that such royal gestures could get beyond empty flourishes. Hamlet's father won old Fortinbras's kingdom of Norway by taking him on in single combat. Even in the theatre a hint of incredulity might creep in. James IV of Scotland, at war with England in John Ford's play *Perkin Warbeck* (1634), sends a challenge to the English commander, the Earl of Surrey, telling him through a herald that his wish is to prevent 'prodigal effusion' of innocent blood. Another English nobleman is sceptical about Scottish courage lasting long, though he declares that any Englishman would welcome such a chance as Surrey is being given

> next to immortality,
> Above all joys of life.

Peace comes, and the matter drops. By the time a doughty Prince of Wales, later George II, took it into his head to call out the King of Prussia, their advisers were able to convince them that such a sparring-match would excite nothing but Europe's derision; though Thackeray, not without a sneaking regard for George, could not help wishing that Europe had been allowed to witness it.[40]

Rival commanders in the field sometimes indulged in the same threadbare heroics. When Mary Stewart's forces were confronting the rebels at Carberry in 1567, there was a proposal that Bothwell as her champion and one of the confederate lords should fight it out. In 1591 when England was taking part in the French civil war Elizabeth's general, the Earl of Essex, sent an invitation to Villars, head of the beleaguered garrison of Rouen. Several letters in high-flown style were exchanged, before Villars backed out, pleading that he was not author-ized to gamble with Rouen.[41] Ordinary officers, or even privates, could be more readily allowed to seek fame in this way. Before battles formal challenges were sometimes thrown out, and on occasion the opening salvo of gunfire was delayed in order to let individuals show their paces.[42] There is a story of Ben Jonson, as a soldier in the Netherlands, killing a Spaniard who came forward from the enemy lines. Far away from Europe there might be an occasional meeting, authentic or invented, between a Christian and an alien champion. During the conquest of Mexico Pedro de Alvarado was said to have killed the chief of the Maya tribe of Quiché in single fight.

---

[39] Gade, 122–4.
[40] Thackeray, *The Four Georges*, 47–8.
[41] G. B. Harrison, *The Life and Death of Robert Devereux, Earl of Essex* (London, 1937), 62–3.
[42] Keen, 165–6.

Fabulous wars, old tales of adventure, could still fascinate men of action as well as armchair readers. Shadows from the age of chivalry haunted Europe, ghosts loitering after cock-crow, unsurprisingly because in all spheres of life it was only very incompletely and stumblingly that the Middle Ages were being left behind. Mountains of rubbish from feudal times, not without veins of precious ore, littered the scene. Amid the chronic wars of the sixteenth century the exploits of Amadis de Gaul and many other old favourites came back to mind by spurts, casting a flickering stained-glass light over the sordid ravagings of the armies. In Spain the reign of Charles V (1516–56) marked the apogee of chivalric literature. The conquest of Granada from the Moors at the end of the previous century had roused enthusiasm, and Fray Luis de Granada put knights who perished in such wars on the same footing as martyrs. Men are always impressed, he observed, by willingness to risk death; hence their flocking to jousts or bullfights.[43] Another conquest, that of Ireland, was the theme of Book V of *The Faerie Queene*[99], that final, overblown flowering of chivalric poetry in England, and in contexts like this the completest exposure of the hollowness of most of its pretensions. Spenser was an official campfollower of the English army, and his 'dark and bloody feelings towards Ireland were uncompromisingly expressed'.[44]

Chivalry was part of the setting within which the early modern duel took shape, one of the siren songs that lured so many to soon-forgotten graves. As often, a class unwilling to quit the stage of history could take refuge in fantasy or, more positively, hearten itself for its journey into the future by hugging rags and tatters of the past. At Rome in April 1645 Evelyn watched 'a Just [*joust*] and Tournament of severall young gentlemen in a formal defy . . . the prizes being distributed by the ladies after the knight-errantry way'. It was exciting, though bloodless.[45] Yet there was a leaven of human vitality in the old romances which could appeal to readers outside the feudal pale. There are touches in *The Pilgrim's Progress* that reveal familiarity with them[46] (and the ding-dong fight between Christian and Apollyon has very much the look of a duel, or ordeal by battle). Milton could enjoy them in his earlier years; it was long after 'L'Allegro' when a changed outlook showed in his contemptuous dismissal of the stock themes of writers content

> to dissect
> With long and tedious havoc fabled knights
> In battles feigned,

[43] A. Valbuena Prat, *La vida española de la edad de oro* (Barcelona, 1943), 59, 68.
[44] C. Brady, 'Spenser's Irish Crisis', *Past and Present*, 111 (1986), 18.
[45] Evelyn, 144.
[46] Milton, *Prose Works*, ed. J. A. St John (London, 1848), iii. 118, Editor's note.

and their 'tinsel trappings'.[47] Even then, his own feigned battles of fabled angels were not without echoes of the clash of knightly arms.

Cervantes had already clapped his extinguisher over the old craze. All the same, Don Quixote's aims were honourable, even if ridiculous; his was the tragicomedy of the good intentions of one era becoming the laughing-stock of its successor. Knight-errantry was gone; the duel, its heir or memento, always kept a measure of the two qualities linked by the term 'quixotic'—absurdity, and idealism. A duellist gave even the most obnoxious opponent an equal chance of victory and life. Thanks in part to this inheritance the duel could perpetuate a compulsive grip of yesterday on today, enchaining men who, because history and society made them what they were, could not emancipate themselves from the past. 'The modern gentleman is still ideally linked with the medieval conception of chivalry.'[48]

Duels of course took place with the more facility because everyone carried weapons, needed for self-protection in disorderly streets and on unpoliced highways; in any sudden fracas swords or daggers would come out like claws. In England the word 'fencing' came into use in the sixteenth century from 'defence', with its cognate 'fence', or barrier. Voltaire looked back on the reign of Louis XIII (1610–43) as a time of universal discord: members of the Parlement wrangled over precedence, canons of Notre Dame brawled with canons of Sainte Chapelle, and 'practically every person was inspired by the passion for duelling', a 'gothic barbarism' which had become 'a part of the national char-acter'.[49]

It did not stand alone among institutionalized forms of violence. Duelling belonged mostly to the advanced or 'civilized' areas, where the individual stood more by himself, manipulated though he might be by invisible marionette-strings of pride and prejudice. In more retarded localities the clan feud still ran its course. In Catalonia, unlike less unruly Castile, the whole nobility was reported to be occupied with vendettas.[50] Italy, in some ways the most enlightened country of Europe, was in other ways as barbarous as any. Family vendettas, Burckhardt wrote, 'extending to friends and distant relations', riddled both higher and lower classes. Feuds pervaded chronicles and novels, especially 'vengeance taken for the violation of women', and, to judge from the authors' comments, revengers had 'the unqualified approval of public opinion'.[51] Noble families had been compelled by the northern city-

[47] *Paradise Lost*, prelude to Bk. 9.
[48] Huizinga, 131.
[49] Voltaire, 17.
[50] J. H. Elliott, *The Revolt of the Catalans* (Cambridge, 1963), 75.
[51] Burckhardt, 307–8.

republics of the Middle Ages to reside within the city walls; there they sometimes built fortified houses, and to claim the right to go on fighting each other over some 'ancient grudge' like that of the Capulets and Montagues was another way of upholding their rank and dignity. Vendetta and duel, in most ways antithetical, could both embody conceptions of honour; in an Italy so corrupt that Machiavelli said men would rather a tyrant killed their father than seized their wealth,[52] the vendetta might be called a rejection of crass materialism. A Tybalt after all had no motive of self-interest for drawing his sword; he was obeying an imperative of duty to the family, or rather its idealized abstraction, an entity higher than himself.

Causes that might bring on a duel were multifarious. Followers even of humble degree might be sucked into their superiors' hatreds, as in Shakespeare's Verona, but the reverse may have been not uncommon. A gentleman might feel obliged to unsheath his sword on behalf of an injured servant,[53] though part of the motive here was a feeling that any wrong to one's servant was a wrong to oneself. Still more self-regarding was whatever concerned property, and the crumbling of the feudal order left many rights debatable. Two French nobles clashed because of a controversy started by their bailiffs over seigneurial claims on the same villages.[54] But when men were in a pugnacious mood the slightest pretext would serve. Two Italian gallants fell out over the rival merits of Tasso and Ariosto; one, mortally wounded, confessed that he had never read the poet whose side he had taken.[55]

Patriotic fever, visible in earlier times, spread as nationalism took hold. In Italy the *patria* was still the native city or province. That fiery artist Benvenuto Cellini fell foul of a young soldier who talked offensively of the Florentines, and who next day sent him a challenge. Cellini took counsel with 'a fine old fellow called Bevilacqua, who had the reputation of having been the best swordsman in Italy. He had fought more than twenty duels in his time.' The offender withdrew, leaving Cellini to feel that he 'came out of the affair with honour'.[56] But there was already an 'Italian' sentiment against foreigners. There were rejoicings in Rome when an Italian defeated a Frenchman, but spared his life, saying that it was enough for him to have guarded the honour of his nation.[57] James I often had trouble with dislikes between Englishmen and the Scots who had followed him to London, and duels were not seldom the outcome of these angry fits.

---

[52] *The Prince*, chap. 17.
[53] Bennetton, 38.
[54] Hutton, 117.
[55] F. L. Lucas, *Literature and Psychology* (London, 1951), 210.
[56] Cellini, 51.
[57] Brantôme, 114–15.

Women were not often onlookers at duels, as they had been at tournaments, but they supplied plentiful apples of discord. At Ipswich lived two good friends and kinsmen, Edmund Withypoll and Anthony Felton. The latter, despite an income of a thousand pounds, did not mind yielding precedence, but his wife objected strongly, and in 1598 the two women got to such a pitch of fury that the husbands were drawn in. It came to an angry Withypoll striking his friend with a 'bastinado' or cane. They were restrained from further hostilities, and the matter went before the Earl Marshal.[58] It was established that though Withypoll had a hundred footmen of the local militia under him, Felton besides being a JP had charge of fifty mounted men, and a military referee declared that a cavalry officer was always the superior. Things ended with an apology from the striker, an example of how things could be accommodated when the parties were willing to listen to reason.

Huizinga dwells on the elaborate formalism of medieval etiquette, as necessary for curbing the excesses of a headstrong society where rude scufflings might take place even at court.[59] Boyish tantrums among pages in great households may be guessed at as the starting-point of some grown-up enmities. It was from a heated atmosphere that the duel emerged, yet as a highly formalized confrontation it could only have sprouted in a late feudal society with an upper class increasingly artificial in its manners and its whole existence. Duelling procedure, gradually evolving, had to impose itself on classes given to unbridled self-assertiveness. At the cost of many lives, it may be credited with bringing their conduct under a salutory discipline that law might have failed to achieve. This could come about only slowly and painfully, the more so because duelling soon became illegal, and its arrangements had to be made clandestinely.

At first it was not unusual for combatants to meet alone and unobserved. The intention might be to evade the law, by a pretence of an accidental encounter, leaving the survivor free to declare himself blameless. But it was early apparent that if duelling deaths were to be easily distinguishable from murder, there would have to be witnesses, and at least a minimum of rules. And a man going to a secret rendezvous might be walking into an ambush. It became customary for each combatant to bring with him a 'second', as an observer and a safeguard against foul play; a friend who would have to be prepared to take his share of whatever legal penalties might be incurred. In Spanish and early modern French he was known as the 'godfather' (*padrino, parrain*). An anonymous work of James I's reign called for two men on each side,

---

[58] See brochure of the 'Christchurch Mansion', built by the Withypoll family in 1548, at Ipswich.
[59] Huizinga, 43 ff.

for better surety, who must be of sufficient position, not less than 'knights or esquyres'.[60]

Taking place on foot, duels could be fought out in town streets or squares, or in nearby fields; also, they were simpler to manage than mounted frays would have been. One precaution carried over from medieval times occurs in Castiglione's anecdote of a duellist being asked by his opponent's second to swear that he was making no use of magic charms.[61] Jousters had enclosed themselves in a more and more impenetrable shell of armour; some duellists were fain to follow their example, according to the same authority, who tells us of poltroons fond of quibbling over points of honour but equally of choosing harmless weapons, covering themselves with enough armour to fend off a cannonade, and staying on the defensive.[62] Protective covering hidden under the dress was before long deemed cheating; as a guarantee against it, as well as for more freedom of movement, both men would often strip to their shirts. It was another indication of serious intentions that shields as well as armour were discarded, though in early days a cloak rolled up over the left arm might do duty for one.

It was between 1550 and 1650 that the greatest variety of weapons were in use. Pride of place went to the rapier, evolving mainly in Italy and Spain, a fairly long and cumbrous sword calling for strength as well as skill. Its slowness must have helped to make feasible the complicated moves and passes devised by the experts, a counterpart to the intricacies of the honour code. Sometimes a pair of rapiers, one in each hand, were used; more often a rapier and dagger were combined, until the latter was discarded in order to leave the duellist free to concentrate on his fencing. Teachers, the majority Italian, found pupils everywhere. 'Prize-players' gave exhibition fights for money. A redoubtable performer at Mantua accustomed to win high stakes was worsted by the Admirable Crichton.[63]

Orderly development of the duel was for long hampered by seconds wanting to take part in the action, instead of being simply invigilators. This seems to have started in Italy; three, four, or even more might be engaged on each side. Brantôme more than once remarks that seconds might join in purely 'par gayeté de cœur', from sheer light-heartedness;[64] a phrase memorable for what it tells of the frivolity, the recklessness, that were thought proper to young bloods. In a celebrated

[60] Bennetton, 20 n. 13. Seconds were Latinized, e.g. by the Council of Trent (Strecker, 24), into 'patrini aut secundantes'.
[61] Castiglione, 184.
[62] Ibid. 62.
[63] Hutton, 88 ff.
[64] Brantôme, 77, etc..

meeting in 1578 between a royal favourite, Quélus, and a rival, with two henchmen on each side, two of the six were killed, two fatally wounded. In its classic form the duel was again to be fought out between two men, but Europe's emergent individualism was still entangled in relationships of earlier origin; and the seventeenth century was in many ways one of decay and retrogression. Many men in a position to command support must have counted on a better chance if they had swordsmen with more skill or experience than their own beside them. One can sympathize with mad old Lear when, thinking he is being captured, he exclaims 'No seconds? all myself?' But Montaigne called it 'a kind of dastardliness' to bring in helpers: third parties should be present, as they used to be, solely as witnesses and umpires.[65] French legislation of the early seventeenth century viewed it as unmanly, and severely censured it. But it went on surprisingly long. D'Artagnan, the Gascon soldier of fortune whose memoirs inspired Dumas, arrived in Paris at the age of sixteen and was delighted to find himself immediately taking part in a three-a-side match. On these occasions when a man was down there was apparently no objection to two turning their blades against one.

Master–servant relations were still semi-feudal, and the line between retainer and menial was unclear. By later duelling standards it must look very odd and discreditable for a domestic to be made use of in an affair of honour, as seems to have quite often happened. No man is a hero to his valet, and the French theatre, often a mouthpiece of newer, middle-class modes of thinking, showed reluctant servitors protesting against being dragged into their employers' unlawful doings.[66] At this rate the duel risked making itself ridiculous, and in the long run it came to be thought proper for only a close relative to join in, and then as proxy, not assistant. In France a man was not expected to fight after reaching the age of sixty; it was usually his son who would take his place, as Diego's son does in Corneille's *Le Cid*.

Peter Burke has described the post-medieval withdrawal of the higher classes from the popular festivities of carnival, miracle-play, folk song, into an élite culture of their own.[67] Duelling represented one aspect of this. It was a private affair of gentlemen alone, even if plebeians might sometimes get a glimpse of it, whereas jousting had been a public spectacle. Like the tournament, but perhaps somewhat quicker because of this privacy, the duel came under refining influences; the aristocratic

---

[65] Montaigne, Bk. 2, chap. 27.
[66] Bennetton, 87–9, 100, 132.
[67] Burke, chap 9, and *passim*.

world, or its more intelligent representatives, had to acknowledge the need of accommodation to the spirit of a changing age. Brantôme set himself to explore the question whether combatants should act on the adage 'Woe to the conquered', or treat their opponents with courteous forbearance. He was a keen enough advocate of the duel to think it disgraceful to come home without fighting, after a last-minute accord.[68] On the other hand he clearly disapproved of the sanguinary custom, a legacy of trial by battle, that put the life of the defeated at the mercy of the victor. In his view Italians, crueller than Frenchmen, were making too small an improvement by recommending that a beaten enemy be only crippled and put out of action for good.[69] Among his own countrymen he singles out a Sieur de Fandilles, so vindictive that he always insisted on having a stake ready and a fire lit, to burn his enemy after rendering him helpless; another killer he refers to as 'un terrible et déterminé exécuteur de vengeances'.[70]

By contrast he holds up examples of magnanimous conduct, and rates highly the credit due to generosity towards the loser; he even admonishes a winner not to trumpet his success ostentatiously.[71] In all this a sound instinct of class shows; it was not merely personal decency that was concerned. Plebeians, who were working out their own notions of 'fair play', would be impressed by seeing or hearing of a well-conducted encounter, with behaviour worthy of gentlemen on both sides. A spectacle of crude butchery would lower their estimate of their superiors instead of raising it. A brave gentleman, it had to be made manifest, could be killed, but he must never be subjected to ignominy or barbarity. And aristocratic fellow-feeling would be undermined by an excess of vicious feeling and brutal conduct, while willingness to take part in the duelling game might well be damped.

The formative period of the duel, and of the classes which practised it, also inaugurated the modern theatre. This had most vitality where it could appeal to all sections of urban society, as it learned to do in Madrid, Paris, London; but everywhere aristocracy had a significant part in shaping its attitudes, either positively or by the criticisms that upper-class behaviour increasingly provoked. Court patronage meant a great deal to the theatre; court life, monarchical self-display, was nothing if not theatrical, and there was an affinity between courtier and actor, visible in the gorgeous costumes, the peacock feathers, sometimes handed on from the one to the other.

In a very particular way this was the great age of modern *tragic* drama. In general, drama and duelling flourished side by side; it is noteworthy, however, that authentic tragedy failed to take root in the

[68] Brantôme, 189.　　　　　　[69] Ibid. 131–2.
[70] Ibid. 5, 13, 94.　　　　　　[71] Ibid. 104, 112, 118.

Spanish or Italian theatre, but blossomed most of all in England, and in a secondary degree, with more indebtedness to the Greeks, in France. It cannot be mere coincidence that France and England were becoming the chosen homes of the duel, whereas in southern Europe, after a dashing start, it fell into the background. In tragedy the purgation by ritual violence of morbid social emotions, more than usually tempestuous in that age of change and dislocation, was apotheosized.

5

The Spread of the Duel

Who could have thought that I, being what I was
A few days back, and what I am; to this
Reduc'd by that name *Honour*; whose nice laws,
Accurs'd be he who framed! ...
And one being vain enough to make the law,
How came the silly world to follow it,
Like sheep to their own slaughter!

Calderón (1600–81), *The Painter of Dishonour*.

DUELLING spread over Europe, taking on varying colours, and some-times different names. Most countries, from England to Romania, made do with a form of the Italian *duello*; Spanish and Portuguese added another word, *desafío*, German adopted also *Zweikampf*, Swedish *envig*, also *tvekamp* which it shared with Danish; in Russia the name that came into use was *poyedinok*. It was spreading because so many lands suffered from the incubus of an aristocracy of feudal origin, restless under political or social strains. This class was responsible for numerous breaches of the law and order that governments were striving to estab-lish, and it was long before a duel, especially with seconds joining in, could be clearly distinguished from other sorts of disorderliness. As a relic of private warfare it held a threat of swelling into something bigger, a factious or seditious tumult. Authority was not yet ready to recognize what was plausible in the argument of Brantôme, Bodin, and others, that a few deaths in well-regulated fights did no harm by comparison with collisions between powerful men bringing troops of retainers into action with them.[1]

Noblemen who took the law into their own hands were defying their rulers as well as each other. On the other hand the perennial ambivalence of relations between throne and nobility gave kings per-sonally, by contrast with kings as office-bearers, a family sympathy with aristocratic foibles, and willingness and need to wink at them. Their usually half-hearted attempts to put down duelling are one index of how inextricably monarchy, with all its more forward-looking

---

[1] Brantôme, 141. Cf. Bacon's objection that when men come to blows openly 'it is a sign the reverence of government is lost', *Essays* (London, 1597, 1625), no. 15, 'of Seditions and Troubles'.

aspects, remained entangled in old feudal habits. Henri III as described by Brantôme was typical: he was always issuing prohibitions, but he was too kind-hearted (*bon*) to punish offenders rigorously; 'he loved his nobility'.[2] If a ban really was being enforced in one country, a rendezvous could be arranged beyond the frontier, and it was one of Brantôme's tenets that a man could not honourably reject a challenge to meet abroad, even if it meant disobeying his sovereign.[3] Monarchy was in any case far less 'absolute' in reality than in name, for want of anything like a modern police machinery.

As yet there was only a limited division between civil and military within the dominant class, but armies were of crucial importance for purposes both of order—or repression—at home and of chronic warfare abroad; rulers could not afford to fall out with the men who led them. Since their wars were as foolish or immoral as any duels could be, in fact very much like duels on an international scale, they were in a poor position to preach. And the contention was soon being heard, as it never ceased to be, that duelling was indispensable for keeping up a proper warlike spirit. Shakespeare's Alcibiades, pleading with the senate on behalf of a comrade condemned for fighting, urges that if spirited soldiers are wanted they cannot be expected to be too tame and docile in private.[4]

Discipline was lax, the chain of command imprecise. Professional jealousies, like Iago's against Cassio, were rampant. But for governments trying to lick into shape the unruly material at their disposal, such disturbances were one more nuisance. Army regulations, in France for instance, included general cautions against them.[5] They were harder to implement because a good many officers, as well as a high proportion of the rank and file, were always foreign mercenaries, drawn from a floating cosmopolitan mass. The prevalence of duelling must have owed much to these footloose adventurers. A climax was reached in the Thirty Years War, from 1618 to 1648, which drew in most of Europe. It helped to spread duelling habits far and wide, though above all among the gentry and soldiery of central Europe. Gustavus Adolphus of Sweden found the craze infecting both officers and men of his polyglot forces. He had a reputation for stern Protestant piety to live up to, and made it a capital crime. When two senior officers were about to fight he is said to have notified them that the survivor would be executed: the dispute was promptly dropped.[6]

---

[2] Ibid. 139.
[3] Ibid. 127–9.
[4] *Timon of Athens*, Act III, sc. v.
[5] See Fourquevaux, *Instructions sur le faict de la guerre*, ed. G. Dickinson (London, 1954), e.g. pp. lxxv ff.
[6] Bosquett, 62–4.

Italian writers might expatiate eloquently on the deportment of a gentleman, but Italian feudings must often have been little encumbered with niceties, even when they rose above the level of murder by poison or stiletto. The national imagination, Burckhardt thought, lent a peculiar subtlety and atrocity to its revenges.[7] Fought sporadically from 1494 to 1559, the 'Italian Wars' brought locust-swarms of foreign soldiers into the country, until Spain finally got the better of France, and must have further inflamed this ruthlessness. The country was badly run by the miniature autocracies which supplanted most of the northern republics, with the prominent exception of Venice; fragmented authority was only partially remedied by the paramountcy acquired by Spain, along with direct rule over Milan, Naples, and Sicily. It was in the south, under foreign rule and suffering economic decay, that assassination kept its ground most firmly. Sicily with its immense proliferation of titles and privileges—Keats's 'most prevailing tinsel'— whose sale amounted almost to a regular wealth tax, was an extreme case of what was happening everywhere under the 'new monarchies'. An alien government had less interest in keeping aristocracy intact, and the class was being too heavily diluted for the duel to be able to provide a congenial and bracing discipline.

Some efforts at policing were made. A story of familiar pattern, dating from 1547, tells of a man at Como under sentence of death for killing in a duel. His wife, to save him, gave herself to the local official, who then broke his word and carried out the execution; the governor, learning of this, compelled him to marry and endow the lady, and then beheaded him.[8] That intrepid traveller Fynes Moryson found that at Mantua, as in most Italian cities, it was forbidden to wear a sword without licence; in some towns under Venetian suzerainty a stranger could carry a sword, but not a pistol.[9] In Florence Cellini, who tells us how when his blood was up he 'joined battle, snorting like an angry bull',[10] was repeatedly in hot water over his ruffianism, but the heat was not excessive. When his brother wounded a man in a sword-fight, at the age of fourteen, and was nearly mobbed, Benvenuto rushed to his aid; they and their opponents were no more than temporarily banished from the city.[11] Even in northern Italy there was less of a feudal-aristocratic tradition than in other countries, and instead a certain businesslike realism whose preference was to wipe an enemy out, not to join him in a polite *pas de deux*.

[7] Burckhardt, 265 ff.
[8] A. Visconti, *Storia di Milano* (Milan, 1937), 431.
[9] Fynes Moryson, *Itinerary* (1617), Pt. 1, Bk. 2, chap. 3.
[10] Cellini, 37–8.
[11] Ibid. 24.

Duelling seems to have found its way into the extensive Venetian territory on the mainland in the early seventeenth century, when Venice was entering on its decline, the merchant oligarchy turning away from the sea to settle down into landowning. There was a plague of *bravi* and *banditti*, some of them hangers-on of nobility. 'Gentlemen called each other out on the most frivolous pretexts', and bullies profited from the fashion by extorting blackmail from the unwarlike.[12] Duels were prohibited under stern penalties in 1535 and 1541, and denounced by the Senate and Council of Ten in 1631, but they went on, mostly over questions of rank and precedence 'and such like inanities', and enveloped in all the formalities prescribed by writers like Muzio; chivalry was reduced to 'the merest casuistry'.[13]

It was in Piedmont that Italian duelling had its sturdiest growth, a fact that must be explained by this small but energetic principality being a meeting-ground of Italian and French life; Savoy was the cradle of its dynasty. A favourite place for duelling was the bridge across the river at Turin, a choice suggestive of a relish for publicity and vainglory. During a French occupation the governor put a stop to this by permitting fights only on the parapet, and forbidding any rescue from the water.[14] A spot where they could be indulged in with the minimum of meddlesome interference was Malta, held from 1530 by the Knights of St John. Like the duel, the Order was a cosmopolitan and aristocratic institution; always under the shadow of Turkish attack, it could hope, like an officer corps, to find in the duel a useful spur to courage and emulation. An eighteenth-century visitor found that some restrictions had been imposed, but counted twenty crosses painted on the street wall to mark places where knights had fallen. He heard of a recent case of a knight who allowed himself to be abused and even struck in a billiard-room quarrel, without challenging the other man: this mean-spirited creature was sentenced to forty-five days of a kind of stool of repentance in church, five years in an unlit dungeon, and imprisonment for life.[15]

Don Quixote was challenged in the end by a 'Knight of the White Moon', a disguised well-wisher from his own district. Galloping into action, he and his old steed collapsed, and he had to fulfil his pledge to go home quietly, if defeated, and stay there for a year.[16] Back at home his wits recovered, and he died a sadder and wiser man, leaving his creator to hope that his book would give knight-errantry its *coup de*

---

[12] W. C. Hazlitt, *The Venetian Republic* (London, 1915), ii. 590 ff.

[13] Molmenti, 71–2.

[14] Steinmetz, i. 183. A variant of this story is given in the *Encyclopédie* article on the Duel (v. 163).

[15] P. Brydone, *A Tour through Sicily and Malta* (London, 1773), i. 332–3.

[16] *Don Quixote*, chaps. 64–5.

grâce. It may have done something to damp, if not quench, ardour
for duelling in Spain. By foreigners, Spaniards were considered more
meticulous than most about punctilio; visitors in later days discovered
that even a labourer could have his *pundonor*, or point of honour, and
a ready knife. A great many Spaniards enjoyed noble status, with the
honorific 'Don', which could be acquired by various means as well as
by birth. They were moreover the imperial race, whose kings reigned
over much of western Europe, the Americas, the Philippines. In contact
with foreigners, as they often were, they cultivated the gravity and
dignity for which Castilian manners came to be noted; this, and Spanish
sobriety, may have left less room for quarrelling.

In Franche-Comté, an inheritance from the old Burgundian state,
between Lorraine and Switzerland, scuffles and duels between local
noblemen and Spaniards were commonplace in the later sixteenth
century, under Philip II.[17] But this was exceptional; Spain did not take
to duelling with anything like the enthusiasm of the French. Colonies
and perpetual war abroad—in the Mediterranean against the Turks,
in Italy against the French, in the Netherlands against rebels, on the
Atlantic against English privateers—drew off most of the more restless
spirits. Internally there was a very long era of peace and, by the
standards of the time, order; and there was a popular monarchy,
unquestioned except during the brief revolt of the 'Comuneros' or
chartered cities in 1520–21. Trust in the monarchy and the justice
it dispensed, after the reforms of Isabella (1479–1504), encouraged
litigation even over issues where men of honour might have been
expected to prefer cold steel. 'A golden moment in the image of the
law' is marked by the flood of cases pouring into the Castilian tribunals
from about 1500.[18] Duelling was firmly prohibited by a law of 1480,
even before the modern mode came in. Manuals of conduct linked
honour with good breeding and recognition of 'the respect due to
others'.[19]

As the seventeenth century went on there was deterioration in every
department, though in literature and the arts it set in less quickly.
Public order was more often disturbed; a reversion to old-style brawlings
between nobles and their retinues can be observed. Seville, the great
city of Andalusia, was notorious for its turbulent mob, and its many
affrays and stabbings at the theatre door.[20] Mme d'Aulnoy, the French
traveller of the late seventeenth century, was told by a Spaniard that his

[17] L. Febvre, *Philippe II et la Franche-Comté* (new edn., Paris, 1970), 100–1.

[18] J. Bossy, 'Postscript', in Bossy (ed.), *Disputes*, 291.

[19] J. Casey, 'Household Disputes and the Law in Early Modern Andalusia', ibid. 206–7. The
strictness of Spanish law was applauded by Voet (p. 215).

[20] H. A. Rennert, *The Spanish Stage in the Time of Lope de Vega* (New York, 1909), 125.

countrymen were passionately revengeful, but preferred assassination to duelling, which meant 'running half the danger'.[21] This sounds like Italy—and there were many Italians in Spain as well as Spaniards in Italy—as though the country in decay was reverting to a Mediterranean norm, divergent from the pattern of northern Europe. An English critic in 1642 accused Spanish duellists of being less honourable than French, and desirous of protecting themselves with quilted doublet and coat of mail.[22] If he was right, it was another mark of a decline that affected the aristocracy most of all.

Plays full of incensed husbands, bent on wiping out stains on their escutcheons, may, it is suggested, have given historians an overheated notion of Spanish 'honour'.[23] Diverse impressions can in fact be culled from the drama. In one of Calderón's plays a Galician expresses surprise at a judge being sent all the way from the capital to investigate a fatal duel, something 'that happens almost every day in Spain'; the judge explains that there has also been forcible resistance to arrest.[24] But in another play a man who has killed a rival in love, in a duel ostensibly over a slight card-table disagreement, tells how he had to take flight to Italy, and only secured a pardon after finding an influential patron.[25] Sometimes at any rate Calderón seems clearly to be condemning the duel, as in one of his best-known works where a sensible farmer gives a Polonius-style lecture to his departing son. 'Quarrel with no one but with good cause': as for fencing-masters and the rest, what we need to learn is not how to fight, but *why*.[26]

In Mme d'Aulnoy's time the bullfight was still an aristocratic sport, regularly known as a 'duel', because the matador must be a gentleman, a cavalier who 'assaults the bull, and fights him in single combat'. Only after the bull 'insulted' him, by molesting him or his mount, could he use his sword.[27]

In France under Louis XII and Francis I (1498–1547), with combative habits stimulated by intercourse with Italy, a beginning was made at setting up courts of honour to adjudicate in disputes. It was in those days that Rabelais was writing his gigantic farce. He was intermittently a priest, more congenially a medical experimenter, and of solidly middle-class stock; his thumbing his nose at antique kings and heroes, and habitual ridicule of war, may be taken as implying a derisory view of aristocracy and its ways, including duelling. Growth of a public

[21] Mme M.-C. D'Aulnoy, *Travels into Spain* (1690; English edn., London, 1930), 67; cf. 289.
[22] James Howell, cited by J. D. Wilson, 406.
[23] Casey, 206–7.
[24] Calderón, *Gil Perez, the Gallician*, in Fitzgerald, 180.
[25] Id., *Beware of Smooth Water*, ibid. 291–2.
[26] Id., *The Mayor of Zalamea*, ibid. 270–1.
[27] D'Aulnoy, 259.

opinion hostile to such things showed in 1560 when the States-General at its meeting at Orleans got Charles IX to declare duelling a capital crime. This session marked an advance in progressive thinking, which had to come mainly from spokesmen of the Third Estate or middle classes. But while England's Parliament was steadily consolidating its place, France's States-General was nearing the end of a precarious life.

The Valois dynasty too was running down, and the chain of civil wars between 1562 and 1598, under religious catchwords, crippled royal authority and allowed duelling, along with all other breaches of the peace, to flourish. Civil wars, here and in England and elsewhere, may have done more than foreign wars to foment duelling, by accustoming men's minds to the thought of strife between fellow-countrymen. An edict of 1566 reiterated the death penalty for duellists of all ranks, and urged disputants to appeal to Marshals or provincial governors as umpires, who would enforce an *amende honorable* or reparation where they found this to be warranted. An edict of 1579 treated the duel as *lèse-majesté*, but was not much more than a dead letter. By espousing the conflicting creeds, noble factions were endowing themselves with a new leading role, and political grudges provided fresh irritants. To kill, Montaigne wrote, was now the desire of every duellist; there were no shades or degrees of revenge, as there used to be. Yet killing, it is rather surprising to hear him say, exposed a man to at least some inconvenience from the law: it left him to 'shift up and downe, runne and trot, and squat here and there', to avoid arrest.[28]

Henri IV came out on top, founding the new Bourbon dynasty. An incident characteristic of him concerned his friend Bassompierre, a future marshal. This cavalier distinguished himself in a three-a-side combat *à la barrière*, a species of tourney and the last of the kind to be held. Henry complained to the Duc de Guise that Mlle d'Entragues, his intended next mistress, 'idolized' Bassompierre for his performance, and belittled everyone else. This might well be called *lèse-majesté*, and, since a monarch could not call out a subject, Guise undertook to break lances with the offender as his proxy. Something like a horseback joust was arranged (technically a *course de champ ouvert*, as distinct from the *champ clos* form of duel of honour) in the courtyard of the Louvre, with king and queen and court looking on from the palace windows. It was the first time such an event had taken place for a century, Bassompierre's memoirs say: he was gravely wounded, which led Henry to forbid its ever being repeated.[29]

It is a curious sidelight on royalty in Europe, by comparison with Asia, and its relations with aristocracy, that a king should have to work

[28] Montaigne, Bk. 2, chap. 27.
[29] *Mémoires du Maréchal de Bassompierre* (Paris, 1665; 1822–3), 344.

off his spleen so circuitously. But the broader measures of the reign
against duelling owed less to him than to his great minister Sully, whose
memoirs supply detail of numerous clashes among the high nobility.[30]
He took an interest in the earlier history of the subject, from the invasion
of the barbarians and their trial by battle, ridiculous enough but at
least well-intentioned, unlike the murderous modern duel. He was
against the death penalty promulgated in 1609 for 'this pernicious and
savage abuse', he says, because he feared that over-severity would make
the law harder to enforce; he blamed his royal master's 'easiness of
temper' for the spread of the evil.[31] Most of Henry's life had been passed
in the camp, among soldiers. His decrees might be harsh, but he nullified
them by granting thousands of pardons, or 'letters of grace'. Chapman
drew a faithful enough picture of him in the scene (Act II, sc. i) of his
play *Bussy d'Ambois,* where Henry hears a long report of an epic fight
between Bussy, with two friends, and three others, and of Bussy alone
of all these 'famous soldiers' being left alive. Bussy enters, with Henry's
brother who has promised to ask forgiveness for him. At first the king
stands firm:

> 'these wilful murders
> Are ever past our pardon',

but after some debate between him and his brother as to whether a
duellist's death really is murder, Bussy is let off with a caution.

It may be suspected that the edicts were meant to impress law-
abiding burghers and magistrates, while Henry's prerogative of setting
them aside enabled him to earn the gratitude of the nobles—many of
them lately his opponents—at no cost to himself. It may be supposed
also that the secretaries of state through whose hands their petitions
passed knew how to get pickings out of the business. An almost incredible number of eight thousand duellists are said to have been
killed during this short reign. 'They'll none of them be missed', some
Frenchmen may have reflected philosophically. Notions of honour
were so refined, said Mandeville, that 'barely looking upon a Man was
often taken for an Affront'.[32]

Duelling on this scale could be a partial replacement, as an outlet
for restless energies, for the civil and foreign wars that came to an end
in 1598. In 1610 Henry was assassinated, when busy planning a new
European war, and down to 1635, when Richelieu launched the country
into the Thirty Years War, French arms found legitimate employment
only fitfully. In 1614 the States-General met for the last time; its

---

[30] Sully, i. 110–14, etc.
[31] Ibid. ii. 367–8, iii. 249–52, 400.
[32] Mandeville, 64.

deliberations had a flood of pamphlets for accompaniment, among them a set of sermons by Bishop Jean Camus denouncing sundry public evils, including duelling which he blamed for causing as much disturbance and bloodshed in a year as two years of war could do.[33] This may sound far-fetched, but since the English invasions came to an end France's wars had been fought mostly on foreign soil, so that Frenchmen suffered only through having to pay for them. The second chamber, of the nobility, was in no self-critical mood, but pressed for all its privileges to be respected. Duelling it declared should be permitted when any grave questions of honour were at stake: an arrangement for regulating other quarrels should be devised by the marshals.[34] Public disapproval was at least extorting an admission that duelling ought not to be resorted to frivolously.

In power from 1624, Richelieu took a firm line against it from the start. He had elbowed his way into office through a welter of court factions; his elder brother perished in a duel in the course of the scrimmagings. It may even be worth recalling that, as a cardinal, he was nominally a Christian, in an era when Catholicism in France was having its belated Counter-Reformation and revival. Duelling became the ground, of more symbolic than practical importance, for a prolonged trial of strength between him and his refractory fellow-nobles. By pouncing on prominent offenders he could hope to overawe the rest. His heaviest blow fell in 1627, a year after another stern edict, when the Comte de Bouteville, an inveterate duellist and a member of the great Montmorency clan, who felt able to laugh at government threats, had an encounter with the Comte de Chapelles. It was a deliberate act of defiance, and despite many appeals on their behalf Richelieu's only concession was to allow them to be beheaded by the sword instead of the axe. Honour came first, he pronounced, except where State interests were concerned.[35]

All the same, he had to confess to the Parlement, the supreme judicial body, when it asked for legislation to be enforced in full, that in the light of experience this was scarcely feasible. A steady frown could at least inspire a feeling that the survivor of a duel would do well to take refuge abroad; but it seems that, even though the edict of 1626 forbade appeals for pardon, a man with strings to pull could look to speedy rehabilitation. Louis XIII may have prized his right of pardon as a way of keeping some independence from his too powerful minister, in these family matters between him and his nobles.

France's duelling mania became notorious abroad. Lord Herbert of

[33] J. M. Hayden, *France and the Estates General of 1614* (Cambridge, 1974), 108.
[34] Ibid. 185.
[35] Powis, 64–5.

Cherbury, himself fond of duelling or at least of bragging of his fondness for it, was there about 1608 and reported that there was 'scarce any man thought worth the looking on, that had not killed some other in duel'.[36] In that country, 'the very seed-plot of all courtesies', according to Ben Jonson every gentleman felt bound to carry a challenge when requested, without asking reasons: to quibble was deemed cowardly, in spite of the fact that he might be expected to take part in the fight.[37] If so, it is a token of the freemasonry that can prevail within a privileged class, however little this may have of real unity. Duelling survived another edict in 1643 from another cardinal-minister, Mazarin. A third cardinal, De Retz, graduated to political buccaneering from a youth spent amid scenes of dissipation and duelling. He was one of a throng of memoirists in seventeenth-century France. Memoir-writing was another symptom of the rise of individual consciousness; the same political and social environment could be favourable both to it and to the duel, and every combatant could hope to be recorded for posterity in someone's pages. Monarchs sought glory from war to keep their memory alive, private men from private battle.

Public opinion was, none the less, slowly asserting itself as a factor, mostly on this issue on the side of the government. One medium through which it could find expression was the drama, though with many cross-currents of feeling. In *Le Cid* Corneille's monarch feels compelled to authorize a judicial duel, but his views are much akin to Richelieu's.[38] Some spectators of noble rank may have taken to heart the lay sermons they heard from the stage. Many must at least have been struck by the point frequently raised that duelling was futile, because it left so much to chance; there could for instance be a case of two men fighting over a woman, one being killed, the other having to flee, the prize falling to someone else.[39] But as a whole, aristocracy reacted unfavourably. Insistence on its right to fight was a means of emphasizing the line of division between itself and the obnoxious upper-middle class, too close to it for comfort. Jealous, besides, of all its privileges, it was likely to be apprehensive that attacks on one of these might be the prelude to attacks on others.

Bourgeois opinion was less effective because the middle classes were heterogeneous, and had no common rallying-point or fidelity to any principle recognized by all. Vincent Voiture, the leading poet of the *Précieux* school, and a salon wit, who came of a bourgeois family, died in Paris in 1648 of injuries sustained in a duel. Also, if the French

[36] Lord Herbert, 52.
[37] *The Magnetic Lady*, Act III, sc. iv.
[38] Bennetton, 21-2, 34.
[39] Ibid. 97.

bourgeoisie was so curiously slow to take over power from the aristocratic state, one reason must have been that peaceful citizens lacked
confidence in their ability to muzzle a still turbulent nobility, in control
of the army and demonstrating by its defiance of the duelling laws its
unwillingness to submit to discipline. Only a strong king could be
depended on to hold it in leash; absolute monarchy became once more,
after the disturbances of the Frondes in mid-century, the lodestar of
prudent thinking.

Bacon tells us in his work on Henry VII that when the king was
preparing for his attack on France in 1492, 'to warm the blood of his
nobility and gallants' he held a month-long tournament at Richmond.
Two gentlemen with a grievance against each other were set jousting:
one had a faulty helmet, and a lance-point got into his mouth. His
death 'was accounted amongst the vulgar as a combat or trial of right'.
A century and a half later Selden, an authority on the history of trial
by battle, held that a judicial duel might still be licensed in England,
though nowhere else; also that if war is lawful, God being sole arbiter
'between two that are supreme', trial by combat must be equally so.[40]
In reality its last, or virtually last, occurrence was in 1571; men were
turning away now from public vindication to the private satisfaction
of the duel.[41]

Habits of earlier days clung to it for long. One of the many duels
that caught Carlyle's eye shows how as late as the 1590s family and
following could still be entangled in a private affair. Sir John Holles, a
wealthy midlands landowner of London citizen descent and later Earl
of Clare, married a Stanhope, and was accused by a rival family, the
Shrewsburys, of jilting their daughter. Their retainers came to blows,
and Holles had to spirit one of his men away to Ireland after a death
on the other side. Sir Gervase Markham, a friend of the Shrewsburys,
taxed him with complicity in murder; Holles challenged him, but
declined to meet him in his enemies' park—a suspicion of treachery
that would seldom have arisen later on, in the golden age of the duel.
Subsequently a chance encounter in Sherwood forest left Markham
stretched on the ground; he recovered, but was emasculated, a grievous
fate for the loose-liver he had been.[42]

Renaissance thinking wavered between pedigree as the sign of distinction, and merit. Bussy d'Ambois insists that nobility has 'no gra-
dation' except of merit (Act III, sc. i). 'Honor', Peacham wrote in his
book on the gentleman, 'is the reward of Vertue and glorious Action
onely'; but he was also strong for social hierarchy, and indignant at

---

[40] Selden, *Table Talk*, 60–1.
[41] Rowse, 229.
[42] Carlyle, 'Two Hundred and Fifty Years Ago', 128–30.

'Every undeserving and base Peasant ayming at Nobilitie', a distemper he saw spreading over Europe. In Naples a groom expected to be addressed as 'Signore', in Venice 'every Mechanique is a *Magnifico*'.[43] Englishmen's minds turned readily to 'complexly mingled ideas about honour'.[44] Terms like 'Honourable' and 'Your Honour' came into complimentary use; in common usage 'honour' was taken in the sense of what inspired men to fight duels. It was thought of as an attribute of the landed gentry, though not exclusively.[45] 'What a gentleman is, 'tis hard with us to define', Selden remarked. 'In other countries he is known by his privileges'[46]—but in England these were less obtrusive, and blood had many shades of blue. Besides the time-honoured path leading a townsman to a country estate, there were many other grounds, of profession, education, property, that could warrant a claim to rank with the highest in the essentials of upper-class status.

Costume and manners ceased to provide a clear dividing-line, as the Elizabethan courtier's lavishly pretentious dress and speech reached their limit. Tax-paying obligations drew no boundary, as they did on the continent. An inclination to claim the duellist's privilege could be all the stronger because the limits of gentility were indistinct, and for those whose claim to status was not beyond query it might seem all too easy to forfeit it by failure to stand on their dignity. In Chapman's comedy of 1599, *All Fools* (Act III, sc. i), a merchant with social ambitions is driven by suspicions of his wife to challenge the courtier whom he believes to have been her guilty partner; knowing little of swordsmanship he is lucky to draw first blood, and then to be parted from his opponent by the bystanders.

A study of how people got on with one another in England from the fifteenth to the seventeenth century indicates that 'at all levels men and women were extremely short-tempered'.[47] If so, this may be taken as one index of the dislocations brought about by the long-drawn transformation of medieval into modern. Witch-hunting was another. London sheltered blackguardism of every kind, and its streets in James I's reign resounded with 'Roaring Boys' and 'Bravaders'. It was one of Europe's largest cities, and swelling uncontrollably. Pugnacious habits could spread from class to class, as did 'swashbuckling', loud beating with sword on buckler. This was more noisy than harmful, but from about 1560 the sharp-pointed rapier was coming in from the continent and displacing the dull-edged broadsword. William Harrison (1534–93)

---

[43] Peacham, 3, 14–15.
[44] Council, 31.
[45] C. L. Barber, 113. Chap. 4 discusses how widely eligibility for duelling extended.
[46] Selden, *Table Talk*, 72.
[47] L. Stone, *Family*, 77; more generally, *The Crisis of the Aristocracy 1558–1641* (Oxford, 1965), 242 ff.: 'The Duel'.

in his *Description of England* said that few Englishmen were without at least a dagger, even 'aged burgesses and magistrates', while nobles, and their serving-men, usually had a sword or rapier as well; and there were some 'desperate cutters' who carried two daggers or two rapiers, ready for use 'in every drunken fray'.[48] It behoved the provident man to learn something of the art of fencing; practice was carried on particularly at Smithfield, where of yore tournaments had been held. Foreign instructors were at hand, with the Spanish and Italian schools competing.[49]

Queen Elizabeth was sometimes supposed to have a certain partiality for the duel, but her authority was several times brought to bear against it. When she heard of the precocious Earl of Essex, at nineteen, picking a quarrel with Sir Charles Blunt (later Lord Mountjoy) over a favour she had given the latter to wear after his performance in a tilt, she 'swore by God's death, it was fit that some one or other should take him down'.[50] As seems to have happened sometimes, the two young men became good friends. When the Earl of Southampton was goaded by Lord Grey into going to the Netherlands to fight him, she interposed and told them they ought to reserve their valour for her service. Late in her reign, in 1597, Southampton and the truculent Earl of Northumberland, who suffered from deafness and 'an exceedingly hot temper', were summoned before the council and forbidden to carry the wrangle between them further.[51]

This Northumberland in a manual composed for his son recommended as the best physical exercises those useful to men 'for the defence of themselves or the service of their country', such as 'managing of all sorts of arms'.[52] In James I's reign there was a marked vogue of martial manners and pursuits, and with them the duel: the word appears to have first found its way into print, in place of 'duello', in 1611 (for long it was often spelled 'dual', as an affair of two men). 'The fury of duels', Hume wrote in his *History,* 'prevailed more than at any other time before or since.'[53] 'Every family of distinction', in the belief of a later writer, 'lost some promising cadet in the early years of the century by duelling.'[54] Taking the country as a whole these impressions may be too highly coloured. It seems, judging by a study of one

[48] L. Withington (ed.), *Elizabethan England* (from W. Harrison's *A Description of England* (London, 1587; London, 1876?), 227–8).

[49] Sieveking, ii. 390, 397.

[50] Sir R. Naunton, *Fragmenta Regalia,* in *Tracts and Pamphlets* (World's Classics, Oxford, 1927), 207–8.

[51] Henry Percy, Earl of Northumberland, *Advice to his Son* (1609; ed. G. B. Harrison, London, 1930), Introd.

[52] Ibid. 63–4.

[53] Hume, 220.

[54] Lord Herbert, 180, in Editor's App. 4, on duelling.

county, Essex, in the seventeenth century that fatal affrays were mostly impromptus, with even knives rarely used, and sticks, stones, or pots snatched up in the heat of the moment playing a bigger part. Further, 'use of the sword, despite that weapon usually being regarded as a gentleman's, shows a surprising lack of class bias'. Only two sword deaths were known to have been inflicted by gentlemen, and no duels, in any strict sense, took place.[55]

Country air may have been less inflammatory than urban. Essex gentlemen probably did some fighting in London; a member of one family was killed there in 1684.[56] After 1604 when the war with Spain petered out, England entered on a long period of inglorious peace broken by a few inglorious attempts at war; a hot-blooded generation grew up on the stories of its gallant forefathers' exploits, and may well have pined, like young Frenchmen after 1815 or young Germans after 1870, for chances to show its own mettle. Naturally passionate and unruly because too full of blood and animal spirits, Bryskett complained in 1606, young men as soon as they think themselves ill-treated 'feare no perill nor danger of their lives, but boldly and rashly undertake to fight'.[57] Foreign example was infectious, and continental textbooks expounded duelling etiquette. Writing in 1617 Fynes Moryson acknowledged that his countrymen, though too choleric, had grown more polished than in sword-and-buckler days, and public brawling was no longer countenanced. Rapiers had made sword-play more dangerous, and legal penalties were another deterrent. Yet he lamented that 'corrupt custom' still made it hard for a youth to win esteem until he had fought a duel, even though it was both a capital crime and a breach of divine law.[58] Any tavern dispute was enough to rouse the 'Martiall *Duellists*', Brathwait wrote in 1630. Some egged young men on to fight; others got money out of nervous youths by pretending to help them to avoid a fight.[59]

Not all of the old aristocracy subscribed to the fashionable ideas of honour. Some may have felt that their eminence set them above the need to trouble about niceties important to lesser mortals. An Earl of Northampton, a Howard, wrote a pamphlet, *Duello Foiled*, dismissing the current notion that 'revenge is necessary to keep the world in good order'.[60] But those who felt duelling to be an evil were likely to think of it as an aristocratic vice. As such it was the more obnoxious to middle-class elements, urban and rural, feeling their growing strength and

[55] J. A. Sharpe, *Crime in Seventeenth-century England: A County Study* (Cambridge, 1983), 128–9.
[56] Ibid. 253 n. 87.
[57] Lodowick Bryskett, *A Discourse of Civill Life* (London, 1606), 100–1.
[58] Fynes Moryson, extract in J. D. Wilson (pp. 128–30).
[59] Brathwait, 39–42.
[60] M. James, 14.

resentful of the ascendancy of those above them; their creed, in the years before they were strong enough to compel blue blood to accept them as a partner, was Puritanism. Fears could still be felt of private feuds compromising public security. John Chamberlain, the Londoner, was nervous about this in 1613: 'the many private quarrels are very great, and prognostic troubled humours, which may breed dangerous diseases'.[61] Apart from war, duelling was 'the most thoughtfully discussed of all forms of violence', more even than rebellion. Its defenders, members of a class 'threatened economically and therefore socially', sharing the education of the higher middle class but anxious to preserve its superior status, tried to equate the duel with the 'just war' of traditional religious teaching.[62]

All such pleas were rejected by the government. Spain's reported success in putting down the duel did not go unnoticed, and James was coming to esteem that country highly. He had lived too close to unlicensed violence in Scotland to see anything romantic or edifying in it. He 'could not abide fighting', and declared that Heaven must have permitted the murder of Henri IV not because he changed his religion but because he tolerated duelling.[63] James was perturbed by the recurrent collisions between Scots who had followed him to London and Englishmen. It was a distress to him in 1612 when two favourites of his, Sir James Stewart and Sir George Wharton, furnished matter for a street ballad by killing each other as Islington.[64]

Sir Edward Coke, the greatest lawyer of the age, drew up a statement of how the common law stood: to kill a man in a duel was murder, but there was no bar to sending a challenge or acting as a second. Following this a 'Proclamation against private Challenges and Combats' saw the light. 'This week here', the shrewd Chamberlain wrote, 'came forth a long proclamation with a book annexed of reasonable bulk, against challenges and duels'; it was at first attributed to Bacon, the attorney-general, but the writer 'did easily see that it came from some higher hand'.[65] James was fond of exercising his pen as well as his tongue. He wanted complaints to be referred to the Earl Marshal, whose long moribund court had continued to be made occasional use of, or to lord-lieutenants; and seconds, or bearers of challenges, were to be subject to the same penalties as their principals. In 1615 the court of Star

---

[61] Cited in Lord Herbert (p. 181).

[62] J. R. Hale, 'Sixteenth-century Explanations of War and Violence', *Past and Present*, 51 (1971), 11–12.

[63] Selden, *Table Talk*, 84.

[64] C. H. Firth, *The Ballad History of the Reign of James I* (London, 1911), 22.

[65] *The Chamberlain Letters*, ed. E. M. Thomson (London, 1966), 130. Cf. J. Spedding, *The Life and Times of Francis Bacon* (London, 1878), i. 705–9.

Chamber, under Bacon's lead, unanimously condemned any idea 'that the private duel in any person whatsoever had any ground of honour'.

But James was always better at huffing and puffing than at steady application, and he was on less firm ground than the Tudors had been for coercing the English upper classes. He permitted Sir Edward Sackville to return to court after his killing of Lord Bruce, and in the same year to succeed to the earldom of Dorset and to hold official appointments. Perhaps he feared that severity towards the English winner would look like partiality to the Scottish loser. His son Charles I likewise disapproved of duelling, though he is said to have been intrigued by the case of one Cashio Burroughs, haunted by the ghost of a mistress he had deserted in Florence, who warned him that he was to perish in a duel, as sure enough he did.[66] An ironical footnote to the anti-duelling legislation concerns Charles's attorney-general Noy, who died in 1634 leaving his painfully amassed gains to his son: this youth, busily engaged in Carlyle's words 'in running through his fortune, was himself run through in a duel: and the Attorney's big Babylon that he had builded, vanished all like a paper castle, and was not'.[67]

The number of recorded duels declined, however, after the second decade of the century. Monarchy and Puritanism together put some check on them: these two ill-assorted forces were not always on opposite sides. Humbler offenders might fare worse than the big fish, and clearly the term 'duel' could sometimes be used in circumstances that later on would not have been thought to warrant it. In a Star Chamber prosecution in 1632 Theodore Kelly was charged with threatening to cudgel another man, 'which the Court held to tend to a duel, which as the Attorney-General pointed out, is "a most perilous thing,—it hath in it apparent danger of both their souls and bodies" '. Kelly was fined £200 and jailed during the king's pleasure. He and his cudgel have an Irish ring, which may have been part of their offence. The Lord Privy Seal and Lord Keeper, who 'found great fault' with his 'long, ruffian-like hair', would have preferred him *topped*, or hanged.[68] On 1 January 1642, when civil war was about to break out, a diarist recorded that 'Mr: Peter Leigh of Lyme was run into the Brest in a Duell in Lambeth feilds by Mr Browne.' On 2 February 'He died of that wound.' On 4 August comes a closing reference to the victim, who probably left no other memorial of his existence than these three: Browne and Mr Mason, his second presumably, were found guilty at the assizes of manslaughter.[69]

[66] E. Maple, *The Realm of Ghosts* (1964; London, 1967), 80.

[67] Carlyle, *Historical Sketches*, 251.

[68] J. R. Tanner, *Tudor Constitutional Documents 1485–1603* (Cambridge, 1930), 278.

[69] Ashmole, ii. 339–41.

Himself by temper very much a man of the sword, Sir Philip Sidney tried in the second version of his *Arcadia*, unfinished at his death in 1586, to sublimate honour into a higher, less unchristian code of conduct. His two heroes fight fiercely hand to hand during a war, not recognizing each other, but after recognition devote their statesmanship to ending the bloodshed. In the second book of *The Faerie Queene* Phaedria separates two knights in mid-combat; but she, in Spenser's allegory, represents indolent enjoyment of life, and flaunts its charms to seduce the hero from his duty. It was on the stage that the subject came in for the liveliest attention. C. L. Barber's meticulous analysis of the seventeenth-century drama reveals what an appetizing theme the duel was for playwrights. Altogether the number of allusions to it more than doubled in the first half of the century, with a marked increase in the years 1611–40; in the earlier years of that period, more closely than later on, duelling was linked with warlike spirit and the martial virtues.[70] Writers made plentiful use of it for comic as well as serious business. They seem to have taken for granted that it was something native to mankind, and must have flourished in all times and places. 'Seventeenth-century duelling conventions are frequently depicted as existing in the ancient world, or in Aztec Mexico',[71] or, as in Beaumont and Fletcher's *A King and No King* (1611), in old Armenia.

Criticism was never absent. There is a warning against hasty quarrels in Marlowe's *Jew of Malta* (1591–2), where Barabas tricks two Christian friends, one of whom has won his daughter's love, into a misunderstanding. They fight and kill each other, while he watches unseen, chuckling. A Christian riposte comes at the end of the play, when the wicked Jew is boiled alive on the stage. One may guess from Marlowe's stormy temperament and violent imaginings that he would have been a ready duellist had he been born on a higher rung of the ladder. As it was, this Canterbury shoemaker's son got into enough scrapes. He and a fellow poet were arrested in 1589 after a clash in which an actor was killed, though their plea of self-defence was accepted. Fights among men of their station must often have been a mixture of imitation of their betters, and vulgar brawling with little heed for rules. Marlowe's own death in 1593 was very much of the second sort, if we set aside its more mysterious aspects.

Robert Greene's brief life had seen enough riotous dissipation and foreign wandering to make a sadder and wiser man of him before, near its end, his play *Friar Bacon and Friar Bungay* came out in 1594. It was composed for a gentry audience, but its condemnation of the duel is unsparing, and the mischief is associated with another, the practice of

---

[70] C. L. Barber, 270, 274.   [71] Ibid. 27.

magic. Fairly late in the rambling story, set in the reign of Henry III, two Suffolk squires and old friends, Lambert and Serlsby, are both suitors to a maid of low degree, and argue until Lambert breaks out:

> I dare thee, coward, to maintain this wrong,
> At dint of rapier, single in the field.

Serlsby agrees. Their sons, likewise fast friends, studying at Oxford, come to Friar Bacon's study there to consult his magic mirror, though Bacon forebodes a 'tragedy'. They see their fathers take the field with sword and dagger, each vowing that if he falls his son will carry on the quarrel—a throw-back from duel to blood feud. Both are mortally wounded; at the sight their sons promptly draw, and kill each other. Bacon is left to deplore the mischief his mirror has done; he smashes it with one of the blood-stained poniards, and bids farewell to all his occult studies.

Early in Shakespeare's *Richard II* a trial by battle is about to be held, after much bombast on each side, when it is suddenly vetoed by the king, for motives not made clear. Near the close of *King Lear* the scene where Edgar comes forward at the summons of Albany's herald, to fight his half-brother Edmund, is a trial by battle in the old tradition as well as a duel in the new style. Various single combats on Shakespeare's battlefields, like those between Hostpur and Prince Hal, Macbeth and Macduff, have much of the character of duels. Challenges are sometimes given and accepted in a fully serious spirit, as in the very different cases of Benedick and Claudio, and Michael Williams the common soldier and the disguised King Henry on the night before Agincourt, when they exchange gloves as gages to wear in their caps. In neither of these cases, however, does a fight follow, and as a rule when Shakespeare talks of duelling it is in a humorous, bantering vein. It is tempting to conclude that he 'deliberately set out to ridicule current practice', at a time when the duel 'almost bore the aspect of a social contagious disease'.[72]

Pistol and Nym vapour and flourish their swords, over Nym's claim of a betting debt of eight shillings, until Bardolph parts them, and they all agree to join the expedition to France, in quest of plunder; neat satire, conscious or not, on the way feuding noblemen were diverted by their governments into attacks on other countries. In the fancy-dress scene at the end of *Love's Labour's Lost* there is clowning over a proposed duel between 'Hector' and 'Pompey': the latter refuses to strip to his shirt, as required, and is forced to confess that he has no shirt. Sir Toby Belch instructs the hesitant Sir Andrew about how to draw up a challenge in intimidating language and 'write it in a martial

[72] J. D. Wilson, 404–5.

hand'.[73] Touchstone the jester makes fun of the jargon of punctilio by relating how he nearly got into a scrape by criticizing the cut of a courtier's beard, but they were able to agree that it was only a disagreement 'upon the seventh cause', or 'upon a lie seven times removed'.[74] One may read a burlesque of duelling into the scene in *A Midsummer Night's Dream* where Lysander and Demetrius draw their swords and blunder about trying to strike each other, each accusing his rival of running away, while Puck darkens the sky and leads them astray with false calls.

Yet Polonius's advice to his son was surely closer to Shakespeare's feeling, and to what became and remained, till duelling disappeared, the view of the more enlightened of those concerned with it:

> Beware
> Of entrance to a quarrel, but being in,
> Bear't that the opposed may beware of thee.

This is not far from Castiglione's maxim that for his own and his friends' sake a gentleman should understand how disputes ought to be handled; he should never embark on a duel precipitately, but must show 'readiness and courage' when no choice was left.[75] In the last resort, for Shakespeare the duel shared with war the essential quality of physical courage, willingness to risk death at the call of whatever men may deem their duty. He was living in a country internally at peace, where the old military feudalism had long been dismantling itself. His complaints of the 'cankers of peace' are a reminder that in the societies of his time (and of ours not much less, it often seems) there was scarcely anything but war to lift men out of the rut of private egotism, concern for their own comforts. War was to retain this appeal to a distorted idealism; the duel could be a similar artificial stiffener for men's higher selves.

But it was clearly better, to Shakespeare's mind, that a man should muster his courage on his country's than on his own behalf. Warlike spirit should be given the rein only in war, Henry V tells his men at Agincourt, and times of peace should breathe 'modest stillness and humility'. As a pioneer prophet of nationalism, Shakespeare foreshadowed the enlargement of 'honour' from personal to public or patriotic. In the debate in *Troilus and Cressida* on whether the war against the Greeks ought to be continued, or halted by restoration of Helen to her rightful lord, Hector rejects the arguments of Troilus and Paris—closely akin to a duellist's reasoning—as the 'mad idolatry' of the individual obsessed with his own feelings, 'the hot passion of distempr'd

---

[73] *Love's Labour's Lost*, Act V, sc. ii, ll. 685 ff.; *Twelfth Night*, Act III, sc. ii; cf. Act III, sc. iv.

[74] *As You Like It*, Act V, sc. iv.

[75] Castiglione, 62.

blood' instead of cool appraisal of right and wrong. Yet while he admits that Troy's cause is a bad one, Hector ends by coming round to support of the war, because it now involves the prestige of the kingdom and its ruling family, 'our joint and several dignities'. As later patriots learned to put it, 'My country right or wrong'. It is also, however, part of Shakespeare's vision that by giving way Hector is sealing his own and his country's doom.

Ben Jonson's earlier life shows resemblances to Marlowe's. A bricklayer's foster-son, he was in jail more than once, and after killing an actor in a duel only escaped execution by pleading 'benefit of clergy'. But he had a much longer run than Marlowe, and was nearing forty when *The Alchemist* was produced in 1610. Subtle the quack alchemist is ready to instruct the bumpkin Kastril in both tobacco-smoking and duelling, two fashionable accomplishments that went together, or so a young ruffler might think; he can cast a horoscope for any quarrel, and supply rules 'To give and take the lie by'. There is a similar derisory tone in Jonson's much later play *The Magnetic Lady* (1632). In Act III long discussions of honour and valour take place. The foppish Sir Diaphanous Silkworm has been rudely struck at the dinner-table by Captain Ironside, and his new costume damaged. A lawyer, Practice, reminds him of the Star Chamber's vigilance against fighting, and advises him to prosecute:

> The reverend law lies open to repair
> Your reputation,

and juries have been known to award £5,000 for small injuries. On the other side, Compass, a scholar, urges him to send a challenge, though it should be in 'generous terms', 'the courtliest kind of quarrel'. Sir Diaphanous resolves to be bold, and wants Bias, a lord's secretary, to carry his defiance, but Bias demurs: he has no wish to get into trouble and forfeit his patron's favour.

In the later, decadent years of the pre-Civil War theatre, duelling was very much in the limelight. If no more, it allowed striking stage effects, which could be reflected in box-office takings, and would have a special appeal to young gentlemen in the audience. Massinger could denounce duelling, but in *A Very Woman*, derived from old Spanish tales of chivalry,[76] he rewards Florisiano with the hand of the lady of his choice, in spite of his having killed a rival in a duel, and been forced to flee and battle his way through other duels, shipwrecks, and so on. In *The Fatal Dowry*, by the same author, there can still be a lingering notion of the arbitrament of the sword coinciding with justice. 'How soon

[76] Roma Gill, 'Collaboration and Revision in Massinger's *A Very Woman*', *Review of English Studies* (May 1967), 138–9.

weak wrong's o'erthrown!' Charalois exclaims, after forcing a fight on the reluctant young Novall, who has been making free with his lady, and despatching him. But in the drama generally the gap between honour and virtue was widening, and honour losing its 'social dimension': rank was of less importance now, but so was social obligation; performance in the duel counted for more than prowess in war.[77] All this was the opposite of what Sidney and Shakespeare, in their different ways, had been advocates for. It meant a self-regarding, and therefore truncated, individualism or egotism, typical of an aristocratic order whose ideology was the first of its outworks to crumble.

Scots were altogether a more backward people than their neighbours, brought up on a peculiar mixture of clan spirit and feudal loyalties, in Lowlands as well as Highlands, which could infect town as well as countryside. Jedburgh had a civic shield—still to be seen on an older stone in the eighteenth-century New Gate—showing a knight in armour at full gallop, as if the burghers liked to look at themselves in a feudal mirror. How a duel among their Border neighbours might turn out can be gleaned from the ballad 'The Dowie Houms o' Yarrow', which begins with a late-night drinking session, leading to a dispute between brothers-in-law and a rendezvous at dawn. The hero's wife, sister to the other man, begs him not to go, but he is obstinate:

> For I maun gae, tho' I ne'er return,

and departs alone, without second or witness. On a hillside he is set on by nine men; he kills five and mortally wounds the rest, but finally is stabbed from behind by 'the stubborn knight', his kinsman. 'Helen of Kirkconnel' records another episode or legend of treachery and ferocity. Helen has saved her love at the cost of her own life from a shot fired by a lurking foe. Lover and assailant meet alone by the water at Kirkconnel:

> I lighted down my sword to draw,
> I hackèd him in pieces sma' . . .

By comparison with such doings a well-conducted duel might be deemed part of a civilizing process, for human beings otherwise irredeemable.

Possibly Adam Bothwell, the sixteenth-century bishop of Orkney and bibliophile, had some inkling of this; his library contained a copy of Muzio's well-known treatise.[78] There were rapiers in Scotland by about 1500, probably imported by the nobility, for use in duelling along with

---

[77] M. James, 89.
[78] D. Shaw, 'Adam Bothwell', in *The Renaissance and Reformation in Scotland*, ed. I. B. Cowan and D. Shaw (Edinburgh, 1983), 167.

'parrying daggers' held in the other hand.[79] But James while still in Scotland was always preaching public order, and, as in England later, he regarded duelling as a menace; it was not only, he declared, 'prohibited and forbiddin be the lawis of this realme', but was banned in every 'wele governit commounwele', and a fight was never likely to lay a quarrel to rest.[80] Counsels of perfection were of little use in his Scotland, however, and in practice, seated on a very shaky throne, he had no alternative but to condone something worse. 'The attitude of the crown was a powerful factor in the survival of the bloodfeud.'[81] It was very near the end of his residence in Scotland that there was legislation against it, in 1598 and 1600.

Only when its suppression was achieved would the way be open for a properly regulated system of duelling, or national phlebotomy. Halting moves in this direction had lately been visible in some quarrels among the nobility. In 1596 the English envoy Robert Bowes reported that Lord Sanquhar had sent a 'cartel' challenging the Earl of Orkney to single fight, and had only desisted from his efforts to provoke the earl 'to field and fight' after a second intervention by the king. His grievances looked trivial. 'But it is whispered', Bowes added, 'that this coal was blown by greater persons aggrieved against Orkney.'[82] If so, a political plot rather than a true duel was in question. Next year English 'advices from Scotland' included news of the Earl of Orkney being at loggerheads with another northern potentate, the Earl of Caithness, 'either accusing other of homicide and perjury'. Caithness had a pair of swords and daggers made at Edinburgh, and offered his enemy a choice of them. Their dispute was likely to 'divide the whole realm in discord for either of them have great friends'.[83]

Holland, very unlike Scotland in spite of the religion they shared, emerged from its war of independence from Spain the most middle-class country of Europe. Not until 1618 was talk heard of a duel, an outlandish borrowing from France. It was a moment of political crisis, pamphlet warfare raged, and inky salvoes between two controversialists led to a challenge. Maurice of Nassau, son and successor as stadtholder or president of William the Silent, intervened to stop things from going further.[84] In Germany too the duel was a loan from France, rather than a native growth,[85] but here a society still heavily feudal gave it a far

---

[79] D. H. Caldwell, *The Scottish Armoury* (Edinburgh, 1979), 23.
[80] G. Donaldson, *Scotland: The Making of the Kingdom, James V–James VII* (Edinburgh, 1965), 222–3.
[81] Wormald, 85.
[82] *Calendar of State Papers Relating to Scotland*, vol. xii (Edinburgh, 1952), 248–9.
[83] Ibid. vol. xiii (Edinburgh, 1969), 78.
[84] Tex, ii. 627.
[85] Prokowsky, 22.

warmer welcome when it made its appearance in the second half of the sixteenth century. Its best carrier was the roving mercenary soldier. German troops took part in many western conflicts; adventurers from western countries like Scotland were equally to the fore in wars in Germany, the Baltic lands, and beyond. Of all armies, or armed rabbles as they still mainly were, that of the Habsburgs, rulers of Austria and elective heads of the Holy Roman Empire or German federation, was the most thoroughly cosmopolitan.

Among the German principalities Electoral Saxony led the way in making the duel illegal, in 1572.[86] In 1617 the emperor Matthias promulgated an edict which firmly condemned duelling and prescribed arbitration instead. Perhaps he and his family nursed a memory of how one of them had been killed in single fight not many years before, if the story is true, by Erasmus Lueger, owner of Predjama, the cavern fortress close to the Postojna caves in Slovenia. He was besieged there by Habsburg forces for two years, and finally, through the treachery of a servant who lit a signal lamp, met an undignified death from a cannon-ball breaking down the wall of the privy where he was seated.

All member-states of the empire were called on to follow the example set by the edict of 1617, but next year the Thirty Years War broke out, and before long all central Europe was plunged into chaos. Mercenary armies came under growing French influence, as the German courts did after the fighting ended. It left them feeble and insecure, nervous of any kind of disorder, and a series of edicts condemned the duel as repugnant to God, humanity, and reason. In Brandenburg-Prussia the first law came out in 1652. In this principality rulers more energetic than most were building up their authority, and were sensitive to any infringements of it. A thunderous enactment of 1688 warned their subjects that duelling was spreading inordinately, especially in court and camp, and depriving the state of useful men; all use of force was reserved by Heaven to sovereigns. Severe penalties were laid down for anyone giving a challenge, and a duel, even if ending without bloodshed, was made a capital crime. Rewards were offered to informers.[87] As usual, the efficacy of the law proved weaker than its intention. In Austria a 'mandate' of 1666 was followed by stern legislation in 1682, which among other sanctions rendered an absconding duellist's property liable to confiscation.

Further east the duel was making its way along with other items of western civilization, such as firearms, standing armies, and hereditary titles. Poland and Hungary had a numerous landowning nobility, susceptible to the appeal of the duel. In Russia the old boyar class was

[86] Prokowsky, 33–4, with text.
[87] Demeter, 120–1; Prokowsky, 82–4.

being supplanted, with the rise of Muscovy and tsarist absolutism, by a new service nobility, still raw and crude. This could only by degrees be educated up to a taste for the newfangled western duel. In the mean time trial by combat, obsolescent in the west, still went on, side by side with a system of monetary reparation for injured honour, graduated by social rank. This was defined in the law-code of 1550. A hundred years later the category of disputes that could be settled by combat was widened, and rules were framed to make encounters more even and keep order among spectators.

Europe was growing more modern, more thoroughly permeated as the years went by with commercial and industrial values or calculations, while its past şelf of feudal times receded into the mists. Yet an astonishing quantity of things from the past were being taken over, by new classes in the west, new nations in the east, along with those two grand opposites, militarism and Christianity. Even newer institutions might be given an archaic cast, much as Victorian mansions might be crowned with turrets and battlements. Part of this 'bastard feudalism' was the spread of serfdom from western Europe, where it was dying out, to eastern regions where it was to last until a century ago. Men's besetting inertia has led them to imitate old patterns of living rather than work out new ones, as well as to build farmhouses with stones from Hadrian's wall. In conditions like those of early modern Europe, with its civil broils and massive insurrections, an added inducement was dread of social change getting out of hand and sweeping away all propertied classes together.

Newcomers to a class, as to a nation, are apt to pick up and exaggerate its hallmarks, and intransigent behaviour in the aristocracy might be worsened by an influx of new members, eager for acceptance. A novelist has written of 'the parvenu's passionate loyalty to an imaginary past'.[88] Burton wrote of parvenus in his day, 'much abashed and ashamed of themselves' because their birth was inferior to their present position, who 'buy titles, coats of arms, and by all means screw themselves into ancient families, falsifying pedigrees, usurping scutcheons . . .'.[89] Because in England social mobility made more room for climbers, such snobbery was exceptionally prevalent there; but everywhere duelling must have owed it a heavy debt.[90]

[88] F. Scott Fitzgerald, *The Last Tycoon* (1941; Harmondsworth, 1960), 142.
[89] Robert Burton, *The Anatomy of Melancholy* (London 1621), Pt. 2, sect. 3, mem. xi (London, 1923), ii. 157–8.
[90] H. W. Dewey, 'The 1550 Sudebnik', in H. J. Cohn (ed.), *Government in Reformation Europe 1520–1560* (London, 1971), 303 n. 38.

6

The Duel at its Apogee

'I am King Tom, Rajah Laut, and fit to look any man hereabouts in the face. I have my name to take care of. Everything rests on that.'

'Mr d'Alcacer would express this by saying that everything rested on honour . . .'.

'Call it what you like. It's something that a man needs to draw a free breath.'

Joseph Conrad, *The Rescue* (1919), Pt. 5, sect. 5.

IN the west generally a critical public opinion was forming, but, as in France, with many fluctuations because the higher middle classes shaded into the nobility or gentry and aspired to the same status. This weakened the response that the Churches, more at one than on most issues in condemning the duel, could command. They may have cheered themselves by finding in their denunciation of duelling a salve to consciences which allowed them to give invariable approval to the wars of their patron governments.

The Catholic Church stood out, not only as the biggest and richest, but because of its monopoly or dominance in most of the duelling countries. The Council of Trent's decree of 1563 held the threat of excommunication over not only duellists but also rulers or authorities who neglected to suppress them. In 1592 Clement VIII added further penalties, among them confiscation of property and 'perpetua infamia'. With the help perhaps of the Spanish hegemony, this seems in time to have made anti-duelling laws up and down Italy somewhat more effective. Catholic strength in Spain may be supposed to have reinforced royal bans there. Brantôme says that some French Catholics felt bound to eschew the new-style duel as well as the old judicial combat.[1]

But Catholic influence at large suffered from the fact that in social terms the Counter-Reformation was fundamentally conservative, or neo-feudal. Its alignment was with monarchy, but still more with landowning aristocracy, and whatever Rome might say it was difficult for a parish priest, or a bishop, himself ordinarily of aristocratic birth, to go against ruling-class feeling. Jesuits in particular, the vanguard of the Counter-Reformation, addressed their militantly Catholic gospel to

[1] Brantôme, 138. Catholic pronouncements are summarized by Strecker, 15–24.

this class, and many belonged to it themselves. They were accused, most weightily by Pascal, of finding loopholes for duelling in their science of casuistry; Macaulay, long after, thought Jesuit confessors of his day easygoing about such peccadilloes.[2]

An Anglican who brought this charge against Spanish and Italian casuists was Joseph Hall, bishop of Exeter and then, under Charles I, of Norwich, and a gifted satirist. Coming forward to endorse government censure of the duel, he pronounced it 'wicked and damnable', murder or attempted murder. Two men drawing swords on each other could decide nothing except which was the better fencer. It was a reversion to the pagan ordeal, or 'a mere tempting of God'. There were no biblical precedents except those of David and Goliath, Joab and Abner, and in each of these cases it was the challenger who lost.[3] In another of his works Hall carped at foreign fashions that made women dress themselves up into 'anticks and monsters', and taught men 'that devilish art and practice' of duelling, to say nothing of sodomy.[4]

In his study of 'cases of conscience' in 1636 the eminent Puritan divine William Perkins refuted the argument that a man declining a challenge was 'disgraced for ever', by insisting that there was no biblical warrant for accepting it. 'Nay, it is rather flat against the Word', and 'it is better for any man to endure a little reproach with some men, than to lose or hazard his life.' For better measure, Perkins rejected the ancient practice of single champions being chosen to decide their peoples' fate, as 'utterly unlawful'. David and Goliath were a special case. A good cause must be backed by the strength of a whole army. The contention that if armies can legitimately fight it must be all right for individuals to do the same, he brushed aside: 'warres and armies are Gods ordinances', duels are not.[5]

Churchmen were shackled by their place in the social hierarchy to this unconvincing logic. In a Jacobean play a pious captain suffers from religious scruples about calling out a man who has talked insultingly of his mother;[6] and there must have been a fair number who took religious admonitions seriously. On the whole, no homilies could make the aristocratic leopard change its spots. The duel rooted itself firmly

---

[2] No. 7 of the *Provincial Letters* attacks Jesuit and other casuists for excusing duels as a defence of honour. Cf. Macaulay, *Essays*, ii. 103.

[3] Hall, vii. 398–400. Voet's book is an example of the fondness for seeking Biblical and classical precedents.

[4] Hall, xii. 126–7.

[5] William Perkins, *The Whole Treatise of the Cases of Conscience* (London, 1636), 294–5. Puritans were not the only religious critics of duelling, but they were the most numerous and emphatic: G. E. Aylmer, 'Collective Mentalities in Mid-Seventeenth-Century England', Trans. Royal Hist. Soc. (1986), 14–15.

[6] C. L. Barber, 35.

and spread widely in the teeth of united condemnation by Church and State.

Over the Europe of the later seventeenth and the eighteenth century, while in some areas the duel was losing its hold, in others, more numerous, it was gaining ground. It flourished where aristocratic styles of living were still unimpaired, but also where new broods of initiates were plentiful, as in England with its perennial crows donning peacock feathers; or where whole new noble classes were coming into being and aping older ones, as in Ireland after the conquest, or in Russia. In both England and France, two leading and always interacting countries, a spell of firm discouragement of the duel was followed by its revival. Those were not the only times when it showed surprising powers of recuperation.

In England it fell off after 1642 when the civil wars broke out, but in the Royalist camp steps had to be taken to curb it. In the Articles of War of the Parliamentary army it was laid down that 'No Corporal, or other Officer commanding the Watch, shall willingly suffer a Souldier to go forth to a Duel, or private Fight, upon paine of death.' If common soldiers were duelling, it sounds as though levelling principles were at work in an unexpected way. The next section deals with 'Drunken and quarrelsome Officers'.[7]

Puritanism in power was free to air its antipathy to the courtly vice of duelling. A Commons committee set up soon after the victory of Worcester in 1651, to remedy 'inconveniences of the law', tabled some draconic remedies: it wanted duelling to be visited with loss of the right hand, confiscation, and banishment—and adultery with death.[8] Civil war left much bad blood between partisans, and foreign influence and fashion could still be insidious. One of the sorts of men Dorothy Osborne did not want for a husband was 'a Traveld Mounsieur whose head is all feather inside and outside, that can talk of nothing but dances and Duells'.[9] Cromwell issued a proclamation against duelling in 1654. Swift had it from some who remembered the Commonweal that he encouraged a 'rude familiarity' or jocularity among his associates, as a way of ridiculing niceties of manner and notions of honour among cavaliers, 'when the smallest word misplaced among gentlemen ended in a duel'.[10]

Thomas Hobbes published in England in 1651 his *Leviathan*, written in France, whither this plebeian had been carried by his royalist connections. An advocate of unfettered state authority, as the only effective

---

[7] C. Firth, *Cromwell's Army* (London, 1902), 418–9.
[8] H. N. Brailsford, *The Levellers and the English Revolution*, ed. C. Hill (London, 1961), 651–3.
[9] *The Letters of Dorothy Osborne to William Temple*, ed. G. C. Moore (Oxford, 1928), 105.
[10] 'An Essay on Conversation'.

muzzle for human beastliness, he was preoccupied with the question of power. He saw as 'honourable' anything that furnished 'an argument and sign of power'. The justice or injustice of an action is irrelevant, 'for honour consisteth only in the opinion of power'. A duel proved courage, and courage proved power; though Hobbes was alive to the paradox always inherent in it, that it was forced on most men by 'the fear of dishonour, in one, or both the combatants: who engaged by rashness, are driven into the lists to avoid disgrace'.[11] His thesis embodies much of the truth; transposed from individual to class, still more. He grew less hopeful, as time went on, of duelling ever being rooted out.[12]

France was standing on the threshold of the era of Louis XIV. With the growing weight of the bourgeoisie, it was approaching something like an equilibrium between the old dominant class and its rival. French good sense, as well as royal megalomania, was part of the spirit of the age. Attitudes to duelling as reflected in literature have a similar twofold nature. Corneille came from a legal rather than aristocratic background, but he seems to waver between disapproval of the duel and admiration of the heroic qualities it could be supposed to stand for. La Rochefoucauld, a duke, had much to say about the psychology of war that can be transferred easily enough to duelling. Death was to him a dark shadow over life, never easily forgotten. Himself an old soldier, he believed that most soldiers expose themselves enough to preserve their credit, but few want to do more. 'The glory of a brave death, the hope of being regretted, the desire to leave a fine reputation'—all these have their charms, but not unanswerable charms.[13] Scarron had more decided views. He came of a well-to-do law family; the youthful accident that left him crippled may have done as much to form them. He composed burlesques of heroic poems like the *Aeneid*, and in a play of 1645, *Jodelet duelliste*, threw ridicule on the notion of honour by making a valet debate whether to call out a rival.[14]

He left a widow to be the morganatic wife of the Grand Monarch. Louis XIV (1643–1715) was a boy when France relapsed into civil strife, the wars of the Fronde, and grew up with a dread of any disorder; his lamentably long reign was an exercise in the familiar game of turning it outward, organizing the country for war and conquest. According to Voltaire's far too eulogistic work on the reign, it was a duel of 1663 in high life that determined him to put duelling down.[15] It must have made a stronger impression because it was one of the kind

---

[11] Thomas Hobbes, *Leviathan* (1651), chap. 10.
[12] Thomas, 192.
[13] La Rochefoucauld, *Maximes* (5th edn., 1678), no. 219.
[14] Bennetton, 37–8.
[15] Voltaire, 328–9.

then entering its twilight, with seconds joining in, three of them on each side. Of the eight men three were killed and all the rest wounded. With the unique prestige and authority that the 'Sun King' built up, and his resolve to reduce all classes to submission to the throne, anti-duelling legislation could for the first time in French history have a real effect. In all he issued a round dozen of decrees. An edict of 1679 codified earlier law; the court of honour, or 'Tribunal des Maréchaux', was given its final shape, and a scale of degrees of offence drawn up: striking a blow, the most grievous of all insults, was punishable with prison. For both fighters and seconds the penalty was to be death.

It was not often inflicted in practice. All early modern legislation in Europe tended to be hortatory, instructional, not expected to be taken literally. Allowance must be made for the ever-present ambivalence of monarchy, between the pulls of past and present; and Louis may have felt, like many rulers, that duelling could help to keep up a martial tone in the intervals between his wars. He was not lavish with pardons, however, like his father and grandfather. As he grew older he grew more pious, or more bigoted; together with a confraternity, the *Compagnie du Saint Sacrament*, he enrolled a band of nobles, among them distinguished soldiers secure against any whisper of lack of nerve, who pledged themselves to abstain from duelling. Many members of the nobility must have been ready to welcome the initiative, men who enjoyed a quiet life, or were willing to listen to anxious parents or wives.

In the preamble to an edict in 1704 Louis could take credit for having virtually extinguished the evil. Most observers admitted the claim. A Frenchman writing in 1720 commended him for having 'cured gentlemen of an obsession which was approaching frenzy', and added, as Hobbes might have done: 'The human race can be reformed only by rigour on the part of its sovereigns.'[16] Voltaire pointed out that Louis' statue in the Place des Victoires, with a chained slave on each of the four sides, which some found fault with as arrogant, was really meant, as its inscriptions proved, to represent 'vices repressed as much as nations conquered', among them heresy and duelling. He himself looked upon Louis's firmness against duelling as one of his greatest services to the nation, and a beneficial example to other countries as well.[17]

There was praise from abroad also. A dialogue-essay of 1711 by Steele, in the *Spectator* (no. 97), looks like a composite tribute to Louis and to Henri IV. Pharamond, 'King of the Gauls', after having 'con-

---

[16] Basnage, Pref. and p. 3. It is noteworthy that the *Encyclopédie* article (v. 163) said nothing of Richelieu, and treated Louis's laws as the first to have real effect. It went into detail about the edict of 1679, as their cornerstone.

[17] Voltaire, 318, 328–9. A century after Louis's death a duellist's widow could pay tribute to the 'immortel auteur de notre législation sur le duel', and the inflexible firmness with which he enforced it (St-Morys, 85, 266).

quer'd France', discusses the problem of duelling with his councillor Eucrate, who argues that only the greatest severity could 'extirpate a Crime which had so long prevailed and was so firmly fixed in the Opinion of the World as great and laudable'. Pharamond dissents, saying that men often fought only 'to save Appearances to the World', without any ill-will. Still he regrets having granted so many pardons, and proceeds to draw up a law denouncing the duel as contrary to Christianity and 'the Rules of Right Reason', and imposing the sternest penalties.

As time went on, and its procedures were systematized and refined, with group fighting abandoned, the duel became in general less obnoxious to authority. It was ceasing to appear a threat to public order; only two men were actively engaged, and once the fight was over 'honour was satisfied'. In this light the duel, almost as highly stylized as the minuet, and a product of the same social atmosphere, could be accepted as a regulated outlet for violent impulses within the classes on which government continued primarily to depend, and whose ethos of the sword it did not want to eradicate. Duelling had the advantage of being self-policing; it was regulated by the seconds, and its élitist character removed any danger of its swelling into a tumult. Authority in any case was coming to be far too firmly established to be imperilled by minor disturbances. Thus the desire of governments to enforce order, and that of the upper classes to enforce self-discipline, could converge.

Hence the French government's willingness to let the duel revive, within limits, after Louis XIV's measures had done their work. Relaxation in fact set in before his death. Of forty-four culprits brought before the Paris Parlement between 1700 and 1725, twelve were acquitted, twenty-six allowed to slip through legal loopholes, only six sentenced, and none of these to execution: the heaviest penalty imposed, though it was indeed heavy enough, was nine years' convict labour in the galleys.[18] Under the Regency following Louis's death in 1715 the anti-duelling edicts remained, but were no longer enforced with any strictness. Before the end of 1715 two captains fought under the terrace of the Tuileries, as it were under authority's nose, but thanks to the Regent's good nature got off with simple dismissal.[19] Over-eagerness among nobles to return to their old sport, which as Saint-Simon noted spread quickly again, provoked a new edict early in 1723, whose promulgation concluded the ceremony at which the new king Louis XV was declared of age.[20]

[18] McManners, 368, 375.
[19] Saint-Simon, iii. 45.
[20] Ibid. iii. 444.

In spite of this, plenty of men, young gallants especially, were ready to fight, if only out of simple bravado. Ironically one of the worst offenders was a Duc de Richelieu, who in 1734 killed a relative, the Prince de Lixen. Once at least he was brought before a court of honour and compelled to apologize. Youth was not always the most to blame. In general, when the atmosphere was becoming unfavourable to duelling (or any other addiction) young men might be the first to turn against it; when conditions brought it into favour, they would be the first to embrace it. Shakespeare's Hector, in the debate on war and peace, cited Aristotle's dictum about young men being 'Unfit to hear moral philosophy'.

Travelling through France in the 1760s Smollett came to think that older officers stood more on punctilio than their juniors, and were apt to egg them on instead of restraining them. Penalties seemed to him easily evaded; after a duel the culprits would pretend that no more than an accidental brush had occurred, and no proceedings would be taken.[21]

Class was a less rigid line of division now, and the thinking of the better-off middle classes was, as always, inconsistent. The Frenchman who praised Louis XIV so highly in 1720 for his firmness admitted that the 'barbarous extravagance' he set his face against could cast a spell even on the most intelligent; and he rebuffed the aristocratic plea that a gentleman is not bound to accept a challenge from a commoner— 'the point of honour must be equal'.[22] One rejoinder might be to send lackeys to teach an impudent citizen a lesson, as happened in the celebrated case of the Chevalier de Rohan and Voltaire. The former subsequently unbent so far as to take up a challenge, but his family stepped in, and Voltaire was shut up in the Bastille (not for the first time) and thence deported to England. As the Revolution approached, and social and financial mingling between aristocracy and bourgeoisie increased, there was coming to be enough equality and fraternity to allow them to fight each other freely. It was an era of Anglomania in France, and English example may have had an influence.

Men without coats of arms were as free as their betters to fight among themselves. Actors seem to have fought at times in the theatre, as well as outside. One of them had the distinction of receiving a wound from that shining light of the profession, Talma. Duelling might well appeal to the histrionic temperament; in eighteenth-century England the great actor James Quin (of Irish origin) was convicted of manslaughter after killing a brother actor in a duel at Covent Garden. The cosmopolitanism of the duel overleapt nationality as well as class, occasionally

---

[21] Smollett, *Travels*, 134–5.
[22] Basnage, Pref. and 15–16.

even race; though it is part of the intertwining destinies of Europe and Africa that black men have been the only non-Europeans to distinguish themselves in this field. In early eighteenth-century France the Chevalier de Saint-Georges, whose mother was a West Indian Negress, won many contests by his swordsmanship, and the admiration of many ladies by his good looks. A later man of colour, Jean-Louis, born in 1784, became an outstanding fencer, one of whose duels was fought in retaliation for an insult to him as a black.[23]

England made far better all-round progress than seventeenth-century France, but while in the later years duelling was being curbed in France by orderly despotism, in England it was running riot under the shaky monarchy restored in 1660. Aristocracy was demoralized by defeat in the civil wars, many of its members by a long spell of exile; it was now bent on reasserting itself. Duelling formed part of a popular royalist reaction, along with wild drinking and prostitution and the reopening of disorderly theatres. Gentlemen of the sort dubbed by Milton

> the sons
> Of Belial, flown with insolence and wine,

were rude to women at the theatre in order to provoke quarrels, or shoved one another off the pavement. Mingling with them were dubious adventurers whom royalist *émigrés* had consorted with, and who were now trying to find a place in what could hardly yet be described as 'polite society'. Addison tells us of 'a very mischievous' association, a 'Club of Duellists'; its president was said to have killed half a dozen opponents, and members took their seats in the order of the number they had disposed of. It did not last long, because most of them were soon knocked off in their turn, or hanged.[24]

A 'grand tour' on the continent was a fashion that obliged Britons to take care of themselves among foreigners more accustomed to military ways. It was on such a tour that a Duke of Hamilton picked up a duelling propensity destined to end in his death, as well as a taste for paintings, and French, and later on Jacobite sympathies.[25] He had recently been taken into Queen Anne's favour and was appointed ambassador to France; unluckily for him he delayed his departure to Paris, and happened to meet and fall out with a drunken Lord Mohun, a desperado whose father had perished in a duel in 1677, and who had three times appeared before the House of Lords on murder charges. A fight in Hyde Park followed, at 8 a.m. on a November morning, 'one of the most celebrated and most savage duels in English history', with

[23] Hutton, 323 ff.
[24] *The Spectator*, no. 9 (10 Mar. 1710–11).
[25] R. K. Marshall, *The Days of Duchess Anne ... 1656–1716* (London, 1973), 143, 228–9.

the seconds on each side joining in. Hamilton though an experienced
fencer was now 54, and like Hamlet fat and scant of breath; but his
enemy, a much younger man, was also killed. Who gave the challenge,
and the reasons for it, have always remained obscure, as have the details
of the fight. There was a lawsuit of long standing between the two, but
Tories suspected a political plot to get rid of Hamilton; a recent
investigator considers this to be unproved.[26] Hyde Park was rising in
popularity as a London rendezvous; Lincoln's Inn Fields and Covent
Garden were the two oftenest chosen. At Kenwood in north London
an old duelling ground is still to be seen, framed by peaceful trees. A
blatantly public spot, St James's Square, was the freakish venue in 1683
for a three-against-three match; the score was three killed and two
wounded.[27]

Like so many other princes, Charles II issued a proclamation against
duelling, but went on pardoning offenders. It was a cheap way of
rewarding loyalists, and humouring the Cavalier faction at large. Pepys
winds up his comments on one affair, in 1662, by saying that 'The
Court is much concerned in this fray, and I am glad of it; hoping that
it will cause some good laws against it.' It was another bloody episode
of high life, between a nephew of the Earl of St Albans and a brother
of the Earl of Carlisle, each with a second taking a hand. Three of the
party seem to have been officers; the survivors fled abroad, but were
able to return after only three months, 'and were acquitted by law'.[28]
Pepys had lately heard details of a fight between Hugh Cholmely,
'first gentleman-usher to the Queen', and Edward Montagu, who had
repeatedly insulted him. Cholmely drove his opponent back until he
tumbled into a ditch and dropped his sword—'but with honour would
take no advantage of him; but did give him his life'.[29] Clearly a victor
was not yet debarred from inflicting further punishment on the loser,
but opinion was moving in favour of magnanimity, which might also
be expected to facilitate an acquittal or pardon. A generation later
occurred the death, recorded in Evelyn's diary in May 1699, of Conyers
Seymour, a spendthrift of twenty-three who had lately stepped into
£7,000 a year. He had resented 'a slight affront in St James's Park,
given him by one who was envious of his gallantries, for he was a vain
foppish young man'.[30]

A month before this an encounter between another pair of young
men about town was the starting-point of a very unusual train of events.

[26] See H. T. Dickinson, 'The Mohun–Hamilton Duel', *Durham University Journal* (June 1965).
[27] Clark, 31.
[28] Pepys, vi. 292–3 (19 Aug. 1662). C. Moore, 246–7, gives the text of Charles II's proclamation of 1679.
[29] Pepys, vi. 280–1 (6 Aug. 1662).
[30] Evelyn, 574.

John Law of Lauriston, an estate outside Edinburgh where his house still stands in its charming park, was living a spendthrift life in England. Rivalry over a lady and other matters led to a fight in Bloomsbury Square with one Edward Wilson, who was fatally wounded. Law was seized, and rather pedantically charged with inflicting the wound 'with a certain sword made of iron and steel of the value of five shillings'. Tried at the Old Bailey and convicted, he was saved by a royal pardon procured by friends at court. Wilson's brother, however, a Lombard Street banker, was firm-minded enough to appeal to the King's Bench, and Law was rearrested. It appears that the authorities, nettled by this flouting of the pardon, connived at his escape. At any rate he got away, drugging his warder and filing off his irons, and reached Paris, where he could afford to laugh at the offer of a reward for the capture of 'a very tall, black, lean, man, well shaped, above six foot high, large pockholes in his face'.[31] Adventures in several countries followed, before Law blossomed into the great financier who gave France its first taste of paper money and bank crashes.

The revolution of 1688, followed by the rebellions of 1715 and 1745, churned up political bile; but notwithstanding real clashes of interest and sentiment between Whig magnates and Tory squires, or competing London cliques, a corporate fellow-feeling was developing among the élite groups, landed or mercantile or professional, who owned and governed England. The Hanoverian advent made no perceptible difference to duelling, which was banned, but ineffectively, in most German states, scarcely at all in their armies. In 1717 when the Prince of Wales muttered some angry words to the Duke of Newcastle, his father's favourite minister, a German accent may have been responsible for the duke misunderstanding them, and hurrying to the king to tell him that he had been challenged to a duel; the prince was placed for a time under virtual house arrest.[32] As George II he saw active service, and had lately won the battle of Dettingen in person when in 1746 his attention was drawn to a fracas between two Scots, a Lieutenant Ferguson and an Ensign Campbell who went to the length of knocking him down. Ferguson put his case before a court-martial, which declared him blameless; but it was felt that he ought to have taken a different course, by calling Campbell out. George made it known to their commanding officer, Lord Albemarle—speaking as a soldier rather than as king—that he shared this feeling, and considered that Ferguson must either fight or forfeit his commission; otherwise all the other officers would be likely to refuse to serve with him.[33]

[31] A. W. Wiston-Glynn, *John Law of Lauriston* (Edinburgh, [1907]), 6–9.
[32] J. H. Plumb, *The First Four Georges* (London, 1966), 55 ff.
[33] George Thomas, Earl of Albemarle, *Fifty Years of My Life* (London, 1876), i. 122–3.

Among British civilians too, a long spell after 1713 without foreign war, as again after 1815, may have favoured duelling, as an alternative excitement. It was winked at in the eighteenth century as it had been in the Restoration epoch, and occasions for it were often as frivolous as before. Under George III (1760–1820) 172 duels were reported; no very large total it may be for a reign of sixty years, but ninety-one of them had fatal results. Legally, in all these fatal cases, murder was committed, yet only eighteen came to trial and executions numbered a meagre two.[34] In 1771 a lawyer affirmed that he knew of no instance in England of capital punishment following a duel properly conducted.[35] Duellists, in short, could kill each other and go scot free, when a poor man could be hanged for stealing a few shillings. Wilkes was a trifle histrionic when at his meeting with a peer of the realm he complained that they met on unequal terms: he knew his lordship had a royal pardon in his pocket, he declared, whereas he himself was to fight with a halter round his neck.

In unmilitary England it might have been expected that the duel would not long continue in fashion; its vogue there is, on the contrary, quite striking. It went with the besetting middle-class aspiration to gentility, nourished since far back in the middle ages by the social currents which carried younger sons of landowners to London and brought rich businessmen to country estates. Martial fame exercised a hypnotic spell, strengthened by the profits that colonial conquests were bringing into the counting-house. In a company of admirals and generals, Dr Johnson believed, that great legal luminary Lord Mansfield 'would shrink; he'd wish to creep under the table'.[36] A collective instinct admonished the higher classes to humour this middle-class foible, and admit to the dignity of the duel men who would otherwise resent it as an invidious monopoly.

In any case the intermingling of property made it scarcely practicable for any distinct caste to fence itself off. Titled aristocrats old or new, or decayed gentlewomen, might see a vast difference between themselves and anyone engaged in 'trade', but such prejudice was a diminishing hindrance to climbers of the slippery pole. Army or navy could be an accelerator. Scott's Lieutenant Taffril frankly owns to having come from 'before the mast', but as commander of a gun-brig he is qualified to serve as a second—though he owns also to having 'little sympathy for that folly'.[37] Jane Austen's supercilious baronet, Sir Walter Elliot, thought the admirals he met looked very vulgar fellows.

---

[34] Steinmetz, i. 38; Gilpin, 27, Editor's note. C. Moore, 248, commented on how openly and unashamedly duelling was carried on.

[35] Bosquett, 30. Cf. p. 94, on an irregular case.

[36] Boswell, *Johnson*, ii. 414, Apr. 1778.

[37] *The Antiquary*, chap. 19.

A man of good standing challenged by one of dubious status might hesitate to decline, for fear of being suspected of a discreditable motive. But such refusals could happen, and Smollett in one novel invents a drolly contrasting pair of cases, one of a man considered too low to give a challenge, the other of a man considering himself too high to accept one. Jery Melford intercepts a love-letter to his sister from the actor Wilson, and abuses him in a strain that provokes a challenge. He had no real title to offer one, Jery tells a friend, 'yet as his behaviour was remarkably spirited, I admitted him to the privilege of a gentleman'. Jery's uncle, Squire Bramble, gets wind of the affair, and brings the mayor to prevent it, just as the couple are priming their pistols. 'The mayor observed that it was great presumption in Wilson, who was a stroller, to proceed to such extremities with a gentleman of family and fortune', and would have sent him to hard labour had not Jery handsomely intervened. In the second case Bramble, invited to dinner by the capricious Lord Oxmington, considers himself slighted by his reception, and, deaf to his nephew's expostulations, sends a challenge. His lordship is staggered—'What! a commoner send a challenge to a peer of the realm! Privilege! Privilege!'—and has the messenger thrown into the horse-pond. Next day the furious squire, with his party and servants, parades in front of the hall, pistols ready, until Oxmington 'with a very bad grace' tenders his apology.[38]

Such questions came up until duelling disappeared from Britain. Very near the end, Lord Cardigan had to bring himself to honour with a challenge a magistrate whom he considered 'no gentleman'.[39] Nicholas Nickleby hears the libertine Sir Mulberry Hawk talking indecently in a hotel room of his sister. He demands satisfaction, insisting on his social right to claim it: 'I am the son of a country gentleman, your equal in birth and education, and your superior in everything besides.' Hawk contemptuously refuses to give his name, they come to blows, Hawk is thrown out of his runaway carriage and left with a broken leg. On his sick-bed he is stung by malicious information of people saying he was afraid to fight, and was given a thrashing. 'Every club and gaming-room has rung with it.'[40]

What happened in England helped to set the tone in England's growing train of dependencies, beginning with Scotland and Ireland. There must have been a reciprocal influence too; Scots and Irishmen might teach their mentors some bad lessons. North of the border feuding and fortified castles were receding in the later seventeenth century, after the salutary Cromwellian occupation. Vendettas that had so often

---

[38] *Humphry Clinker*, 11–13, 268 ff.
[39] Woodham-Smith, 61.
[40] *Nicholas Nickleby*, chaps. 32, 38.

harassed the countryside, like the one in Ayrshire at the end of the sixteenth century between hostile branches of the Kennedy clan, were now things of the past. Two Jacobite rebellions, however, or Highland irruptions, helped to keep fighting habits from fading quickly. So did Scotland's surplus of impecunious noblemen, younger sons, bonnet-lairds, Highland tacksmen or cadets of clan chiefs, who gave the country its prominent share in the conquering and running of the empire. Writing of the 1730s, Walter Scott observed that 'Duels were then very common in Scotland, for the gentry were at once idle, haughty, fierce, divided by faction'; they had a fitting place for their encounters in the 'deep, wild, grassy valley, scattered with huge rocks and fragments', that runs through Holyrood park at Edinburgh.[41]

Common soldiers were not averse from following the custom of their officers.[42] In ordinary society Englishmen sometimes found tempers unexpectedly hot. An English student at Edinburgh, when president of a medical society in 1776, noted in his diary that he had been in danger of 'having a duel on my hands, for no other reason than having done my duty to the Society'.[43] There was another side of the Caledonian temperament, it is true, which Dean Ramsay had in mind when he wrote of his countrymen being apt to take a 'cool, and deliberative view of a question'. He related a story of a Scot humorously turning off a challenge from an irate Englishman whose marvellous tales of India, including a tiger more than forty feet long, he had made mild fun of.[44] Another anecdote concerns a Lieutenant Smith, some years after the battle of Prestonpans in 1745, taking exception to a song by one Adam Skirving of Haddington, in which he was accused of running away. In reply to a challenge, Adam said he would meet Smith 'and take an observation. If he found he could fight him, he would; if not, he would turn his back and make off as the lieutenant had done before.'[45]

James VI's statute of 1600 had made duelling without royal sanction a capital crime, even if no death ensued. A century later, near the close of Scottish independence, an Act of 1696 subjected to banishment and confiscation of movables anyone concerned in the giving or accepting of a challenge, whether or not a fight took place. Both laws were repealed in 1819, but even during their long lifetimes they had been toothless, because they conflicted with upper-class sentiment. As a legal commentator put it, killing was murder even in the most fairly

---

    [41] *The Heart of Midlothian*, chap. 11.
    [42] J. Prebble, *Culloden* (London, 1961), 22.
    [43] S. Neville, 241.
    [44] Ramsay, 18.
    [45] *The Diaries of Helen Graham 1823–1826*, ed. J. Irvine (Edinburgh, 1957), 86.

conducted duel, and principals and seconds were equally guilty; 'but there is no modern instance of a capital conviction on such a charge, where there has been nothing dishonourable in the conduct of the accused'.[46]

A combatant might, indeed, feel obliged to withdraw from the country, and sometimes the result was permanent exile. One evening in April 1790 Captain James Macrae, whose home in Edinburgh was a centre of gay private theatricals, while escorting a lady from the theatre fell foul of the tipsy servant of his friend Sir George Ramsay, about which of them had prior claim to a sedan chair. An angry correspondence passed between Macrae and Ramsay; on the 14th they met at an inn on the edge of the golf-links at nearby Musselburgh, and walked down to the beach. Their seconds 'placed' them at fourteen steps; Macrae was bruised, Ramsay mortally wounded. Macrae fled to France with one of his seconds, an officer; failing to appear for trial, he had no choice but to remain abroad until his death in 1816.[47]

Records of several members of the ramifying Gordon 'family', or clan, end with their having to seek refuge abroad for the same reason.[48] It was not on their native heath only that they fought. During the American War hopes were long cherished by the British that more loyalists might be rallied to their side, and in 1780 a force including a Guards battalion marched out from New York to test the feeling of the inhabitants. Its only achievement before being compelled to retire was to burn the town of Springfield. Lieutenant-Colonel Thomas of the 1st Guards impugned the conduct there of Colonel the Hon. Cosmo Gordon, of the Scots Guards, who appealed to a court-martial and was exonerated. This was not enough for the second son of an Earl of Aberdeen, and in 1783, the war over, he called Thomas to account. They met on 3 September at the 'Ring' in Hyde Park, and moved towards each other firing at will. Thomas was left a dying man. Gordon was tried for murder, but acquitted because the judge held that the provocation he had received justified his action.[49] A paper written by Thomas the night before the contest made a deep impression on Boswell; it expressed a hope that God might pardon 'the irreligious step I now (in compliance with the unwarrantable customs of this wicked world) put myself under the necessity of taking'.[50]

Boswell stands out in his journals as a man stimulated and tormented by complexities, contradictions, dilemmas. Few men can have left so

---

[46] R. Bell, *A Dictionary of the Law of Scotland* (Edinburgh, 1807–8), 'Duelling'.
[47] J. Grant, *Edinburgh*, iii. 138–42.
[48] Information from Miss Joanna Gordon, formerly custodian of the Gordon records.
[49] Maj. Gen. Sir F. Maurice, *The History of the Scots Guards* (London, 1934), i. 184.
[50] Boswell, *Johnson*, iii. 245 n.

graphic an account of their sensations when a duel was in prospect; he was at risk half a dozen times though never actually obliged to come up to the scratch. On 6 October 1774, at Edinburgh, he received a demand for an apology for a press article reflecting on the Lord Justice-Clerk, from his son William Miller, a stripling of nineteen. Boswell's first impulse was to ignore it, but his wife was distraught, and he caught the alarm from her. 'We lay awake in a sort of burning fever all night, suggesting various schemes.' Next day he took heart, calling to mind 'how many duels had been fought without any hurt, or without much hurt'. He felt further relieved when they went to consult his uncle Cochrane, an old soldier, who talked of the matter with 'coolness, indifference and ease'. Boswell's closest friend, the bottle, was another comforter. 'I eat a good dinner, and drank freely of excellent claret, and by degrees I felt myself firm.' After more consultations he thought it not beneath him to write to Miller saying that no offence to his father had been designed. On Saturday night he was 'much intoxicated', next morning he had to sit through a sermon on the 'gloomy subject' of sudden death. At last, on the 18th, Miller wrote insisting on seeing him. His poor wife 'was like one in a kind of delirium'. All ended amicably; a nervous reaction followed. 'After so many days of warm living and agitation I felt a sort of depression.'[51]

Restoration manners found particularly easy entry into the Anglo-Irish landowning class created by what in all its stages was a very brutal colonial conquest. Duelling was soon 'an everyday occurrence' in the life of 'the hospitable, feckless, hard-drinking, fearless, fox-hunting, fire-eating Irish landlord', a stereotype growingly familiar and 'probably no caricature'.[52] To the extent that there was a strong Protestant, even Puritan, element in the original Anglo-Irish composition, its downward drift into jolly blackguardism makes an instructive case-study in the natural history of ruling classes established by force. Ironside fortitude turned into the animal courage of the habitual duellist or steeplechaser. Such a class, its alienness perpetuated by its religion of anti-popery, had to keep up its confidence in its own vitality, and impress the subject masses with it. Fighting, along with insatiable drinking, raised its spirits and invested its sordid rack-renting existence with a spurious glow.

Froude's portrayal of these landowners in the eighteenth century cannot be dismissed. There is much in his observation that they came to resemble 'Irish chiefs of the sixteenth century in modern costume'.[53] A dominant class, however proud of its separateness, tends to be drawn into playing the role its subjects expect of it; English nabobs in Bengal

[51] Boswell, *The Ominous Years*, 11–25.
[52] E. MacLysaght, *Irish Life in the Seventeenth Century: After Cromwell* (London, 1939), 95–6.
[53] Froude, ii. 194; cf. ii. 446.

collected harems and lumbered about on elephants. Irish chiefs of old were always at war with one another; these Anglo-Irishmen held one obligation sacred, as Froude says—'to send or accept a challenge, with or without reason, at any place and at any time'. If some eccentric magistrate was conscientious enough to interfere, 'he was encountered by a challenge to himself from one or other of the parties aggrieved'.[54] Chief Justice for twenty-seven years, starting near 1800, was John Toler, whose 'scanty knowledge of law, his gross callousness, and his buffoonery',[55] were reckoned no handicap, and he progressed to the title of Earl of Norbury and the reputation of being 'the most active and deadliest pistol-fighter of his era'.[56] It is the less surprising to read of lawyers quitting the court-room to take a shot at one another.

Duelling in short was 'part of a gentleman's code, and no one could take his proper station in life until he had "smelt powder" '.[57] Kings had to fight wars for very similar reasons. A Lord Mountmorris came home from a fight slightly damaged, but cock-a-hoop at having made his courage known. 'In fact never did any person enjoy a wound more sincerely!' He kept his room for a month, 'inconceivably gratified' by the many enquirers after his health, though half of them were really laughing in their sleeves.[58] An ancestor fallen on the field of honour may be supposed to have given a family a certain romantic aura. A Stewart of the actively self-propelling family from which Castlereagh, himself a duellist, and later the marquises of Londonderry were to come, was one who lost his life. Wolfe Tone, the early martyr of Irish patriotism, was balked by his coachmaker father of an ambition to join the army, and found student life at Trinity College, Dublin, a dull substitute. He acted as second in a duel in which a class-mate was killed. 'The University authorities', a biographer remarks, 'were in no very strong position for taking severe measures, seeing that some of themselves, including Provost Hutchinson, had set an example of duelling.'[59] A sylvan suburb of the capital was for some time the fashionable meeting-ground; a traveller wrote of passing 'a fine grove called Clontarf Wood, a place where men of heart go to bleed one another in duels', others to take their mistresses for a breath of air.[60]

On the English stage the Hibernian had to be distinguished by an Irish or pseudo-Irish name and brogue, which might disguise an Anglo-

---

[54] Ibid. ii. 194.
[55] DNB.
[56] Andrew, 39.
[57] Maxwell, 21.
[58] Barrington, i. 125–7. For his own duels, with Richard Daley, 'balloonist and fop', and Councillor M'Nally, see ii. 3 ff., where he writes of the Irish passion for duelling, and ii. 29 ff.
[59] F. MacDermot, *Theobald Wolfe Tone* (1939; Tralee edn., 1968), 9.
[60] Cited by MacLysaght, 379.

Irish identity. Fourteen years before Sir Lucius O'Trigger, a seafaring
Captain Terence O'Cutter trod the boards. Bearing a challenge from
Lord Trinket, he suggested a fight at the same time between himself
and the other second. He loved fighting, he confessed, 'better than salt
beef and biscuit', better even than grog.[61] In the Irish mummers' plays
can be recognized a version or parody of the duel, mixed up with
fragments of folklore and Irish history, and with variants to suit Catholic
or Protestant preference.[62] When the Grand Turk rushes in, intent on
a bout with Prince George, we see the time-honoured fantasy of rulers
in single combat. Cromwell makes appearances, in the congenial
company of Beelzebub. At the end, when the defeated champion is
brought back to life, an ancient faith in resurrection peeps out, together
with the reconciliation that sometimes followed on a duel.

Early British India resembled Anglo-Ireland in many bad ways.
Anglo-Irish and Scottish cadets were numerous there, and habits
carried out from home by them or by English youths were not easily
shaken off. An English writer on India in the mid-nineteenth century
took as cheerful a view as he could by saying that towards 1800 the
worst things that 'utterly disgraced the British name in India' were less
obtrusive. 'Open fraud, mid-day violence, heartless tyranny gave way
in due course to bribery, peculation, gambling, horse-racing, drinking,
and duelling.'[63] In an atmosphere so sordidly depraved, duelling might
at least be reckoned an injection of something higher, questionable
though notions of 'honour' might be; something ennobling, however
misguided, to preserve society from total degeneracy. War has had,
more stridently, the same appeal.

In official attitudes to duelling Europe's overseas possessions show
some sharp contrasts in behaviour, related to social structures in the
metropolitan countries and also, one may guess, to the ease or difficulty
with which native populations were controlled. In bourgeois Holland's
East Indian settlements, planted among island peoples, many of them
warlike, there was a death penalty, and it was enforced. In Ceylon each
of the Portuguese garrisons had a place near its camp where duelling
was licensed.[64] They were confined to the lowlands, fairly easily held
down. Bengal, the first Indian province occupied by the British, proved
reassuringly easy to hold down and exploit, so that there could seem
not much need for its masters to forgo dissensions among themselves.
But duelling among men high up, pillars of a still shaky polity, was not

---

[61] George Colman, *The Jealous Wife* (1761), Act IV.

[62] See Gailey.

[63] J. Capper, *The Three Presidencies of India* (London, 1853), 467.

[64] C. R. Boxer, cited by Clark, 42. On the Netherlands East Indies, cf. 'Multatuli', *Max Havelaar* (1860); trans. W. Siebenhaar (New York, 1927), 192.

without its inconveniences. Lord Macartney as governor of Madras in the 1770s could not see eye to eye with the commander-in-chief in the south, Major-General James Stuart, over their respective prerogatives. These two Scots were discreet enough not to push things too far until after their return to Britain, when Stuart would not be put off without a duel. Having only one leg he had to be propped up against a tree, while Macartney was short-sighted; neither did the other much harm.

Recognition of the unwisdom of too much lack of team spirit brought some efforts to put a stop to duelling, as William Hickey the Calcutta memoirist discovered. Having an affair on his hands, he enlisted his friend Major Cairnes, a well-connected Irishman, as his second. Cairnes produced a pair of pistols, observing that they had 'more than once performed their duty admirably, and he sincerely hoped they would not prove less decisive upon the present occasion'. But Hickey was called away by a summons from Mr Justice Hyde, who read him a lecture on his rashness and on the impropriety of a deputy-sheriff planning a 'most outrageous breach of the law', and made it clear that government was now determined to treat offenders of all ranks 'with the utmost rigour'.[65]

Not much later an Ensign Davison made the risk of legal proceedings his excuse for declining a challenge, when taxed by a fellow-member of the 'Bucks' with scurrilous talk about the club; 'whereupon Prendergast said he was a pitiful scoundrel, and immediately gave him a severe horsewhipping'. A fight was now unavoidable; they met next morning in the neighbouring Dutch settlement of Chinsurah, to be out of East India Company jurisdiction, and at the second shot Prendergast was hit in the thigh. 'The surgeons put him to extreme torture in their fruitless endeavours to find and extract the ball', and he was lucky to survive. Davison was generally condemned, and expelled from the club. 'The fellow was vexed to the soul at this issue of the business.'[66]

There is an occasional lighter note. During the long voyage out to India quarrels often led to vows of hostilities; by the time the parties got ashore their tempers had time to cool, but 'contemporary prejudice obliged them to make a show of a duel'. Two frightened cadets were thus bullied into squaring up to each other, but their bearleaders made a joke of it by giving them pistols without bullets.[67]

In other parts of eighteenth-century Europe the duel was having mixed fortunes. In Sweden it seems to have dropped out curiously quickly after the seventeenth century. A nobility largely of foreign extraction was now being assimilated; Sweden's grand military epoch

[65] Hickey, iii. 265–7.
[66] Ibid. ii. 337–9.
[67] D. Kincaid, *British Social Life in India 1608–1937* (1938; 2nd edn., London, 1973), 87–8.

was ending in disaster; the 'Caps', or bourgeois party, were coming to the front in politics at the expense of the 'Hats'. In southern Europe there was less activity than formerly. In its morbid way the duel was an index of vitality, not precisely in either aristocracy or nation, but in the two interacting. France, Prussia, Russia could in diverse ways be called dynamic, Italy and Spain decadent. Spain had sunk from the first place it once held in Europe; nonentities tied to the apron-strings of the court made up its effete peerage. Its feeble army was officered chiefly by middle-class men in want of a profession. So was the British army, still more the navy, but with a colouring borrowed from an aristocratic tradition still very much alive.

How foreigners saw things beyond the Pyrenees may be suggested by the episode in the French novel *Gil Blas* where a jealous Portuguese duke has a Spanish gentleman thrashed by his lackeys, and the Spaniard plans in return to assassinate him.[68] A like view of Italy shows in Molière's short comedy-ballet *Le Sicilien*, performed at court in 1667 with the youthful Louis XIV taking part in the final dance. In scene xiii a French gentleman's Turkish slave, in disguise, consults the Sicilian Don Phèdre (played by Molière), complaining of having been slapped on the cheek, and asking whether he should seek revenge by fighting his assailant, or having him murdered. 'Assassiner, c'est le plus court chemin', replies Don Phèdre without hesitation. Italy had professional cut-throats for hire, the south especially, and there was still the vendetta, private and secret instead of open and acknowledged like the duel.

In the Hanoverian period Britain was an extensive employer of German troops, whose officers' susceptibilities had to be considered. In 1742 Horace Walpole, to whose gossip-letters duelling news lent a plentiful seasoning, reported to a friend a quarrel between Lieutenant Robert Rich and Lieutenant-Colonel Gilbert Vane, of the 1st Foot Guards, serving in Flanders. It led to Rich—a baronet's son—boxing Vane's ear, in front of the regiment, while their commander was endeavouring to placate them. 'They were immediately put in arrest, but the learned in the laws of honour say they must fight, for no German officer will serve with Vane till he has had satisfaction.'[69] In 1756 when German troops were stationed in England Walpole thought that 'both Hessians and Hanoverians are rather popular', but a Hessian officer had created an incident by wanting to fight a Hampshire magistrate who arrested one of his men.[70]

Kipling wrote a poem about the time and cost needed to produce an officer whose utility could be cut short by one bullet on a wild frontier.

[68] A. R. Lesage, *Gil Blas de Santillane* (1715–35), Bk. 3, chap. 7.
[69] Walpole, xvii (Walpole to Sir Horace Mann, 7 July 1742).
[70] Ibid. xx. 563.

Frederick the Great (1740–86) had a similar notion of duelling in his army, as depriving him of lives that could have been sacrificed more usefully, with more profit that is to himself. Abroad a notion got afloat that, taking a leaf out of Gustavus Adolphus's book, he put a stop to the duel by compelling practitioners to go on fighting till one dropped, and then hanging the other. Frederick did confirm an edict of 1713, which itself reproduced much of previous Prussian legislation, though with somewhat mitigated penalties. He even toyed with the idea of procuring an international agreement to refuse asylum to duellists on the run.[71] Late in his reign he set up courts of honour, on the French model, requiring duels to be approved by the regiments concerned. But enforcement was difficult. His officers were landowners, with more ancestors than acres, and he could only shrug his philosophical shoulders over their mania for trying to kill one another. There was method in their madness, for, as Vagts points out, the practice served their interests as a class, by helping to keep out competition from non-nobles.[72] How jealously exclusive an officer corps could be, against interlopers of any kind, is illustrated by Smollett's anecdote of an Englishman in Piedmontese service, who met with so many affronts from his fellow-officers that he was 'obliged to hazard his life in many rencounters with them, before they would be quiet'.[73]

East and west Europe remained, as always, in many ways apart, but integration on a certain level was going on. Poland had a still bigger swarm of gentry than France, many of them impoverished and reckless, and trying to cling to their status by hook or by crook. Central authority was disintegrating as the partition of the country by its three neighbours approached. Clan feuds were rampant. In Mickiewicz's epic, or verse novel, about life in the Lithuanian part of Poland in the early nineteenth century, we hear an old diehard busy stirring up once more a grudge between two clans; a young listener, thrilled by his gory reminiscences, recalls what he has read of bloodily romantic tales from England, Scotland, Germany.[74] Elsewhere in the poem, when two men after a hunt are wrangling over which of them shot the bear—in reality it was neither—the judge's deputy declares that 'according to the ancient custom we give you our permission for a duel'. But he goes on to make them laugh by relating a story of a similar dispute when the two parties, after fighting with sabres, 'swore to shoot at each other over the hide of a bear: that was in true gentleman's style, almost barrel to barrel'—

[71] Demeter, 122–3.
[72] Vagts, 72.
[73] Smollett, *Travels*, 131.
[74] Mickiewicz, Bk. 2.

and how he restored peace by a trick taken from Virgil.[75] A tale that circulated abroad went one better than the bear's hide: two Poles, each resolved to be the other's quietus, agreed to sit side by side on a barrel of gunpowder, each with a match to set it off.[76]

Russia had no age of chivalry to look back on, and the *pomeshchiks* or service gentry, who started as mounted troopers, had no pretensions to gentility until by the later seventeenth century they managed to establish themselves as hereditary owners of the fiefs and serfs granted to them. They could then blossom into a minor nobility, fusing with what was left of the older aristocracy, and sharing with it the titles that were being adopted from the west, and with them foreign fashions of dress and the use of foreign languages instead of Russian. For such a *parvenu* class duelling could set a seal on their respectability. In the mean time it was confined, even more than in Germany, mainly to the army. Peter the Great (1689–1725) in his military regulations did his best to keep it out. He could be far more high-handed with his officers than Frederick, and made the sending of a challenge a hanging matter. He must have feared that duelling would be bad for discipline in his raw forces, and may have feared that it would intensify frictions inevitable between foreigners serving in them and native Russians.

Catherine the Great (1762–96), that self-appointed empress or usurper, granted a Charter of the Nobility which gave it further, long-coveted privileges. She was a German, priding herself on her European culture, and her *Nakaz* or draft law code of 1767 showed her less uncompromising about the duel than Peter had been. In her view the right way to restrain it was to treat the challenger as aggressor, and punish him.[77] This was a speciously simple distinction; clearly it might be the challenger who was forced into action against his will. The way would soon be open for Russia to become one of the chosen homes of the duel. With its spread from St Petersburg to the provinces, boorish manners could be varnished or transfigured by patrician feeling. As Macaulay wrote of seventeenth-century England, a rustic gentleman might talk and behave like a carter, yet be 'punctilious on matters of genealogy and precedence, and ready to risk his life rather than see a stain cast on the honour of his house'.[78]

In the course of the eighteenth century aristocracy and its allies or understrappers were establishing themselves firmly in control of Europe. Resistance both from the masses, chiefly the peasants, and from subject

[75] Mickiewicz, Bk. 4.

[76] Geddes, 32–3.

[77] W. F. Reddaway (ed.), *Documents of Catherine the Great* (Cambridge, 1931), 253 (*Nakaz*, para. 234).

[78] Macaulay, *History of England*, chap. 3 (1848).

nationalities like Ireland or Bohemia, was beaten down. This pacification was accomplished far more by coercion than by reform, and brought armies very much to the front. One of the indulgences that had to be allowed them was duelling, which had the important function of helping to stiffen the morale of the indispensable officer corps, the firmest bastion of class rule. This corps was itself a microcosm of the dominant classes, reproducing the amalgam a successful class must achieve of collective feeling and competitive individual ambition. Duelling as an institution reflected and preserved the class allegiance common to all officers. The honour code linked Europe together across national lines, with the aid of France's now established position as *arbiter elegantiarum* of European culture, as well as linking higher and lower sections of the upper classes. It was a part of what made Europe one whole; it emanated from aristocracies which in many ways perpetuated the thinking of a pre-national past. Their Europe was for them a republic of swords, as for scholars it was a republic of letters. All higher classes felt more kinship with one another, irrespective of nationality, than with their humbler compatriots. Built into Europe's social and economic foundations was the necessity of war between nations; yet only repeated and mounting explosions, after 1789, could by stages disrupt the fraternity of blue blood.

Warfare and duelling helped to sustain each other. Patriotism might help to brace a duellist's nerve, not only when he faced a foreigner: a man who shrank from the test would bring some discredit on his country. Governments might well come to consider that the willingness of officers to 'defend their honour' was necessary to keep up their zest in fighting, their readiness to defend the reputation of the army and the interests of their country. In the kingdom of Sardinia-Piedmont it came to be obligatory for officers, while outside the armed forces duelling was forbidden. In general, regulations with regard to officers underwent a steady turn towards greater indulgence, and then positive approval.

There had to be careful adjustment to the requirements of discipline. One mischief which proved hard to check was of officers on active service wanting to fight each other straightaway instead of waiting till the campaign was over. Captain Ochterlony of the 60th Foot, mortally wounded during an abortive British attempt on Quebec at the end of July 1759, had received an injury the day before from Captain Wetterstroom of the Grenadiers.[79] A second point hard to hammer home was proper respect for differences of rank; equality of right to challenge a superior was less easily accommodated to the military

[79] Hibbert, 93, 96. A Japanese analogy in 1600 can be found in S. R. Turnbull, *The Samurai: A Military History* (London, 1977), 237.

hierarchy than among civilians. As a rule junior officers were not supposed to challenge their seniors. There were symptoms in the East India Company forces early on of young officers hungry for promotion being tempted to clear the way by calling out men above them and shooting them down. In 1824 the Duke of York as commander-in-chief struck a subaltern named Battier off the half-pay list for his presumption in sending a challenge to a senior, and reprimanded Lord Londonderry for meeting him.

All over Europe officer corps were being built on the same plan, but with wide variations of temper. In an army like the Prussian, officers thought of themselves as the bodyguard of their royal chief. In Britain their mentality was coloured by the strength of parliamentary insti-tutions, which enabled them to feel that they had citizen rights of their own; this comes out very distinctly in the published apologia of the mutinous officers of the Madras Army in 1809.[80] But men like these, largely from the professional middle classes, were being in many ways assimilated into the habits of their forerunners and tutors, the gentry, just as the upper-middle class in civil life was; and in this process the duel had a special place, as initiation into the traditional code. In the British navy materials were still more mixed, and the creation of a homogeneous officer cadre was a more protracted task. Captain Marr-yat's novels belong to a time when 'better' men were joining the service in numbers, with the result that the quarterdeck was becoming less ill-mannered, but more haughtily aloof from the forecastle.

In the trade of war physical courage could easily be hailed as the supreme virtue. Macaulay contrasted the decay of the military qualities in late medieval Italy with the esteem in which they were held further north. 'Among the rude nations which lay beyond the Alps, valour was absolutely indispensable', and cowardice 'the foulest reproach'.[81] Before 1789 a young entrant to the French army was expected to prove himself by taking on an expert swordsman, though he could usually hope to be let off with a few scratches. It was from the armies above all that this ethos spread to the rest of the social strata from which officers came; and honour really often boiled down to nothing more than the necessity of showing indifference to physical danger. In a divided society like Europe's it was proper for some to be bold and combative, and for the rest to be resigned, patient, and submissive.

Lady Emily in Susan Ferrier's novel was 'too fearless and independent to be deterred by the world's dread laugh from doing what she thought right'.[82] Not many men had this quality; physical courage was no

[80] Anon., *Discontents of the Madras Army* (London, 1809), e.g. 100, 258–9.
[81] *Essays*, i. 17–18.
[82] Susan Ferrier, *Marriage* (1818), chap. 60.

assurance of moral courage. So far as worship of it, as the *suprema lex* of the gentleman, influenced military tactics, it can only have had a retarding effect, like the tournament earlier. Conrad's obdurate duellist, General Feraud, remained 'A mere fighter all his life, a cavalry man, a *sabreur*,' who saw war very simply as 'a massed lot of personal contests, a sort of gregarious duelling'.[83] German student duelling in the form of the *Mensur*, a test of nothing but stoical endurance of pain, was a suitable preparation for the insane heroism of the Prussian Guard at Gravelotte in 1870, when it tried to advance up a slope swept by French fire and lost eight thousand men. Most of the war of 1914–18 was a ding-dong struggle for bits of muddy trench as worthless as the 'little patch of ground' disputed between Pole and Norwegian in *Hamlet*. Years after it was over Haig was still full of faith in the cavalry charge as the key to victory.[84]

Mental attitudes clung to by social strata falling behind the times become more and more archaic, and in the end self-destructive. They may share the same weakness that besets adolescent classes or peoples under stress, the proneness to 'voluntarism' that enables them to believe in the power of will and courage to achieve what rational calculation shows to be impossible. This was the gospel preached by the Mao of the Cultural Revolution. Chinese Boxers, fanatic Mahdists, Zulus, brought to bay by more advanced military forces, made up for what they lacked by priding themselves on spirit and endurance, and threw themselves against Europe's machine-guns. In no very different way the military section of Europe's upper classes, falling behind in education and intelligence, pinned their faith to 'character', most easily defined as ability to face shot and shell, or the duelling sabre or pistol, undaunted. It was a philosophy not without practical returns, over a long period. Small European forces conquered a great part of the world; what mattered much more, almost all attempts at revolution inside Europe were crushed. As something that helped to build up the morale which made these achievements possible, the duel is entitled to its share in their halo.

[83] Conrad, 233.
[84] J. Ellis, *The Social History of the Machine Gun* (London, 1975), 56.

7

Grudges and Grievances

I must marry another—and yet I must love this; and if it lead me into some little inconveniences, as jealousies, and duels, and death, and so forth—yet, while sweet love is in the case, Fortune, do thy worst, and avaunt mortality!

Dryden, *Marriage-à-la-Mode* (1673), Scene 1.

OCCASIONS requiring formal reprisals in accord with recognized conventions, publicly approved expectations, have abounded from the earliest times. Human beings can quarrel in any environment; but in modern Europe, it is probable, they found it easier to do so because of the spread of urban living. By the eighteenth century it was customary for well-off families, if not permanently resident in towns, to pass part of the year there; preferably, if they could afford it, in a metropolis, London or Edinburgh, Paris or St Petersburg. There they herded together in monotonously narrow company. Only on some sides is man a social animal; he is also a natural solitary, accustomed through almost the whole of his long evolution to live by himself, or with very few others. Crowding together has been found to have unbalancing, hysteria-inducing effects, even on children,[1] not to speak of animals. On adults the result of herd-living, combined with strict rules of behaviour, must be to dualize consciousness, dividing it into two existences, public and private, outward and inward. Necessary self-control in some areas may make men petulant, capricious, even childish, in others. Horace Walpole congratulated himself on being old enough to be free to do as he pleased, when he reflected on the lack of freedom of his juniors: 'Young men must conform to every folly in fashion, drink when they had rather be sober, fight a duel if somebody else is wrong-headed, marry to please their fathers ...'.[2]

Niceties of Italian punctilio were left behind in course of time, but a doctrine of what was truly honourable and worth fighting about never made much headway. Men capable of taking a higher view of the subject were seldom among those likely to be personally engaged. Some issues of social life came to be generally reckoned grave enough to warrant, even to compel, a challenge; the great majority of ruptures

[1] Desmond Morris, *The Naked Ape* (London, 1968), 87–8.
[2] Walpole, xxxi. 305 (to Hannah More, 1789).

came from much smaller, even insignificant matters. Hazlitt tells a story of a backgammon player so furious at losing a game that he threw the board out of the window; it hit a passer-by, who rushed in with sword drawn, clamorous for 'instant "satisfaction"'. Luckily he too was a keen player, and on learning what had happened readily excused the loss of temper.[3]

The triviality of many disputes, which satire could scarcely exaggerate, and the willingness of so many men, young men in particular, to risk death, maiming, or exile, on the spur of the moment, suggest an infantile mentality, minds incapable of serious thought, and reacting to any stimulus like automata. Such minds belonged to a class bereft of any social function, or any healthier one than war, that could not be better performed by others, and drying up mentally or morally well in advance of its material decline. One might even credit some members of it with something like a 'death-wish', or instinctive conviction that the best one could do with one's life was to gamble with it. An affinity between duel and suicide comes out in Stendhal's remark on the pangs of despised love, and the self-contempt engendered by it, as a prime cause of suicide. 'You kill yourself to avenge your honour.'[4] Like suicide, a duel might beckon to a young man like Pan Tadeusz as a way out of his troubles.[5] But the duelling propensity points also to a fund of irritable discontent, awaiting chances to erupt in a discharge of bad humours. Among untutored people like the Pygmies bickering and squabbling may go on all the time, and, with wife-beating thrown in now and then, supply an adequate outlet for disgruntlement.[6]

A great deal must be allowed for sheer boredom. Burton of the *Anatomy of Melancholy* believed that far the most of those belonging to Europe's leisured classes suffered from low spirits.[7] Boswell noticed how the dull vacuity of gentry life in the countryside made him look forward all the time to the next meal, as a break in the monotony. Risking death as a mode of adding spice to life would reach its limit in the escape from ennui known as Russian roulette. In Ireland the inanity of a landowner's existence was at its most complete, and must have done much to feed the appetite for duelling; but the same blight was at work everywhere, and about the end of the last century a German count challenged his father-in-law 'because, at a game of billiards, the latter hesitated to accept his statement that he had made a cannon'.[8]

Most yawners, it may be supposed, would relish a combat between

---

[3] Hazlitt, 'On Great and Little Things', in *Table Talk* (1821–2).
[4] Stendhal, *Love*, 118.
[5] Mickiewicz, 206 ff.
[6] Montagu, 178.
[7] *The Anatomy of Melancholy* (1623; London, 1923), ii. 161–2.
[8] Whitman, 77.

a pair of neighbours or acquaintances more than one they were themselves concerned in; and men could gossip about challenges and their
likely outcome much as women could chatter about Venus and her
secrets. Such diversions were not limited to idle gentlefolk. When the
two gold-rush partners in Bret Harte's story, known to have parted
company, passed each other in the street without exchanging shots,
the bystanders were disappointed, the fire-eating Colonel Starbottle
disgusted.[9]

Town life was less insipid, but offered frequent occasions for taking
offence, and a wider audience, more reputation to be earned or lost.
That amiable old squire Sir Roger de Coverley had once been 'what
you call a fine Gentleman', who 'fought a Duel upon his first coming
to Town, and kick'd Bully *Dawson* in a publick Coffee-house for calling
him Youngster'.[10] So long as duelling was a fashion, a young man of
spirit would judge it the best way to win his spurs and the right to think
well of himself. There were men who never found a better way of
making their mark, and grew into inveterate quarrellers.

There were others who enjoyed the sensation of the thing, when they
could do so with impunity. One such, in an account preserved by
Smollett, was the Duke of Buckingham of Charles II's time: he provoked
a weak Earl of Shrewsbury by insults, and killed him, but when
challenged by Lord Ossory found a pretext for missing the rendezvous,
confident that the House of Lords would interfere and save him from
having to fight.[11] A cheap success could be won by humiliating a victim
afraid or unwilling to retaliate, such as Hamlet suspects himself of
being:

> Who calls me villain, breaks my pate across,
> Plucks off my beard and blows it in my face,
> Tweaks me by the nose, gives me the lie i' th' throat?

Ireland was fertile of bullies, as well as of more sporting duellists.
'Fighting Fitzgerald' left Eton to travel abroad and pick up more vices
before returning to Ireland in 1775. He had been caught cheating with
dice at Versailles, which might have been expected to disqualify him
as a gentleman; none the less he ran up a total of more than thirty
duels, galling men by rudeness, even blows, in London clubs or Dublin
theatres, on one occasion shooting a man's wig off his head. Settling in
County Mayo he terrorized the neighbourhood, and his own family,
until he went a step too far by having a local rival murdered. He was
sentenced to death by the redoubtable John Fitzgibbon, later Earl of

[9] 'The Iliad of Sandy Bar', in *The Luck of Roaring Camp* (1868).
[10] R. Steele, *The Spectator*, 2 (1711).
[11] Smollett, *Travels*, 140–1.

Clare; his trial and hanging aroused much interest, and no doubt pleasure.[12]

Another celebrity of those days was Beauchamp Bagenal, whose tinder-box temper earned him 'a reputation almost European'. In 1773 he requested leave of absence for a relative serving in America with the army. He received a civil reply from Colonel Blaquiere, government secretary at Dublin, that the viceroy had no power in the matter. To his extreme surprise, Bagenal instantly challenged him. 'When Irish gentlemen made requests they were to be granted.' Blaquiere had no choice but to agree, and they met in Phoenix Park; Blaquiere fired in the air, while his assailant after two misfires managed to put a bullet through his hat. He could not get Blaquiere to fire at him, and was left looking ridiculous when the seconds intervened to end the affair; Blaquiere was left 'the most popular secretary that had ever held office'.[13]

In Ireland or Scotland the old feudal ties kept their meaning longer, and a wrong to an underling was an affront to his superior. An Irish landlord might feel it behoved him to come to the defence of a tenant by calling out, or letting his son call out, a man who injured him. At Kinsale in County Cork two officers fought because one had beaten the other's servant, and the aggressor was killed.[14] Some were just as ready to stand by their dogs, and in 1803 Captain Macnamara killed Lieutenant-Colonel Montgomery by way of setting things right after a scrap between their dogs in Hyde Park.[15] The mettlesome pair in *Pan Tadeusz* who wanted to fight over the bear were also given to endless argument about the merits of their hunting-dogs, though 'in friendly fashion, like men of honour, who were on their way to settle a mortal quarrel'.[16] Descending a step further in the scale, two French officers of the Guards fought on a Paris *quai*, soon after Louis XIV's death, in broad daylight, about a cat.[17] Both came from families of the *noblesse de la robe*, or magistrature, and may have been in a hurry to signalize their entry into the nobility of the sword.

Laurence Sterne's father, a ne'er-do-well Irish ensign of hasty temper, fell out at Gibraltar—in a fortress under siege—with a Captain Phillips over a more useful creature, a goose. They drew their swords indoors, and Sterne was pinned to the wall; 'upon which he quietly asked, or is said to have asked, "*Do* wipe the plaster off your sword before you pull

[12] Maxwell, 52–4.
[13] Froude, ii. 145 ff.
[14] Steinmetz, i. 242–3.
[15] Baldick, 97–8.
[16] Mickiewicz, Bk. 2.
[17] Steinmetz, i. 250.

it out of me." '[18] He survived, to be sent to Jamaica, where the deadly climate soon cooked his goose.

Of all European armies Bacchus was the patron saint, and the great days of the duel saw his reign at its palmiest. Lord Herbert prefaced the story of his abortive quarrel with Lord Howard de Walden during the siege of Juliers in 1610 by saying that it started at a feast accompanied by 'liberal drinking'.[19] Samuel Butler in his verses 'Upon Drunkenness' spoke of the tippler neglecting all better things:

> For madness, noise, and bloody fights;
> When nothing can decide, but swords
> And pots, the right or wrong of words.

Intoxication was a licensed release from the irksomeness of artificially stilted manners. Thackeray remarks that men of the Restoration era might spend a quarter of their time drinking;[20] they can seldom have been perfectly sober. This may have saved lives, as well as jeopardizing them; drunken quarrels were sometimes fought out at once, or early next morning after a brief, often sleepless night, when marksmanship must have been at a low ebb.

There were close psychological links too between duelling and the massive social drinking that persisted, in Britain, down to mid-nineteenth century, both ending about the same time. It was typical of a parasitic upper class that it should want to congregate round the bottle for hours every day, somewhat as Europeans far away in their colonies huddled together in mess or club. Alcohol provided an artificial bond, a spurious fraternity, and like duelling acquired a ritual of its own, the burdensome formalities described, in Scotland, by Dean Ramsay.[21] Irritable topers were naturally many. When the obnoxious Ensign Davison grew drunk and unmannerly at a party in Hickey's house at Calcutta, the latter ordered him out. Davison got up, 'putting his hand to the hilt of his sword, which upon his attempting to draw I knocked him down'. Everyone felt that he had behaved like a perfect host, and would be under no obligation to accept a challenge; but when a second arrived, desiring an apology, he felt he must fight.[22] On some occasions the drinking was one-sided, as in the farcical episode in 1813 of Lord Mount Charles, a Trinity College student, travelling from Cambridge to London in a coach driven by one Hellfire Dick. It was a time of agrarian disturbances round Ely, and the boisterously tipsy undergraduate started an altercation with 'a stout, farmer-like man seated

---

[18] L. Hartley, *Laurence Sterne* (Chapel Hill, N. Carolina, 1943), 11–12.
[19] Lord Herbert, 62–3.
[20] *Henry Esmond*, Bk. 1, chap. 12.
[21] Ramsay, chap. 3.
[22] Hickey, iii. 263.

opposite to him', accused him of being a rioter, and brought out a pair of pistols, 'insisting on their exchanging shots across the high-road'. Dick, a peacemaker despite his nickname, succeeded in quietening him down.[23]

Drinking often went with gambling, though shrewder gamesters took care to keep their heads cool. Each pursuit was in its way a challenge to be met, a test of nerve and the demeanour proper to a gentleman. The duellist too had to be a *beau joueur*. High stakes were another cure for boredom, and another means of getting the better of a rival. Money so lost had to be paid, as a 'debt of honour', and failure to pay invited punishment as well as ignominy. An Irish peer, Lord Belfield, was called out by an English MP who was dunning him; they met in London, with both sword and pistol, and it was the aggrieved party instead of the defaulter who was wounded.[24] In the museum of the Irish National Stud at Tully, near Kildare, is a record of the grand race for a thousand guineas, at the Curragh in September 1751, between the horses of Sir Ralph Gore and the Earl of March. Gore won, but the verdict was contested, and the earl wanted satisfaction. His opponent duly presented himself, bringing a coffin inscribed with the earl's name; this chastening hint brought a hasty withdrawal.

More serious issues might arise from libel, in days when legal restraints on it were inadequate. A duel would often be resorted to in preference to the law's delay, uncertainty, expense, and from a conviction that a man ought to rely on himself to protect his honour. Early newspapers gave themselves a very wide latitude of abusiveness, which might not be easy to retaliate against. It seemed to Macaulay, writing of a duel of 1777, 'almost incredible that any human being should ever have stooped to fight with a writer in the *Morning Post*'.[25] Professional grudges erupted readily. During the long-drawn 'Douglas Cause' in the High Court at Edinburgh, between the ducal dynasties of Douglas and Hamilton, an advocate on the Douglas side—later Lord Thurlow, the Chancellor—commented acrimoniously on the methods employed by his learned friend Andrew Stuart, who promptly called him out; 'the pair fought a savage but bloodless battle'.[26] Thurlow was a clergyman's son, sent down from Cambridge for misconduct, but not cured of his vulgar arrogance, profanity, and loose living; it was this *cause célèbre* that started him on his legal and political career.

By an odd reversal of the 1774 episode when he was the recipient of an unwelcome challenge, in March 1776 Boswell convinced himself

[23] L. and H. Fowler, *Cambridge Commemorated* (Cambridge, 1984), 173.
[24] Steinmetz, i. 243.
[25] Review of Croker's edn. of Boswell's *Johnson*.
[26] Pottle, 397–8.

that the Lord Advocate had spoken objectionably of his father's conduct in another law case, and that it was his disagreeable duty to bring the slanderer to book, even though his father cared nothing about it. Family spirit was very strong in Boswell, and he may have felt that he ought not to be less ready to live up to it than his former challenger, young Miller, had been. This time he could not confide in his wife, and on the eve of a journey to London confided instead in his diary. One has to die some time, he reflected. 'My wife and children will be consoled in a short time ... If I am wounded, my spirits will be raised by a sense of honour and a sort of gallant vanity which a duel justly fought inspires. My greatest uneasiness was the fear of fear.' In London his anxiety was speedily laid to rest by Sir John Pringle, who dissuaded him from 'quixotism'. ' "Everybody here", said he, "is abused in public and it is never thought there should be a duel on that account." '[27] Times were changing, indeed, but Sir John must have been stretching the truth out of kindness to his young friend.

Early in Handel's career, in 1704, he was taking part in the production of an opera called *Cleopatra*; the versatile composer, Mattheson, was acting both as Antony and as conductor. Having duly given up the ghost, Mattheson wanted to take his place at the harpsichord; Handel refused to surrender it, and an impromptu sword fight took place at the stage door, with most of the audience looking on. Mattheson might have perished a second time that evening, or cut Handel's career short, 'had God's guidance', he piously set down, 'not graciously ordained that my blade, thrusting against my opponent's broad metal coat-button, should be shattered'.[28] Never can a button have served humanity better. If professional actors were sometimes irascible, even the smell of the footlights was enough to ignite some tempers. When amateur theatricals came in at Calcutta after 1765 there were duels between gentlemen jockeying one another for the best roles.[29]

Sons of Mars had more than their share of touchiness. They were not very liberally paid, and had to be compensated by other perquisites: in time of war medals and plunder, in peacetime uniforms as eye-catching as female finery, and to many women irresistible, social standing, the privilege of duelling. There could be no shortage of sore spots among men cooped up together with, in peacetime, little to do with their time. Saint-Simon mentions a set-to in Paris in 1717 between two officers who had long detested each other. One was badly hurt, and much influence had to be brought to bear, and much time and money spent, to save them from disciplinary measures. They were then wisely

---

[27] *The Ominous Years*, 245–54.

[28] J. Keates, *Handel: The Man and his Music* (London, 1985), 24.

[29] Calder, 765.

separated, by being assigned to different corps.[30] A few years later, when the Cameronians were encamped on the links at Edinburgh, Captain Chiesley and Lieutenant Moodie fell out, and, happening to meet in the Canongate, drew their swords. Both were wounded beyond recovery—'Mr. Moodie's wife looking over the window all the while this bloody tragedy was acting'.[31]

After Wolfe's death at the capture of Quebec in 1759 the command devolved on the Hon. George Townshend, a clever caricaturist chiefly good at making enemies. He penned an unimpressive report of the victory, and sailed home in the same ship with the hero's corpse; in England he was heavy-handedly critical of Wolfe's tactics, and seemed disposed to claim more than his own fair share of credit. He was attacked in a pamphlet, the work he suspected of another high-ranking officer, the Earl of Albemarle; they were on the point of fighting when a royal messenger came to stop them: Townshend's second had babbled.[32] Such a duel at such a moment would have marred the patriotic rejoicings. Townshend came in for much derision, but thanks to his abler brother Charles, Chancellor of the Exchequer, in 1767 he obtained the lieutenant-governorship of Ireland. He had a stormy time of it, and when his term ended in 1773 he was beset by a spirited young Irishman, Lord Bellamont, smarting at being refused an audience at Dublin. Delicate negotiations smoothed the matter over, but whisperings followed, until there was nothing for it but a fight.[33] Again Townshend seems to have been unlucky with his second, Lord Ligonier, who according to Horace Walpole muddied the waters by issuing a confused statement about his principal's answer to the challenge.[34] Townshend was luckier with his shot, which hit Bellamont in the groin; he was still in distress from the wound when he put on his splendidest costume to be painted by Reynolds.

An army case that made a stir, partly because the culprit, Major Campbell, was a cousin of the Earl of Breadalbane, took place in northern Ireland in 1808. He quarrelled with a brother officer, Captain Boyd, in the mess, and in the fight that immediately ensued mortally wounded him. Campbell absconded and lay low for some months in Chelsea, before giving himself up and being sent back to Ireland to be condemned by a morose Presbyterian jury. Strenuous efforts were made to save him, and Lord Moira wrote a long letter to place the facts before the Prince Regent. Campbell had served for twenty-seven years,

[30] Saint-Simon, iii. 118–19.
[31] J. Grant, *Edinburgh*, iii. 30.
[32] Hibbert, chap. 15.
[33] Steinmetz, i. 328 ff.
[34] Walpole, xxxii. 93 and n. 6.

with an excellent record, and there had been no bad blood between the two men previously. What happened was 'wholly imputable to the madness of intoxication'; they and a couple of others went on sitting too long over their wine at the end of a review dinner, after all the rest had 'retired overcome'. The cabinet had gone into the matter, Moira explained, and decided that justice must take its course. The duel was a highly irregular one, fought hugger-mugger that same night, in a room, at seven paces; Boyd was given no time to find a second, or settle his affairs.[35] It must have weighed with the government that such behaviour at such a time, with the country at war, and in such a place as restless Ireland, was more than usually irresponsible. Campbell went to the gallows on the same day that Moira's letter was written; the neighbouring gentry flocked to look on, in mourning clothes.

Naval men were not behind in readiness to cavil, like Hotspur, on the ninth part of a hair. A novel founded on personal experience described how its narrator, on a beach in the West Indies just after a hard brush with the enemy, watched two officers land and prepare for a duel. Captain Pinkem was demanding an apology for some words spoken by a junior years ago, when he was too young to remember them. The latter was conciliatory, but could not apologize because, Pinkem being known for a first-rate shot, withdrawal would look unmanly. 'Violent and headstrong' though he was, Pinkem felt enough compunction to warn his inexperienced opponent to stand in the correct sideways posture. The young man fired first, at random; Pinkem stood rigid for a few seconds before dropping, his pistol going off and the bullet burying itself in the sand. 'He fell with his face turned towards me, and I never shall forget the horrible expression of it.'[36]

Despite disharmonies, every regiment or warship worth its salt had a strong feeling of its identity, and feuds between them might easily break out, as in former times between clans. In France one regimental champion was Ney, before the Revolution a hussar trooper and a brilliant fencer, later one of Napoleon's marshals. Each corps had its fencing-master, who might be tempted to welcome duels as a chance to show his skill. Between some regiments 'quarrels were hereditary', and their officers were bound to fight whenever they happened to be posted within reach of each other.[37]

Politics supplied an increasingly fertile ground, a fact that helps to explain the vitality of duelling in Britain, where parties were the first to blossom and take the place of court cliques or local factions, and where election contests provided a prime chance to do rivals down and

[35] Aspinall, vi. 300–1.
[36] Michael Scott, *Tom Cringle's Log* (1836; London, 1915), 120–2.
[37] Bosquett, 68; Massi, 138 ff., 'On the barbarous custom of Regimental Hereditary Feuds'.

get rid of boredom—and money. Once again Ireland may be said to have set the pace. Electioneering there included 'duels between gentlemen and rioting among the peasantry', as a matter of course.[38] In February 1787 Sir John Colthurst received a mortal wound from Dominick Trant, whom he had challenged as writer of a pamphlet accusing unnamed Protestants, Colthurst by implication among them, of complicity in recent disturbances in Munster.[39] Politicians disappointed of promised favours were quick to show their resentment. In 1780 the lord-lieutenant, the Earl of Buckinghamshire, was recalled, having proved 'quite unable to cope with the difficulties of his position in Ireland'.[40] One of them followed him to England, in the shape of an abusive letter, threatening a challenge, from Sir Henry Cavendish, lately appointed receiver-general for Ireland but still not content. There was talk in London of a prosecution, but the attorney-general advised against it. 'In Ireland the scandal of exposure would be certain—a conviction would be extremely uncertain.'[41]

In eighteenth-century England the combatant most in the political limelight was the democrat or demagogue Wilkes. The meeting he had most cause to regret was in 1763, with Samuel Martin, secretary to the Treasury. Wilkes suffered from a squint which made him unlikely to be a good marksman;[42] he received a ball in his stomach. This gave him a painful excuse for not returning to England next year to stand trial for charges against him, but it was rejected, and he had to lurk abroad.

Patriotism could breed disputes, as in earlier days, and Anglo-Scottish prejudices were still lively. Wilkes underwent a challenge when in Paris, though he was able to steer clear of it, from a Captain Forbes who took umbrage at some articles in his paper the *North Briton* as disrespectful to Scotland. More exceptionally, piety led a lawyer to call out a tippler for indulging in profane talk.[43] The defender of the faith was fatally injured.

Among primitive peoples a wife's abduction may be the commonest of all apples of discord. Higher up the scale too, few departments of life can have justified better than duelling the maxim *cherchez la femme*. Women might be mistresses with rival suitors, or respectable wives, sisters, daughters insulted by improper advances, or besmirched by

---

[38] Maxwell, 49.

[39] M. J. Bric, 'The Rightboy Protest in County Cork 1785–1788', *Past and Present*, 100 (1983), 120.

[40] *DNB*.

[41] Froude, ii. 271–3.

[42] A suggestion I owe to Prof. G. Rudé. Charles Churchill's long, declamatory poem *The Duellist* (1764) applauds the patriot Wilkes and denounces Martin as a tool of the foes of liberty.

[43] Steinmetz, ii. 44–5.

scandal, or seduced, or jilted. All these circumstances could lead to hostilities, and one of the most interesting features of the duel is the insight it offers into the spirit and working of the patriarchal upper-class family, in its peculiar European forms. In the classical French drama few explanations of duels ever emerge except points of honour and love.[44] Duelling could sustain the prestige of a class, but also of the male sex, by designating it as woman's natural guardian, protector, possessor.

This was a species of machismo more creditable at least than most others, which have run to bullying women rather than impressing them by manly courage. It went with the fact that by contrast with Afro-Asia, European women, especially north-European, were relatively free, both visible and mobile; upper-class women, frequently though not always, more than others. Outside Europe women were too closely immured, at least those cloistered in wealthy harems guarded by eunuchs and slaves; though women of the poorer classes might be able to throw some dust in their husbands' eyes, as they did in the Egypt described by Edward Lane and Richard Curzon, or in the *Arabian Nights*. In Europe the partial freedom of women gave a man a more intelligent companion, and possible access to other bedrooms; but his 'honour' was liable to be tarnished by his wife's conduct, since he was still supposedly lord and master, and to let himself be cuckolded would be like a governor allowing his subjects to flout him. He was compelled to live dangerously. Any assumption of superiority over others, whether by kings or by lesser folk, carries with it its own liabilities. With power was mixed up that perennial creeping weed, property, and fear of patrimonial succession being bastardized. A wife was herself a species of property.

By one line of descent the duel derived from the chivalrous ideals or fancies of feudalism, which had a long life. While Herbert was serving in the Low Countries in 1614 a cavalier in the Spanish camp threw out a challenge 'for the sake of his mistress', and Herbert says he sent a 'trumpet' or herald with acceptance, but the enemy commander Spinola vetoed it.[45] He was a Genoese, of a great banking family, with shrewder notions than most grandees of how wars should be conducted. Herbert came in for a wittier snub when he took a dislike to a Frenchman, Balagny, and wanted to fight him and prove that he had a 'worthier mistress'. Balagny proposed a better way of deciding which was 'the abler man to serve his mistress'—they should get a couple of wenches, and 'he that doth his business best' would be the winner.[46]

[44] Bennetton, 138.
[45] Lord Herbert, 79–80.
[46] Ibid. 65.

A better legacy of chivalry was the knightly duty of defending a woman, whether from bodily danger or—as England's highest order, the Garter, reminds us—from slander. Seldom was this duty more admirably performed than when Thomas Otway the playwright, if the tale is true, challenged young John Churchill, the later Duke of Marlborough, for 'beating an orange wench' at the theatre. Both men were wounded, Churchill more gravely.[47] Novelists found opportunities here. In Samuel Richardson's *Clarissa*, after the heroine has been persuaded by the profligate Lovelace to elope, and left to die of shame, he is called out and killed by her cousin, Colonel Morden. In such situations officers were given the *beau rôle*, which must have redounded to the credit of the army in readers' eyes. Jane Austen's solitary duel is undertaken (off-stage) by another colonel, a family friend indignant at the jilting of a fatherless girl. In Meredith's *Diana of the Crossways* sundry threats hang in the air, though none of them results in an encounter. Some are comic, like the stage-Irishman's talk at a ball of calling a man out because he has failed to keep an engagement with a young lady for one of the dances, but others are seriously meant to frighten mischievous tongues out of traducing women.

Christianity, while severely condemning adultery—in practice chiefly in women—unlike some other religions or cultures set up no fixed penalty for a breach of the spouse's lawful monopoly. It might be called an advance of civilization that men should seek to revenge this on the interloper, rather than on the erring wife. 'Revenge', however, is an inaccurate term, better fitted to the murder of an Italian seducer by a husband who would scarcely prize his wife enough to risk his own life over her morals. Custom or convention, if not law, warranted a European husband in killing both wife and lover caught *in flagrante delicto*: but this situation would not arise often. What the code of honour granted him was not a reprisal, but 'satisfaction', which might bring about the death or injury of the culprit, but equally his own.

Reluctance to be obliged to fight may have scared off some Lotharios. Some philanderers did pay a heavy price, like the profligate Marquis de Sévigné who, estranged from his wife the letter-writer, perished at last in a duel over a licentious married woman. On the other hand many husbands may have hesitated about complaining, especially the elderly kind, common in Catholic countries, with young wives immured in a convent before marriage and now eager to enjoy life. Such men could hardly think themselves a match for dashing young Don Juans. Assassination could give them a short cut, and avoid publicity.

Still, a wronged man who braved the seducer protected his self-

[47] Antonia Fraser, *The Weaker Vessel: Woman's Lot in Seventeenth-century England* (1984; London, 1985), 465–6.

respect and reputation by the mere fact of calling him out and facing the consequences. If he were killed or wounded the woman would be disgraced, and only the most hardened libertine would be likely to continue the liaison; and sympathy would be with the victim, unless he had been a notoriously bad husband. Thus in a way he would be punishing the trespasser, like a Japanese committing hara-kiri at his enemy's door. Sometimes sympathies must have been divided. A young officer of a garrison on the Arakan coast of Burma in the 1840s flirted, not too seriously, with a married woman, as lonely young men in such God-forsaken spots were apt to do. She had a row with her husband, and rushed to his house for shelter. He foolishly let her stay, and stayed with her. A challenge followed, 'as the night the day', and he died after lying for some weeks paralysed by a bullet, aged twenty-one.[48]

Fathers and other close relatives of unmarried women might have tribulations of their own. Goldsmith's Chinese traveller, escaping from inner Asia to Moscow with a lovely female he has fallen in with, learns that she came from Europe, and had been betrothed to an elderly friend of her father, who suddenly abandoned her to marry a fortune. This was no disappointment to her, but her father, 'stimulated by a mistaken notion of military honour, upbraided his friend in such terms that a challenge was soon given and accepted'. Summoned at midnight to the scene of the encounter, she found her father dying and, worse still, upbraiding her with his last breath from a misguided suspicion that a lapse from virtue on her part was responsible for her desertion.[49] An eighteenth-century diary tells of a lover in raptures about his fiancée, until the newspapers 'announced his being obliged to fight a duel on the breaking-off of the match' by the lady 'and the rudeness of her brother and relations. How uncertain', the diarist concludes, 'are human hopes and expectations!'[50] Stendhal reckoned jealousy the worst of all human ills. Most suitors are not too deeply smitten, he observed, and can often be got rid of by a quiet hint of a challenge; if not, 'you can find a pleasant diversion in risking your life', and 'play with the idea of killing your rival'.[51]

In all this there were not only wide regional variations, but fluctuations between one social era and another. A man who knew high society in England as well as other countries in the late seventeenth century, Count Gramont, came to the conclusion: 'Every man who believes that his honour depends upon that of his wife is a fool who torments himself, and drives her to despair.' He had in mind the

[48] Pughe, 83.
[49] Goldsmith, *The Citizen of the World* (1762), Letter 60.
[50] S. Neville, 148–9 (1772).
[51] Stendhal, *Love*, 112–13.

Catholic lands of southern Europe. Spaniards 'tyrannize over their wives', and shut them up; Italians still more closely and ingeniously, but most of them with a conviction that the best safeguard of all is the murderer's knife. Only the 'courteous and indulgent nations' where husbands take no notice enjoy peace and quiet.[52] Gramont's memoirs are a labyrinth of amorous intrigue in England and elsewhere, yet the number of affairs of honour figuring in it is surprisingly small.

As Thackeray wrote, apropos of a duel in *Henry Esmond* caused by a fiancée's unguarded conduct, 'Few men were so jealous about the point of honour in those days', and many 'thought a royal blot was an ornament to their family coat'.[53] Young married women, once they had furnished their new family with an heir, could hope to have their own rooms and go about in their own carriages; the arrangement may have been acceptable to some husbands because it left them free to look the other way. Not all were so acquiescent. Vanbrugh and Cibber's comedy *The Provok'd Husband* (1728) opens with a wrangle between Lord and Lady Townly. He grumbles at her gadding about, and demands to know whether wives should be under less restraint than single women. 'Oh my lord, they are quite different creatures', she retorts. 'Wives have infinite liberties in life, that would be terrible in an unmarried woman to take.'

On the whole, marital fidelity seemed not worth fighting about, on condition that wives were reasonably discreet and their partners not degrading. In one view this state of affairs may be seen as, like the duel, an expression of upper-class freemasonry. In another light it may be that when men cease to be jealous they are really losing faith not merely in women, or love, but in the whole moral fabric of their society, little as they may wish its material structure to be altered. A Muslim peasant in the Punjab will explain his religion's ban on pork on the ground that boars are disgustingly careless of their females' behaviour.

Yet a man of rank, above the folly of fighting for love, might be ready to fight in order to make it clear that he was not to be trifled with. Jealousy, a young marquis in a nineteenth-century French play tells his middle-class wife, is a feeling *du dernier bourgeois*—middle-class to the last degree.[54] But such phlegmatic indifference might conceal the real meaning, that jealousy is inconvenient in a woman. Gramont had a good deal to say about the celebrated fight between the Earl of Shrewsbury and the Duke of Buckingham, whose mistress the countess had long been. She had already been the cause of a bloody combat near Barn Elmes, and in Gramont's opinion was a beauty who 'might have

---

[52] Gramont, 165 (chap. 6).
[53] Bk. 1, chap. 2.
[54] Augier and Sandeau, Act II, sc. 4.

a man killed for her every day, and she would only hold her head the higher for it'. Lord Shrewsbury, 'too polite a man to make any reproaches to his wife, was resolved to have redress for his injured honour'.[55] While he was losing his life the lady it was said was looking on, in male attire, and holding her lover's horse.[56] Fashions came from France; and it may of course be that the curbing of the duel by Louis XIV helped to embolden the philanderers of the age.

If an Englishman's marriage went wrong, he could get out of it. A divorce became a possibility for a deceived husband fairly early. An Italian could not hope for one; a Frenchman could, after the Revolution, but many of the old ruling class would be loth to take advantage of a legal right repudiated by their Church. Without this remedy, a duel might seem a more pressing choice. Also, English law, guided increasingly by habits of mind bred by business, was prepared to compensate the husband financially, and debit the seducer. This might indeed represent the chief risk run by an eighteenth-century amorist.[57] From the aristocratic point of view it was sacrificing honour to mercenary calculation, however; and jealousy was not, after all, extinct.

A foreigner who discovered this was Alfieri (1749–1803), the Piedmontese nobleman and author who travelled over Europe, regaling himself with the sweets of love, and whose memoirs reveal a temperament well suited to the writing of tragedies of the more melodramatic sort. In England he fell in love with the fascinating Penelope, daughter of Earl Rivers and wife of Lord Ligonier, a very jealous military consort. He 'lived in a perpetual delirium', he records, and was guilty of many indiscretions. One evening at the Haymarket theatre the husband cornered him in his box, intent on reprisals. They walked to Green Park, then a 'large meadow' off St James's Park, and drew their swords—still worn habitually at the time—as dusk was falling, without witnesses. Alfieri was a poor fencer, and his left arm was in a sling, from a riding accident; he wanted to be killed, he tells us, but his antagonist was not inexorable, and broke off after inflicting a slight wound. What mortified the poet was to discover that the lady had been having a three-year liaison with a groom of her husband's; and it all got into the press. Ligonier obtained a divorce; he did not care to sue for damages, 'as the laws of that country allow; for every wrong has its tariff and for cuckolding it is highest of all'. This was lucky for Alfieri, who confesses that he might have been reduced to penury.[58] His most

[55] Gramont, 1.
[56] Pepys, vii. 265 n. 3.
[57] Stone, 317.
[58] Vittorio Alfieri, *Autobiography*, trans. Sir H. M. McAnally (privately pub., 1949), chaps. 10, 11. See also *DNB*, 'Ligonier'. Macaulay and others situate this duel in Hyde Park.

remarkable capture was still before him, that of the youthful bride of the ageing Young Pretender. The erring fair one who cost him a scratch in Green Park entered matrimony again, after many years, this time with a trooper at Northampton.

Whatever aristocratic scruples there might be, the availability of pecuniary satisfaction must be one reason for the early demise of the duel in England. When Lord Brudenel, the later notorious Earl of Cardigan, in 1823 appropriated the wife of Captain Johnstone, the latter sued, and was awarded £1,000. Brudenel must have felt that he was entitled to something better, and offered to fight; Johnstone replied that he had already given him the fullest 'satisfaction', by relieving him of an unpleasant partner.[59]

No doubt some women were piqued by the cooling of their husbands' jealousy, and even if Lady Shrewsburys were few, vanity could be tickled by the thought of men fighting over them. Steele wrote an amusing skit about a flirtatious widow and her budding daughter, competing for admirers. An elderly suitor, Crastin, ruffled by insinuations as to his age, sends young Tulip an invitation to meet 'in *Hide-Park*, or behind *Montague House*, or ... *Barn Elmes*, or any other fashionable place that's fit for a Gentleman to dye in'. Alarmed, the ladies drive all over London to prevent bloodshed; at last Crastin is discovered waiting in the park, while Tulip has decamped to the country. '*Flavia* tears her Hair for his Inglorious Safety, curses and despises her Charmer', and joins her mother as a devotee of old Crastin.[60] A story got afloat in London of a young lady watching two men fight for her hand. No grass, it was said, ever grew again on the spot where she stood.[61]

From this to instigation of quarrels would not be a long step. Love was not always the motive. Evelyn heard much talk about a Scotsman named Laws, condemned for murder after killing a young man unfairly in a duel; he had been set on to it by a woman with a grievance against the youth, the owner of a lodging-house where Laws's mistress lived.[62] A much later writer warned against mischief-making by 'artful, dangerous and vicious females, and inflammatory mistresses, who pride themselves much in being the object of a duel'.[63] Some may have taken a vicarious pleasure in stirring bad blood between men not connected with them, and their schools for scandal must have fomented many a misunderstanding. But there must also have been a multitude of women

---

[59] Woodham-Smith, 20–1.

[60] *The Spectator*, no. 91 (1711).

[61] Bayne-Powell, 48. Trollope tells a similar story of his *femme fatale*, Signora Neroni, in *Barchester Towers* (London, 1857), chap. 9.

[62] Evelyn, 22 Apr. 1694.

[63] Bosquett, 19.

who burned to see justice done, or get their own back, on men who wronged them, and could see no other way to it. In Goldsmith's novel the vicar's son George gets into a fight at the urging of his 'deluded mother', whose dazzling hopes of a marriage between her daughter and a depraved but wealthy profligate have been dashed by his only wanting to trifle with her.[64] Between the sexes in upper-class life relations have always been liable to embitterment from the men's free access to women of lower status—in the extreme case to slave-women, as in Rome, Arabia, or Virginia. In Europe and its offshoots a wife could retaliate by compelling him to risk his life.

A few women took up arms themselves. Nearly always it was to fight one another; there is something symbolic here of the long failure of womankind to combine against its oppressors. Male fantasy, however, suggests a relish for the notion of women trying to fight men, being worsted in a literal 'battle of the sexes', and brought back to their duty of submission. Hippolyta, daughter of the war-god and queen of the Amazons, was defeated and made his wife by Theseus. Tancred the crusader, in the legends that encrusted his memory, had a long struggle with a Saracen girl disguised as a man who finally, outmatched and dying, begged him to give her baptism. Beaumont and Fletcher achieved a fine theatrical effect at the end of the *The Maid's Tragedy* (1611) by making their wronged heroine Aspatia don men's clothes and confront the faithless Amintor, pretending to be her brother, come to avenge her. He is too conscience-stricken to want to fight: she has to cuff him, and then lets him wound her without defending herself. Dying, she discloses herself, and he commits suicide in remorse. In Handel's complicated opera *Partenope*, about a queen of Naples, a man taunted for reluctance to accept a challenge, from an enemy whom he knows to be a woman in disguise, gets out of it by promising to fight if both of them are stripped to the waist.

Flesh and blood women in England were sometimes seen fighting for money, with quarterstaffs or swords. More romantic episodes are heard of in seventeenth-century France, at times with a woman of rank in the limelight. A baroness was contemptuous of a bourgeoise who declined the honour of a duel with her.[65] In 1650 a fight between two sisters, near Bordeaux, was followed by their husbands fighting: in each case one died of wounds.[66] Actresses were the best known for their prowess; they were among the first liberated, self-reliant women, along with prostitutes, between whom and themselves there was no hard and fast line. Two French actresses fought with swords in the theatre, and one

[64] *The Vicar of Wakefield*, chap. 30.
[65] Bennetton, 36 n. 13, 67.
[66] Baldick, 69–70. Leguina, 15 n. 4, refers to a challenge between ladies at Naples.

was wounded; another pair with pistols, at which Louis XIV is said to have condescended to be amused.[67] Mlle de Maupin, of the Paris opera, who died in 1707, was the most famous in this line; she learned fencing from a lover, and was said to have taken on men, and killed several of them. Théophile Gautier made a novel out of her life.

Usually women fought over a man, as men so often did over a woman; doubtless men appreciated the flattering tribute as much as women did, though some might balk at a mistress of such militant disposition. A French play of 1651 showed two ladies in male dress about to fight over a lover, when prevented by the brother of one of them. A plebeian imitation could be made use of to ridicule duelling still further, as in a 1715 play with two maidservants wanting to fight.[68] But about the same time two *grandes dames*, the Comtesse de Polignac and the Marquise de Nesle, fought with pistols, one being grazed by a bullet, to decide their claims on that thoroughbred duellist the Duc de Richelieu, whom they could expect to be suitably impressed. In Venice, whose convents were known for their laxity, 'two abbesses fought a duel with stilettos over the elegant abbé de Pomponne'.[69]

If women could take to duelling, others outside the pale could do so too. Like many other habits or tastes, this one could percolate quite far down in society. There was nothing new about the horny-handed coming to blows, but the spectacle of how the gentry conducted its affairs could put more modish ideas into their heads. In some French legislation it was felt necessary to prohibit duels among all classes, not the nobility alone; and there was a case in 1666 of a lackey challenging a citizen, and threatening to beat him if he would not turn out.[70] In the French army the officers' passion for duelling infected other ranks; General Hoche of the Revolutionary army had a fight, when still a private, with a brutal corporal.[71] Goya painted a 'Duel with cudgels', showing two Spaniards knee-deep in sand, clubbing each other to death.

Despite the gulf between officers and men in the British army, some imitation by the latter of their superiors' habits could take place, including duelling, no doubt in rougher and readier fashion and more among NCOs than privates; more perhaps also among Irishmen than others. When the Royal Hospital at Kilmainham, near Dublin, was founded by Charles II, as an Irish Chelsea Hospital or Hôtel des Invalides, one of the regulations debarred the inmates from duelling.

[67] Bennetton, 107.
[68] Ibid. 96, 106.
[69] Bassermann, 154.
[70] Bennetton, 58, 62.
[71] Vagts, 71.

In English civil society imitativeness had been precocious. Everyone has grown so refined, Hamlet exclaims, 'that the toe of the peasant comes so near the heel of the courtier, he galls his kibe'; and in *Henry VI*, Part 2, Shakespeare makes fun of underlings aping their betters with his rebel Cade, pretending to be the true king, who knights himself as Sir John Mortimer so as to be on a footing to fight the commander of the government forces, Sir Humphrey Stafford. Attorney-General Bacon expressed a hope that noblemen would give up duelling, now that it was being adopted by barbers and butchers.[72] These groundlings must have caught fire partly from watching exhibitions of 'buckler-play', by 'prize-fighters' who used swords not over-sharp and tried to avoid damaging one another; some blood had to be drawn, to convince onlookers that they were getting their money's worth.[73]

Those in close contact with the gentry, like servants of the more favoured sort, were especially likely to copy their ways. There has been a long-standing tradition of this in English literature, more preoccupied than that of any other country with niceties of class behaviour; the middle classes could make up for their own snobbishness by deriding more vulgar snobs. Sheridan's footman conveys urgent news of an impending duel in the floweriest, most long-winded language he can rise to. But lower-class duelling could be as serious as any other kind. In 1780 two Negro servants fought in Hyde Park: neither was much hurt, but a few years later a pair of footmen were both badly injured.[74]

A fight with knives got the slang name of 'chivy duel'. A nearer likeness to the true duel, in some ways, was the English mode of settling differences by a fist-fight, with at least rough and ready rules, and some refereeing; in professional bouts there were also 'seconds'. Aristocratic influence had its place here too. A disapproving Mr Gilpin watched a contest between two pugilists, on a high platform surrounded by a crowd, and by the carriages of choicer spectators. They shook hands, 'grinning horribly', and one made an 'oration', promising fair play— but there was soon a cry of *foul* against him, led by the Duke of Hamilton and endorsed by the umpire. His Grace, Gilpin adds, 'is the great patron of the pugilists and often amuses himself with sparring with them'; also with bear-baiting.[75] Possibly his ancestor's fate made him prefer these sports to duelling.

[72] Steinmetz, i. 33.
[73] John Brand, *Popular Antiquities of Great Britain* (new edn., London, 1854), ii. 400.
[74] Lady D. Nevill, 159.
[75] Gilpin, 109–10.

8

Procedure and Etiquette

The celebrated Bully Egan ... fought another duel with Curran,
and when on the ground complained of the disadvantage in which
he stood, Curran being like a blade of grass, and he as broad as a
haystack. Curran declared that he scorned to take any unfair
advantage. 'Let my size be chalked upon your body', he said, 'and
any shots of mine which hit outside the chalk shall not count.'

Correspondence of Daniel O'Connell, ii. 489.

F R O M being what it often was in early modern times, a mere explosion
of bad temper, the duel was rescued by its chivalric leaven, by pressure
of the law, and by a gradual refining and polishing, if without any true
moral change, of the upper classes whose prerogative it was. Members
of an élite class claim respectful treatment from one another; as their
class matures and learns to cultivate the art of living, its manners—
within its own ranks—become more polished. Any audible friction in
its social life is felt as a disturbance to tranquil enjoyment of the *douceur
de vivre*. Politeness once developed can be flatteringly extended to
outsiders, when this appears judicious. Good manners are prized the
more when the effective power of an aristocracy is diminishing, as in
eighteenth-century France or in late Mughal India. They are likely
then to turn into obsession with minutiae of deportment, precedence,
and so on. St Simon, the chronicler of Louis XIV's court, stands near
the close of 'an exhausted tradition', where everything is 'frozen into a
ritual exactness and exclusiveness'.[1]

A duel was a breach of the façade of harmony required to impress
inferior classes, but when properly draped and stage-managed its disruptive character could be greatly softened, or even reversed. It shared
the urbane creed of *toujours la politesse*; what occasioned a fight might
still be vulgarly trivial, but the duel itself grew into a ritual, as formal
as a church service. It enshrined the philosophy of a dominant class,
and could thereby uplift and ennoble the most banal dispute, the most
blockish combatant, somewhat as the royal uniform transformed its
commonplace wearer. Formerly the individual subordinated himself to
duty to a lord: now this was depersonalized into loyalty to a code of
conduct shared by the heirs to the feudal order.

[1] Brinton, 283.

Gentlemen must be ready to fight, but with decorum and dignity, not like the noisy plebeians they had too often resembled. Everything in the ceremonial of the duel was of a kind to stamp it as the affair of an élite. If aristocracy was to survive and hold on to privileges that had less and less justification, it must distinguish itself by an appropriate carriage, which the man in the street could recognize as proof of superiority, however incomprehensible the code that duelling was linked to. Beau Nash, master of ceremonies at Bath from 1704, discouraged the swords that rustical gentlemen were wont to bring with them to a ball. He had been in the army, and knew how quickly swords could fly out of their sheaths. Without their constant presence there might not be many fewer duels, but there would be far fewer unseemly impromptus.

The aristocratic mode of living hid under a well-tailored exterior much raw egotism, and the necessity, which Tolstoy came to find so crippling, of coercing and exploiting others; the contrast was epitomized in the duel, with its smooth formalities and its blade or bullet biting into flesh. A gentleman could not retaliate with crude physical force against someone who pulled his nose or trod on his toes; instead of knocking an aggressor down, as an ordinary man would want to do, he had to exchange cards, name his second, and be ready to appear in Hyde Park or the Bois de Boulogne and exchange sword-thrusts or shots. Written challenges had to be courteously worded; combatants saluted each other before the action began, as though acknowledging a visionary flag of class and honour.

As life grew more orderly, duellists had to take account of public opinion as well as good manners. In any circles like the Anglo-Irish where duels were common they were sure to occur often between friends and neighbours, who after the meeting was over would want—if both were still alive—to resume their former intercourse; a duel conducted in due form would make this easier than a vulgar set-to. It could even come to be held that the duel, partly by being so politely conducted, had a civilizing influence on social behaviour at large. Recommending politeness in conversation, Swift paid tribute to the duel as the gentleman's means of upholding his right to be treated civilly.[2] A century later a British writer on the duel was convinced (not all would have agreed with him) that in places where duelling was most in vogue, such as, in the case of Ireland, Dublin or Galway, 'the gentry were the most polite and friendly, and the middle classes the most civilized and respectful': even the lower classes, taking pattern from their betters, were 'tractable and good-natured to excess'.[3] Stendhal had something

[2] Swift, 'Essay on Conversation'.
[3] Bosquett, 21.

of the same kind to say about Corsica and the frequency of murders there. 'Thanks to the admirable law of the rifle, great politeness prevails'.[4] Officers, likeliest of all to be found duelling, prided themselves on a varnish of good manners. Dr Johnson could allude to 'that courtesy which is so closely connected with the military character',[5] as something generally admitted.

For a long time combatants might have associates fighting side by side with them. For still longer, they might come to grips on the spur of the moment, with no witnesses; this too came to be viewed with increasing disfavour. An example was the clash between Byron's great-uncle and a neighbour of his, Chaworth; it took place by candlelight in a London tavern. Chaworth's death was found only manslaughter by the House of Lords, and as a peer Byron got off scot-free. A shilling publication was promptly advertised in the *Gentleman's Magazine* under the title 'A circumstantial account of a late unhappy affair which happened at the Star and Garter in Pall Mall'. A duellist of lesser rank could hope for indulgent treatment, but it would have to be established that a casualty was a bona fide offering to the code of honour. 'Let us be sacrificers, but not butchers, Cassius.'

With the coming of age of the true modern duel, two men were left to face each other, but under scrutiny of representatives of their world. The affair concerned their single honour, and began and ended with them, quite unlike a clan or family feud which drew men in willy-nilly. In trial by battle proxies had been allowed in many cases; a duellist had to do his own fighting, except in rare cases, when it was most likely to be a son who—provided that the father was not the aggressor—was allowed to take his place. In one of Meredith's novels a French friend takes the place of an Englishman who has been called out by another Frenchman, after duelling in England has come to an end.[6]

From one point of view we see a code of honour derived from the feudal past asserting itself; from another we see the bourgeois (and Protestant) rule of the strict accountability of the individual. Duelling evolved with the gradual advance of European life, bringing about an intricate counterpoint of the ethics of two jarring but related epochs, the feudal and the bourgeois. It was the individual who held the sword or the pistol, but very often less of his own volition than under the silent compulsion of a law he had taken no part in framing. As witnesses of his conduct there were, at the least, his second and his opponent's. After being frequent participants, seconds reverted to their proper function as counsellors, observers, and directors. Though on opposite sides, they

---

[4] Stendhal, *Vie de Napoléon* (1837; Paris, 1928), 6.

[5] Johnson, *Journey*, 30.

[6] *Beauchamp's Career*, chaps. 25 ff.

were in a real sense colleagues. They were assisting the combatants, but they were also delegates of the class to which all concerned belonged, and whose standards of conduct all of them were taking the field to vindicate. It was part of the institution that seconds should be guided by a gentlemanly sense of fitness, rather than by narrow partisanship.

A second stood, none the less, in a very special relationship to his principal, all the more exacting if the two were personal friends, as well as, for example, fellow-officers. It became a conventional phrase to talk of a man 'putting himself into his second's hands', or 'entrusting his honour to his second'. In one light he could be said to be abdicating his moral responsibility, agreeing to act blindfolded like a believer obeying his priest. The honour of both seconds was also on trial, and they had need of a trust in each other's integrity only possible between members of the same chosen class. It is seldom that we hear of a neutral umpire, or *juge de camp*, in addition to them. The replacement of the sword by the pistol left him, besides, with less to do.

The primary duty of seconds was to guarantee fair play, an equal chance for both their men, by agreeing on time, place, weapons, and procedure, and seeing to it that no illicit advantage was taken. Swords had to be the same length, pistols had to be given the same charge of powder, the sun must not be in either man's eyes. In early days, if there were no scrutineers, irregularities must have been common. A ludicrous case detailed in an early seventeenth-century pamphlet is that of a Henry Welby who fell out with his younger brother. Henry's pistol missed fire, he seized his brother's and got it away from him, and found it double-loaded. This struck him so sharply with the thought of how close he had been to death that he shut himself up in his house in Grub Street and never quitted it through all his remaining forty-four years.[7]

In its classic days the duel was a secluded meeting, with few if any spectators; this was necessary to avoid police interference, but it was testimony to those subject to the honour code that its representatives could be trusted to manage the proceedings on their own. It was another responsibility of seconds to be ready to testify to the regularity of these proceedings. Where important personages were concerned a written record might be needed and other witnesses enlisted. When a duel took place in 1854 between the French ambassador and American minister at Madrid, the British minister Lord Howden helped to draw up a *procès-verbal* to be forwarded to their governments.[8]

A combatant's reputation, in his own little corner of the world, would depend for the rest of his life on how he had come through the ordeal. One may wonder what use was a clandestine encounter ending without

---

[7] S. Heath, *In the Steps of the Pilgrims* (1911; new edn., London, 1950), 83–4.
[8] See despatches in Foreign Office archive, Series 72 (Spain), vol. 842.

harm done; in such a case the duel may seem little more than a mysterious rite. Yet reports of what happened were always likely to be afloat before long, making the round of the London clubs or Paris salons, and requiring the evidence of the seconds, as accredited observers, to rectify them. There might be difficulties about this, as when a duel had to be arranged abroad, to obviate legal consequences. In 1830 George Bingham, later the Lord Lucan of the Crimean War, went to Ostend to face a Major Fitzgerald who had called him out. It appears that the challenger had second thoughts, but whispers circulated that it was Bingham whose resolution failed him.[9]

Seconds as agents for their principals had a distinct resemblance to lawyers negotiating such a matter as a marriage contract. Their *pourparlers* provided an interval, brief as it might be, for cool reflection. It came to be the practice in French legal actions over insult or libel for the court to order the offender to make public withdrawal, by *amende honorable* and *réparation d'honneur*. Something similar was what a second would be aiming at. He had no judge or jury to appeal to, but the code of honour, the opinion of the well-bred world, supplied an equivalent. In all this may be seen one aspect of Europe's remarkable legalism and litigiousness, unknown in other continents.

It was an accepted part of the duty of seconds to examine the facts of the case, and co-operate in seeking a peaceful solution, if this could comport with the self-respect of both disputants. Most issues could be resolved, it was often held, by judicious management. Between them the seconds could constitute a small court of honour. In Conrad's duelling story a returned French émigré, a nobleman of the old school, reassures his daughter's fiancé, who is under a challenge: 'I tell you that *entre galants hommes* an affair can always be arranged.'[10] An example of how a pointless fight might be averted can be found in the Heber family's correspondence, at the end of an intricate narrative beginning with a lady jilted by a man who, when brought to book, felt obliged to stand on his dignity as an officer of Fencibles.[11]

There must have been many men who after giving way to a fit of temper were very willing to be extricated from an unpleasant situation. A disagreement between two Scottish lairds over hare-shooting rights lasted until the *pustles*, or pistols, made their appearance, when one of them, 'not relishing the thought of half an ounce of lead in his thorax, accepted of a very slim apology'.[12] Occasionally seconds seem to have concluded that a fight would be ridiculous, and taken their own steps

[9] Woodham-Smith, 35–6.
[10] Conrad, 242.
[11] Cholmondeley, 100–1.
[12] Tennant, 36.

to prevent mischief. When two foreign officers taking part in the Carlist war in Spain in the 1830s were bent on fighting, their seconds set them to fight on the beach at San Sebastian, on sand too loose to enable either of them to shoot straight.[13] Occasionally the principals, it was rumoured, took their own precautions, by privately agreeing not to shoot too straight; though it was also said that at times one of them had been known to break such an agreement, and fire with unpleasant accuracy.[14]

There were seconds who could be accused of egging their men on to fight, for however unrighteous or nugatory reasons, rather than forgo the excitement of a combat. By taking an uncompromising tone and insisting on action instead of accommodation, they could feel more important and make a parade of vicarious courage. Bosquett was one authority who warned his readers earnestly to choose their seconds very carefully, and above all not to rely on a man with a grudge of his own against the other principal. He had often, he asserted, witnessed 'not only the most ignorant, but the most infamous and blood-thirsty conduct', in men always, 'at bottom, cowards and poltroons'. He related a story of how he served as second to one of a couple of Dublin doctors who had fallen out at the theatre the night before. His co-second was very fierce, and threatened that if his man was killed he would at once challenge the winner to a second combat; Bosquett told him that he must withdraw this highly improper threat, or else fight *him*. After one exchange of fire he persuaded the two medicos to let things drop, to the disgust of the man of blood, who protested that 'the town would call it a shabby business if they did not proceed'.[15] Other Irish seconds struck visitors as needlessly bellicose;[16] it was after all the land of Sir Lucius O'Trigger.

It was a land too where the duel might be expected to take some extravagant or atavistic shapes. Lord Herbert in his novitiate in Elizabeth's time was taught horseback duelling, where the object was to work round behind the antagonist and strike at his unprotected left side.[17] This was abandoned before long, but in Ireland Sir Jonah Barrington recalled his grandfather, as late as the eighteenth century, taking to the saddle with pistol and short sword, after a silly squabble with a man named Gilbert, and dismounting him by stabbing his horse. It ended with their becoming 'intimately attached and joyous friends'.[18] Less happy was the outcome of an affair indignantly described by

[13] Beasley, 92–4.
[14] Geddes, 4.
[15] Bosquett, 4 ff.
[16] Baldick, 38–9.
[17] Lord Herbert, 40.
[18] Barrington, ii. 54 ff.

Barrington between his younger brother William, aged 20, and one M'Kenzie, following an after-dinner row. According to this account, they exchanged two shots, and then M'Kenzie's second, a Captain Gillespie, carried away by the spirit of the occasion, drew his own pistol, fired at William, and killed him. An extraordinary trial took place, but Gillespie lived to win fame by a career of 'glorious butchery' in India.[19]

Castiglione included wrestling among the accomplishments fitting for a gentleman, but the physical contact it involved made it unsuitable to an affair of honour, just as plebeian buffets or quarterstaff-blows would have been. (A similar consideration lay behind Stevenson's preference for a goad over a stick, when driving his donkey; it permitted 'a gentlemanly fence'.[20] Still more relevant, Honour was a Moloch only to be placated by encounters where men's lives were at stake. The choice had to be between deadly weapons, and the man challenged had the benefit of the choice.

It was never in fact very wide, since the weapon had to be an 'honourable' one. A carpenter's axe was far too prosaic, and a quarrel dissolved in laughter when, about 1660, Sir William Petty the pioneer economist, who was very myopic, proposed to fight with one, in a dark cellar. He had been challenged by Sir Hierome Sankey, a former soldier, knighted by Cromwell, and still a preacher: the two had 'printed one against the other'.[21] Less preposterous, but still not genteel enough, partly because duellists ought to be close enough to look each other in the face, were the longbow of the English archer, slowly expiring in the sixteenth century, and the crossbow of the Genoese mercenary. Superseded in warfare by the pike and musket, which were to coalesce in the bayonet, the sword was left to become part of an officer's insignia. It became the premier weapon of the duel, in the shape of the rapier, whose sharp point drank blood copiously in spite of the weapon's initial weight and bulk. This drawback must have helped to make fencing as complicated as the code of honour it accompanied; pedants turned it into an artificial science, bolstered by mathematical diagrams, and produced 'vast and complicated encyclopaedias which were of little practical use, if any, in a real fight'.[22] As time went on the rapier shed some of its size and became 'the slender feather-weight arm which is now recognized *par excellence* as the "small sword"',[23] the *épée de combat* of the late eighteenth- and nineteenth-century duel and of modern fencing.

[19] Ibid. i. 161 ff.
[20] R. L. Stevenson, *Travels with a Donkey in the Cevennes* (1879), chap. 4: 'I Have a Goad'.
[21] Sutherland, no. 48.
[22] Sir T. A. Cook, 'Fencing', in *Harmsworth's Encyclopaedia*.
[23] Hutton, 232.

Few exercises had a longer vogue than fencing. Boswell considered his countrymen good at the art, and himself took lessons at Utrecht from 'an old Italian who gave his age as ninety-four, and said he had fought in the Battle of the Boyne'[24]—perhaps he had forgotten on which side. Thanks in part to its association with the duel, fencing could be a mark of gentility by itself. We cannot suppose that a sober citizen like Monsieur Jourdain, when he took it up, was contemplating anything so outrageous as fighting; what he was looking to was a gentlemanly deportment. Plebeians given to thinking may despise the body, and wrap themselves up in their minds or souls; the man of rank is imbued with a pervasive self-esteem which extends to his limbs at least as much as to invisibles. Fencing or dancing have seemed to him far from undignified, because they foster an easy grace of carriage, in contrast with the awkward bearing of the lout or bumpkin.

Still, a reputation for proficiency might be an insurance against receiving too many challenges. Fencing became so skilled an art that a tiro had little chance; here must be one reason why the sword gave way by degrees to the pistol, earliest in unmartial England. Among the military the older weapon held out longer. In one of Farquhar's plays, produced in 1706, the reluctant Brazen tries to get out of a contest with Mr Worthy, who has brought a case of pistols, each double-loaded, by saying that as a foot officer he can only fight with the sword.[25] In France the pistol was regarded for some time as barbarous.[26] Most French civilians were reconciled to it by the end of the eighteenth century, while officers in the French and other continental armies, always conservative, preferred cold steel, with the sabre coming in to rival the straight sword. It is not often that we hear of sword or sabre duels in Russia, where there was no aristocratic tradition linked with those weapons.

Pistols had been tried long since, sometimes in Brantôme's day from horseback, where they proved capable of scoring some hits; but it was an argument against all early firearms that they were so erratic as to be a menace to bystanders as well as antagonists.[27] Gunpowder started life indeed with aristocratic prejudice against it, as an indiscriminate killer of high and low. When firearms spread, the musket was a rank-and-file weapon, like its successor the rifle. It was left to self-respecting pirates to settle their differences, in the words of Scott's corsair, with sixty yards of sea beach and a brace of rifles.[28] On the other hand the pistol was coming to form an item of an officer's equipment, partly

[24] Pottle, 125.
[25] George Farquhar, *The Recruiting Officer* (1706), Act V, sc. vi. Comic allusions to duelling are scattered through the play.
[26] Smollett, *Travels*, 140.
[27] Brantôme, 62–3.
[28] *The Pirate*, chap. 17.

because of its utility for keeping his men under control in action. Cavalry always enjoyed a higher status than infantry, and in the nineteenth century all French horsemen carried pistols. In French drama pistols made their first appearance in 1655, when a man armed with one confronted a man with a sword; the former was killed.[29] Less uncommon was the use of both weapons together. In an affair in 1778, arising from one man contradicting another in an argument, each sported a sword and two pistols:[30] not surprisingly, with such armaments, one was killed and the other badly wounded.

Europe was moving into an industrial age, and the pistol represented modernity. Perpetual warfare in Europe brought improvements, and helped to keep technology advancing. Duelling pistols could not have been produced by any non-European craftsmen. These specialized weapons were available by the 1770s. It is one more sign of the ambiguity of legal and social attitudes that although nearly all countries had laws against duelling, these tools for its service could be manufactured and sold without let or hindrance. They were on the cumbrous side at first, though like a sword-hilt they could be given an artistic shape and finish. The number surviving in Britain is an indication of how brisk a demand there was for them; many must have been bought as 'status symbols' by men who privately hoped they would never have to use them.[31] It would be a distinction to possess a well-cased pair of them, and in a family of rank they might be handed down from father to son, embellished with stories of the good work they had done.

There were blockages against further technical improvement. An ancestral weapon was likely to fall behind the times. By and large, duels were less often inspired as time went on by a desire to kill or maim an opponent; this was only incidental to the aim of securing 'satisfaction'. When rifling of the barrel was transforming the smooth-bore musket, the same improvement for pistols designed for duelling was frowned on, especially in Britain, although disapproval might be circumvented by the barrel being rifled along the part further from the muzzle and out of sight. Also regarded as unsporting was the hair-trigger, which permitted a steadier if slightly slower fire. When Lord Cardigan wounded Captain Tuckett in 1840 it was felt by some to be discreditable that his weapons had rifled barrels and hair-triggers, while Tuckett's were ordinary duelling pistols.[32] Neither sort may have been excessively dangerous. An authority calculated that in two hundred British duels only one life was lost in every fourteen cases, one man wounded in

[29] Bennetton, 126–7.
[30] Steinmetz, ii. 19–20.
[31] Wilkinson, 53.
[32] Woodham-Smith, 83–4.

every six.[33] Very many duels which left no business for the coroner must have gone unregistered.

In some ways the pistol, compared with the sword, was an equalizer: in Smollett's eyes a saving grace.[34] In times when growing numbers aspired to the privilege, anyone who could press a trigger could be a duellist, and many took the field without ever having handled a weapon before. The shorter the range, the better chance the amateur had of hitting his mark. For those determined not to miss there was the form of duel *au mouchoir*, with the antagonists close enough for each to hold a corner of a handkerchief; equivalent to a suicide pact, it can never have been popular. Skill no doubt varied, but much less than in fencing, if only because pistols, down to about 1800, were too little dependable. We hear of habitual duellists who practised at targets and learned to allow for a weapon's *dispart*, or 'throw'. 'Always level low', was an expert's advice, 'and fire the instant the word is given'.[35] But whereas fencing could be a pastime, pistol-shooting was something it may have been thought unbecoming to practise too much. Army men would have some advantage over civilians, and duels between officers might be expected to result in more fatalities, but it does not seem that their marksmanship was at all remarkable. Not all duels, at any rate, had so dramatic a finish as the one suggested by the old catch-phrase— remembered for example at the 'Dove' tavern at Hammersmith, backing on a narrow lane reputed to have been a duelling resort— 'Pistols for two and champagne for one'.

A bullet's direction being less predictable than that of a sword-thrust, possibly some of the more religiously minded, or fatalistic, found it easier to see the hand of Providence, or fate, on a trigger than on a sword-hilt. But if the pistol was a leveller, it was so most of all perhaps between generations. Duelling started as, most often, an indulgence of fiery youth; but as social conventions hardened, older men were drawn in too. For them the pistol was clearly more suitable; they could form a dignified part of the tableau, whereas an elderly gentleman sparring away with a rapier would be an unedifying spectacle. Duelling spread downward from the aristocracy; it spread upward from young to old, sober Age learning from rash Youth instead of the other way about.

In the Middle Ages the judicial duel was impressively organized by authority; the early modern duel was anarchical; in the classical era strict formality returned, with the combatants themselves, through their seconds, responsible for it. The turn from steel to powder was one factor favouring this evolution. Unlike modern Americans, gentlemen

[33] Wilkinson, 45–6; Steinmetz, i. 89–90.
[34] Smollett, *Travels*, 140.
[35] Grant, *Romance*, chap. 34.

were not likely to have pistols in their pockets all the time, as they formerly had swords at their sides. This by itself made a pause necessary. With firearms, moreover, duels had to be kept semi-secret, and therefore more carefully managed; they could not be carried on in the street, like a sword-fight, because of the noise and the risk to passers-by. Above all, pistols favoured the ritualizing of the duel into a calm, passion-free encounter, especially as it became more customary for the combatants to stand still instead of moving back to or forward from their marks. This may be truest of England, and the *milords* whose *sang-froid* made such an impression on excitable foreigners.

With society changing in so many ways so rapidly, it could not always be clear to a gentleman, not fond of fighting for its own sake, what he ought to do when drawn into a quarrel. He might have no experienced second to turn to. A compendium of rules would be helpful, and a number were composed at various times. As in most spheres having to do with the use of arms, regulation owed most, after the early Italian primacy, to France; from the seventeenth century procedure was frequently discussed in French writings. At the same time a good part of the vocabulary of war and diplomacy was coming to be French; a remoter parallel may be detected in the French passion for imposing fixed rules on the drama, with which also the duel had so much in common.

Once again Ireland made itself heard. Sundry foreign regulations were consulted when in 1777 an Irish code was drafted which came to be known as the 'Twenty-six commandments'. It was the work of men who happened to be gathered at Clonmel for the summer assizes, a revealing sidelight on Anglo-Irish attitudes to the law of the land and the private law of the ruling class. For some offences an exchange of two or more shots was held to be the minimum purgation. Cheating at cards was one of the crimes equivalent to a blow. An enlightened provision was that challenges should not be delivered at night, 'for it is desirable to avoid all hot-headed proceedings'. Irish heads were usually too well heated at night with claret.

Some resemblances may be noticed between this sort of legislation and the drawing up of rules to govern sports like cricket or football, and—half-way between play and fight—boxing or wrestling. It was here that England, a country where law was in most though not all ways held in respect, could make its mark. Looking at Europe as a whole, the codification of duelling forms a parallel with the development of laws or conventions governing international relations. A duel was a miniature war, a trial of courage and training concentrated into a few intense minutes in the lives of two individuals—sometimes their last minutes. The two things were evolving side by side, with men from the same classes taking the lead in both; duelling etiquette and the polite usages of modern war have alike marked the officer class of Europe as a freemasonry, with claims rising above the merely national. Brantôme recommended magnanimity towards the private enemy; Velásquez's painting of the surrender of Breda, with its courtly gestures, shows the same spirit in the realm of war. It came to be the right of an officer dying as a prisoner of war to be borne to the grave by four enemy officers of the same rank.

Monarchs embodied the cosmopolitanism of the upper classes. They might detest and attack one another, but they addressed one another as 'my brother'. In the days of chivalry a threat or declaration of war was delivered by a herald; a second conveying a challenge performed the same role, and in early modern times might, like a herald, receive a handsome gift. Seconds clearing up the grounds of a quarrel and seeking an accommodation were like lawyers, but still more like diplomats, who were coming from the sixteenth century to form a distinct profession, another exclusively European phenomenon. There were diplomats, just as there were seconds, who embittered disputes, from dislike of their *chers collègues* or other motives, instead of pouring oil on troubled waters. Rules for the field of honour would help to suggest thoughts of subjecting the battlefield likewise to regulation, and 'laws of war' were, if tardily and imperfectly, being recognized. In both cases a third party might come forward to mediate; and the concept of an international court of justice had an analogy with, and may even have owed a debt to, the courts of honour set up in several countries to prevent unnecessary duels.

Once resolved on, combats took place with only brief delay. Waiting for the ordeal would be painful to most duellists and their friends, while injured honour required prompt salving, just as physical injury called for prompt surgery. Any long interval would suggest to busybodies that one or both parties were hesitating. The customary hour of dawn, when few people would be about, helped to ensure the least publicity. Fairly secluded spots could be found in most cities, and became the favourite choice. At Paris the gardens of the Palais Royal were for long the usual resort. 'Duelling pistols or swords', it is said, 'were always in stock at the cafés' round about.[36] Later on it was found judicious to remove further afield, and the Bois de Boulogne naturally suggested itself; Dubliners, by the late eighteenth century, were meeting at a clump of thorn-trees in Phoenix Park.

Pistols made their decisions quickly; preliminaries took some time, the final point being for the seconds to decide how the signal was to be

---

[36] Bassermann, 195.

given: it might be by a word or words, or by the dropping of a handkerchief. In George III's England a coin was usually tossed to decide who should fire first, and this went on longer in France and elsewhere; but what came to be accepted was the obvious method of letting both men fire together, or just as they chose within a specified time-limit, which might be twenty seconds. One variant was for the combatants to stand back to back, walk away from each other, and at a signal turn round and fire. It can hardly have made for cool, steady aiming. Perhaps it was not intended to. Much importance was attached—only Sir Lucius O'Trigger dissenting—to a sideways stance, as offering the narrowest target.

One duty of seconds was to arrange for a surgeon to be on hand. They could hardly arrange for a clergyman, since all Churches condemned duelling so firmly; and it was a convention that medical men should not be actual onlookers, for fear of their being involved in any legal trouble that might follow. They seldom seem to have felt any repugnance. Army doctors would be course be expected to officiate in military duels, even though they were only grudgingly being admitted, during the nineteenth century, in the more high-toned British regiments at least, to the status of gentlemen. Mr Winkle's challenger in *Pickwick* was the regimental surgeon, Dr Slammer.

How far apart to stand was a point that could give rise to argument, especially it may be when one or both men were not burning for the fray. A Canadian affair, stemming from a gambling dispute, was talked out when an officer, accused of hanging back, proposed to fight at four paces; his challenger declined, but was ready for ten; the officer would not hear of more than five.[37] A customary distance was twelve paces. What this meant is not always clear, since a 'pace' might be either the thirty inches of a single step, or the sixty of a movement of both feet. Bosquett is explicit, however, that it meant sixty inches,[38] so that twelve paces would be twenty yards, nearly the length of a cricket pitch. Marksmen being often inexperienced or their nerves shaky, and pistols unreliable, the chances of a miss were not bad. This could be the less regretted when emphasis was shifting away from revenge on an enemy to 'satisfaction' of an impersonal concept of honour. There had undeniably to be a sufficient element of risk to keep duelling from becoming a joke. 'Deloping', or firing in the air, might be generous, but might be taken as an admission of being in the wrong; if both men deliberately fired wide, things became farcical. How long a fight should continue was at the seconds' discretion. They might be averse to letting it go on after the first shot, unless both principals were clamorous for another.

[37] Riddell, *Richardson*, 123–4.
[38] Bosquett, Notes, i.

Two shots were customary, but a second might 'take his man off the ground'—the phrase favoured on these occasions—rather than consent to more than two. Where swords remained in use, hostilities usually ended, in the later days, as soon as blood was drawn. Since through most of the duelling era the stock medical remedy for nearly all ailments was bleeding, the loss of a small quantity of blood would not be too disturbing.

Still, it must always have needed good nerves, or self-command, to preserve a cool demeanour before the fray, especially at the chilling hour of dawn. A cigar was often resorted to. Sword-play would soon set the blood tingling; with pistols, men had the nervous strain of standing apart, each alone. It was an essential of the performance that the combatant had not merely to risk his life, but to do so with composure, an air of being as indifferent to danger as an officer in battle. Such imperturbability was part of the carriage of the superior class, which in Europe's empires became that of the superior race; the 'lower orders', or native peoples, both had to be impressed. It has been characteristic of aristocracies at all times, but especially in times when their pretensions have come under scrutiny, and they have not been free to behave unselfconsciously. To seem only casually concerned by anything that happens, to float far above the agitations of ordinary mortals, unruffled even in the tumbril, is a way of asserting a superior quality. It is the imperturbability of a class wishing, like the Serene Highnesses of old Germany, to be thought beyond the reach of accident or surprise. Scott was nettled by fashionable readers who considered it beneath them to feel admiration for anything; he called their pose, borrowing a Latinism from Shenstone, *flocci-pauci-nihili-pili-fication*— or, as we might say, 'don't-care-a-rap-or-a-damn-or-a-farthing-ism'. Dickens's young gentleman in *Hard Times* thought 'indifference' the hallmark of good breeding.

A duellist's air of cool indifference to life or death was a fine exhibition of this demeanour. The pose could outlive the duel, and survived into the twentieth century, though it may have to be looked for in popular fiction more than in life. Bulldog Drummond's highly class-conscious young friends in the 1920s, busy lynching trade unionists and other subversives, made complete suppression of any outward emotion their fetish.[39] One of the clichés running through Frank Richards' engaging tales of public school life, the pabulum of two generations of juveniles, turns on 'the calm repose that stamps the caste of Vere de Vere'. A less than usually unsuccessful Tory premier of recent decades lived on a reputation for being 'unflappable'.

[39] 'Sapper' (H. C. McNeile), *Bulldog Drummond* and its sequels.

In Lover's best-known Irish novel a duellist positively bent on killing his man, or inflicting a serious wound, is held up to censure.[40] In France on the other hand, down to the later eighteenth century, an older, more vicious spirit persisted, and a man might wait for a wounded opponent to recover and then call him out again. A serious offence must be punished by death, or the avenger perish in the attempt, and Smollett heard of two officers fighting five times over, until one was killed.[41] Joseph Conrad may have overlooked this tradition when he wrote his long story, sprouting from a germ of fact, about an officer of Napoleon who, spurred on by an unquenchable hatred, keeps forcing a challenge on an enemy, at every interval in the wars, and after their end, when they have both risen to be generals. In Britain anger could be consigned to oblivion after a single meeting; everywhere, later on, a determination to keep a feud alive came to be viewed as reprehensible. A man who had given satisfaction ought not to be made to answer for his fault again, just as he could not be put on trial again on the same charge.

Rather, it was proper for each man to do his quixotic best to shield the other from prosecution. They had after all joined in a conspiracy to flout the law. Public-school honour, in the same spirit, forbade any tale-telling, however much at daggers drawn two boys might be. The northern Ireland case of 1808, in which Captain Boyd's dying words helped to bring Major Campbell to the gallows, has been cited as one of the very few of 'a British combatant failing to try his utmost to screen and exonerate his opponent'.[42] Boyd's bitterness was understandable, but it contrasts sharply with the conduct of Lord Camelford four years earlier. This grand-nephew of Chatham was an intelligent student of mathematics, chemistry, and—more surprisingly—theology, who somehow frittered away his gifts; he went into the navy, where he must have found himself in uncongenial company, and made his mark chiefly by ill temper and quarrelsomeness. He quarrelled for the last time, with a Mr Best, at the age of 29; but two days before being mortally wounded in the fields behind Holland House, he added a codicil to his will declaring himself 'fully and entirely the Aggressor as well in the spirit as in the letter of the Word', and solemnly forbade friends or relatives, in case of his death, to institute proceedings; if Best was arraigned, the statement was to be laid before the king, to induce him to grant a pardon. Best, 'noted as a deadly shot', had in fact done all he could to avoid a clash, and an indictment against him was thrown out by a grand jury.[43]

[40] *Handy Andy*, chap. 19.
[41] Smollett, *Travels*, 135–6.
[42] Steinmetz, ii. 208 ff.
[43] Lady D. Nevill, 160–3.

In a community of self-isolating individuals—as the rich, far more than the poor, have always been—two men coming together to fight, under agreed protocols sanctioned by their peers, might be brought closer to each other than they would ever have been in ordinary life. The most idealistic purpose a duel could serve was to enable a man conscious of having erred to expose himself to chastisement by standing fire. Turgenev expressed willingness to act in this spirit when he received a challenge from Tolstoy and reproached himself for some hasty words that had led to it.[44] Even if a man had no such feeling beforehand, combat and shared risk might produce a kind of catharsis of morbid jealousies or enmities which would otherwise have gone on growing more inflamed. Wartime enemies have sometimes experienced a similar alteration. An account of his duel written in 1613 by Sir Edward Sackville praised the dying Bruce for not letting his surgeon attack him, when he was wounded and helpless.[45] Laertes at the point of death begs Hamlet to 'exchange forgiveness'; Valmont in Laclos's novel with his last breath exculpates his weeping enemy and takes leave of him as a friend;[46] Captain M'Intyre in Scott's novel asks pardon, when he lies bleeding on the ground, for having dragged his unwilling opponent into the fight. Wilkes after being wounded by Martin admitted that he had behaved honourably. Once he had stood fire a man could feel free to express regret he could not have acknowledged before, under threat of a challenge. Having stood two shots and been slightly wounded by the first, Fox assured Adam that he had meant no offence by his words in the House.

After his duel with O'Connell at Dublin in 1815, D'Esterre, who had provoked it, lingered for two days, 'and with his last breath confessed that O'Connell was blameless'; his second, Sir Edward Stanley, gave an assurance that the family had no desire to press for a prosecution.[47] It is observable that the legal outcome might depend in some measure on private initiative, or silence; and all duellists were members of one great family, whose standing would suffer if the uninitiated were brought into its affairs. A dying man was making his peace with heaven, but he was also paying his last respects to the class he was proud to belong to, and the code of honour that was the breath of its nostrils.

In the Irish mummers' plays the dramatic core consisted of two champions boasting and coming to blows, one being killed, and finally a doctor being summoned to bring him back to life. Irish divisions could be healed in folk-fantasy, if in no more humdrum fashion. A more

---

[44] Maude, i. 230.
[45] Carlyle, *Historical Sketches*, 102.
[46] Laclos, Letter 174.
[47] O'Connell, i. 32–3.

workaday Irish peacemaking is described in a letter from O'Connell to his son about a row at Ennis and one man knocking another down. 'They then fought, fired a shot each, came home safe and arm-in-arm together, got tipsy in company with each other, went together to the ball and danced till morning.'[48] Bacchus was responsible for many ruffled feathers, but he could help to smooth some down.

[48] Ibid. i. 47–8.

9

The Psychology of Honour

'Méfiez-vous de ces préjugés nouveaux et des prétentions de messieurs les parvenus! Ils auront beau dire et beau faire, un homme de rien ne sera jamais vraiment noble de cœur ... Vous ne le verrez jamais sacrifier sa fortune et sa vie pour une idée, pour sa religion, pour son prince, pour son nom.'

George Sand, *Le Marquis de Villemer* (1861), chap. xi.

ANY social structure is in perennial danger of losing its firm shape, sagging at the joints. An aristocracy in particular requires many artificial props and braces. Formal manners have been more and more important as a supplement to fine dress, even displacing it as the chief blazon. In a class still sturdily growing, as aristocracy was in some areas in modern times, notably in England, its members go through the daily movements it imposes on them with little consciousness of constraint; when it is growing arthritic, its patterns of behaviour losing meaning, the individual (if of some intelligence) is more and more aware of being compelled to go through actions, make set speeches, perform gestures, mechanically. To lend conviction to such artificialities, something of a different kind is called for. In Europe an obsolescent and for most purposes useless class had to exert itself to move, or at least appear to be moving, with the times; but it also had to reinvigorate itself by looking back into its feudal past.

This was more than half imaginary. On the one hand medieval Europe was little known or understood by its descendants until quite recently; on the other hand, very few aristocrats of modern times were really descended from the medieval chivalry whose heirs they purported to be. In many ways they were pretenders strutting in borrowed plumage to hypnotize themselves and overawe others. Duelling was a way to make the charade more convincing to both; it brought a note of stern reality into make-believe. It is only comprehensible in terms of Europe's social and political complexities; in its fully ritualized form the duel was one of the most fantastical things in human annals.

William James pointed out that aristocracies have cherished, sentimentally at least, a notion of personal qualities like courage, generosity, sense of duty, as their hallmark, antithetical to soulless pursuit of wealth; and that this thinking has survived in the ideal image of the soldier.[1] The duel harmonized with it, by stripping the individual of any adventitious assets and leaving him to confront his destiny supported by nothing but his pride in membership of a chosen section of mankind, and fidelity to the duty this laid on him.

Few ever actually fought, but each encounter did something to buttress the whole class, until public opinion outside it grew robust enough to brand duelling as either wicked or ridiculous. This came about with surprising slowness. Aristocracy was persisting by virtue of qualities that won admiration, however reluctant; like monarchy, it grew more and more into an actor, playing an elaborate part. Its mannered style of living, not without elements of permanent human value, could dazzle the aspiring bourgeois, as could its bravery in war. Duelling was a feature of the 'noble' life that could enhance these attractions.

One point was its being normally illegal, especially for civilians. The duellist put himself above the law, and demonstrated that his self-respect, or, what came to the same thing, his respect for his class, mattered more to him than any external fiat. He spoke of 'being out', when he went to fight; a Jacobite rebel would boast of having 'been out in the '45': each was self-outlawed. In what he deemed questions of honour the gentleman stood outside any social contract binding on the common man; he belonged to a superior social order which made its own rules. Absolute monarchs compelled their nobles in early modern Europe to submit to many restraints, but noblemen obstinately insisted on keeping one area of freedom, symbolically vital to them if practically meaningless.

A class detached from its original setting is likely to adopt customs that represent once serious occupations in a vestigial or emblematic form. Feudal nobility was devoted to the business of war. When most of its descendants retired from this, for a long time they liked to have their portraits painted in outdated armour, often incongruously combined with lace sleeves and wigs. An artist of the late seventeenth century kept a suit of it in his studio, ready for any client.[2] Nearer our own day, when British cavalry regiments were turned into tank units, officers had to be authorized to go on wearing spurs. In the Second World War they were fond of calling assault groups of tanks 'sabre squadrons', crews 'mounted' their machine, and if it was knocked out the commander might report himself 'unhorsed'.[3] Apart from such outward marks of identity, men of blue blood had to find activities that

---

[1] Williams James, 313.

[2] S. Stevenson and D. Thomson, *John Michael Wright, the King's Painter* (Edinburgh, 1982), 42, 70-1, 94-5.

[3] D. Orgill, *The Gothic Line* (1967; London, 1969), 98-9.

could seem to show them still invested with the old sovereign virtue, willingness to risk life or limb in the pursuit of their vocation. Duelling met this need most literally. Next to it might be placed hunting, in its 'nobler' forms which always contained a spice of danger. 'They were selfish, drunken, socially useless if you like', a recent commentator writes of Britain's fox-hunters, but they had the saving grace of being always ready to risk their necks.[4] If the chief ordinary occupation of members of the duelling class was killing animals, it might be felt as no great departure if they occasionally tried to kill each other, by way of a change.

Another opportunity for neck-risking was the steeplechase, or cross-country horse-race. Heavy wagers often depended on the result, a further hazard shared with other kinds of racing. Gambling was one refuge from the ever-looming cloud of boredom. Man is endowed, through freaks of mutation, with a miraculous brain which he does not need and seldom knows what to do with, and he may be led by its Mephisto-counsels into all kinds of erratic behaviour. How little the refinement of manners was accompanied by growth of intelligent interests, to provide occupation for it, can be seen in the alcoholism of upper-class society, the chronic relapse from polished gentility to the boorish level of Squire Western.

A country gentleman ruining himself on the turf, as in Thomas Warton's 'Newmarket' poem,[5] was a familiar topic of English satire. Gambling fever, on green turf or green baize, must have hastened the turnover of county families. A man had to be able to hazard his fortune on a turn of the cards as coolly as his forefathers risked their lives on the luck of battle. Card-tables at Versailles, where millions of *livres* were yearly staked, offered a new tournament ground for blood to show its quality. There were a good many gamesters, of course, with purses not as long as their pedigrees, who looked to the cards for an income, as jousters used to count on the spoils of victory in the lists. But to a gentleman money (which he did nothing to earn) was, in principle, merely filthy lucre; and a loser's unwillingness to pay his 'debt of honour' was a grave sin, not only because a gentleman's word ought to be his bond, but because it signified ignoble reluctance to part with money. To cheat at cards was even worse, and meant immediate ostracism.

Closely related to both gambling and duelling was the willingness in eighteenth-century England of county families, which in the Wars of the Roses or the Great Rebellion battled it out at the head of their followers, to risk bankruptcy in order to defeat each other, by litigation

4 J. Moore, Introd. to 'Nimrod', 10.
5 Thomas Warton, 'Newmarket, a Satire'.

or, still more, expensive bribery in parliamentary elections. There could be solid profit in being a county member, in days when gentlemen had no objection to bribes with decent pseudonyms, but the prime reward was status, together with the excitement of the contest. Even drinking could be another competition; at the end of a day competing in the chase, men spent the night trying to drink one another under the table. A gentleman could no more flinch from the bottle than from the bullet.

Behind all the doings of the higher class lay the code of honour which supported its confidence in itself and in its capacity to rule. A sense of 'honour' could be thought of as an innate virtue, or as conformity with stereotyped rules of conduct. The two notions were seldom congruent, as ideally they were supposed to be. The second was simpler, and in practice an individual's honour, like that of a nation, had little to do with any ethical convictions; its meaning was much closer to 'prestige', so incessantly invoked by modern governments as a mainspring of action. A duellist, like a government, had to impress his underlings, as well as his peers. The nicely defined points he was concerned with belonged to a more and more dessicated social morality. Heroic ages and virtues pass away, wrote Carlyle—'A spontaneous habitual all-pervading spirit of Chivalrous Valour shrinks together, and perks itself up into shrivelled Points of Honour.'[6]

From one side of its ancestry, in the half-mythological world of chivalry, duelling inherited the task, social as well as personal, of punishing wrong-doing. In the old Germanic poems, as in many early societies, private revenge was felt to be at the same time a duty to the community. So Othello felt it: 'she must die, else she'll betray more men'. When more than punctilio was in question, a duellist might be commended for taking a stand against misconduct discreditable to his class. But the gentleman's morality was always equivocal. It was dishonourable for him to let his wife or daughter be seduced, but far less so, if at all, for him to seduce someone else's. Nobody thought much the worse of a man for debauching his neighbour's daughter, Dr Johnson believed. Still less did it occur to anyone that a gentleman ought to be called out for ruining a servant-girl or abandoning her children. All morality grows warped, the more it is compressed into the limits of one class and its self-love. It was not easy therefore to mount a high moral horse, and the purpose of fighting was much less to penalize a wrongdoer than to demonstrate readiness to resent an injury or insult. The irrationality that was part and parcel of the classical duel was an admission that justice was unattainable in this imperfect world: what could be had, at a high price, was the respect of society.

⁶ 'Characteristics' (1831), in *Scottish Miscellany*, 192.

This was only too easily forfeited. Satire found one of its favourite butts in the man who pretended to a daring he did not possess. Far-quhar's highwayman in *The Beaux' Stratagem*, after robbing a coach, displays with the rest of his booty two silver-hilted swords: 'I took those from fellows that never show any part of their swords but the hilts' (Act II, sc. ii). Every such witticism was a reminder of what was expected of the gentleman, and of how joyfully tongues would wag at his expense if he were found wanting. A story told of the philosophic La Fontaine bears witness to the pressure of opinion. Much against his will he felt obliged to undertake a fight with a friend, an officer rumoured to be too attentive to his wife. Never having held a sword in his hand before, he was disarmed after a slight skirmish, and the pair went amicably home. The duel meant in fact an extreme form of social compulsion exerted on the individual; that the groups accepting it should be willing to submit voluntarily to the discipline, when they had so long and fiercely refused to be dragooned by their governments, helps to explain their tenacity of collective life. Noble rank in its formative years every-where rendered a man liable to military service, as it did in Russia well into the eighteenth century, and a degree of moral obligation to serve might linger on. In other ways too members of the upper class were habituated to compliance with social demands, because they were so closely constrained by family authority, patrimonial property, the duty of making suitable marriages.

In all élite classes the individual as such has only a limited right to exist. He finds whatever side-roads to freedom are left open to him, like the old-time German student's charter to drink too much beer and fall asleep in the gutter. Amorous adventure was another of the licensed outlets that enabled a gentleman, especially in youth, to feel as free as a bird, even if they were no better than substitutes for a moral freedom he was deprived of by his social position. For women there were fewer relaxations, though they were allowed in some countries to join in sports like hunting, and to go to balls and dance with different men. A standard of 'honour' of their own was set for them; its essential canon was to preserve a 'reputation', to be believed in other words to be chaste, or faithful to a husband. His duty was to perform certain actions, a woman's was to abstain from certain others, and her reputation like her youthful bloom could be protected by skilled devices. A forcible trespass on her virtue was 'a fate worse than death', to which a truly self-respecting woman would prefer suicide, just as a man was expected to prefer death on the duelling-ground to loss of honour.

To decline a challenge, for whatever reason, was to face 'the dreaded stigma of the censorious world'.[7] This was morally much the same as

---

[7] Bosquett, 23.

the medieval ceremony of the degrading of a recreant knight. A gentleman of Bordeaux, on the eve of the French Revolution, who refused a
challenge on account of religious scruples, was so cruelly taunted and
baited that at last in desperation he turned on one of his tormentors,
and was killed.[8] It is impossible to know how many others rejected a
challenge on conscientious grounds, or from timidity, or out of sheer
common sense, and subjected themselves to derision. Many who did
not must have regretted it later, if they lived to do so. What Morley
wrote of religious conformism, and fear of the world's frown, would
have suited their case well. 'Consider the triviality of life and conversation and purpose, in the bulk of those whose approval is held out
for our prize ... the empire over them of prejudice unadulterated
by rationality ... unrelieved by a single leavening particle of fresh
thought.'[9]

'The Russian's personal freedom is much greater than the Englishman's', Somerset Maugham felt, visiting tsarist Russia early in
this century.[10] Others too felt that while there was no political liberty in Russia, there was much more absence of social restraints, for
young women as well as men. It may be that every society works out
a sort of balance, and that freedom, like water, finds its own level;
that only people like Victorian Englishmen, priding themselves on
political and national independence, could want to load themselves
with rigid conventions, Sabbatarian gloom, marital fetters, top
hats, as though in dread of too much enfranchisement. All men's self-
respect in any case depends a great deal on what others think of
them, or they suppose others to think. Individuals of an upper class ruling more or less directly, not through a powerful bureaucracy as in
tsarist Russia, may fancy themselves more individualistic than others,
but in many ways are more closely hemmed in by convention, because
of their need to stand before the multitude in impressive postures.
Very likely each one of them at some moment sees through the commandments of his order, and would like to break away; but he is seldom able to summon up enough resolution. The more unnatural
the rules he is subjected to, the more severe must be the penalties for
defiance.

For men with no better lights of their own, the Giant Custom
had the value of marking out a boundary-line, a limit beyond which
withdrawal with self-respect was impossible. An individual lacking any
perceptible claim on his own account can find a niche in the common
consciousness of his class (as, in other contexts, of his nation, or race).

[8] Steinmetz, i. 292.
[9] John Morley, *On Compromise* (1874; Thinker's Library, London, 1933), 119.
[10] *A Writer's Notebook* (Harmondsworth, 1949).

Banishment from this is a sort of extinction, leaving his mirror to show him only his friendless, mediocre self. Likewise, for a gentleman in danger of sinking into social disgrace, his readiness to fight, or being believed to be ready, and encouraging others to do so, could be the last refuge of a scoundrel. Of this species the two seconds in the fatal duel in *Nicholas Nickleby* were exemplars. 'Both utterly heartless, both men upon the town, both thoroughly initiated in its worst vices ... they were, naturally, gentlemen of unblemished honour themselves, and of great nicety concerning the honour of other people.'[11]

As at earlier stages of European history, there was downward as well as upward mobility at every social level. Poverty rather than scoundrelism was the commonest cause of claimants to gentility having to fear decline into the plebeian mass. In Poland the lower gentry were sinking, by the eighteenth century, into dependence on the magnates, or coming to be no better off than peasants, ploughing the few fields left to them with a rusty sword in their belt to show that their blood was still blue. Everywhere inequalities within the noblesse, always prominent, were widening with the unequal distribution of incomes; and the humbler categories were swollen by a multitude of portionless younger sons, and bastards more or less acknowledged by their families.

Proust's Duc de Guermantes could look down, privately, on the common run of his class, unworthy of his exalted notice. But the feudal relationship of lord and vassal had long since melted into a sort of *corpus mysticum* within which assertion of equal rights, on a certain level, could not be repudiated even by the highest. The duel was its most forcible expression. It continued to be the great leveller of noble ranks. *Cursory reflections on the single combat or modern duel*, an English publication of 1774, was addressed to 'gentlemen in every class of life'. All of them had access to the 'satisfaction' it afforded; and while they were sheltered from having to measure swords with social inferiors, at the risk of coming off worst, it must have been one of its charms for the small fry that no difference of title or fortune debarred them from firing a pistol at a peer—slight as their chances might be of getting close enough to a peer to pick a quarrel with him. As in the earlier, formative days of the duel, this continued to represent a source of strength to the aristocratic principle, by investing a fragmented upper class with a unique kind of solidarity. If they were to have any corporate survival in a Europe moving faster and faster into modernity, those at the top needed more than ever a loyal following. 'Matiness' could outlast the duel that helped to nurse it. At table in a Cambridge college some years ago a duke prefaced a remark to a mathematician with the words, inclusive

[11] Chap. 50.

of the two of them: 'In *our* class ...' His surprised hearer could detect no hint of insolence[12].

At each level it was proper for those above to keep the respect and attachment of those below them; and for some of them to display on occasion a willingness to meet gentlemen of more modest station on the field of honour, as well as, more habitually, in the rivalry of the hunting-field, was a useful condescension. Those of the highest grade were not infrequently 'out'; French dukes and marquises, English coronets, were well represented, and even members of royal families might take the field, a Comte d'Artois, a Duke of York, or two together, a Duc de Montpensier against a Duque de Sevilla. In this sphere as in others the maxim of *noblesse oblige* held sway, and the leaders of society had to prove themselves no whit behind the rest when honour called.

If the man with right on his side (supposing there were any right or wrong in the matter) was killed or wounded he had made a sacrifice for virtue; if it was the offender who suffered, he could be said to have expiated his fault. But both ran the same risk; the duel cannot be made to look rational in terms of the individual, but only as an institution from which a *class*, a social order, benefited. It was this class that vindicated its collective honour by summoning both parties to undergo the ordeal prescribed by it, and thus purged itself of a stain. In the microcosm of army life this spirit displayed itself very explicitly: two officers who quarrelled had to fight, whether they wanted to or not, because otherwise the regiment was dishonoured. The antagonists were partners in a joint duty of defending the treasured values of their kind in a philistine world. The duel set the gentry class above all others, as possessing a courage and resolution no other could emulate, and a code of conduct none but it could live up to.

Thus viewed, duellists belonged to a nameless order of chivalry, owing fealty to ideals incomprehensible to an encroaching world of egotism and materialism. In their ceremonial sacrifice to these ideals they went beyond both private retaliation and public principle. Winning or losing, and however deep their animosity, the two opponents, and their seconds, could still feel that they breathed the same air and shared the same creed. In a Restoration tragicomedy Lord Beaufort and his second Sir Frederick arrive for a fight with a hated rival in love, to find him and his second being assailed by bandits. Beaufort at once calls on his friend to help him rout these caitiffs and rescue their opponents:

> Their blood's too good to grace such Villains Swords.

[12] I had this anecdote from the don thus honoured, the eminent mathematician Professor Hardy, of Trinity College.

As soon as the riff-raff have beeen dealt with, the duel goes forward as designed.[13]

In higher poetical language the loser in a duel might be called 'a Roman by a Roman valiantly vanquished'; and as at the close of a Shakespearian tragedy, a man might have perished, but his world went on, hallowed and strengthened. Conversely, any failure of nerve on the part of a member of the élite reflected on the whole body, and if often repeated would undermine it. There can be detected here the instinct of a garrison, such as any dominant class in a sense is, encamped in the midst of a population always passively or actively hostile; a lurking premonition of a day of wrath when the masses will rise up against it and it will have to fight for survival like the gods of Valhalla. Obliquely the duel was a warning to Demos that the same weapons were ready to be turned against *him*. War has been a magnification of the same threat. Logically enough, the penalty for rejecting a challenge was far more severe than any condemnation by the élite of its members' lapses from the morality of parsons. Security for any dominant class, as for a ruling race like the British in India, depends a great deal on its psychological ascendancy, its unblurred image.

The duelling classes might have strong inner bonds, but when their members fought it was among themselves; the ultimate hallmark of gentility was the right of gentlemen to kill each other. Within any class or community impulses of tension and antipathy as well as of fraternity are interwoven with its psychological fabric. Duelling was part of this complex of feeling; it brought to light 'intraspecific' enmities, as feudal strife, the Wars of the Roses for example, did more noisily. A class with overweening pretensions must impress both itself and others by its strict discipline over its members; the heavier the pressure for conformity, the stronger the reaction, normally suppressed though this is. The duel may be seen as a channel for working off lurking rebelliousness, by directing it against a substitute target, even if it was fought in the name of the class whose values both combatants subscribed to. Or we may think of the morbidities of a parasitic class working themselves off against individual scapegoats. The readiness of 'society' to hound and expel a dissident revealed both its spirit of uniformity and its inner discords. There was a feminine parallel in the alacrity with which ladies pulled to pieces on the slightest pretext the reputation of one of themselves.

'Moral' pressure on its members to risk their lives in combats, often against their grain, was the most insistent binding force of the duelling class; there is proof here of how ill-founded its claim to superiority was,

[13] Etherege, Act IV, sc. iv.

how abnormal its outlook. A class guilty of the sin of hubris, of elevating itself above common humanity, claimed an immunity from law that could be a menace only to its own members. There was something of masochism in this, traceable, it may be suspected, to an uneasy conscience which had to be appeased by a species of mortification. It could not admit to itself the real nature of the sinfulness that it vaguely confessed to on Sundays, the guilt of exploitation of Hodge the farm labourer, of slaves on West Indian plantations, of women abandoned to pauperism or prostitution. Consciousness of all this could only take disguised shapes. In the mature age of the duel religion was at a low ebb, but the duellist's morbid sensitivity to other people's opinions suggests a persistence of the neurotic self-consciousness and self-criticism that Reformation and Counter-reformation had bred. Boswell is an excellent specimen of this nagging unease. Formerly men like him had practised mortifications and austerities. In modern history, above all in 1914–18, the grand expiation was war; on the battlefield the sword-bearers were predestined to be the heaviest sufferers. The duel could have the same psychological function in little.

No doubt one thing that helped to keep it fresh was that some men, in braggart youth or when protected by grey hairs, were fond of recalling with additions the number of times they had been 'out', just as others might like to hint at the number of women they had made prize of. Duelling could serve for self-parade and boasting. But it may be seen as sometimes a medium for self-assertion of a more meaningful kind. In one light the duellist was a slave of convention and opinion, a prisoner of his caste. In another, he was a solitary being drawing on moral as well as physical courage by defying the law in the name of a principle of private right or duty. Like the blood feud, a duel might be intended to set right an injury to a family or other group, and bravery shown in it enhanced the group's reputation; but it concerned directly only two individuals. In Europe's evolving society, more and more geared to an economic individualism that affected even a class self-enclosed like the aristocracy in its traditional thinking, there was being generated the instinctive feeling, so potent in romantic literature, Elizabethan or Byronic, of the individual pitted against the world, man against society, the riddle of the isolated self.

If the old ruling class was subject to influences from the bourgeois competitive economy, there is a reciprocal influence to be recognized, thanks to which some qualities borrowed from the older class could inspire or invigorate the newer, or at least its chosen spirits. Among them were those that entered into duelling; the sentiment of personal honour, the willingness to defy law in defence of it, the proud indifference to consequences. In the constitutional history of Europe feudal 'liberties' paved the way for modern, more democratic rights; in its moral history aristocratic intransigence was also a precursor. If duelling was a disease, it was also a remarkable manifestation of the refusal to compromise. The Scotsman who wrote that paean to national independence, *An Account of Corsica*, was stuffed with feudal notions. His book opens with a panegyric on Liberty, and Boswell is soon proclaiming that 'Liberty is indeed the parent of felicity, of every noble virtue, and even of every art and science.'[14] Burke, the middle-class Irishman, preferred to ascribe these blessings to the State. Boswell's fellow-countryman Walter Scott thought of feudalism as pervaded by 'an ardent spirit of liberty', though he acknowledged that it left too many rights to be monopolized by the higher ranks.[15]

An English gentleman addressed his sovereign, and his son addressed *him*, as 'Sir'. He was himself in his small way a sovereign, with inviolable rights. A European bowed to his king, as he did to any other gentleman; an Asiatic prostrated himself on the ground before him, as he did to God. Desire for distinction is innate in mankind, wrote Montesquieu, but the pole it turns to varies from man to man and from nation to nation. A Frenchman will shake off his feet the dust of a court which flouts his self-respect, and in republics the sentiment is still keener; among Persians, on the other hand, it cannot arise, because their status is not their own but depends entirely on royal caprice.[16] In both East and West dominant classes had a continuous existence, but in Asia their membership changed far more rapidly, and its fortunes were not anchored so firmly to landed estates such as in Europe might belong to the same family for centuries. The European's self-respect was founded on the respect paid by law and custom to his property, and by extension to that of the trading classes. Morier's celebrated novel reminds us that a minister of the Shah might be summarily sentenced to the bastinado, with no better hope than of being able to bribe the executioner, between blows, not to be too zealous.[17] Such a man had far too little independent existence to think of acting, as the duellist did, in obedience to an invisible code instead of an all too visible master. It would be impossible for him to comprehend the ideal that Shakespeare summed up, at the end of the age of chivalry and on the threshold of the duelling age, in Hamlet's reflection that a man worth the name ought

> greatly to find quarrel in a straw,
> When Honour's at the stake.

[14] Boswell, *Corsica*, 4.
[15] *Anne of Geierstein*, chap. 27.
[16] Montesquieu, no. 90.
[17] James Morier, *Hajji Baba of Ispahan* (1824).

This unyielding temper could feed the self-admiration of a class, but it could soar higher. It had its roots in a physical courage which was for Shakespeare, if not the supreme virtue, the ark of the covenant of all virtues, and which a sympathetic philosopher might think of as the crude adolescence of moral courage. With the coming of the bourgeois era of utilitarianism, cash nexus, and scramble for money, there was value in anything that could remind men of higher motives, stemming from concern for the social whole. This was strongest in tribal times, when most elementary; after men divided themselves into classes it was truncated, but it could survive as respect for ideal principles transcending material self-interest, conceptions chiefly religious, sometimes absurd. The concept of honour lay open to all Falstaff's gibes, but it derived from a very old emotion of obligation to community or country, like that of Shakespeare's republican Romans.

In them we see it constricted into a narrower mould, the mind of a class, but still harbouring the spark of a universal principle. Duelling contracted it much further, yet here too an ideal element is recognizable. It is part of the history of the most noxious, at any rate least useful, section of modern European society, yet this section was capable through individuals here and there of precious contributions to the rest. It gave England its Hampdens, and Europe a galaxy of writers and thinkers, hard though it must be to trace the intricate nervous links between the élitist pride and self-reliance so evident in the duel, and the finer, more truly aristocratic things into which it was capable of being transmuted.

Confessedly designed to supply not justice but 'satisfaction', the duel was losing most of any moral flavour it could pretend to, but it was taking on a genuine touch of the tragic. In the dawn of religion sacrifice, animal or human, was at its centre. Blood had to be shed, if the gods were to be convinced that their worshippers were in earnest. In Carthage during national crises more children were offered up, and more of them were children of the nobility. Aztec warriors braved the perils of war, and killed their captives in ritual single fight, in order to sustain the order of Nature and assure the bounty of the harvests and the continuity of the human race;[18] also, implicitly, that of the social hierarchy, and it was to this, and its permanence, that the duellist more modestly dedicated his blood.

Men have written solemn pledges with blood for ink. Something of an ancient sense of the paramount significance of death, inflicted or undergone, seems to have lingered into the modern psyche. William James speaks of mankind's overriding reverence for 'heroism': whatever

[18] See I. Clendinnen, 'The Cost of Courage in Aztec Society', *Past and Present*, 107 (1985).

a human being's frailties, if he risks—still more, suffers—death for his chosen cause, 'the fact consecrates him forever'.[19] Hence much of the mystique of war, and the laurel-leaves of the warrior. Hence too the adoption of the duel as the acid test of a man's right to belong to the 'noble' class, a right which could not rest securely on birth and rank alone, still less on wealth. Death in itself is not tragic; the duellist's gamble with it has tragic undertones because it is imposed on him by the tyranny of social demands, but also is accepted by him as a necessity of his being.

At such moments the individual rises above himself, or rather feels as if 'rapt', or 'transported'; he has a sensation of the superhuman, as if he were part of a force far greater than himself, because the total involvement of his faculties and energies makes him a different being from the half-awake creature of every day. Captain Ahab at the end of *Moby Dick* is at his highest pitch of resolve, and the fever of action, but it is now above all that he feels himself most firmly held in the grip of destiny, as no more than an actor performing a part set down for him before the oceans rolled. Life and drama merge into one.

But in the greatest of all psychological dramas Hamlet's suffering comes from inability to incorporate himself with the destiny that seems to hurry him on. He has throughout the tormenting consciousness of one challenged by fate, as though to a duel, to prove his resolution by a desperate and dubiously righteous deed. Concentrated in his figure are the tensions that have run through human history between social loyalties that the individual prizes, and duties inseparable from them that he shrinks from but cannot shirk. Hamlet's soliloquies are laden with the fear of loss of self, of identity, of a place among men, through a hesitancy which cannot but seem to him, because it would seem to others, at bottom mere cowardice. It is very appropriate that his drama should end in a kind of duel, muddied by the plottings of a murderous uncle.

[19] William James, 353.

10

Honour and Enlightenment

Express malice ... takes in the case of deliberate duelling, where both parties meet avowedly with an intent to murder: thinking it their duty as gentlemen, and claiming it as their right ... and therefore the law has justly fixed the crime and punishment of murder on them, and on their seconds also.

Blackstone, *Commentaries on the Laws of England* (1765-9), Bk. 4, chap. 14, sect. 3.

THE eighteenth century, when duelling came to maturity, was, more than most, an era of divided soul. On the one hand it was the time of full bloom for aristocracy, with the storm and stress of the previous centuries left behind. On the other hand it was the age of Enlightenment, in whose eyes everything medieval was 'Gothic', or uncivilized. With its descent from trial by combat and jousting, the duel came in for a good share of the opprobrium. Feudal lords of old were 'unlettered, and ignorant to a degree of stupidity; they were fierce, untractable, and cruel', said a British writer.[1] A Frenchman, while not gainsaying that the old nobility of his day was entitled to respect, thought it ridiculous for men to want to fight in order to uphold the renown of their mail-clad ancestors. Shedding one's blood does no good to one's forefathers, and in any case genealogies had been much tampered with.[2]

Pope may be suspected of having the duel in mind when he wrote in the *Dunciad* (Book 3) that 'fool with fool is barb'rous civil war'. Whatever virtues the duel might possess, as a mode of settling differences the Age of Reason could not but frown on it. Criticism of it had a part in the progressive current of thinking, the growth of the bourgeois, anti-feudal consciousness with its European citadel in the Encyclopaedia edited by D'Alembert and Diderot. It must, however, be remembered that the intellectuals of any class are always likely to be far in advance of its solid, stolid bulk, which lives less on ideas than on instincts, nose to the ground like a dog's, not pointed towards the horizon. A dominant class is the least capable of learning from experience and reflection, except in such fields as political manœuvre. As with an individual growing older, its life-lessons become more heterogeneous, ill-assorted,

[1] Bosquett, 44-5.
[2] Basnage, 8, 15.

but always with a thick sediment from the time of youth when impressions were vividest and thinking simplest. It seldom finds leisure or energy to sort out its notions and try to arrange them logically. Old convictions may come to seem less plausible, but it is another thing to shake them off.

There were, moreover, many cross-currents. In France part of the nobility was absorbing the spirit of the Enlightenment, part of the bourgeoisie was emulating aristocratic behaviour. Fights went on between nobles, between nobles and commoners, and between commoners.[3] Reason had even better cause to look askance at war than at duelling, but with little effect, partly because philosophers themselves were inconsistent. Voltaire could not withhold some admiration of military triumphs when he came to write of Louis XIV, that plague of Europe, or Catherine the Great, that plague of the Turks.

Against duelling, Enlightenment ideas were the less penetrative because they accompanied a further increase in élitism, or the drawing apart of the higher ranks from the commonalty and its habits of thinking and behaving. In some ways the change was for the better, as when the higher ranks ceased to encourage the lower to hunt for witches. But their self-segregation meant that their own standards of conduct remained in many ways fixed in old twisted patterns. It brought with it psychological strains also, to add to those that lack of occupation subjected the idle to. Western Europe in the eighteenth century seems to have been more than usually infected by the disease of melancholia. Himself a sufferer from it, and from the religious neurosis that often accompanied it, Boswell during his travels came on frequent cases. He cannot have been alone in finding it worsened by the collision between religious and social injunctions, whenever a duel loomed up. Emotional instability was one of the byways leading towards Romanticism and its glooms and hectic flushes.

A hint of the further withdrawal of the élite from the many-headed can be detected in Marvell's famous line on Charles I on the scaffold:

> He nothing common did or mean:

common was acquiring its uncomplimentary sense, of vulgarity. Rochefoucauld claimed Reason as an endowment of gentlemen, though they might give way privately to some *belles passions*; the masses were swayed by emotion alone. He had in mind not a faculty of abstract reasoning, but self-control, urbanity, recognition of the claims of equals; altogether, acceptance of society as it was, or could be made by further surface polishing. His class, it is true, was beginning to feel the breath of bourgeois common sense. This deepened in the eighteenth century, but

---

[3] Kelly, 244.

without modifying the élitist quality of the prevailing culture; the wealthier bourgeoisie too was firmly averse to anything 'low', and in most ways could harmonize far better with the aristocracy than with the people.

Current opinion on the duel fluctuated. It was often debated; those who troubled their heads about it were likelier to be critics than defenders, like the writer who gave his work in 1753 the neat title: *A home thrust at duelling*. There was always reprobation of the habitual quarreller, regularly associated with other bad qualities, like Thackeray's character, long abroad as a soldier of fortune, who had picked up habits of 'duelling, brawling, vice and play'.[4] Equally there was censure for the spineless bully like Diderot's Chevalier de Morlière with his long sword, ready with an insult for anybody not carrying one, but quite tame if you gave him a rap on the nose—yet from old habits of bravado quite unaware of his own cowardice.[5] The swashbuckling captain was a stock figure of the *Commedia dell'arte*. There could be respect for the man who took the field only on valid occasion; and a properly conducted duel was orderly and dignified, perpetuating a privilege of blue blood without harming anyone else. It might stir curiosity, even admiration, rather than dislike.

Contradictory views were reflected in legal attitudes. Thirty years after the stern French edict of 1723 not a single death sentence had been passed on a duellist.[6] Another thirty years on, a nobleman in Laclos's novel, who has killed his opponent, is sent an anonymous warning that the case has been discussed at the public prosecutor's office: 'although this sort of affair is normally looked upon with indulgence, there is always, none the less, a certain consideration due to the law'.[7] In Spain, now under a branch of the Bourbon dynasty, the old law against duelling was reinforced in 1716 and 1757, with a death penalty attached; the ban may have been more effective than in France. In Venice opinion, as reflected in Goldoni's plays, was critical; this provoked some counter-criticism, and in 1739 the Council of Ten had to repeat its prohibition. 'But on the whole the Venetians preferred to arrange their disputes, rather than to fight.'[8] Venice was sinking into its decline, and decadence could sometimes be on the same side as philosophy.

In England the jury system ought to have been another ally; but three distinct juries might have to consider a duelling case. Only when

<hr />

[4] *Henry Esmond*, Bk. 1, chap. 2.
[5] D. Diderot, *Le Neveu de Rameau* (1762–73); ed. A. Adam (Paris, 1967), 92–3.
[6] Kelly, 24.
[7] Laclos, Letter 167.
[8] Molmenti, 73.

it had a fatal ending was it likely to be considered at all, and then the first to be concerned was the coroner's jury, convened in haste from the neighbourhood. It appears that its members were 'usually of middling rank, mostly husbandmen and craftsmen'.[9] Such citizens might be less willing to give the killer the benefit of any doubt there might be (unless they happened to depend on him for their livelihood) than the members of the petty jury who would try him; while the grand jury which determined whether he ought to go on trial had the highest social standing. Service on it entitled a man to call himself thereafter 'Esquire', and in Ireland until 1898 the grand jury also had charge of local government. Apart from British reverence for the nobility and gentry, jurymen might themselves be entitled to the privilege of the duel, and might some day have to brave its legal hazards.

Some judges were not deaf to enlightened ideas, and might indeed be more open to them than a run-of-the-mill jury. This seems to have been so in an unusual case in 1780, where, however, the jurymen might well plead extenuating circumstances in their favour as well as the defendant's. A Captain Hanson forced a quarrel on a man named Donovan, out of anger at the latter interfering to prevent a fight between him and someone else. Hanson was killed, and Donovan put on trial; the judge admitted that he had shown merit, but emphasized that 'it was false honour in men to break the laws of God and their country', and that duelling implied 'a deliberate resolution to commit murder'. The verdict was only manslaughter, and a £10 fine ended the matter.[10]

Bentham's treatise on *Morals and Legislation*, in 1789, and his Utilitarian philosophy, mark the direction in which progressive thought was moving. He had a good deal to say about reputation, as 'a kind of fictitious object of property'. Social status affects temperament, he saw, and 'the quantum of sensibility appears to be greater in the higher ranks of men than in the lower'. Those who resented an affront by fighting, to avoid 'the shame of being thought to bear it patiently', would be credited by some with 'honour', by others with 'false honour'. Bentham himself was prepared to see 'a not unsalutory association of ideas' in the habit of deeming it cowardly to cling to life more than to reputation; and he recognized that sermons against the duel had little effect—'the influence of the religious sanction is known to be in general but weak', especially among the duelling classes.[11] Bentham of course

[9] M. MacDonald, 'The Secularization of Suicide in England 1660–1800', *Past and Present*, 111 (1986), 65.

[10] Steinmetz, ii. 27.

[11] Jeremy Bentham, *An Introduction to the Principles of Morals and Legislation* (1789), ed. J. H. Burns and H. L. A. Hart (London, 1970), 65, 106–7 n., 193.

could not do other than censure it as a preposterous substitute for justice, but he allowed that reputation was entitled to protection, and transgressors should be penalized, with the punishment fitting the crime.

How firm a hold the duel had taken on the European imagination may be gleaned from the metaphorical use of the word by writers of many sorts. In 1588 Leno Zanchi wrote a treatise in the form of a debate between a soldier and a divine on the 'duel', or controversy about the meaning of Matthew, chapter 5, on non-violence. In 1631 Donne preached a funeral sermon at St Paul's, before Charles I, on 'Death's Duel'. Milton eclipses all others in his use of the image, particularly with reference to the trial of strength between Christ and the Tempter—first towards the close of *Paradise Lost*, where Adam is warned not to expect it to be one of physical force, and then early in *Paradise Regained* when the angels sing a paean to

> the Son of God,
> Now entering his great duel, not of arms,
> But to vanquish by wisdom hellish wiles.[12]

In ludicrous contrast with this sublimity, a chapter of *Tom Jones* devoted to relations between Mr Partridge and his virago is entitled 'One of the most bloody battles, or rather duels, that were ever recorded in domestic history'.[13]

Human beings are in general remarkably obtuse about one another, and in need of go-betweens, terrestrial or celestial; and it is only in the thick of unwonted action, or the spectacle of it, that the process of life shakes them into awareness. Theatre and novel exercised a steadily growing influence on the feelings, and in a lesser measure on the behaviour, of the more literate and leisured. Young ladies like Sheridan's Lydia Languish may have been the most impressionable, but young men were not far behind. It was under a novelist's spell that the disappointed young lover in Aksakov's story threatened suicide.[14] Many must have owed their subjection to the code of honour to ideas culled from similar circulating-library sources. At any rate the duel was a theme dear to imaginative literature.[15] A society must be well stored with materials of conflict if it is to be able to cultivate literary forms like the drama or novel. It had the advantage of standing at a point of convergence between social classes and their ideas; it could be viewed from many angles, and range from the tragic to the risible.

Duelling could be introduced for its own sake, to furnish an exciting

---

[12] *Paradise Lost*, Bk. 12, ll. 386–7; *Paradise Regained*, Bk. 1, 173–5.
[13] Henry Fielding, *Tom Jones* (1749), Bk. 2, chap. 4.
[14] Sergei Aksakov, *A Russian Gentleman* (1846; World's Classics, Oxford, 1982), 90.
[15] See also on this subject Baldick, chap. 12, 'The Pen and the Sword'.

episode, though it might also be treated seriously and critically. Or it could serve playwrights simply as a convenient device, as in *The Beaux' Stratagem* where Archer accounts for his 'master' being down in the country by saying that 'he fought a duel t'other day in London, wounded his man so dangerously that he thinks fit to withdraw till he hears whether the gentleman's wounds be mortal or not'.[16] As entertainment the duel found an easy way into opera, a less realistic art than drama. A challenge has a place in the *Orontea*, by the Franciscan composer Cesti, produced at Venice in 1649. A Restoration version of *The Tempest* found room for a duel, besides bestowing a sister on Miranda. King Arthur in the play by Dryden with music by Purcell settles a dispute with a hostile ruler by defeating him in single combat. Visual art was not neglectful of the theme. A drawing attributed to Hogarth, for an illustration to a novel, shows a man in full dress under a tree, with sword upraised, while his opponent stands disarmed, weapon lying on the ground.[17] There was even a place for the duel in early essays at 'programme music'; an Italian suite of chamber music contained an *agitato* movement representing a fencing contest, followed by one where a surgeon was supposed to be treating the wounded.

In eighteenth-century France the mixed groups forming the upper bourgeoisie were approaching parity in resources with the nobility, itself heterogeneous and from early times diluted with bourgeois blood and money. In such an uneasy balance, literature could have an exceptional influence on opinion, and in France the duel, as a social problem, was taken seriously in the theatre. This had a central place in the nation's culture as a clearing-house of ideas; like Shakespeare's theatre it formed a bridge between court circles and public. Molière had set a firmly anti-duelling tone for others to follow. His middle-class background and professional life predominated over any infection that court employments might bring, especially as his patron Louis XIV was no friend to the duel. His Don Juan turns duelling into a farce by first evading a challenge from the brother of a girl he has seduced, who wants him to marry her, on the pretext of meaning to retire into religious life—then taking up the challenge with hypocritical protests that heaven does not wish him to fight—and finally failing to keep the rendezvous. Laclos's Chevalier Danceny, who has been deceived into a quarrel that proved fatal, ends by retiring abroad, with a real intention of taking vows.[18]

Only a rare voice was lifted in reasoned defence of the duel. An apologist argued that Nature wishes man to be strong, and ability to

[16] George Farquhar, *The Beaux' Stratagem* (1707), Act III, sc. iii.
[17] A. P. Oppé (ed.), *The Drawings of William Hogarth* (London, 1948), 32.
[18] Laclos, Letter 174.

brave death is a strengthening lesson to learn.[19] A historical study of duelling published in 1720 was far removed from this survival-of-the-fittest argument. Its author looked back at the barbarian invasions, the Lombard laws, the adoption of ordeal by battle: for him the duel was an offspring of the Dark Ages. He repudiated the cult of valour, that 'idol' of the duellist: 'it is a cruel delusion of the human mind to make merit consist in killing men'.[20] Genuine honour is the fulfilment of our social duties; it cannot be tarnished by any insult, as the 'Chevalier Duellistes' fancy. Yet even so decided a polemist could not keep clear of the inconsistency of maintaining that a worthy commoner has as much right to fight a duel as a nobleman: 'the point of honour must be equal'.[21] It was an anticipation in one way of the Equality demanded in 1789.

Montesquieu blamed a French national appetite for 'glory' for the vogue of 'a certain *je ne sais quoi* known as the point of honour', especially among military men, and commented that its exigencies were formerly so severe that to infringe the code in the smallest detail brought obloquy crueller than death. He was sardonic about how a second invited to join in felt complimented, and would risk his life for a fellow he would not have given four guineas to save from the gallows. Montesquieu goes on in a strain implying that at the time he was writing—1721—French law was often disregarded, but was by no means a dead letter. A Frenchman might find himself in a painful dilemma. 'If he obeys the laws of honour, he perishes on the scaffold; if those of justice, he is banished for ever from the society of men.'[22] Rousseau added his later voice, in the sentimental-humanitarian strain he was master of, in *La Nouvelle Héloïse* (1760). His *Confessions* show him at one time taking fencing lessons, but finding he had no aptitude.[23] Whether or not this helped to turn him against duelling, his early life in republican Geneva must have done more, cruel stepmother though his native city was.

In England elasticity of social boundaries, which opened the door wider to would-be duellists, could be expected to widen the field of debate as well. It provided comic writers with much easy fun. One target was the man who, like Bob Acres the landowner, felt obliged to live up to his position, but found his courage oozing away when most wanted. A satirist's moral could be read variously: men ought not to be pushed by society into such situations; but they needlessly make themselves ridiculous when they aspire to a dignity they are unfit for.

[19] Kelly, 239.
[20] Basnage, 21–2.
[21] Ibid. 15–16.
[22] Montesquieu, Letter 91. The passage was quoted by the writer of the short article in the *Encyclopédie* (xii. 873) on 'Point d'honneur'.
[23] Rousseau, *Confessions*, Bk. 5.

Sir Nicholas Cully in the Restoration comedy *The Comical Revenge* owes his knighthood to Cromwell, in other words is a bogus gentleman. He is led by the nose, by a pair of gamblers and cheats, into undertaking a duel, over a gambling debt alleged against him; when the time comes he wishes he had let his friendly neighbour Colonel Hewson know about it: he would have sent soldiers to prevent it. His second, one of the cheats, remonstrates—'this wou'd not secure your Honour. What wou'd the world have judg'd?'—to which Cully sensibly replies 'Let the world have judg'd what it wou'd.' When his opponent arrives, looking fierce, Cully decides to admit the debt and pay up, pretending that his conscience would not let him 'fight in a wrong Cause'.[24]

Sir Courtly Nice, in another play of the 1660s, is all right in point of birth, but as an unwarlike fop only looks foolish when he takes umbrage at Mr Surly and wants to call him out. 'I desire the Honour of your Company, Sir, tomorrow Morning at Barn-Elms, Sir—please to name your weapon, Sir.' He is quenched by the derisive answer: 'A Squirt'.[25] But a graver vein of criticism was provoked by Restoration excesses, the muddy flood of vice and violence brought back with them from exile by returning royalists, much given to duelling in a country where it had been at a low ebb for two decades. Writing on drama in 1672 Dryden observed that great poets like Homer and Tasso made little of 'the *point of honour*, so much magnified by the French, and so ridiculously aped by us'.[26] Puritanism was not yet a spent force; censors could gather encouragement from the Revolution of 1688, and the duel may have been more vigorously denounced about the end of the century than later on, after it came to be managed with more propriety.

Jeremy Collier was a 'non-juring', or anti-Revolution, divine, but louder than anyone else in denouncing profanity and immorality on the stage. His attack on the duel was equally robust. It took the form of a dialogue between Philotimus, lover-of-honour, who has a quarrel on his hands, and Philalethes, lover-of-truth, who tries to dissuade him from accepting a challenge. He protests that this will ruin his reputation, something 'worse than being buried Alive'. 'Don't stake your Life against a Nut-shell', rejoins his friend, 'nor run into the other World upon every Fop's errand.' Duellists are 'Murtherers by *Principle*', worse than highwaymen who are only plying a trade. France is full of proud noblemen, he points out, yet there 'Duelling is absolutely suppressed'. His hearer takes refuge in the thought that he has nothing to fear from the law. 'If we kill *fairly*, we have always Interest at Court to bring us off.' But he ends by yielding to good sense and promises to drop his

---

[24] Etherege, Act III, sc. v.
[25] John Crowne, *Sir Courtly Nice*, Act IV, sc. i.
[26] 'Of Heroic Plays' (1672).

1*a* Knights jousting, on the church port of St Zeno, Verona
Alinari

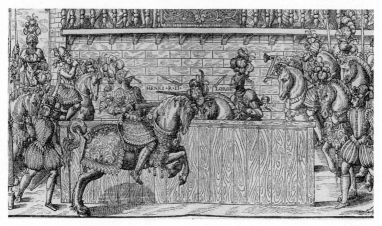

1*b* The death of Henri II of France, 1559. From a French woodcut
Photographie Giraudon

2*a* A German training-school, from a sixteenth-century handbook
on fencing
Bodleian Library, Oxford. Douce M672 f.xcvi

2*b* Fencing positions, from a French seventeenth-century handbook

3 'Duel between two women' by José de Ribera, *c.*1636
Prado, Madrid

4a A students' duel
From the album of Johann Jacob Haller von Hallerstein, 1740
British Library

4b A nineteenth-century German students' duel
Mary Evans Picture Library

5a Sir Philip Francis wounded by Warren Hastings, 1779
Mary Evans Picture Library

5b Alexander Hamilton killed by Aaron Burr, 1804
Culver Pictures

6*a*   An illustration to Molière's *Le Bourgeois Gentilhomme*
by C. R. Leslie, *c.*1841
Victoria and Albert Museum

6*b*   'O'Toole versus O'Callaghan' by John Leech
The Mansell Collection

7a *La Rixe* by Ernest Meissonier
Reproduced by gracious permission of Her Majesty the Queen

7b *Suite d'un bal masqué* by Jean Léon Gérôme, 1867
Lauros-Giraudon

8*a* An illustration to Scott's *Rob Roy*
BBC Hulton Picture Library

8*b* Tenniel's illustration of Tweedledum and Tweedledee for *Through the Looking-Glass* by Lewis Carroll

quarrel, only hesitating because he fears his enemy 'will post me up for a Coward, and how then?'—an early allusion to the later widespread practice of 'posting'. Treat him as a madman, the robust Philalethes replies.[27]

Swift had the characteristic notion that the right thing would be to let furious fighters go on exterminating one another.[28] In one of Steele's parables about the humane king Pharamond, a conscience-stricken duellist is admitted to his presence and tells him he has just had the misfortune to kill his best friend; he upbraids his ruler for having tolerated the evil—'a Tyrant Custom, which is misnamed a Point of Honour', so potent that even the judge who sentences a fighter really approves his conduct. 'Shame is the greatest of all Evils; what avail Laws, when Death only attends the Breach of them, and Shame Obedience to them?'[29] Steele had felt the tyranny himself, when he was drawn into a combat while serving in the Coldstream Guards. He recurred often to the subject in the *Tatler*, and the last scene of his comedy *The Lying Lover* (1703) bristles with duelling talk. Its plot came from the Spanish stage, by way of Corneille, a small token of how cosmopolitan a theme the duel furnished.

Defoe was another who used strong language about it; but in *Atlantis Major*, his political burlesque of 1711, he accused the Duke of Argyll of rudeness to another nobleman, whom he once challenged but then backed out of fighting, 'choosing to risk his Honour rather than his Life'. Defoe was excoriating the Scottish peers, who then held the scales between Whig and Tory, as needy and greedy for court favours, and prepared to submit to humiliation in order to earn them.

In the next generation a like ambiguity can be felt in Fielding. He was fond of reducing the duel to caricature, yet recognition of the self-respect and integrity that ought to be its mainspring somehow remains. This can be said even of the low-life scene of gambling, pocket-picking, mutual abuse, and gentlemanly rant, which is calmed at length by Jonathan Wild with a philosophical speech about Honour, 'and what pity is it that a word of such a sovereign use and virtue should have so uncertain and various an application'.[30] In *Joseph Andrews* the view presented is that while braggarts often prudently retreat, 'many a grave and plain man will, on a just provocation, betake himself to that mischievous metal, cold iron'. We are given a specimen of *just provocation* when Beau Didapper makes improper advances to Fanny, until honest

[27] Collier, 115–45.
[28] Bosquett, 74–5.
[29] *The Spectator*, no. 84 (1711). See also *Tracts and Pamphlets by Richard Steele*, ed. R. Blanchard (Baltimore, 1944), 501, 513–17.
[30] Fielding, *Jonathan Wild* (1743), chap. 13.

Joseph boxes his ears, and offers to meet him with any weapon; while Parson Adams steps between them, seizing up the lid of a kitchen-pot as shield against the incensed Beau's sword.[31] Manly feeling and absurdity jostle together.

Smollett was one of not a few writers whose literary activities brought them on to, or close to, the field of honour. An admiral took exception to a severe review of his pamphlet defending his conduct in an unsuccessful expedition, though things ended with no worse than £100 damages and a short prison sentence.[32] There is a *reductio ad absurdum* of duelling in his tale of a young clergyman, Tom Eastgate, who at Oxford has sucked up to a landowner named Prankley in the hope of a good living in his gift. When Prankley fobs him off, Eastgate reacts so angrily that he is forced to resent it, and pistols are agreed on for six o'clock next morning. While they walk up a hill together towards a clump of firs, Prankley loses heart, and tries to persuade his companion that a clergyman ought not to shed blood. Eastgate merely pulls out a big horse-pistol. Prankley's hand shakes too much for him to be able to prime his weapon, and he begs a day's delay to make his will—this, he mentions, is to contain the promised living for his old friend. Eastgate promptly responds that he cannot dream of firing at his benefactor, and is left 'not a little pleased with the effects of his own sagacity'.[33]

What struck Smollett the novelist most was the ridiculous side of duelling, although Squire Bramble is sufficient reminder that he could understand a man of sense feeling obliged to resort to it. It is in the *Travels* that we come on his sweeping condemnation, one of the most energetic ever penned, of 'the folly and the mischief which are coun-tenanced by the modern practice of duelling'. He recalls cases known to him of 'whole families ruined, or women and children made widows and orphans', and ends by recommending a special court, with wide penal powers: anyone proposing a fight will be banished, anyone killed will be gibbeted, the killer hanged, both corpses handed over for dissection.[34]

Richardson in *Clarissa* was distinctly unsympathetic to duelling. Various arguments are urged against it, such as the absurdity of giving a man who has done you a small injury a chance to do you a great one.[35] At the end the repentant heroine implores both her brother and

---

[31] Fielding, *Joseph Andrews*, Bk. 2, chap. 14; Bk. 4, chap. 11. Cf. the duel in his *Amelia* (1751), Bk. 5, chap. 5: 'Containing much heroical Matter'.

[32] Sutherland, no. 175.

[33] *Humphry Clinker*, 69–72. In earlier novels Smollett's duelling episodes are more conventional, but show no liking for the custom; see *Roderick Random* (1748), chap. 69 and *Peregrine Pickle* (1751), chaps. 40, 63.

[34] *Travels*, 138–40.

[35] *Clarissa*, i. 368. Gilmour (p. 28) refers to Richardson's emphasis in *Sir Charles Grandison* (1753–4) on the greater courage needed to refuse a challenge.

her cousin Colonel Morden not to seek to punish Lovelace; and Morden hesitates for long before resolving to follow the villain to the continent and bring him to book. Their encounter follows the rules of polite conduct admirably. Morden offers the choice of place and weapon, and they debate the claims of sword or pistol, each concerned not to seem to be seeking an advantage. Rapiers are agreed on; they meet in 'a little lone valley', and fall to 'after a few compliments', both perfectly cool. Lovelace is run through; before his death, amid delirium and convulsions, he tells Morden 'You have well revenged the dear creature.'[36] Thus the duel ends by being presented in its best colours, and despite the author's admonishments the reader's sympathy is likely to be with Morden, who has acted on principle and after due deliberation.

It may have been Sheridan's comic masterpiece of 1775, *The Rivals*, that struck the shrewdest blow. He was only twenty-three when he wrote it, but with his Irish background he must have known a good many of the O'Trigger family; and he too had personal experience, having been very recently compelled—by a motive as good as any could be, to protect the woman he was marrying from slander—to fight a Captain Matthews twice over. Goldsmith was another Irishman, and, however improbably, once came near at least to having to fight. He was induced by an army friend to resent a newspaper attack by calling on the publisher and striking him with a cane. Luckily this led to legal proceedings instead of a challenge, and Goldsmith retreated to a handsome apology.[37]

In *The Vicar of Wakefield* dispraise of duelling is mixed with a sort of nostalgia. The vicar's son George, having become factotum to a dissipated but not over-bold man about town, Squire Thornhill, is requested by him to fight on his behalf a man who pretends that his sister has been wronged. (One may wonder how many 'shotgun weddings' took place under threat of a challenge from truculent brothers or fathers.) George complies, only to discover that the 'sister' was a prostitute and the man her bully-boy. For his pains he is sternly reprimanded by Thornhill's uncle, Sir William, a conscientious opponent of duelling. Subsequently he learns that Thornhill has been trifling with his own sister, and sends a challenge, but is seized by a band of the squire's men, and in the scuffle wounds one of them. Sir William, arriving as *deus ex machina*, reproves him for wanting to be a duellist a second time. 'You imagine, perhaps, that a contempt for your own life gives you a right to take that of another.' Yet he cannot help taxing his nephew with cowardice; when reminded of his 'repeated

---

[36] *Clarissa*, vii. 316–22.
[37] *Boswell for the Defence 1769–1774*, ed. W. K. Wimsatt and F. A. Pottle (London, 1960), 165–6.

instructions' not to fight, he can only hum and haw, and musingly remark that young Thornhill's father would have acted very differently—'My brother, indeed, was the soul of honour.'[38]

Because duelling was so virulent in Ireland, it provoked one of the earliest attempts at organized opposition. In legend at least, the 'Order of the Friendly Brothers of St. Patrick' was born in the early seventeenth century, in the western town of Athenry, much troubled by wars and disasters. Its first recorded meeting was in 1750; it may be probable that Quakers, those oddities among Ireland's odd inhabitants, took a hand. In 1763 a set of 'Fundamental Laws' was published, in a solemnly inflated, very un-Quakerish, style. There was to be a 'Grand President', responsible for the 'Government of the ORDER diffused through the Universe'. Rule XX, recognizing that the best of men are carried away at times by passion, set forth that no member should 'presume to decide his own Quarrel, according to the Laws of pretended Honour, by the barbarous Practice of DUELLING, unknown to the politest, and bravest Nations' (the Greeks and Romans, presumably—possibly also the Chinese), but should submit to the decision of the brethren.[39] It was not long before this clarion-call was answered by a more strident trumpet, the Irish duelling code of 1777.

Scotland's transition from feudal to modern was unusually brusque. Its sword-bearing classes might prize the duel all the more as a link with their martial past; at the same time, the moral dilemmas it raised could be felt the more sharply. Scotland's great philosopher Hume was a man of old family as well as an apostle of the Enlightenment; he had lived long in France, and had worn the king's uniform. He had a clear eye for what was laughable in medieval notions, but his verdict makes allowance for the other side of the case. 'The great independence of men', he wrote of the Middle Ages, 'made personal honor and fidelity the chief tie among them', while 'the solemnities of single combat' lent decorum to their contests. 'These ideas of chivalry ... let modern *gallantry* and the *point of honour*, which still maintain their influence, and are the genuine offspring of those ancient affectations.'[40]

Antiquated modes of thinking were broken in on by the Union with England in 1707, followed by the exodus to London of a drove of the ever-hungry nobility, in quest of pickings from the public purse. With the partial removal of this feudal incubus Edinburgh was left to be the gathering-point of the minor landowners, who rubbed elbows there

---

[38] Goldsmith, *The Vicar*, chaps. 20, 28, 30, 31.

[39] Mrs A. M. Fraser, 'The Friendly Brothers of St. Patrick', *Dublin Historical Record*, 14 (1955–8), 34 ff. I am grateful to the Museum authorities at Belfast for a copy of this article.

[40] Hume, 40. Cf. C. Moore (223–4) on chivalric origins, 'the bitterness of whose fruits are still tasted in the modern duel'.

with its professional classes, legal and clerical and medical. Scots now had to think of how their country could be saved from turning into a mere English backwater; and, more pressingly, of how their own incomes could be brought up nearer to the English level. Decades of eager pursuit of material improvement followed, with a belated agricultural revolution as its bottom. Need for haste made new ideas of all kinds more welcome than they usually are. When Hume, Adam Smith, and others founded the Select Society in 1754, as a discussion centre for the cream of the intelligentsia, it quickly acquired high status and drew the attention of many of the gentry.

By 'an astonishing qualitative change' in Edinburgh life, the small band of literati, or innovating thinkers, found themselves towing the widest-awake of the landed gentry.[41] But there was something fallacious in this relationship. In England the professional groups were too largely an offshoot of the county families; in Scotland far more so, above all in the case of the higher legal corporation, because any authentic middle class, before the industrial revolution, was much smaller. Among the Select Society's members gentry-connections, like Hume's, were prevalent; a majority of the younger ones stood to inherit estates.[42] An educated group so entangled in the past could not be well ballasted, or look to an independent future. Gentry values would impose themselves more on balance than bourgeois; the absence of aristocrats who would have kept advocates and professors more at a distance only accentuated this. Lairds were learning to be progressive landholders, in other words learning how to exploit their soil and their labourers more efficiently, and acquiring a smattering of interest in things of the mind; intellectuals, serving as their bearleaders, were hindered from developing on their own lines. They had no links with any stirrings of popular feeling that could provide a counterweight; their deepening isolation from common humanity was reflected in the spreading adoption of English speech, and the migration from the grimy vitality of old Edinburgh to the prim-and-properness of the New Town.

An index of this situation was an abrupt declension into a kind of fatalistic mood. In Edinburgh between 1750 and 1780 'determinism suddenly emerged as the ideological norm of polite culture'. Smith and Hume insisted that man was 'psychologically and sociologically' confined, with little scope for purposive, creative activity; the writers Mackenzie and John Home derived a parallel doctrine very largely from Greek tragedy, unfolding under the dominion of fate.[43] All this

[41] N. T. Phillipson, 'Edinburgh and the Scottish Enlightenment', in *The University in Society*, ed. L. Stone (Princeton, 1974), ii. 424. [42] Ibid. 444–5.
[43] N. T. Phillipson, 'Towards a Definition of the Scottish Enlightenment', in *City and Society in the 18th Century*, ed. P. Fritz and D. Williams (Toronto, 1973), 137, 141; cf. C. E. Davie, *The Scottish Enlightenment* (London, 1981), 16.

was in one way a secularized theology, the ghost of Calvinist pre-destination. It differed widely from Marx's 'historical determinism' in leaving very little room for human volition. Man was the prisoner of his social environment, because no class force able to alter it was discernible; here precisely was the experience of an intelligentsia drawn away from its true 'mission', or natural bent. Individuals can feel free only while the class or community they belong to feels free to remake its corner of the world.

Landowners, with very little wish for change except where their own comforts were concerned, could find in determinism a handy way to shrug off responsibility for the condition of small farmers reduced, as in England much earlier, to farm labourers. Adam Smith was not the only observer who realized or glimpsed at times that the material expansion sustaining the Scottish Enlightenment was benefiting only a few. It continued, but Scotland's distinctive contribution to European progress was not to last long. Its social foundations were too narrow; the talents that might have kept it going followed the example of their superiors and removed to London. One facet of this decline was Scotland's failure to give a firm lead towards abolition of the duel. There was no one of sufficient eminence to denounce it as whole-heartedly as Wilberforce in England—Walter Scott came nearest—, and the impulse towards its abolition came mainly from south of the border.

Boswell was a lawyer, a judge's son, a keen reader and writer, very much a modern-minded intellectual, widely travelled, with many London contacts. He was also acutely conscious of his old blood and feudal ancestry, and their claims on him. These opposite tides and their conflicting pressures helped to give him his third dimension, a morbid piety. He was at one time smitten with ideas of a military career and fame, and may have indulged in fantasies about himself as a dashing duellist. Signor Romanzo, his romanticized self carrying on a fictional propaganda on behalf of his admired Corsica and its struggle for freedom, is challenged at one point by a French duke, because he has been talking too enthusiastically of the British and their sovereign; the duke pays the penalty of his impertinence with a serious wound.[44] When a flesh and blood duel was in prospect Boswell was painfully hesitant. This happened half a dozen times, yet somehow the crisis always passed off, leaving him to wonder anxiously whether his dislike of violence was cowardice; a duel was at least a touchstone of manhood.[45]

He told Rousseau all about the first occasion, which arose from his irritating a Frenchman by heedlessly abusing France, and asked for

[44] Pottle, 305.
[45] Ibid. 155; Introd. to Boswell, *The Ominous Years*, xvi.

Rousseau's opinion about duelling in general.[46] But it was of course Johnson that he turned to most expectantly, bringing the subject up with surprising persistence. His mentor also took a marked interest in it. It is hard to suppose that the Doctor, at sixty-six, can have been subjected to a challenge; but his famous letter to the author of *Ossian* was a rejoinder to one couched in a style 'very different from the language of literary contest'. Boswell never saw it, but he thought Macpherson greatly mistaken if he fancied that Johnson could be intimidated, 'for no man was ever more remarkable for personal courage'.[47] His approval of duelling, however qualified, accompanied High Church and high Tory convictions; it must have owed a good deal also to his native argumentativeness and love of contradiction.

One evening in 1772 he was a guest, with Boswell and Goldsmith, at dinner with General Oglethorpe. Boswell started the question of whether duelling could be squared with Christian morality. 'The brave old General fired at this, and said, with a lofty air, "Undoubtedly a man has a right to defend his honour."' Goldsmith was flippant; Johnson took up the problem in 'a masterly manner'; his argument, as recollected by Boswell, looks a good deal less than convincing, and has relevance only for his own day. Its gist is that in a polished state of civilization 'an affront is held to be a serious injury', and 'men have agreed to banish from their society one who puts up with an affront without fighting a duel. Now, Sir, it is never unlawful to fight in self-defence.' Society's present 'superfluity of refinement' may by regrettable; 'but while such notions prevail, no doubt a man may lawfully fight a duel'. Boswell appends his own rider, that this only covers the injured party. 'All mankind must condemn the aggressor.'[48] Johnson would scarcely have dissented from this. But neither of them asked why it was often the innocent party instead of the aggressor who was threatened with ostracism.

On a later occasion, in 1783, Johnson maintained the same stand when Boswell tackled him with more than usual urgency, having recently been recalled to London from Burke's country house by news of a duel between two officers, one of them a close relative of his, who had killed his antagonist and himself been dangerously wounded. Even in face of this catastrophe, Johnson argued that Scripture forbids revenge, not self-defence; revealing, we may perhaps guess, an obscure feeling of a man who had met with many injustices in a long life, and may sometimes have had day-dreams of reprisals. 'No, Sir, a man may shoot the man who invades his character, as he may shoot him who

[46] Pottle, 196.
[47] Boswell, *Johnson*, ii. 101 (1775).
[48] Ibid. ii. 15–16 (1772).

attempts to break into his house.' Boswell thought an aggressor killed in a duel could have little chance of heaven; the sage was not so sure.[49]

Exploring the Highlands could give Johnson livelier impressions of a society far removed from his over-refined England, and his veneration for old ways cooled somewhat. He came in contact with a martial ardour that might have useful outlets, but concluded that anyone who 'places honour only in successful violence, is a very troublesome and pernicious animal in time of peace'.[50] During their tour he and Boswell came back more than once to the duel. He dwelt on a redeeming feature confined to sword-play: in England there was no need to go to extremes, because the winner could satisfy his honour by disarming the other man, and it was reckoned cowardly to force a beaten man to go on fighting. 'A man is sufficiently punished, by being called out, and subjected to the risk that is in a duel.' But when his disciple objected that the injured person was equally at risk, 'he fairly owned that he could not explain the rationality of duelling'.[51] It is a striking case, though by no means the only one, of mankind hugging for centuries a practice that nobody could account for.

That Johnson was deeply religious, and yet so pertinaciously ready seek justification for duelling, is one illustration of how limited was the success of the Churches against it. One reason must be that, tied as they were so closely to the society they worked within, they could not attack too energetically. Swift may not have been very religious, but he was at least a dean; yet his comments on duels within his own circle suggest no moral concern. What impressed him one morning in London when he breakfasted with the Lord Herbert of his day, and was given a present of a velvet cap, was that his host was 'as merry and easy as ever I saw him, yet had received a challenge half an hour before, and half an hour after fought a duel'.[52] Swift was 'infinitely concerned' at the news, early another morning, of the demise of the Duke of Hamilton, 'a frank, honest, good-natured man' whom he 'loved very well'; but there is no Christian reference when he goes on to say that reports differed as to whose hand caused the death of the duke, who died before he could be carried to 'the cake-house by the ring in Hyde Park', but that 'the dog Mohun was killed on the spot'.[53] A dean of this cut would not much alarm the consciences of the Anglo-Irish duellists who called their simulacrum of a church the 'Church of Ireland'.

Had the duel been less firmly entrenched, it ought to have been more

---

[49] Boswell, *Johnson*, iii. 245 (1783).
[50] Johnson, *Journey*, 83.
[51] Boswell, *Hebrides*, 201–2 (19 Sept. 1785).
[52] Swift, *The Journal to Stella*, Letter 12 (Jan. 1710–11).
[53] Ibid., Letter 55 (15 Nov. 1712).

seriously shaken in the eighteenth century, for it was one of the few issues on which religion and enlightenment could see eye to eye. Not much less remarkable, it was one on which Catholic and Protestant could agree. Scipione Maffei's work dedicated in 1710 to Pope Clement XI has been called 'the best of all the books against duelling';[54] and Catholic teaching has been particularly strict and detailed. As summed up in a modern manual, it leaves only one very small loophole, for a duel approved by public authority in the common interest as an alternative to war. 'Fighting a duel on *private authority* is mortally sinful', even if undertaken as the only way to avoid loss of rank or position. Anyone engaging in it, or giving or accepting a challenge, or acting as a second, or looking on and not interfering, lays himself open to excommunication. So does a doctor or priest standing by, though not one called after a fight, nor a cab-driver, who cannot choose his passengers. Books forbidden to the faithful include all that palliate suicide, divorce, or duelling.[55]

Funeral oratory, a branch of literature much cultivated in *ancien régime* France, gave preachers scope for enforcing such principles; their audiences had a taste for topics of current interest such as duelling.[56] Yet doctrine might be muffled, as in earlier years, by the Church's social structure and connections. Great men had household chaplains, who would not be far from the scene when a duel was in progress. Regimental chaplains likewise might stretch a point or two to oblige an officer. They were 'seldom rigid Casuists', Mandeville remarked, and few of them saints themselves.[57] What Rome said, Macaulay pointed out when arguing for abolition of the anti-Catholic penal laws, fell on many deaf ears. 'She commands all her followers to fast often, to be charitable to the poor, to take no interest for money, to fight no duels, to see no plays. Do they obey these injunctions?'[58]

Prelates in seventeenth- and eighteenth-century England were socially a more mixed body than in Catholic lands, many coming from middle-class professional families; and nonconformists had less reason still for any tenderness towards duelling. Sermons of the later eighteenth century frequently bracketed duelling with suicide, as offences to God, the creator of all lives.[59] Anglican clergymen on the other hand were for the most part a torpid race of time-servers, unlikely to bark very loudly at their masters, or to have much weight with them if they did. We even hear of a Revd Mr Bate, editor of the *Morning Post*, taking the

[54] Clark, 39.
[55] Jone, Sect. 5, chap. 3.
[56] McManners, 228–9.
[57] Mandeville, 151.
[58] *Essays*, i. 136.
[59] Information from Dr Olive Anderson.

field in 1777 at the Adelphi tavern with a Captain Stoney, because of some articles reflecting on the lady whom the officer was about to marry; both were wounded.[60] This was only one of Bate's three duels, which did not hinder him from rising to be a dean. A Revd Mr Allan was acquitted by a jury, in defiance of the judge, after killing a man in Hyde Park. 'His bishop does not seem to have taken any notice of the matter.'[61]

Religion addressed its admonitions against duelling to the higher classes, whose belief has always been that the function of religion is to tell the lower classes what to do or not do. It must have restrained a certain number of individuals from fighting; and it may have had an indirect share in the refining and humanizing of the duel, somewhat as it helped in feudal times to refine men's images of love. Only a new social order, bringing with it a new outlook, would put an end to something so inextricably entangled with conservative thinking as the duel. As things were, the wide gap between Christian professions and the real tenets of the dominant classes in Christendom was always an embarrassment to those who, like Boswell, or Scott, liked to think of themselves as both gentlemen and Christians.

Of the less articulate sections of the community, whose views are harder to decipher, women of the higher classes were the most closely affected. How they felt, we can know or guess chiefly from what men were saying about them, or for them. Serious women could hear their opinions expressed by preachers; also by journals like the *Spectator*, which had a numerous female readership and wanted to appeal to it. There may be ground for thinking that a current of reforming opinion on this subject was taking hold among women more quickly than among men, especially after the religious revival got under way. Addiction to duelling would be associated in many of their minds with other habits, especially drunkenness and libertinism, obnoxious to wives and apt to drive them to piety for consolation. The mother of the Duke of Hamilton, killed fighting, duchess in her own right until she renounced the title in his favour, befriended persecuted Covenanters. But no concerted movement of protest emerged, any more than, among women of any rank, against war; and on both subjects views no doubt fluctuated.

In the time of the ceremonial duel, two Spanish captains paid the French commander at Ferrara, the Duc de Nemours, the compliment of requesting him to preside over a combat. Such a spectacle could be watched by ladies, and the charming Duchess of Ferrara was present, and saw with distress one of the men's lives in danger. She begged Nemours to halt the fight; he explained that he could not, it must run

[60] Steinmetz, ii. 17–18.
[61] Bayne-Powell, 49.

its course; the loser's second then took it on himself to offer a surrender, and all ended happily.[62] But for women proud of their descent, as well as for men, a duel in their own family was something they might feel obliged to accept as a consequence of rank. When Leonora, in Calderón's play, is assured that her brother was killed in a fair fight, and asked whether in view of this she still wishes his opponent to be prosecuted, her answer is:

> No, sir; for though the laws of duel are
> For men alone, I know enough of them
> To pardon all that was in honour done.[63]

Very similarly, Laclos's Mme de Rosemonde, aunt of the man killed, is shown letters proving that an unscrupulous woman was to blame, and accedes to Danceny's request to leave the affair to oblivion, instead of prosecuting.[64] Here again we see that whether the law was set in motion or not depended a good deal on whether a dead man's family or friends wanted to jog the authorities into action, or had enough influence to do so. When Tatiana and Onegin meet again, near the end of Pushkin's poem, and she sermonizes him as he once did her, she makes no allusion to his duel; there are no reproaches for his friend Lensky's death.

Another Leonora, in an agony of grief at her lover being run through in a duel, is quickly consoled by her mirror, which assures her that her 'cursed charms' alone could have been the destruction of so fine a gentleman.[65] A woman not herself concerned, the wife of an English clergyman-schoolmaster, could think cordially of a meritorious duellist, as William Gilpin reports that his mother did after one affair: 'she says Mr W acted like a man of great courage and honour and also like a good man'.[66] It would be less easy to take so liberal a view if family income as well as honour was at stake. When Jane Austen's Mr Bennet goes off in chase of an eloped daughter, his wife is in dread of news of a duel, and his death, and their being turned out of the family's entailed property.[67]

Opposite reactions, masculine and feminine, come out in a Goldsmith comedy when Leontine and Olivia are eloping, and have a Mr Honeywood to blame for their troubles. 'We shall have satisfaction: he shall give me instant satisfaction', exclaims the hero. Olivia remonstrates, much like Clarissa Harlowe. 'Whatever be our fate, let us not add guilt

---

[62] Brantôme, 22–4.
[63] Fitzgerald, 192 (*Gil Perez*, Act III).
[64] Laclos, Letters 169, 171.
[65] Fielding, *Joseph Andrews*, Bk. 2, chap. 4.
[66] Gilpin, 27.
[67] *Pride and Prejudice*, chap. 47.

to our misfortunes.' Honeywood enters, and Leontine accosts him with 'Draw, villain!'[68] A story about Garrick's brother George shows a woman not simply remonstrating but cutting a duel short. He was fighting a fellow actor, whom he had been misled into suspecting of making love to his wife, when she rushed on the scene, in time to stop them after one exchange of fire.[69] Tears of regret could be a feminine offering, when it was too late for any other. As a child Jane Welsh, Carlyle's future wife, could be seen in the churchyard at Haddington 'weeping bitterly and impartially over the graves of a young army officer, Sutherland, shot in a duel, and of little Ann Cameron who had been burned to death'.[70]

We have glimpses of popular interest in duels of the more sensational kind, or in high life. When Swift sent to St James's Square to enquire about the Duke of Hamilton's death, 'a great rabble was about the house'.[71] Later in the eighteenth century a ballad was made about a woman named Deborah, hanged for aiding her lover's escape to Holland after a duel; she died feeling ill-used, not unreasonably considering how few men were ever hanged for duelling. Ordinary folk may have thought of gentlemen and fighting-cocks as birds of the same feather, and relished details of a well-fought combat, or still more the spectacle itself, if they could get close enough to watch. A display of skill and nerve may have impressed the lower orders more than it did middle-class critics. They have always had ambivalent feelings about their social superiors, which an event like a duel would throw into relief. We can only guess how often there was an obscure sense that the gentry were proving their mysterious right to be looked up to as 'the quality'; or, conversely, that any harm they came by was well-merited retribution for their arrogant treatment of their inferiors.

[68] Goldsmith, *The Good-Natur'd Man* (1768), Act V.
[69] Steinmetz, ii. 14.
[70] Hanson, 13.
[71] As n. 45.

I I

Decline and Rebirth

I find in one memoir a note of a newly-joined ensign after mess
addressing the assembled officers as follows: 'By Jasus, gentlemen,
I am conscious you must have the meanest opinion of my courage.
Here have I been no less than six weeks with the regiment, and the
divil of a duel have I fought yet. Now, Captain C., you are the
senior captain, and if you please I will begin with you first: so name
your time and place.'

Oman, *Wellington's Army*, 201.

DESPITE the apparent ineffectiveness of legal bans and spiritual
rebukes, there must have been many who had qualms about duelling,
and the prospect of being branded by both earthly and heavenly law
as a Cain. Bellicose combatants were increasingly a minority, while
most men would only throw out challenges under pressure of opinion
or persuasion of officious tongues, or accepted them because they could
see no decent way out. With newer currents of opinion so critical of
aristocratic assumptions, and of the 'point of honour' as one of the most
pernicious, hesitation about being drawn in, even indirectly as a second,
must often have been painful. There were no doubt many unevennesses
in the trend. Duelling is in fashion, Horace Walpole remarked in a
jocular letter of 1774.[1] In 1791 young Coleridge was writing from
Cambridge to his brother the Revd George about 'a dreadful circumstance': two Pembroke men had gone to Newmarket to settle a
difference, and one was killed. 'A fellow of our college made a very just
observation, that formerly students of Colleges were censur'd for being
pedants—but that now they were too much men of the world.'[2]

Still, the number of encounters would seem to have been falling off
in the later decades of the eighteenth century. Young William Gilpin,
enjoying the social whirl at Bath in 1773, had high praise for the master
of ceremonies, Captain Wade, for his prohibition of sword-carrying in
public places, 'which is the bane of civil society: he always interposes
in every quarrel and has been known to sit up all night to prevent a

---

[1] Walpole, xxxv: to Sir William Hamilton, 22 Feb. 1774.
[2] Coleridge, *Collected Letters*, ed. E. L. Griggs, vol. i (Oxford, 1956), 19.

dual'.[3] In the didactic novels of the back-to-Nature and Noble Savage school, the hero might resort at times to direct action against a miscreant, but not in the style prescribed by convention.[4] Some straggling rays of enlightenment were finding their way even into Ireland, where Arthur Young on tour in 1780 thought that drinking and duelling were going out of fashion.[5] He was too sanguine. In 1801 a visiting clergyman was much pleased with Dublin and its people, except that, he wrote to a friend, 'the vile custom of duelling is as much in vogue among them as ever'; every gunsmith's shop advertised duelling pistols warranted to hit their mark at any given range.[6] As to Scotland, a Bishop Geddes complained in a pamphlet in 1790 that 'the groundless prejudice in favour of duels' was 'very common in these times', and easily seduced weak-minded young men. Scotland had strict laws, but they were ignored; government ought to be enforcing them, with the backing of public associations like one lately formed at Norwich. Opinion compelled men to stand in a field and shoot at each other, it was said: what if it bade them 'dance naked through the streets at mid-day'?[7]

A stronghold of opinion, as in other countries, was the army. One day in May 1789, when at Versailles the States-General was meeting for the first time since 1614, no less a person than the Duke of York was to be seen on Wimbledon Common with a Lieutenant-Colonel Lenox, whose bullet grazed the royal hair without his deigning to return the fire. Lenox had accused the duke of maligning him, and forced him to give satisfaction by actually shouting a complaint on the parade-ground. His fellow-officers of the Coldstream Guards—Steele's old regiment—decided that he had shown spirit, but not judgement, and he soon exchanged into a new corps, fighting another duel *en passant*.

Novelists high and low have found the theme of royalty condescending to measure swords or pistols with men outside the charmed circle an enthralling one;[8] but according to Fox, when news of their son's prank reached the king and queen 'the first showed very little and the second *no* emotion at all'.[9] A few years later the duke was made commander-in-chief, a billet he was at least less unequal to than his former one of prince-bishop of Osnabrück, in Hanover. Possibly he

---

[3] Gilpin, 26. Gibbon's diary for 6 April 1764 shows him too playing peacemaker, and reflecting that his day could not have been better spent (*Autobiography* (World's Classics, London, 1907), 140–1).

[4] Information from Dr P. D. Tripathi.

[5] A. Young, 205–6.

[6] Cholmondeley, 179–80.

[7] Geddes, 3, 8–9, 36 ff, 47.

[8] Examples: Scott, *Woodstock*, chap. 28; Thackeray, *Henry Esmond*, Bk. 3, chap. 13; R. L. Stevenson, *Prince Otto*, chap. 4; Anthony Hope, *The Prisoner of Zenda* (1893), chap. 1.

[9] Walpole, xxxix. 464 n. 1.

reckoned a duel a good way to live down his pseudo-ecclesiastical past. He might have thought twice about taking on a common or garden officer, and such a nobody might have hesitated to fire at royalty; but Lenox was heir to a peerage of royal origin, and his escapade did not prevent him from rising to the highest posts. Years later we find him, as fourth Duke of Richmond and lord-lieutenant of Ireland, playing the part of Satan rebuking sin by upholding a death-sentence for duelling: 'We shall never quiet the thing till a punishment has taken place.'[10] He was at Waterloo, and died at last of hydrophobia, while governor-general of Canada, brought low, after braving so many bullets, by the bite of a fox.

In France too swords were being seldomer worn, and duels, partly as a result, becoming less frequent. In the mild sunshine of the Enlightenment old ways of feeling and acting could gradually fade. In Languedoc for instance disputes over property and other contentious matters were being oftener settled by compromise; 'a settlement might even take the place of a duel', as when a challenge from a nobleman was rejected, though both men concerned were former officers. All this can be seen as part of 'the passage from a private to a public order', acceptance by the individual of the reign of law.[11] There was, it is true, a contrary tendency before 1789 which has been dubbed the 'feudal reaction', but this was mainly a pursuit of material benefits like enhanced feudal dues, and closer restriction of commissions in the army to the old nobility. When 1789 came the nobles, despite their control of the army, made a poor showing, like sorcerers' apprentices paralysed by the flood they had unloosed with their factious opposition to the monarchy. Horace Walpole was disgusted at the spectacle of how they 'ran away on the first panic, and are now littering Europe. The French can stab, but not fight.' He recalled how in Paris in 1765, in a discussion of a play where a father approved of his son fighting a duel, Diderot quoted to him a recent dictum that 'Louis XV would find it as difficult to re-establish duels, as Louis XIV had to suppress them'.[12]

Paradoxically it was the Revolution, which as the triumph of progressive ideas ought to have given duelling its *coup de grâce*, along with feudal dues and so many other museum pieces, that galvanized it back into life. Together with the ensuing quarter-century of European conflict, it gave the duel a further long tenure, as something that aristocracy could cling to as a fragment from the wreckage of its past,

---

[10] Aspinall, vi. 301. On Lenox (or Lennox) see also *D.N.B.*

[11] N. Castan, 'The Arbitration of Disputes under the "Ancien Régime"', in Bossy (ed.), 226, 229, 258. C. Moore (pp. 238–40) cited Mercier's *Tableau de Paris* on diminution of duelling in France.

[12] Walpole, xxiv. 180–1.

and that its overthrowers could adopt as part of their gains. Events at the outset had a running accompaniment of fights between individuals, who fell—in Carlyle's words—'mutually skewered through with iron, their wrath and life alike ending', and died as fools die.[13] For want of better arguments royalists, in person or through hired swordsmen, were trying to intimidate 'patriots' by thrusting challenges on them, which some declined on principle. Mirabeau received a string of them, and was badly hurt in one fight he failed to avoid. As a renegade marquis heading the revolution he was peculiarly obnoxious to his class.

Soldiers siding with the reformers volunteered to take on their enemies. The Paris municipality begged the Assembly for a ban on duelling, but no legislation against it came into effect. A deputy eloquent in favour of the proposal, Barnave, soon found himself, in August 1790, having to fight the royalist Cazalès. They met in the Bois de Boulogne, where Cazalès's stiff hat saved him from Barnave's bullet; Barnave's neck had no such protection when the wheels of history had rolled on for another three years and his turn came for the 'national razor', or guillotine. Meanwhile the revolution was collectivizing standards of conduct, substituting patriotic duty and honour for the self-regarding code of aristocracy.[14] In Year II of the new calendar the National Convention resolved that duelling was illegal and ought to be put down; the Jacobin regime of 1793–4 discountenanced it in the army,[15] which by then had half Europe to fight. But the onward march of revolution was halted by the *coup d'état* of Thermidor, or July 1794; under the rule of the Directory, from 1795 until the coming to power of General Bonaparte at the end of 1799, the duel blossomed afresh. Businessmen and speculators were digesting their profits, and their 'gilded youth' posed as a new élite, with duelling for one of its borrowed plumes.

An era was opening when youth grew accustomed, as Ségur said, to risk everything for glory, and Napoleon himself 'lived on glory above all'[16]—as might be said of the whole long aristocratic ascendancy. Napoleon was fond of referring to himself in private as a nobleman born, on the strength of the dubious family claim that got him into the officers' college at Brienne; he would even declare, truthfully or not, that as a lieutenant he had once been out, and would talk of the sword as a nobler duelling weapon than the pistol. In power he put a check on duelling; it was not outlawed by his new Codes, but in his eyes it

[13] Carlyle, *French Revolution*, Bk. 3, chap. 3: 'Sword in Hand'.

[14] N. Hampson, 'The French Revolution and the Nationalisation of Honour', in M. R. D. Foot (ed.), *War and Society* (London, 1973), 199 ff.

[15] Kelly, 250.

[16] Ségur, *Aide de Camp*, 84, 325.

was a wasteful nuisance. He was displeased when a useful General Régnier was killed in 1802 by General Destaing after recriminations about the Egyptian campaign; but his tactics of fostering ill-will among his army chiefs, for fear of their combining against him, would not help to mend such matters. Baron Marbot's memoirs tell of a 'deplorable scene' between two marshals during the battle of Aspern against the Austrians in the hard-fought campaign of 1809. Bessières had been placed under the command of Lannes, who sent him a peremptory order to attack; Bessières resented this, Lannes accused him of hanging back, Bessières demanded satisfaction on the spot—and the two were seemingly about to fight in full view, when they were pulled up by the blunt intervention of a senior commander, Masséna. Lannes then reported his insubordinate colleague to Napoleon, who sent for Bessières and gave him a stern dressing-down.[17]

A smaller flare-up might take place even closer under the emperor's nose. At the end of 1807, during the campaign in Poland, his aide-de-camp Ségur had to make a report to him, in a wretched cottage within range of the Russian cannon, and on coming out from his room into a rough corridor stumbled over a sleeping officer, who jumped up and broke into abuse. A duel had to be arranged for next day, and was only forestalled by Ségur's capture by the enemy.[18] The disgruntled officer was a Piedmontese; outbreaks of temper in Napoleon's cosmopolitan armies may often have been fanned by national frictions. Others might be traced to class discords. Duelling must have received a fillip from Napoleon's policy of welcoming men of the old regime like the Comte de Ségur into his service, and inviting émigrés to return to France. Men whom the revolution had raised up from the ranks could hardly be expected to welcome these yoke-fellows. Underlying the obsessive hatred of Feraud, in Conrad's story *The Duel*, for the man he harasses with endless challenges, is the fact that he is by birth a nobody, a blacksmith's son, just the kind of soldier to be an idolater of the self-made Napoleon, and to harbour dark suspicions that the well-born D'Hubert 'never truly loved the emperor'. On such lines the French officer corps long continued to be divided.

Duelling spread among men of the rank and file as well; it had been democratized by the upheaval instead of being swept away. In that very realistic novel *A Conscript of 1813*, a young soldier Zebedee refuses to be bullied by an older one. Ears are boxed, whiskers pulled out, experienced comrades pronounce that there must be a duel, and the company captain agrees; as the fencing-master says, 'to fight was an honour for new recruits'. In spite of a warning that 'all these veterans

[17] Baron de Marbot, *Memoirs* (English edn., London, 1929), 214–16.
[18] Ségur, *Aide de Camp*, chap. 22.

have some terrible tricks of fighting', picked up abroad, Zebedee takes his stand unflinchingly; he is saved by a stumble, and by his sabre running through an opponent caught off guard. Zebedee is left staring at it, pale as death. The same day, the regiment marches off.[19]

Not only soldiers might pick up the germ. In remote Shetland in 1802 a poor crofter indited a formal challenge to a neighbour, Eric Laurenson: 'Dear Sir, I Ola Smith chalang yow and your brother both to meet me 13th of March on the Ouns of Gord at half 12 o clok, man for man at fear play over a rop or over a stick or any yow pleas.' Ola or Oliver may have imbibed a fighting spirit from his father, who had an exciting time in 1779, during the American war, when he and his brother were picked up as pilots by the daring American raider John Paul Jones, then commanding a small French squadron, and survived the action off Flamborough Head. Laurenson instead of taking up the defiance went to the sheriff court, and Ola was bound over; three years later his unruly temper led to his banishment from Shetland.[20] A folk instinct for duelling would seem to have lingered there from Norse times. At Christmas in 1848 half a dozen 'tinsmiths or travelling merchants' at Lerwick were charged with a brawl that led to their exchanging challenges and marching off a mile or so to a public highroad, where they did 'wickedly and riotously fight with and strike and beat and bruise each other', to the 'disturbance and alarm of the lieges'.[21]

During the wars of 1793–1815 half a million Britons saw service, many of them reluctantly, in the armed forces, and warlike ideas were stamped in an unaccustomed fashion on the nation's mind. The country swarmed with foreigners, many royalist émigrés among them, besides mercenaries like the men of the German Legion. A refugee from the Austrians, not the French, turned up in 1814, the Greek-Italian poet Ugo Foscolo, an old soldier of Napoleon's who died at Turnham Green in 1827. This choleric bard on one occasion wanted the great actor Macready to carry a challenge from him to a careless translator. In the heated wartime atmosphere ministers and other politicians might feel that to keep the esteem of the men in uniform it was for them to show that they were as intrepid as any, even if not very useful. Before the encounter of Canning and Castlereagh in 1809, Pitt as prime minister in 1798 gave cause for some doubts about his sanity when he accepted

---

[19] E. Erckmann and L. G. Chatrian, *The History of a Conscript of 1813* (1864; trans. R. D. Gillman, London, 1909), chap. 10.

[20] Information from Dr Brian Smith, a collateral descendant of Ola Smith. He informs me also of a letter preserved in *Shetland Archives*, 24 Jan. 1910, from a Shetland landowner to a friend in 1808, wishing that a man who had been challenged had 'avowed manfully and christianlike that his principles did not permit him to take the life of another or rush into eternity himself without orders'.

[21] *Shetland Archives*, SC. 12/6/100/20; another reference supplied by Brian Smith.

a challenge from his Whig critic George Tierney; their bloodless bout was watched by his friend Addington, the Speaker.[22] In 1800 Henry Grattan the Irish patriot took the field with Isaac Cory, in 1807 Sir Francis Burdett the radical with James Paull.

In the armed forces, however, a fresh vogue of duelling could not but be felt, as it was by Napoleon, as a nuisance in time of war. When Sir John Moore was serving in 1795 with the marines attached to the Mediterranean fleet, he was conscious of no love being lost between marine and naval officers, and he recorded three duels in his diary. Naval captains seemed to him very overbearing. 'Their manners at best when on board of their ships are not the most amiable.'[23] When the one-armed Nelson was chosen in 1798, on the recommendation of Admiral Lord St Vincent, to command the fleet intended to intercept a French move towards the Levant, some other aspirants were aggrieved, and one, Sir John Orde, challenged St Vincent; a fight was only prevented by royal order.[24] In the army tempers were at least as inflammable. We have the Edinburgh sheriff's statement of his expenses when investigating a duel in Holyrood Park on 2 August 1798, between Lieutenant-Colonel Neville, of the Rutlandshire Cavalry, and Baillie, late of the same corps, in which Neville suffered a grave injury.[25] In 1813 when a Lieutenant Blundell was killed by a Mr Maguire, the latter and both seconds were condemned to death; the sentence was not carried out, but those belonging to the army were cashiered.

It was in the Peninsula that British troops were chiefly employed, from 1808 on. According to Oman duels were less frequent than might have been expected, fewer than in England in the same years, 'not to speak of Ireland and India, where they were beyond all reason common'. Wellington disliked them, and good commanders took pains to smooth disagreements. Oman admits that duels were not easily brought to light. Seconds, usually the only witnesses, had to keep quiet for their own sakes, and the few courts-martial held always decided that the charge was non-proven. 'The whole matter was clearly a solemn farce.'[26]

The young English officer at Dublin, in a Lever novel concerned with that era, who suddenly found himself in for a duel, had often heard of such things, and had come to suppose them 'more or less imperative': to reach a certain age without having been out was to be suspected of over-caution. 'Such was, in a great measure, the tone of

[22] Lord Rosebery, *Pitt* (London, 1891), 138–9.

[23] Sir John Moore, i. 157.

[24] O. Warner, *A Portrait of Lord Nelson* (Harmondsworth, 1963), 144–5.

[25] Scottish History Society, *Papers from the Collection of Sir William Fraser* (Edinburgh, 1924), 278–80.

[26] Oman, 201–2.

the day.'[27] A humorous remark by Palmerston, writing home from a tour on the continent soon after the peace, with his friend Sir George Shee, is evidence of how ready the duellist's weapon was to float before men's minds, like Macbeth's dagger. 'We quarrel all day like cat and dog yet as we left our duelling pistols at home no fatal consequences have yet ensued.'[28]

Wilberforce had begun by desiring a reform of Parliament; under stress of the war years and their social as well as national perils, he moved towards wanting a reform of the aristocracy, from the Prince Regent down. In this he was a forerunner of Carlyle, and like him suffered disillusion; unlike the racialist Carlyle, he transferred his hopes and energies to the anti-slavery cause. The middle classes he himself belonged to had minds open to religious light, he came before long to feel, but among those higher up it could not compete with the dictates of honour. His book on standards of Christian conduct appeared in 1797, and had much influence on the next generation, as a part of the Evangelical revival.

Duelling was inevitably one of his targets. He saw the men of fashion all round him happy in their emancipation from the 'base and servile villeinage' of religion; lacking any sense of responsibility, they made it their chief business to fill up the vacancy of their lives with sport, cards, theatre-going, and worse. Among them 'a quick feeling of injuries, and a promptness in resenting them', were admired as proper pride.[29] Worldly credit was their supreme good, worldly shame their worst evil. It was a disgrace to a professedly Christian society that duelling should so long have been tolerated, 'with little restraint or opposition' or reproach from Christian moralists. Its essential blot was that it meant rating man's approval above God's. Guilt was far from being confined to those who actually fought, Wilberforce argued: its sum total was incalculable, because it was shared by all those whose 'settled habitual determination' was to fight if occasion required—something that could not be said of any other crime. Laws against it seemed powerless; the best he could propose was a court of honour, with parliamentary backing, and discouragement of duelling by the crown and in the armed forces. In the mean time a good man must prepare his mind for 'disgrace and obloquy' by meditating beforehand on the probable necessity of one day having to stomach them.[30]

Wilberforce himself was the recipient of one challenge, from a captain trading with the West Indies, where his campaign against the slave

[27] Lever, *Jack Hinton*, chap. 13.
[28] Palmerston, 143 (Cambrai, 20 Oct. 1818).
[29] W. Wilberforce, chap. 4, sect. 2.
[30] Ibid. sect. 3.

trade won him many enemies.[31] In 1809 he was disgusted by the
Canning–Castlereagh duel, as humiliating to the country, but had
enough sense of the droll to be amused by a detail he heard—of a noble
earl on the spot picking up and carrying off, with 'provident parsimony',
one of the pistols thrown aside after firing, while his gardener made off
with another.[32] In his own circle Wilberforce was always ready with
admonitions. A man in need of them was his brother-in-law James
Stephen, who confessed one night at dinner that 'his strongest temptations were to duelling'.[33]

In Austria duelling was ignored in Maria Teresa's criminal code of
1768, but it was dealt with in detail in that of her son Joseph II in
1787. Capital punishment had been abolished; the maximum prison
sentence, for murder, was awarded to a challenger who killed his
opponent, despite the fact that it was very often the injured party who
felt obliged to offer the challenge.[34] A new Austrian code in 1803 shared
a tendency becoming prevalent by then to soften penalties for duelling;
but special note might be taken of cases where there had been a compact
to fight to the death.[35] The sanguinary taste for combat *à outrance* was
still not altogether a thing of the past.

In Prussia in 1785, near the end of Frederick the Great's life, stiff
punishment for duelling except by warrant of a tribunal of honour
was being considered; but reaction soon followed, and in 1791 army
tribunals were abandoned. Under the code of 1794 duelling was a
crime, except for noblemen and officers. For the first time, as Demeter
says, the government was as good as admitting a contradiction between
the law of the land and the code of a class.[36] After their ignominious
defeat by Napoleon at Jena in 1806, Prussian officers had to find ways
of regaining face, and must have been in a mood to fall out with one
another. A modern-minded group in the government which was trying
to reform army and nation was unable to enforce a ban; the most that
could be done was to urge commanders to exert their influence. A
decree in 1808 set up a court of honour in each regiment, but with only
limited functions.

Army modes had juvenile mimics in the student fraternities so much
a feature of German universities. Drinking and duelling were their
chief pursuits, as Crabb Robinson found during 1802–04 when he was
studying German culture, chiefly at Weimar, and meeting Goethe. He
watched numbers of duels, and at times needed some care to avoid

---

[31] R. I. and S. Wilberforce, *The Life of William Wilberforce* (London, 1838), i. 355–6.
[32] Ibid. iii. 426.
[33] Ibid. ii. 93.
[34] Prokowsky, 114–15.
[35] Ibid. 130–1.
[36] Demeter, 126.

having to take the field himself. At the neighbouring university of Jena duelling was very common, but not very dangerous: 'it is but a silly boy's play'. Nearly a hundred duels took place there within six months in 1803; a few students had serious wounds, and at Halle one managed to get killed.[37] The craze went on worsening through the war years, if Treitschke can be believed that in one week in the summer of 1815 there were no fewer than 147 duels at Jena, in a student population of 350. This 'ineradicable German love of brawling', as he calls it, had been coming under censure from more serious students, and teachers like Fichte, who felt that energies ought to be harnessed to the service of the Fatherland.[38] Hence the setting up in 1815 of the 'Burschenschaft' clubs, inaugurated at Jena with a procession in traditional style through the little town, headed by young men who had fought as volunteers in the 'War of Liberation' of 1813–14 against the French. One of its aims was to curb the excesses of the duelling cult; a fight was only to be permitted if sanctioned by a 'council of honour'.

With wars nearly continuous from 1792 to 1815, Europe underwent a thorough militarization. Conscription spread everywhere; hitherto as a rule it had been practised only on the poor, like England's press-ganged Jack Tars or Holy Russia's serf-soldiers, but now many of higher station were drawn into the net. It was, in Conrad's words, and for Frenchmen above all, 'one long, intoxicating clash of arms, unique in the magnitude of its glory and disaster'.[39] Conrad like General Bonaparte was understood to have fought a duel of his own; he was fascinated by the Napoleonic era, and wrote his long story *The Duel* as an attempt to recapture its spirit. National animosities were intensifying, and might find vent on occasion in duelling between others than soldiers. Shortly before the outbreak of hostilities between France and Russia in 1812, the French envoy at Naples, where Napoleon had installed his brother-in-law Joachim Murat as king, resented his Russian colleague's venturing to take precedence over him, and demanded satisfaction. Their seconds joined in the fight, in the old style—perhaps not having much faith in their principals as men of action—and the Frenchman, General Excelmans, was badly wounded.

At the end of the wars, with an Allied army of occupation in France, the duel offered Frenchmen opportunities for retaliation. Whatever the misconduct of some of the Prussians and Cossacks, this was nothing like a Nazi occupation; on the plane on which officers lived and moved the old conventions still held sway, and French speech and manners represented a common medium. French swordsmen, sometimes it was

[37] Robinson, 104, 127–8, 138.
[38] Treitschke, 99.
[39] Conrad, 223.

said regimental fencing-masters in officers' uniforms, picked quarrels with members of the allied forces. Britons were seldom their equals at sword-play, and sometimes came off worst at shooting too, like a Lieutenant Gordon shot dead at Cambrai. A ghoulish incident lingered in English memories long enough to find its way into the recollections of Gladstone's secretary Sir Algernon West. A young Englishman rashly undertook to face a French duellist of the more brutal sort in what was known as a contest *à la barrière*. A rope was stretched between the two men, and they walked towards it, each free to choose his moment. The Englishman impetuously fired at once, missed, and walked on steadily to the rope. 'Pauvre jeune homme, je plains ta mère', said his antagonist, and shot him through the heart.[40]

The prolonged conflict with Napoleon, a despot, but still, as he proclaimed, the heir of the Revolution, accentuated all Europe's con-servatism, not least in the two countries that did most to overthrow him, tsarist Russia and oligarchic Britain. After his fall, when 'kings crept out again to feel the sun', they could be expected to look sym-pathetically on a custom so dear to so many of their adherents, as Charles II did in England after the Restoration. Duelling could be one means of stiffening the morale and advertising the determination of the aristocracy to reassert itself; in particular, that of its military wing, the officer-corps of Europe. Everywhere patriotism had been fanned, armies had established themselves as, more than ever before, admired national institutions, and civilians could find their duelling more infectious.

The officer was the nation's defender and champion. He might too easily come to think himself its master. There had been a long period during which armies were unpopular, everywhere deservedly among common people, in England among Tories because of memories of Cromwell and his major-generals. England in fact suffered least from the incubus, partly because the wider distribution there of the 'privileges of the gentleman' meant that the man-at-arms was less at liberty than in many countries to ride roughshod over the civilian. But every officer was apt to feel that as wearer of the king's uniform he personated the king, and must not permit his sovereign to suffer any slight. He could not, of course, fight a man of inferior social status; he might not object to kicking him. In some lands, like Spain with its *fuero militar*, he was sheltered by being amenable only to army rules and tribunals. After Spain's defeat in the war of 1898 with the USA some officers broke into the premises of a newspaper which ventured to find fault with the army's performance;[41] out of the duellist's 'honour' had sprouted the

---

[40] West, 47–8. Episodes of that time in Lever's novel *Harry Lorrequer* were taken from actual events (Preface to revised edn., 1872).

[41] J. C. Ullman, *The Tragic Week* (Harvard, 1968), 24.

sacred honour of the army, outraged by the mildest criticism. In
Germany as in Spain, or Japan, the army became a state within the
state. 'The institution of the duel was the sharp reminder of this group
independence and power.'[42] An officer corps could thus form an élite
of aristocracy, not numbering many of the highest titles or fortunes,
but exercising the strongest claim to respect, or fear, and the strength
to uphold class ascendancy and the rights of property in general.

In 1814 a book by a romantically conservative French aristocrat
expounded the view that the true national character had been at its
best in the Middle Ages, and argued against any fettering of the duel.[43]
Everything Gothic had been out of fashion in the eighteenth century,
but the Romantic movement had a strong medievalizing vein, with a
naïve admiration for feudal chivalry. Like the religious revival nourished by the long wars, it was a reaction against the cult of Reason;
partly against its narrowness, so that romanticism could be in some
ways a supplement to enlightenment, though in others its negation.
Enlightenment stood for cautious, piecemeal adaptation to a changing
world; after the Revolution those most eager for change, with ardent
youth in the vanguard, were not content with gradualness, but wanted
a new heaven and earth on the spot, though they might be not at all
sure in what direction to look for it. Europe was moving backwards as
well as forwards. Past as well as future can be given a bright coat of
paint, in contrast with a dreary present; and on this side romanticism
could be an ally of aristocracy, and endorse its claim to stand for higher
things than money-grubbing. Aristocracy was entering on its final
phase, before the later nineteenth-century submergence in plutocracy.

Romanticism brought with it too a kind of existentialist preoccupation with experience, sensation, a fondness for intensities of
emotion, even something like an infatuation with fantasies of death.
Whisperings of fate, individualism with its sharpened self-consciousness,
admiration of self-exposure to danger, longing for ideals to serve, as
knights of old served their mistresses—all helped to make the duel a
perfect meeting-point of romanticism and conservatism. It fed also on
a new idealizing of love, in place of the triviality to which amorous
passion had been reduced, and it could seem quite natural once more
for men to fight over women. In Russia duelling, so sternly prohibited
by Peter the Great, was in fashion under Alexander I, who in his later,
reactionary days cherished sundry mystico-chivalric whimsies. At the
Congress of Vienna which drew up the 1815 peace-treaty he and
Metternich, the Austrian chancellor, are said to have wanted to fight

---

[42] Vagts, 69–70.
[43] Comte de Montlosier, cited by M. S. Anderson, *Historians and Eighteenth-century Europe 1715–1789* (Oxford, 1979), 10.

a duel, not about the territorial rivalries that almost plunged Europe back into war, but about a lady.

Duelling had the further, unpremeditated advantage that it might help to wean some sections of the middle classes away from radicalism, and bring them under the social sway of the élite. Thermidor had shown the French bourgeoisie, or a part of it, ready as in former days to play the sedulous ape, and take over some of its forerunner's habits. Its chief beneficiaries were speculators profiting by the windfall gains to be got from the immense quantities of land confiscated from the Church and other owners. As always, land-buying brought bourgeois investors closer to the old landed nobility—though all landowning was now being commercialized—while industrialization, the legitimate sequel to a bourgeois revolution, was retarded by half a century.

All revolutions are premature, in the sense of taking place before the class they are to benefit is mature, and 1789 was a 'bourgeois revolution' without a solid enough bourgeoisie to take command. This makes it easier to comprehend Marx's aphorism, one of very far-reaching application (to England, for instance, as well as to France), that 'Bourgeois society reproduces in its own form everything against which it had fought in feudal or absolutist form.[44] Again the ambivalence of the bourgeois about his predecessor was showing itself. He hated the aristocrat, but admired aristocracy, seeing in it—largely though not altogether bemused by its surface airs and graces—a higher, richer mode of being than his own. Goethe's young middle-class hero Wilhelm Meister, full like his creator of cultural aspirations, ponders on this, and wishes he had been born into the nobility and so been better able to escape one-sidedness, or defective harmony of personality.[45]

To the common run of a prospering middle class, the kind of emancipation or enlargement craved by the bourgeois soul always seemed attainable far more easily by imitation than by independent striving, such as Puritanism, for example, once inculcated. As his biographer Morley wrote, Cobden set out to inspire his fellow businessmen of Lancashire with visions of their own, but was driven to conclude that they 'seem only to desire riches that they may be enabled to prostrate themselves at the foot of feudalism'.[46] His friend Bright the Quaker was outraged by a 'pious banker' he met in the north of England who believed that the Corn Laws must be kept up and the poor kept hungry because the vital thing was to 'maintain the hereditary aristocracy'.[47]

[44] *Theories of Surplus Value*, English edn. by G. A. Bonner and E. Burns (London, 1951), 176. Much of *The Eighteenth Brumaire of Louis Bonaparte* (1852) might be called an expansion on this theme.
[45] *Wilhelm Meister* (1795–6), Bk. 5, chap. 3.
[46] John Morley, *The Life of Richard Cobden* (London, 1881), ii. 482.
[47] John Bright, *Selected Speeches*, Everyman edn., (London, 1907), 257.

A short cut, if a crooked one, to the aristocratic garden of perfection was to take up duelling, or if not actively then at least to view it with approval. To the middle classes the duel had been objectionable as a privilege of those above them; now there was nothing to exclude them, and bourgeois France could adopt it from the old ruling class much as it continued the aggressive foreign policies of the old monarchy. Duelling could percolate to humbler strata than the *haute bourgeoisie*. 'We understand', Carlyle wrote at the end of his history of the Revolution, 'all Frenchmen have the "right of duel"; the Hackney-coachman with the Peer, if insult be given! such is the law of Public Opinion. Equality at least in death!'[48]

After the restoration of the Bourbon monarchy in France there were frequent collisions between royalists and Bonapartist or other malcontents, often half-pay officers. One poor ex-officer acted as second to Stendhal's plebeian hero Julien, when he resolved to have it out with a M. de Beauvoisis whom he believed to have insulted him in a café: in reality the offender was that gentleman's coachman, who gave Julien a card of his master's. Leaving the house after learning this, Julien ran into the man and tried to chastise him, which was enough for Beauvoisis to consider ground for a duel. They drove off together to pick up a friend of his, who guided them to a quiet spot, Julien all the time admiring their elegance and easy unconcerned conversation. The contest was over in a moment: a wound in his arm was bound up, and he was seen home by his courteous opponent, who soon became a friend or patron. 'Mon dieu!' he was saying to himself on the return journey, 'un duel, n'est-ce que ça!'[49]

In Germany the progressive, mostly middle-class student societies were before long suppressed, and the older snob type revived.[50] Among the nurselings of this university life were Marx, with his youthful duel, and Engels, who at twenty wrote to a friend, in his strain of comic exuberance: 'I am now fencing furiously and will soon hack you all to pieces. I have had two duels here in the last few weeks', and given the second fellow 'a real beauty above the brow.'[51] In another letter of those days Engels mentions a pair of noisy little boys he knew at Bremen. 'The other day they started dancing on the linen chests, each armed with a gun and a sword; they challenged each other to a duel.'[52]

The years after Waterloo, when the Holy Alliance of reactionary governments tried to make Europe a well-drilled prison, were in spite

[48] Carlyle, *French Revolution*, final chap.
[49] Stendhal, *Le Rouge et le Noir* (1830), Bk. 2, chap. 6.
[50] Samuel and Hinton, 119.
[51] *Letters of the Young Engels 1838–1845* (Moscow, 1976), 181 (1841).
[52] Ibid. 41 (1838).

of it a stormy time of economic change, social unrest, political tension. Middle-class liberalism wrestled with autocracy and repression; it often had nationalist movements for partners, since a large part of Europe had been left by the Congress of Vienna under foreign rule after the powerful stimulus given to national feeling by the Napoleonic wars. It could count on backing from the industrial bourgeoisie. In its youth this class, growing up first in Britain, had a far more intransigent faith in its own ways and ideas than the older species of capitalism, mercantile or financial, continuing side by side with it, and as always finding it quite natural to gravitate towards aristocracy.

But industry had a two-edged effect, because employers felt at least as much antagonism towards the new working class as towards the old ruling class, and fear of it would eventually turn liberalism into conservatism. In the meantime the landed aristocracy, particularly in England, could best hold on to its position by posing as protector of the unwarlike mill-owner against the spectre of social revolt. For this it had to maintain a martial aspect, fortified by its hold on the army, and the prestige it had earned by its dogged resistance to Napoleon. Duelling could be a reminder to all that the master-hand was still ready on the trigger. 'Any elite', Pareto wrote, 'which is not prepared to join in battle to defend its positions is in full decadence' —like the French *noblesse* of the eighteenth century, softened by 'sensibility'. He saw the same ailment creeping into aristocracy in his own day.[53]

The revolutions of 1848, though all were defeated, gave the whole European pattern a shaking up. Industry, science, modernity were spreading everywhere now, quickest in Britain, and there by mid-century, with social crisis left behind, the duel was extinct. Fine points of 'honour' wilted in the climate of cotton-mill and Stock Exchange, and pecuniary satisfaction was preferred to that of the pistol: damages obtainable from the courts for libel, or wife-enticement, or breach of promise. In France the duel lingered on, but in the later part of the century its character was changing; after 1789 it could not, after all, shake off for long a degree of unreality or attitudinizing, and it tended now to decline into a stunt, serving to get a politician's or a journalist's name into the papers. For such purposes it welcomed publicity, and might attract a gallery of appreciative spectators.

In its more serious meaning the duel was retreating from its western cradle to its haunts further east, with the armies always its chief practitioners. In modern conditions it is the army, Durkheim wrote, that 'most recalls the structure of lower societies', as 'a massive, compact

[53] Pareto, ed. Finer, 136.

group providing a rigid setting for the individual'.[54] In Germany and in the Habsburg empire and Russia duelling went on compulsively. Human beings cannot be entirely mechanized, and no doubt the calls of honour might be comfortably vague at times, and individuals comfortably sluggish about responding to them, like Turgenev's character who wonders whether he is bound to demand satisfaction for something, decides that he is not, and sets his mind at rest by stuffing himself at the café with bread and butter.[55]

As the nineteenth century wore on, tension between the requirements of the duel and the moral consciousness of Europe intensified; but this aided the duel to extend its hold on the European imagination, as a theme for writers and artists who found in it a certain archetypal relevance to the human condition. Here again there was rebirth, after a tendency in the eighteenth century towards desiccation. As the social relations that gave birth to the duel withered, its cultural accompaniments had also shown signs of drying up. They too were survivals from an earlier day, like the stilted tragedies in verse kept up in eighteenth-century France and England in deference to aristocratic taste. Romantic literature was a far livelier vehicle, and the duel was an all the more eligible subject because fiction and drama were so largely concerned with high life, where the duel was most at home. Here is one of many indications of how keen a curiosity the middle classes, which provided most of the readers and audiences, felt about the contours of life among those above them. A good many novels after 1815, when so many British families had members who had served in the Peninsula, were written by military men, who could be relied on not to neglect the story-telling value of the duel.

John Pettie painted an old-time sword and dagger fight. A motif that attracted more than one artist was a duel arising from a masked ball, with the combatants still in their fancy dress. A more realistic drawing of the 1820s by Cruikshank showed two men just after firing, one wounded, the top-hatted seconds hurrying towards him, a waiting carriage in the rear under the trees. In the opera it was a conventional motif always ready to be drawn on, tragedy reduced to a neat stylized form. Music could lend it wings, and in Russia duelling was still active when music was having its grand efflorescence. Rossini in his opera founded on Scott's *Lady of the Lake*, Offenbach in *Hoffmann*, found it a rewarding asset; so did Verdi, in *La Traviata*, and more theatrically in *La Forza del Destino*, with Alvaro, mortally wounded by the hermit he has compelled to fight him, begging to be shriven by his enemy.

Families with means, in countries like France or Spain, were always

[54] Durkheim, 234.
[55] Turgenev, *Smoke* (1867), chap. 19.

ready to buy their sons off from military service. With the propertied, class has usually counted more than nation, and they do not seem to have been nearly so eager to restrain their sons from fighting duels. Nor do women. 'There is too much reason', an English critic of duelling lamented, 'to fear that some young men think it a feather in their cap, with the female sex especially, to have fought a duel.'[56] A rosy glance from the fair sex must have been part of the reward that innumerable duellists looked forward to, like knights in tournaments long before them, and the exalting of the military virtues during the quarter-century of European warfare before 1815 added to its attraction. Clearly this would give women the power to put a damper on the duel, by withdrawing their tribute; and if Tolstoy was right, 'It is women who form public opinion, and in our day women are particularly powerful.'[57] It would be agreeable to think that with their status and education improving, their pleasure at men fighting, about them particularly, would diminish.

Vanity and inertia stood in the way, and on the whole it would seem that upper-class women, now as earlier, seldom found it hard to accept the conventional behaviour of men of their class. In Lermontov's novel the young lady's mother sees no objection to her marrying the man who has just killed an acquaintance of theirs; true, this other man, spiteful from disappointment, had been speaking ill of her daughter. Jerome K. Jerome when staying at Freiburg found that football, introduced by his secretary as a substitute for the *Mensur*, caught on quickly with young men, but the young women who liked to see an admirer's face smothered in bandages 'shrank from him when he came back from the football field dirty and dishevelled'.[58] A face disfigured by scars was a passport to a good marriage, with a middle-class heiress very likely; a comment on both bourgeois and feminine susceptibility, and the wealthier middle class's lack of any firm tenets or principles. As always, female snobbery in this class helped to fuel its desire, so much a part of European history, to assimilate itself to aristocracy.

A woman might have good reason for welcoming the bullet that put an end to a man in her life. A German gentleman, accused by a notorious bully of rudeness because he was smoking in the presence of ladies, in the resulting duel by some fluke shot the ruffian dead. He received a grateful letter from his wife or mistress.[59] There must have been some women who took steps to procure such an outcome, for a variety of motives, oftener to be found in fiction than in recorded fact,

---

[56] 'Nimrod', 351.
[57] Tolstoy, *What Then Must We Do?* (1886; trans. A. Maude, London, 1934), 350.
[58] Jerome, 156–7.
[59] Whitman, 77–9.

but perhaps not much oftener than in the invisible history of the unrecorded. Or, at any rate, suspicions of plots against them may have often occurred to men uneasily conscious of too much trifling with women, just as those conscious of exploiting the masses have lived in fear of reprisals. In a melodramatic Bulwer-Lytton novel of high and low life, the young Englishman Pelham becomes an admirer of a French duchess. Having to take refuge one day, on her husband's approach, in a room off her boudoir, he lights on a wig and false teeth. Furious, she bribes a Frenchman, with a promise of her favours, to pick a quarrel with him and kill him. Pelham makes light of their pistol-fight in the Bois de Boulogne, from which of course he emerges victorious: a French duel is a casual incident, soon over, whereas in England it is 'a thing of state and solemnity—long faces—early rising—and will-making'.[60]

In Kuprin's novel the junior lieutenant Romashov has fallen in love with the charming vampire Shurochka, in spite of hearing her talk far from charmingly of a recent army duel to the death before a crowd of spectators, including ladies and a photographer. She thought this bad, not because it was the man insulted who died in agony, but because the publicity would help the puling, sentimental critics of duelling, a necessary institution in her opinion for an army with such a riff-raff of officers as the Russian. At the end, when Romashov has resolved to quit his detestable profession rather than fight her husband, she comes in secret to persuade him to fight—assuring him that neither need come to harm—because a duel will be good for the army career of her husband, whom she looks down on but is ambitious for. Romashov is disgusted, but consents, and lets himself be killed, without pulling his trigger.[61]

'But what would you?' an older woman in another Russian story asks, after telling of a fatal duel. 'Man is not master of sin.' This worthy woman of modest birth, wife of the commandant of a remote garrison, expresses a feeling that many women must have shared, resigned acceptance of men's wildness or folly. Her daughter, whom two officers are fighting about, protests more energetically. 'What strange beings men are! For a single word, which they would probably forget a week afterwards, they are ready to murder each other and to sacrifice not only their life, but their conscience', and the happiness of those they love.[62] Pushkin, the writer of these words, was one of many men who risked or lost their lives for the sake of women unworthy of them. The aptest of all comments on duels like theirs might be Jerome's anecdote

---

[60] E. G. Bulwer-Lytton (Lord Lytton), *Pelham, or Adventures of a Gentleman* (London, 1828), chaps. 23, 27, 28.
[61] Kuprin, 57–8, 341 ff.
[62] Pushkin, 'The Captain's Daughter', chaps. 3–4 (in *Prose Tales*).

(related in support of his view that men are better-looking than women) of a young officer at Munich going to a ball in his sister's clothes, and two fellow-officers as a result meeting next morning in the Englische Garten, and one being killed.[63]

Easier to respect than the woman who provoked a quarrel for selfish purposes was the occasional one who did her own fighting. Female bouts occasioned by jealousy persisted into the nineteenth century. In 1828 there was a pistol fight between a French and a German woman, both in love with a painter;[64] whether he or his pictures deserved their devotion is not said. But by now there were beginning to be women with better motives than jealousy. When Bonaparte was in Egypt he ordered a surgeon who showed fear of catching the plague to be dressed in female attire and paraded through Alexandria on a donkey. A naval captain's wife, 'an athletic beauty of twenty-seven', resented this as an affront to her sex, and declared that she would like to fight the general.[65]

Under the *nom de guerre* 'James Miranda Stuart Barry' a woman born in 1795 is said to have studied medicine at Edinburgh disguised as a man, served abroad as an army surgeon, and faced courts-martial for fighting duels with men who mocked her low stature and high-pitched voice.[66] When feminism was making its claims heard more openly, one sometimes raised was that, instead of having to rely on male defenders, women should be emancipated enough to fight their own battles. Not surprisingly, it was in high society, from families inured to the code of honour, that two champions came forward to vindicate this right most dramatically, when a Princess Metternich and a Countess Kilmannsegg, who had disagreed about arrangements for an exhibition at Vienna, engaged in a duel; each came off slightly the worse.

[63] Jerome, 144.
[64] Steinmetz, ii. 125-6; and see Baldick, chap. 11: 'Women Duellists'.
[65] J. C. Herold, *Bonaparte in Egypt* (London, 1962), 209.
[66] M. Alic, *Hypatia's Heritage* (London, 1986), 105-6.

12

Britain: The Final Decades

[The Revd. Dr Tennyson, the poet's dipsomaniac father,] kept a large knife and a loaded gun in his room, and he was with difficulty persuaded not to fire the gun through the kitchen window ... In a kind of waking delirium Dr Tennyson began even wilder imaginings than before; at one point he was convinced that he was about to have a duel with Mr Vane, a friend of his father's.

R. B. Martin, *Tennyson, The Unquiet Heart* (Oxford, 1983), 64–6.

TRIAL by battle was thought worth abolishing in England by an Act of 1819, after Abraham Thornton saved his neck by throwing down a gauntlet that no one cared to pick up. On duelling the state of the law, or rather of the law-courts, remained confused. It was forbidden, but the gap between ban and enforcement was as wide as before, and judgements and penalties, when there were any, were puzzlingly arbitrary. Chief Justice Abbott, ruling on a moonlight fatality in 1821 at Chalk Farm, after an inquest had found wilful murder, pointed out that a sudden killing in hot blood might be deemed only manslaughter, but a duel was a premeditated crime. None the less the jury found J. H. Christie not guilty. Other juries were not sorry to reduce murder to manslaughter. If there was no grave injury, justice was usually able to close its eyes altogether.

After all, duelling was a heritage of the upper classes, and of the very highest of them among the rest. In 1822 the Duke of Bedford made a forcible speech in favour of parliamentary reform, and taxed the Duke of Buckingham at a county meeting with political jobbery: this drew a challenge, and led to a duel which, as the radical Scottish landowner Kinloch observed, 'terminated without any ducal blood being shed'.[1] In fact his Grace of Bedford, it was said, fired in the air, and his Grace of Buckingham not at all; this perhaps sole encounter between a brace of English dukes was less thrilling than it ought to have been. A challenger or his second could 'post' a man who declined to fight, by publicly accusing him of cowardice, without fear of any consequences. Duels were reported in the press with monotonous frequency, no fewer than fourteen for example in *The Times* in the last three months of 1835.

[1] Tennant, 192.

'No country is at present more addicted to duelling', Bosquett wrote in 1817.[2] Hyde Park was too populous to be a meeting-place now, and some other hallowed haunts had been built over. Chalk Farm was a magnet; Hampstead Heath was convenient, and in the 1830s and 1840s Wimbledon Common came into favour.

Regency habits of 'hard living' survived in the army when elsewhere they were being abandoned.[3] So powerful an institution can prolong the mentality of one age into another, and England was a medley of eras as well as of regions. Young officers were not intellectual, the army's historian confesses: 'sport, horseflesh and women' were their interests, and from time to time 'they varied the monotony by quarrelling and fighting duels, generally after some foolish controversy over their cups'.[4] Duelling allowed youth to dramatize itself and its sillinesses, as youth has always hankered to do (with its heroisms as well), spinning out the 'let's pretend' games of childhood. Army regulations were moreover unequivocal about an officer's obligation to 'defend his honour', which was at the same time the honour of his regiment. Captain Macnamara of the navy, who killed an army man in 1803, won acquittal by pleading an officer's need to sustain his character for courage.[5] It cannot have been thought equally praiseworthy for officers to take on civilians. Yet in 1818 when a major and one of his seconds were tried for murder, the victim being a young civilian, they were convicted of no more than manslaughter, and let off with three months.[6]

It was a concomitant of economic progress, in England ahead of other countries, that so many offences could be, as in primitive times, estimated in cash terms, and redeemed by payment. In many ways this was acceptable enough, as common sense. The sticking-point came oftenest where family honour, a wife's seduction, was concerned. Damages might be liberal;[7] but to be content with cash might be said to imply that a wife was a piece of property, which had lost part of its value; though this was scarcely the reason why sticklers felt it demeaning to pocket money, and an injury to their honour with it. He had never known a self-respecting man, Bosquett affirmed, willing to sue for damages against a seducer. 'For these and such like offences the law can make no adequate retribution.'[8] To the aristocratic mind, payment

---

[2] Bosquett, 85. Cf. Howard, 54–5, on young gentlemen learning by the age of 20 to keep Joe Manton pistols and send friends to demand explanations.

[3] W. S. Hamer, *The British Army, Civil–Military Relations 1885–1905* (Oxford, 1970), 82.

[4] J. W. Fortescue, *A History of the British Army*, x (London, 1923), 37.

[5] Baldick, 98.

[6] Steinmetz, ii. 240.

[7] In the celebrated Norton case in 1836 the sum demanded was £10,000; see I. O'Faolain and L. Martines (edd.), *Not in God's Image* (London, 1973), 334 ff.

[8] Bosquett, 17.

was a bribe to keep quiet, by contrast with the nobler act of inflicting or endeavouring to inflict punishment. Whether to be called out as a philanderer would be felt as a disgrace, might be another question. Duelling was credited with inducing men to be polite or discreet, rather than to be virtuous. Of course the seducer might be a true romantic lover, and the husband an unpleasant beast.

There was no legal redress for debts of honour. A notorious case leading to a duel arose from Lord George Bentinck, the grand panjandrum of the turf, accusing George Osbaldistone of cheating in a race he rode in: Bentinck refused to pay a debt of £200, and recriminations brought on a challenge. Osbaldistone seems to have had difficulty in enlisting a second, because as a crack shot he was expected to hit his target; apparently men shrank more from offending the ducal house of Portland than from breaking the law. The fight proved oddly innocuous; the seconds may have agreed to leave the pistols unloaded.[9] What is interesting in the tangled story is that it brought to light some of the hanky-panky indulged in by gentlemen careful of their honour but inclined to spend beyond their means, and full of crafty tricks, invented by them or their stablemen and trainers, for making money out of the sport of kings. The noble racketeers of Epsom or Newmarket were counterparts of the sharks gorging themselves in the City; both species would make a contribution to England's united plutocracy, whose constituent elements were drawn together far more by their worse than by their better qualities.

In the mean time an aristocracy 'not very different from that of the eighteenth century' still reigned, little shaken by the first Reform Act and buttressed not only by the House of Lords but by army, civil service, judiciary, and church.[10] All these, and the equally unreformed universities, and the empire, were increasingly staffed by scions of the gentry making their way into the professions, but priding themselves on adhering to the canons of gentility. Landed influence thus benefited, and the persistence of duelling was aided, by the continued sway of primogeniture in the transmission of landed property, which pushed so many cadets into other walks of life. Many they consorted with there were only too ready to imitate them. Among writers, some were born under the same stars; others, and the swelling cohorts of 'gentlemen of the press', were eager to claim a place beside them, like a Hindu caste-group floating itself up the scale. Doubtless many men socially not disqualified from duelling never dreamed of pulling a trigger. All the same, qualifications, always exceptionally elastic in England, were now becoming still more so. In a perceptive scrutiny of the English character,

[9] J. Welcome, *Infamous Occasions ... Some Famous Racing Scandals* (London, 1980), chap. 2.
[10] Guttsman, 35, 111–12.

Coleridge dwelt on the wide uniformity of dress and manners, and the effect of this 'absence of any cognizable marks of distinction' in making each class or stratum 'more reserved and jealous', and giving Englishmen the 'haughtiness' and stand-offishness so much disliked by foreigners.[11]

Duelling could cast its spell wide enough to appeal, in fantasy at least, to clerks, shop-assistants, and the generality of the lower-middle classes, the same who were to derive so much vicarious enjoyment from the empire and the thought of Britannia ruling the world. Readiness to admire or mimic the duellist was one aspect of the British snobbery that has done so much to give Toryism its astonishingly long life. Dickens invented a scene of young fellows behaving in what they think the proper style for gentlemen, a social evening in the course of which Miss Sophy tries to incite Dick Swiveller into a declaration by making him jealous of Mr Cheggs. Dick retreating into a corner, the ruffled Cheggs follows him. 'Have the goodness to smile, sir, in order that we may not be suspected.—Did you speak to me, sir?' Dick looks him up and down superciliously. 'No, sir, I didn't.' Question and answer having been repeated, they cap the 'tremendous dialogue' with menacing frowns.[12]

Such comic scenes were not altogether fanciful. Shortly before this novel was written, in August 1838, two hempen homespuns met at Wimbledon to fight about a girl. Mirfin was killed, Eliot fled; the former's second got a year's hard labour. A good many such fights may have taken place, without bloody endings, among them some resembling the one in Thomas Hood's poem 'The Duel, a serious ballad'. There Mr Clay and Mr Bray were about to fight over a lady, when

> Fear made them tremble so they found
> They both were shaking hands—

and they agreed to fire in the air, as all good duellists ought to.

There was besides, to keep duelling green in England, the example of foreign countries, and the invigorating influence of Scots and Irishmen; this was felt especially in the army, many of whose units spent very long periods overseas where other activities were often lacking, but it was felt also in the political arena. In Scotland, with its surviving clan or kinship ties, anyone who cared to could boast of being at least tenth cousin to some petty laird, and hence of being a possessor of Honour, that second soul of the gentleman. Political wranglings may have grown more embittered because the country was sliding further

---

[11] Coleridge, *The Friend* (2nd edn., rev., 1818), Sect. 3, Essay 5.
[12] *The Old Curiosity Shop* (1841), chap. 8.

towards absorption into England, and the barkings and bickerings of its factions were increasingly parochial and irresponsible. They set a good many bullets flying, not always with much accuracy. At Ravelston, on the edge of Edinburgh, in 1829 there was a meeting between a pair of fiery editors, Mr Maclaren of the *Scotsman* and Mr Brown of the *Caledonian Mercury*, following 'a wordy warfare in the columns of these papers'. A harmless exchange of shots took place, and then 'the seconds declared that the matter should not be carried further'.[13]

A much greater stir had been caused a few years previously by the death of Sir Alexander Boswell, son of James the so frequent near-duellist, who inherited his fondness for printed squibs and snipings. For some time one of the targets of scurrilous Tory abuse had been James Stuart of Dunearn, who was charged, among other sins, with refusing satisfaction to a Tory journalist. Stuart discovered that some anonymous attacks on him were the work of Sir Alexander, to whom he was related and with whom he had been on good terms. Boswell had been an MP, and got a bill passed repealing two old Scottish statutes against duelling. More recently he had been a zealous champion of authority against the people, as commander of the Ayrshire Yeomanry Cavalry during the unrest and attempted insurrection of 1820. He was also a writer of humorous songs in the vernacular, some of them current today.[14]

Stuart challenged him, received no apology, and met him at Auchtertool in Fife on 22 March 1822. He had scarcely ever touched a pistol, but luck often counted more than skill, and his second shot inflicted a mortal wound. It often proved good policy to lie low for a while and let the dust settle; Stuart went abroad briefly, and then returned and surrendered to justice. 'No Scotch trial in my time', wrote the celebrated judge Lord Cockburn, 'excited such interest', and Stuart's conduct had been so blameless, 'and the necessity, according to the existing law of society, of acting as he did' was so clear, that immediate acquittal was the only possible verdict.[15]

One thought that sustained James Boswell on the edge of a duel was that he had heard Dr Johnson defend duelling as not anti-Christian.[16] We may wonder how Johnson would have felt if his young disciple had fought and fallen, or if he could have known of the fate in store for Boswell's son—or how this son felt if he ever read the diary pages about his father's ordeals.

[13] W. M. Gilbert, *Edinburgh in the Nineteenth Century* (Edinburgh, 1901), 92.

[14] P. B. Ellis and S. Mac A'Ghobhainn, *The Scottish Insurrection of 1820* (London, 1970), *passim*.

[15] Lord Cockburn, *Memorials of his Time* (abr. edn., Edinburgh, 1945), 226–8. On the Tory journalism of that envenomed time, cf. R. M. W. Cowan, *The Newspaper in Scotland ... 1815–1860* (Glasgow, 1946), 63–6. See also Karl Miller, *Cockburn's Millennium* (London, 1975), 33–4.

[16] Boswell, *The Ominous Years*, 13.

Ireland was still, observed Stendhal (who noted also its scandalous misgovernment by England), 'in that curious state ... when people who are breakfasting cheerfully with one another may meet two hours later on the field of battle'.[17] A towering figure among men of the true Hibernian breed was the redoubtable Richard Martin, 'King of Connemara', where his family owned vast tracts, and friend of his brother-monarch George IV. He had come through 'such a prodigious number of duels that he earned the nickname of "Hair-trigger Dick" ';[18] he also earned a visit from Maria Edgeworth and a place in her novel *Harry Ormond*. A niche close to him may be claimed for the father who urged his young son into a challenge, after a steeplechase dispute in 1841, loaded the pistols, and saw the boy shot.[19] This travesty of Roman parental fortitude is not the only case of the sort. A higher version, in one of Scott's tales of the Border, concerns an old clan head who dies of grief after watching his son defeated and killed in single fight by an English champion—grief not for his 'degenerate boy', but for the loss of the treasured family sword.[20]

In politics as in other departments Ireland furnishes some of the choicest examples. In 1807, when there was keen rivalry in a Wexford county election, John Colclough the Whig was shot dead by William Alcock the Tory, 'for trespass in canvassing the freeholders of an elderly widow'.[21] Hundreds gathered to watch the contest between this pair of old friends, among them several magistrates. However, as the whole business was 'reckoned fair in Ireland, it created no sensation', wrote Arthur Wellesley, newly back in Dublin as chief secretary.[22] Judge and jury were unanimous against any conviction, and another Tory candidate was found, who triumphed at the poll. In Lover's novel *Handy Andy* (chapter 19), when a weak sheriff fails to prevent an election duel, the author comments that any interference at such a time would have been thought 'a very impertinent, unjustifiable, and discourteous interference with the private pleasures and privileges of gentlemen'.

Such behaviour can have done nothing to deter the 'faction-fighting' rampant among the peasantry in the first half of the century, a sort of collective duelling between bands of men armed with heavy sticks, sometimes nursing memories or legends of clan or district feuds of long ago. 'They went out to prove their manhood and their skill in battle',[23] just as gentlemen did. Hard knocks were plentiful, deaths not rare. As

[17] Stendhal, *Love*, 149–50.
[18] Maxwell, 56.
[19] Steinmetz, ii. 362.
[20] 'Death of the Laird's Jock'.
[21] Bolton, 38; see also Barrington, i. 298 ff.
[22] Elizabeth Longford, *Wellington: The Years of the Sword* (London, 1969), 130.
[23] P. O'Donnell, *The Irish Faction Fighters* (Dublin, 1975), 47.

with duelling, magistrates were sometimes ready to wink at the practice, while the Catholic church denounced it. Both exercises came to an end about the same time.

Some of the dispossessed Catholic landed families had kept up the duelling habit; their frequent links with service in Catholic armies abroad must have confirmed it. Others were joining in now, as in England. Middle-class Catholics shared a too prevalent disdain for 'trade', and a desire to escape from useful exertion into landowning or law. They like others could buy their way into genteel acceptance; to shoot their way might be a quickener. Irrespective of Catholic or Protestant, men of position were not always prepared to oblige an upstart. Lord Lucan contemptuously refused to fight an agent dismissed from his Mayo estates, who retaliated by going about with a big stick and threatening to give his lordship a cudgelling.[24]

A more valuable pair of lives were at risk when a poet and his critic locked horns in 1806. Thomas Moore, son of a Catholic grocer and wafted into the drawing-room, like Burns, by his poems, may have felt that he was defending the dignity of the native Muse as well as his own when he called out Francis Jeffrey, of the *Edinburgh Review*, in reply to an acerbic criticism of these poems. In his memoirs he owned to 'a certain *Irish* predilection for such encounters, or ... a dash of vanity'.[25] A meeting at Chalk Farm was duly arranged, and Moore, who had hardly seen a pistol before, laid in a stock of powder and bullets at a shop in Bond Street. He and Jeffrey were having a friendly chat while the seconds loaded, an operation that seemed to take an inordinately long time, when the police, who had been tipped off by someone, rushed out from behind the trees.

The pair were conducted to Bow Street, and bound over. Moore says he felt that he 'would rather have lost a limb', but worse was to follow, because a humorous Irish newspaperman altered 'bullets' to 'pellets', and this got into all the journals. 'Were you not amused with the duel between Jeffrys [*sic*] and Anacreon Moore', Palmerston wrote to his friend Sulivan, 'loading their pistols with pellets of paper was an excellent idea.'[26] Rogers, the literary banker, negotiated 'a treaty of peace' between the foes; they met at his house, Jeffrey gave 'the most satisfactory apologies', and they became good friends. Rogers was 'playing his favourite part of peace-maker',[27] not one where he had many competitors. Most writers of the time, apart from Byron and

[24] Woodham-Smith, 105–6.
[25] *Memoirs, Journal, and Correspondence of Thomas Moore* (London, 1853–6), i. 199 ff.
[26] Palmerston, 66.
[27] P. W. Clayden, *Rogers and his Contemporaries* (London, 1889), i. 41–2.

Shelley, came from the middle classes; Rogers had the further virtue of being the son of a Dissenting businessman.

Irish nationalism was a rising tide. Underlying it was the discontent of the peasantry, and attacks on landlords or their bailiffs came to be one feature of the agrarian unrest. The spectacle of gentlefolk so ready to shoot one another might well encourage a feeling that there could be no harm in others shooting them. On the political side the Irish movement was led by Daniel O'Connnell, whose duel in 1815, when he fatally wounded D'Esterre, was one of its most dramatic episodes. He had been lambasting the corruptions and jobberies of the Dublin Corporation, and it was said that D'Esterre, as a good shot, formerly in the navy, was put up by some members to silence him. 'An extraordinary amount of publicity and delay attended the quarrel', says the editor of O'Connell's correspondence, from which it appears that D'Esterre followed him about for a week, between his house in Merion Square and the Courts, flourishing a whip and collecting a crowd of gapers.[28]

In the summer of the same year O'Connell responded to a challenge from the chief secretary for Ireland, Peel, known for his anti-Catholic fervour as 'Orange-Peel', and the target of some of O'Connell's fiercest vituperation. It is of course in its way a tribute to British political manners, compared with most of Europe and all of Asia, that a man high in the government should be obliged to resort to such a means of venting his spleen, instead of simply ordering his heckler's arrest or execution. Because O'Connell had been bound over, and Peel must have felt it judicious to avoid the limelight, a meeting abroad had to be arranged; the police were in time to prevent it, and O'Connell had an exceedingly uncomfortable night journey back from Holyhead to Dublin. 'I lay on the cabin floor as sick as a dog', he wrote to his wife, 'with three gentlemen's legs on my breast and stomach, and the sea water dripping in on my knees and feet.'[29]

This experience may have joined with compunction over D'Esterre's death to keep him from any more fighting. Later on when Lord Alvanley objected to being dubbed 'a bloated buffoon', O'Connell's son offered to deputize for him, probably without his sanction. Alvanley consulted friends, who were divided, the diarist Greville learned; he resolved to accept, and they met that very day in Arlington Street and set off in two hackney coaches. A touch of the ridiculous prefaced their business: an old Irishwoman asked for money as a fee for her attendance, and a Methodist parson, the only other bystander, 'exhorted the combatants in vain to forego their sinful purpose', until Alvanley told him

[28] O'Connell, i. 277 ff.
[29] Ibid. i. 144–5 (30 Sept. 1815).

to mind his own business. At the start a shot may have gone off accidentally; Alvanley's second, to his great though suppressed indignation, foolishly agreed to let the fight go to three exchanges. Morgan's second, in Grenville's opinion, 'acted like a ruffian, and had anything happened he would have been hanged'.[30] In the end no harm was done. That other gossip, Creevey, was strongly critical of Alvanley, who had after all made a political attack on O'Connell and his allies in a speech in the Lords. 'I *know* that this arose from spite', disappointment at failure to get a post he wanted in the royal household. 'Then the publicity he has given to his challenge of O'Connell is against all rules.'[31] Clearly duellists were expected to observe a proper reticence. Morgan declined a later challenge to his father from the young Disraeli, who may have thought that a duel in his *curriculum vitae* would help to make him a shining light of Toryism.

Among dignitaries who felt no need to hide their light under a bushel by going abroad to fight, the most eminent of all was Wellington, when premier in 1829, at the age of sixty. His sparring-partner was the Earl of Winchilsea, who had belaboured him over his—and Peel's—conversion to Catholic emancipation, as apostasy. Since both fired wide, their meeting served little visible purpose, and seemed to reduce 'satisfaction' to a sham. They of course suffered no worse penalty than caricaturists could inflict, like the well-known cartoon by 'Paul Pry', or William Heath. The storms of the first Reform Bill were about to break; at the centre of one of their minor squalls was Tennyson's uncle Charles, Clerk of the Ordnance. He won a heated election at Stamford in May 1831, on the reforming platform, against Lord Thomas Cecil. The defeated candidate complained publicly of his canvassing methods, charging him with hiring gangs of bullies. Goaded by this, and by an anonymous letter taunting him with cowardice, Tennyson called Cecil out, and on a June evening a harmless exchange of shots took place at Wormwood Scrubs. While leaving, they were taken into custody, but the case was dismissed.[32] The aggrieved man had earned only derision, the booby-prize of not a few who ventured on to the field of honour.

There had never ceased to be opposition to the duel, and both Utilitarian thinking, that heir of the eighteenth-century enlightenment, and Evangelicalism, helped to fill its sails. An unusually intelligent young aristocrat, Lord William Bentinck, later governor-general of

---

[30] *The Greville Memoirs: A Journal of the Reigns of King George IV and King William IV*, by Charles C. F. Greville, ed. H. Reeve (London, 1874), iii. 256–7.

[31] *The Creevey Papers: A Selection from the Correspondence and Diaries of the late Thomas Creevey, MP*, ed. Sir H. Maxwell (London, 1912), 646–7.

[32] R. B. Martin, *Tennyson, the Unquiet Heart* (1980; Oxford, 1983), 143–4.

India, when a stripling officer was sensible enough to accept an apology instead of insisting on a combat, because he did not want, he said, to make his 'entrée into public life in the character of a duellist'.[33] Some critics thought the practice wicked, others silly, particularly when imitated by individuals not to the manner born. There may be a hint of this in C. R. Leslie's well-known painting of Monsieur Jourdain fencing with his maid-servant. It may be guessed that some were turning away from duelling because in England, where so many were eligible, it was in danger of becoming vulgarly popular, as it already was in America where everyone was eligible. Perhaps it was beginning to be left to older men, brought up on stricter principles of honour, while some of their juniors were tiring of it; much as Archdeacon Grantley of Barchester was nettled by his son's not wanting to sit lengthily over the wine with him after dinner.

With all this, and a gradual permeation of the atmosphere with ways of thinking generated by economic change, there were symptoms of the duel losing its vitality, and of its apologists being thrown onto the defensive. It was 'quite chimerical', Bosquett stoutly maintained, to suppose that any law could put duelling down. 'It has been a custom from the earliest ages to decide differences and avenge injuries by single combat.' Apologists for war have made copious use of the identical argument. But Bosquett was a man standing between two epochs; another work by him was on 'New Systems and Inventions', for 'the mercantile and maritime world'. In the next breath he declared that judicious seconds could make fighting unnecessary in almost every case.[34] Confessing, with some reluctance he said, to having himself fought four times, and served twenty-five times as a second, he was happy to be able to add that 'life or honour were never lost in my hands'. There should be a court of honour, backed by stern rules, to protect individuals from having to fight without good reason or else undergo 'the dreaded stigma of the censorious world'.[35] A man like Palmerston, politically so aggressive, could discuss the same question of how quarrels should be handled, with much more concern for common sense than for abstract honour.[36]

While duelling was being little by little undermined, there was a growing cult of sport, in the newer and better meaning of the word, games rather than hunting. Boxing found many to extol it, as a more truly British and less unchristian thing than duelling; amateur boxing in particular, as distinct from the pugilism which inherited from

[33] J. Rosselli, *Lord William Bentinck* (London, 1974), 35.
[34] Bosquett, 16.
[35] Ibid. 123–4.
[36] Palmerston, 255 (1833).

professional fencing matches the title of prize-fighting. Upper-class participation was helping to refine a popular pastime. Regency bucks, or 'Corinthians', improving on their eighteenth-century precursors, took lessons from leading exponents like 'Gentleman Jackson', and were proud of their ability to take on any comer, however rough a customer he might be, and 'tap his claret'. The Prince Regent was 'a great patron of this national sport', like his great-uncle Butcher Cumberland, until a boxer he was watching at Brighton lost his life.[37]

Boxing had spread to the public schools. In his memoirs the Earl of Malmesbury, a Foreign Secretary of the 1850s, recalled life at Eton in the early 1820s, when 'the immortal Dr. Keate' held sway. Bouts among the youngsters were so spirited that 'The Windsor and Slough coaches used to stop under the playing-field wall to see these duels'. A 'very desperate one' was won by the younger boxer, destined to lose his life in the storming of the Redan at Sevastopol. In another, 'young Ashley, a most gallant boy', son of Lord Shaftesbury, was killed.[38] It must be this death that occasioned Keate's comment, when informed, that it was regrettable, but his pupils must know how to defend themselves. In the same spirit officers were made aware that they must know how to 'defend their honour'.

To the upper classes boxing could appear a still better thing for the lower classes, weaning them away from worse forms of violence which might some day erupt against their masters; and if the masters went on peppering one another with bullets, this antidote might lose some of its efficacy. It was reported in 1829 that when Wellington and Winchilsea were cocking their guns, some workmen in Battersea Fields came up and recommended them to use their fists instead.[39] A professor of moral philosophy who plumed himself on his proficiency with the gloves was John Wilson, or 'Christopher North'. In one of the *Noctes Ambrosianae*, a series of dialogues mostly by him in *Blackwood's Magazine* between 1822 and 1835, there is a eulogy of boxing, under fixed rules, as an innocent mode of settling disputes.[40]

Mr Pickwick was startled by his cabman's readiness to offer to fight him, but in a general way such pugnacity could be viewed as laudable, and in keeping with England's relatively peaceful record and law-abiding habits. In one of his novels Scott observed that 'the lower orders of London' had always been noted for their love of 'club-law, or fist-law, and for the equity and impartiality with which they see it

[37] Thackeray, *Four Georges*, 125.

[38] Lord Malmesbury, *Memoirs of an Ex-Minister* (Leipzig, 1885), i. 21.

[39] Steinmetz, ii. 342.

[40] *Noctes Ambrosianae* (Edinburgh, 1892), iv. 189 ff. (1834). Among midshipmen, however, boxing seems to have given way to duelling (Howard, p. 317).

administered.[41] If pugilism owed something to aristocratic guidance, it may be a converse truth that duelling owed some part of its well-regulated machinery to awareness on the part of the gentleman that the man in the street had definite, if rough and ready, standards of fair play. A directly political moral is drawn by Captain Barclay, in a work of fiction of 1832. He is eloquent in praise of boxing, as 'a display of manly intrepidity' and many other virtues, and argues that if government suppresses it there will be an end of the common Englishman's 'sense of honour, and spirit, and gallantry'. Fists will give way to knives, and 'the lower orders will become a base rabble of cowards and assassins', who (the real sting in the tail of the argument) will abandon the higher classes, instead of standing by them, should a foreign invasion take place.[42] There is much in the same book in dispraise of duelling.

As criticism of the duel mounted, one line of attack was that it was a practice kept going by a class privileged to break the law. This was the more damaging because the old order was coming under heavy pressure of both middle-class and working-class opinion for many other vices too, like rotten boroughs and sinecures and Corn Laws. For a long time a rooted instinct made Toryism feel that to abandon the time-honoured right to private combat would be a perilous surrender, setting its feet on a slippery slope. But the Reform Act of 1832 meant defeat by the better-off middle classes, and it was soon followed by the rampant Chartism of the workers. It might well seem now that an outpost of aristocracy like duelling was no longer a bulwark, but a source of weakness, a hindrance to the closing of ranks among all the propertied which the times so loudly called for.

In the army, its chief stronghold, there were incidents that did it little credit. The brother of Sir George de Lacy Evans, commander of the British Legion in Spain during the Carlist War of the 1830s, was wounded in a duel in London by a young officer whom he had maligned in Spain, and whose case was sustained by the United Services Club[43]— which could sometimes act as an arbiter or court of honour. A crucial event was the affair in 1840 of Lord Cardigan, a notorious duellist and bully, who took a dislike to an officer in his regiment, provoked him into a challenge, and got him court-martialled and cashiered. Captain Tuckett, lately of the regiment, gave Cardigan his deserts in the press, and drew a challenge from him. At the windmill on Wimbledon Common, Tuckett was wounded by the second shot; Cardigan was

---

[41] *Peveril of the Peak*, chap. 32.

[42] 'Nimrod', 226–7. Cf. the praise of boxing, by comparison with knife or poison, in George Borrow's *The Romany Rye* (London, 1857), App. chap. 8. Chaps. 4–7 of the App. are concerned with English gentility and snobbery.

[43] Beasley, 72, 83.

arrested and, public feeling being aroused, committed to trial.[44] In the House of Lords he had a sympathetic jury; the prosecution managers were also helpful, and Chief Justice Denman had no choice but to direct his acquittal. Denman was no reactionary Tory, but a Broughamite with an active political life behind him.[45] But the obvious miscarriage of justice raised a clamour.

Before the trial Cardigan's counsel, Sir W. Follett, consulted the well-informed diarist and diner-out Croker, for many years Secretary to the Admiralty. They evidently felt that duelling was now on the defensive, and Croker recommended that if it became necessary to 'parry an attack on the general system' Follett should not defend it, but urge that what was needed was more stringent legislation rather than the penalizing of an individual for obeying common custom. He put together some historical notes, though premising that a full picture would be hard to assemble. 'Duels are seldom matters of record.' In the past hundred years six men who reached the premiership had been 'out': Lord Bath, Lord Shelburne, Pitt, Fox, Canning, Wellington; and Peel had twice been a challenger. Croker believed that in recent years there had been a marked decline, and doubted whether more than half a dozen living peers had ever fought.[46]

Opposition to duelling was becoming irresistible. In 1839 Lord Powerscourt, MP for Bath, had to eat humble pie when reproved by the archdeacon and his clergy for taking part in a duel, an act which they refused to condone in any parliamentary character.[47] Not to be outdone, the bishop of London thundered in the House of Lords against 'the barbarous, wicked, and unchristian practice'.[48] An anti-duelling association had been set up in 1810, without much effect; a far stronger one took the field in 1843, and enrolled respected figures willing to serve as arbitrators. A good proportion of members belonged to the services, among them thirty-five generals or admirals.[49] Smaller than some others in Europe, the army had a prestige conferred by its victories over Napoleon, now being continued the length and breadth of Asia. Its officer corps moreover, or at least the top echelons, enjoyed a high social standing. Wellington's generals had been 'a remarkably socially homogeneous group', with numerous affiliations to the peerage.[50] In 1838 when Britain could boast 548 peers, fifty-eight of them held

[44] Woodham-Smith, 67–79.

[45] T. H. Ford, 'The Trial of Lord Cardigan', *History*, 198 (1975).

[46] *The Croker Papers: The Correspondence and Diaries of John Wilson Croker*, ed. L. J. Jennings (London, 1884), ii. 407–8.

[47] Andrew, 432.

[48] Steinmetz, ii. 361.

[49] Vagts, 176.

[50] G. Harris-Jenkins, *The Army in Victorian Society* (London, 1977), 49–50.

commissions, and together with close relatives made up a total of 462, out of 6,173 officers in all on the active list.[51] If the army itself were to show signs of a waning attachment to the duel, the moral repercussion would be great.

There had always been a kind of taboo on fighting between close relatives, linked very likely with the feudal primogeniture which stirred so many resentments in younger brothers and might have caused much fraternal bloodshed. In one of Scott's novels Lord Etherington, who has jockeyed his half-brother Tyrrel out of title and estate, meets him by chance, forces a contest on him, and wounds him: this, he admits to his experienced confidant Captain Jekyl, was a wild act, and he believes Tyrrel did not fire at him—his pistol must have gone off as he fell. Jekyl, deputed to negotiate with Tyrrel, takes for granted that another fight between them is out of the question.[52] With the Victorians the family took on a special middle-class sacredness, and a weighty impetus was given to the abolitionist cause by a duel at Camden Town, in the summer of 1843, from the fact of the combatants being brothers-in-law, Colonel Fawcett of the 55th Foot and Lieutenant Munro of the Household Cavalry. Fawcett died of his wound; Munro, it was known, had fought only under provocation, and in deference to military convention. The case came up in the Commons, where Sir Charles Napier, an admiral with a heroic record, and a naval reformer, said that the best way to stop duels would be to allow them only across a table, with lots drawn for the pistols and only one of them loaded, the survivor to be hanged.[53]

On Prince Albert's initiative the question was discussed by army and navy chiefs. A 'general order' for the army was drafted, which the queen 'attentively perused' and approved, she informed Wellington, then commander-in-chief, adding that it ought to be extended to all the armed forces.[54] The outcome next year was that the Articles of War were altered so as to make duelling, or offering a challenge, a grave offence, for which seconds as well as combatants would be cashiered. It would no longer be a reproach to any officer to be willing to tender an apology; and it came to be understood that a man who thought himself affronted should appeal to the senior officer present, and that every officer was empowered to stop a fight and if necessary arrest the transgressors.

Conservatism was making one of those tactical retreats that it showed itself so adept at in nineteenth-century Britain. (Catholic emancipation

[51] Ibid. 39.
[52] *St Ronan's Well*, chaps. 26, 29.
[53] Lady D. Nevill, 159.
[54] *The Letters of Queen Victoria*, i (London, 1908), 450, 484.

had been granted in 1829, the Corn Laws were swept away in 1846.) Many officers, of the more professional type, must have been glad to be relieved of an invidious part of their obligations. Once the army had come to the conclusion that duelling must end, civilians could make no more than a few spluttering efforts to keep it going. In 1844 Charles Lever the novelist was abused, as editor of a journal, by a Mr Hall. 'A man who wrote so much about duelling', as his biographer Fitzpatrick said, 'was not likely to pocket such phrases as those levelled at him', and he came over from Ireland to London to deal with his critic. A rendezvous at Chalk Farm was arranged, but a peaceful settlement averted it. 'We were not such fools', Hall told Fitzpatrick later on, 'as to shoot at one another ... A duel would have been an absurdity at that period ... it was tolerated only when cases were desperate.'[55] Even Irish landlords might be shocked out of some of their 'pleasant vices' by the frightful famine that began its ravages in 1845.

It was another sign of the times when, one night at Lady Palmerston's after the opera, Sidney Herbert came up to Lord Malmesbury 'in a great state of excitement' to tell him that his quitting Peel's party was 'unworthy of a gentleman', and worked himself into 'a frantic passion'.[56] Not many years earlier an emissary would infallibly have been calling on Herbert next morning, but this was 1846, and Malmesbury simply shrugged it off. Two years later a friend of another Sir Charles Napier, conqueror of Sind, doughty controversialist, and cousin of the admiral, was agreeing with a member of the family that Sir Charles must be restrained from calling out any of his *bêtes noires*. 'His age, his position, and the present state of public opinion', were all against it.[57] He was sixty-six. One diehard, George Smythe, was nearly called out in 1849 by the writer Monckton Milnes, for a press attack on him, and three years later fought what has been called the last duel in England, over an election dispute, with Colonel Romilly. It was an appropriately burlesque event, with the two men and their seconds having to share a station fly at Weybridge. As Algernon West was to say, 'ridicule at last did more than morality to kill duelling'.[58]

Burning with rage as he thought of his enemy, and of how he would enjoy 'shooting him down like a mad dog', the hero of a novel of the Crimean War years could only remind himself regretfully that such a

[55] Fitzpatrick, ii. 54 ff. Lever never ceased to be a defender of the duel—'he continued to the end true to the trigger' (ibid. ii. 59–60).

[56] Malmesbury, i. 177–8.

[57] Rosamond Lawrence, *Charles Napier: Friend and Fighter 1782–1853* (London, 1852), 172.

[58] West, 47. To 1847 belongs the farce by J. M. Morton, *Box and Cox*, later turned into the Sullivan operetta *Cox and Box*, with its pair of journeymen who talk of a duel but decide to throw dice instead.

procedure 'was no longer approved of now in England'.[59] It was still for a while possible to think of going abroad and fighting; a sporting journalist named Dillon, who had the honour to be killed in a sword duel in 1862 by a French duke, was one of the last Britons to do so. In a Trollope novel a few years later Lord Baldock alarmed his mother by telling her that a penniless Irishman was after her niece, and that he and Lord Chiltern had been over to Holland and fought about her. 'Fought a duel about Violet!' she exclaimed. 'People don't fight duels now.'[60]

Duelling was indeed being relegated to the realm of fantasy. Lord Frederick Hamilton remembered how in 1868, at the age of eleven, when his father was viceroy at Dublin and he a page-boy, the Prince and Princess of Wales made a visit, and the pages were given new silk suits and small swords. He and one of the others, later a general, promptly went out into the garden to fight a duel, starting with the 'vague flourishes' they supposed, from pictures, to be 'the orthodox preliminaries'. They were soon apprehended, and orders given by 'the highest quarters' for their steel blades to be replaced by wooden ones.[61] In high life duels might still float through a few grown-up minds, the aristocracy being the most cosmopolitan section of society, as the royal family was of the aristocracy. In 1876 Lord Aylesford was hurrying home from a shooting-party in India to shoot the Marquis of Blandford, son and heir of the Duke of Marlborough, who had made too free with his wife; Lord Randolph Churchill, the maverick politician, came to the aid of his brother Blandford by threatening to disclose some love-letters to Lady Aylesford from the Prince of Wales. The Prince, then at Cairo, sent Randolph a challenge to a pistol-fight on the French coast; the mischief-maker relished the chance to mock him 'for suggesting a duel he knew to be impossible'.[62]

His own American consort was one of many ladies who caught the roving royal eye, and a penchant for melodrama seems to have run in the family. Towards the end of a Devonshire House ball in 1897 where Lady Randolph masqueraded as a Byzantine empress, her seventeen-year-old son Jack, got up as a courtier from Versailles with a rapier, disappeared into the garden, with brother Winston for second, to do battle for a lady against a crusader with a double-handed sword. Jack came off worst, his mother heard, with 'a nasty cut on his silk stocking'.[63]

With the cessation of duelling 'the concept of gentlemanly conduct altered', to something less aggressive: in the army this entailed an

[59] James Grant, *Under the Red Dragon* (London, 1875), 191.
[60] *Phineas Finn* (1869–70), ii. 47. Irishmen could no longer be depicted as always thirsting for a fight. Gilmour (p. 29) points out that Phineas fights only once, and then reluctantly.
[61] *The Days before Yesterday* (1920; new edn., London, 1937), 98.
[62] Leslie, 51–5.
[63] R. G. Martin, *Lady Randolph Churchill* (London, 1972), 91–2.

'increasingly paternalistic concern of officers for the welfare of the other ranks'.[64] Changing manners were viewed by some men of the old school with distaste. Far away at Calcutta in 1855 the governor-general, a Scot of military parentage, wrote to a friend at home: 'Times must be changed indeed when such repartees as you describe, between Lord Cardigan and Sir Robert Peel, lead to nothing harder or sharper than words. I don't know either of them, and don't wish to.'[65] Crimean War squabbles could have been expected to produce a crop of duels a few years earlier. When it ended in 1856 the commander-in-chief in India was the Hon. G. Anson, a pillar of the Jockey Club who had been 'in demand in England as an arbiter of social disputes and affairs of honour', like Gladstone's minister the Marquis of Hartington later.[66] It was a twilight era when questions of 'honour' still counted, but had to be settled in a new style, and a trusted individual of high rank could unite the conciliatory functions of two seconds.

Abandonment of the duel was a not insignificant symptom of the approaching demise of the long-drawn aristocratic ascendancy in England; it had barely a generation to survive before the sharp decline of land-rents, from the 1870s, completed its supersession by a very mixed *tutti frutti* plutocracy. When Meredith's hero Nevil Beauchamp had to admit to M. d'Orbec that there was no duelling now in England, the Frenchman 'imagined the confession to be somewhat humbling', and a heated argument followed.[67] Treitschke must have been only one of many Europeans who believed that Englishmen, playing games instead of learning to handle weapons, were growing effeminate. Britons from the sort of families formerly subject to the code of honour had to be all the more careful to strike manly attitudes. They took cold baths every morning, and sent their sons to boarding-schools to be flogged by professionals. They could still advertise their 'pluck', as they were fond of calling it—a euphemism for *guts*—by hunting, with the empire's population of big game awaiting their challenge.

It would be interesting to know whether ladies' 'reputations' were scrutinized more vigilantly by their custodians when philanderers no longer had the fear of the pistol before them. In Pinero's play of 1899 the middle-aged roué Lord Quex is indignant at discovering that his fiancée is being besieged by a young officer. His grandfather in like case would have called this rival out; now, his convivial army friend 'Chick' can give no more robust counsel than 'Punch his head'.[68]

[64] E. M. Spiers, *The Army and Society 1815–1914* (London, 1980), 26.

[65] *Private Letters of the Marquess of Dalhousie*, ed. J. G. A. Baird (Edinburgh, 1910), 349.

[66] C. R. Hibbert, *The Great Mutiny, India 1857* (1978; Harmondsworth, 1980), 72.

[67] *Beauchamp's Career*, chap. 25.

[68] *The Gay Lord Quex*. Cf. the lavatory fist-fight between two MPs in John Galsworthy's novel *The Silver Spoon* (1926), Pt. 2, chap 2.

Englishmen could give up duelling earlier than most lands where it took root, because their seldom-broken history had allowed a unique accumulation of other aristocratic institutions or symbols or ceremonies, presided over by the monarchy and ensuring the desired continuity. England suffered a resulting rigidity, a stereotyping of character and loss of initiative; tradition was making men, instead of men making tradition. Yet thanks to a long interplay of two class ideologies England was able to enrich Europe, and at least one Asian country deeply influenced by it, India, with a term and an idea elsewhere lacking. Over the rest of western and middle Europe a man of birth had conventionally been known as a man who rode a horse. Greeks and Romans gave the title of *Hippeis* or *Equites* to their substantial upper-middle citizens; feudalism promoted the man in the saddle to the highest status, as 'chevalier', 'caballero', 'Ritter'. English had 'cavalier', but in the civil wars this word lost its chance of attaining a similar rank by turning into a party label. French, Spanish, Italian had besides their 'gentilhomme', 'gentilhombre', and 'gentiluomo', derived from *gens*—family or clan—but with a meaning limited to station and manners.

In England by contrast, where 'nobility' was reserved to a very few, the 'great dividing line' was between 'gentlemen and the non-gentlemanly class'.[69] The term could denote either family descent or social culture, but implied an ideal of conduct owing something to both; something less artificial than an honour code blazoning mere pride of blood, less self-regarding or self-preserving than the promptings of mere intelligence and ability. It clothed an élitism imbued with more of a moral flavour than any other such secular denomination. Religious revival in early nineteenth-century England deepened this. Carey the Northamptonshire shoemaker and pioneer missionary in Bengal could draw a picture of the perfect gentleman.[70] Henri Taine the conservative French historian struggled with the word in his *Notes on England*: 'it is constantly occurring and it expresses a whole complex of particularly interesting ideas', with a moral core, a nobility 'of the heart'.[71] Relinquishment of duelling, as the cachet of the gentleman, helped to liberate this higher quality from some of its old social bonds. Patriotism lent it a further polish, as something peculiar to this favoured island. An 'English gentleman' belonged, in the eyes of English gentlemen and their admirers, to a very special category. At the end of one of Rider Haggard's novels Sir Henry Curtis, now king-consort of a white nation somewhere in Africa, writes to his old friend at home that he still takes

[69] Guttsman, 113–14. He discusses various English definitions of 'gentleman'.

[70] G. Smith, *The Life of William Carey* (London, 1909), 130–1.

[71] W. L. Guttsman (ed.), *The English Ruling Class* (an anthology; London, 1969), 36–9.

more pride in being an English gentleman than he could have felt in being born on the steps of a throne.[72]

Yet the name of 'gentleman' could find adoption among foreigners reared far away from English skies. Bazarov, the young scientist and positivist of Turgenev's novel of 1861, had an unexpected visit from an acquaintance wanting to fight him. He was baffled, but assured his caller that there would be no need of the cane he had brought with him. 'You can go on being a *gentleman*, and I will accept your challenge in the same *gentlemanly* way' (*po-dzhentl'menski*).[73] Still more remarkable is the use of the word in the mysterious farewell letter left by the Crown Prince Rudolph, heir to the Habsburg empire, before his suicide at Mayerling in 1889. Writing in Magyar to a Hungarian friend, he said that the only choice now left him, as a 'gentleman', was to die. Fifty years later the general secretary of the Communist Party of India was not displeased to be able to tell me of a British official saying of him: 'Joshi is at least a gentleman.'

[72] *Allan Quatermain* (1887).
[73] *Fathers and Sons*, chap. 24.

13

Walter Scott and Honour

A friend warns me that Gourgaud is described as 'a *mauvais garçon*, famous fencer, marksman, and so forth. I wrote in answer, which is true, that I would hope all my friends would trust to my acting with proper caution and advice; but that if I were capable, in a moment of weakness, of doing anything short of what my honour demanded, I would die the death of a poisoned rat in a hole, out of mere sense of my own degradation.'

Scott, Journal, 17 September 1827

IN Britain in the first half of the nineteenth century the duel raised moral problems more acute than anywhere else, because of the disharmony between it and growing sections of the public, and because of its wider social diffusion than anywhere else except in France. Men who might seem in the highest degree unlikely to have anything to do with it were at some point or other of their lives brought close to it. One of the unlikeliest of all was Coleridge, who at the age of forty, during his break with Wordsworth and Montagu, told Lamb that if Montagu persisted in denying the truth of his charges, 'what must be the consequence, unless I am a more abject Coward than I have hitherto suspected, I need not say'.[1]

Another improbable was Macaulay, who showed all a respectable citizen's dislike of duelling as a typical vice of aristocracy in his description of the libertine Alfieri and his duel with Lord Ligonier.[2] Macaulay's style, however, was very much that of a duellist, and in his essay-writing years, when as his nephew wrote 'his spirit was high, and his pen cut deep', several people 'displayed symptoms of a desire to meet him elsewhere than on paper'. On these occasions, we are assured, he manifested 'a quiet but very decided sense of what was due to himself', and brought things to 'an honourable and satisfactory issue'.[3] How this squaring of the circle was achieved is not explained.

A time was drawing on when only the most frivolous of the upper classes, or heedless young neophytes, could turn out for a duel as light-heartedly as in days before Wesley and Wilberforce, Arkwright and Stephenson, Robespierre and Napoleon. For other men a grave question

---

[1] Molly Lefebure, *Samuel Taylor Coleridge: A Bondage of Opium* (London, 1974), 472.
[2] 'Moore's Life of Lord Byron' (1831), in *Essays*, i. 164.
[3] Sir G. O. Trevelyan, *The Life and Letters of Lord Macaulay* (1876), chap. 3.

of conscience would arise, and a tug of war between allegiance to time-honoured rubrics and the maxims of religion, good sense, and modern civilization. Few individuals felt it more poignantly than Scott, and the shadow of the duel falls heavily across many pages of his novels, and some chapters of his own life. Apart from Byron, he was the best known to Europe of all the British writers of his day, better known probably than any other except Shakespeare. In Lermontov's novel Pechorin, far away in the Caucasus, calms his nerves on the night before his duel by reading *Old Mortality*, and surrendering to Scott's spell. The fact that to a man like Sir Walter the duel could seem, for good or ill, so crucial a thing in men's social life, is an emphatic reminder of its vitality, coupled with the still tenacious hold of aristocracy. At home and abroad his views on it must be credited with wide influence.

A lawyer's son, himself a law officer—though it was always on moral, not legal, grounds that he debated the duel—and a self-made landowner, Scott was all his life a mixture of urban professional middle-class thinking, and of hankering for the rank of landed gentleman to which he felt his ancestors summoned him. He was in youth his own Disinherited Knight. Literary fame meant nothing to him, his son-in-law and biographer tells us, compared with the status of a Border laird, and the respect, Lockhart might have added, of a parcel of blockheads 'spacious in the possession of dirt'. His young hero in *Redgauntlet*, ignorant of his family and descent, torments himself with wonderings about who he really is; Scott may be said to have done the same. He lived half in the workaday present, an up-to-date businessman ready to serve as chairman of a gas company, half in day-dreams of a heroic past. He had one foot in the Enlightenment, one in the Middle Ages.

Working his way up with his pen into the gentry, ensnared in a spider-web of notions as musty and mouldering as Smailholm tower, the memento of his family's past, Scott was always very conscious of duelling as a distinction of the rank he so obsessively aspired to. He had a bourgeois *alter ego* in Monkbarns in *The Antiquary*, proud to call German printers his forebears, and rational on all subjects except Roman antiquities. Monkbarns once narrowly missed having to fight Sir Peter Pepperbrand, for doubting the existence of a ghost in his castle; 'but I humbled myself and apologized ... even in my younger days I was no friend to the *monomachia*, or duel'. In a homily to his Highland nephew Captain M'Intyre on it—'of all the absurdities introduced by the Gothic tribes, the most gross, impious, and cruel'— he fondly recalled an essay he composed when the town clerk and provost, or mayor, of the neighbouring township 'chose to assume the privileges of gentlemen, and challenged each other'.[4] Scott realized

---

[4] *The Antiquary* (1816), chaps. 9, 19.

that duelling was spreading, not simply surviving. One of his lawyers remarks on the foolish copying of a custom formerly confined to the gentry, when 'men who had no grandfathers never dreamed of such folly'.[5]

In a passage in *Peveril*, a tale of late seventeenth-century England, Scott sums up fairly and forcibly the incongruity between 'noble' and bourgeois values. Peveril believes himself to be conferring an honour on Major Bridgenorth the Puritan by admitting him to the duelling privilege; Bridgenorth declines it, on principle, from common sense, and because he is well on in years. As human beings these two men can comprehend and respect each other; as representatives of antithetical classes they are as far apart as chalk and cheese. Yet there is a corner of Bridgenorth's mind that regrets the necessity of refusing, and letting Sir Geoffrey the old Cavalier take comfort for defeat in the civil war by thinking plebeians capable only of herd courage, when drunk on sermons, not of the personal bravery exacted by the duel.[6] Another Puritan feels no scruple about drawing his sword when, on business from the parliamentary commissioners, he is attacked by an intransigent Cavalier; after speedily disarming Sir Henry he is content to reprove him, all the time with no change in his 'sour and grave composure', as if 'combat of life and death' was no more than part of a day's work.[7] A like confrontation is the wrestling between the rebel Covenanter and Sergeant Bothwell, who has tried to humiliate him and finds he has met more than his match.[8]

If the duel calls for more bravery than war, no sort of fighting needs very much, an executioner asserts. Any 'paltry curs' will fight, but to face the block and the axe, alone, in cold blood, is the true test of nobility.[9] There is, moreover, far more courage than Sir Geoffrey allowed for in not a few of Scott's humbler characters; and the lively bout at quarterstaff between the miller and Gurth the serf forms a foil in *Ivanhoe* to the jousting of the knights.

There is a recurrent counterpointing in the novels of the notions of Honour and Honesty, which had been diverging from their common root since the fourteenth century. Scott deeply respected both, even if his own business dealings as partner in a printing firm may not always have been above reproach.[10] He felt his bankruptcy as a disgrace, as well as misfortune, and laboured unsparingly to pay off his debts. Hard work, the 'bourgeois ethic', was practised by this Scots laird as

[5] *St Ronan's Well*, chap. 15.
[6] *Peveril of the Peak* (1822), chap. 9.
[7] *Woodstock* (1826), chap. 2.
[8] *Old Mortality* (1816), chap. 4.
[9] *Anne of Geierstein* (1829), chap. 14.
[10] See E. Quayle, *The Ruin of Sir Walter Scott* (London, 1968).

strenuously as it was preached by the Scots peasant Carlyle. His self-made Halbert has more taste for useful land-improvement than for blood-letting, or 'idle fame derived from dead ancestors'; his better-born wife dismisses such unworthy fancies.[11] But in Baillie Jarvie, the Glasgow businessman, contempt for gentility is mixed with a sneaking respect for it, and for his own family connection with it; and if the scuffle in the Highland tavern looks like a burlesque of duelling, when the baillie fails to get his rusty sword out of its sheath he snatches up a hot fire-iron and makes a brave enough show.[12]

Scott admired the class he longed to incorporate himself with, but he was also critical of it. As a Tory he endorsed its politics, as a well-informed and liberal-minded citizen he wanted to improve its pattern of life. He was anxious to see the old Scotland of the landowners preserved as far as might be, but he understood that to survive it must overhaul itself, morally if not politically. As a pathfinder of Victorian respectability, when thinking seriously he judged 'gentility' in terms of conduct far more than of caste, even if his prejudices in favour of lineage could never be shaken off altogether. He was teacher and educator as well as entertainer, desirous of refining the standards of his time; particularly the conduct of men to women, and, second only perhaps to this, the prevailing concepts of 'honour'.

These had a special relevance to the officer, one of the social types to which Scott's novels helped to lend definition, and prescribe a norm; a type in much need of recasting and polishing. He had felt in youth the attraction of a military career, and by putting his elder son into the army he was in a way fulfilling an old wish of his own. He was enrolling young Walter in a profession where to fight a duel might at any time become an obligation, and awareness of this must have lent urgency to his later reflections on the subject. His letters to his heir breathe a wish to see him a perfect gentleman, adorned with all the middle-class virtues. One may guess that the commonplace young fellow was relieved by his escape with his regiment to India, from where he never returned.

Unlike later novelists for whom the duel was a fading memory, he lived in a society where it was a contemporary reality, something that might rear its head in his vicinity at any time. How seriously he took it would depend on circumstances. There is a mixture of amusement and half-comic regret in his narration of a challenge received in May 1818 by his worthy associate the Ettrick Shepherd. 'Our poor friend Hogg has had an *affair of honour*', he wrote to the Duke of Buccleuch, head of the Scott clan. Two deputies arrived from Glasgow bearing a defiance: he locked them up, and came in consternation to consult

---

[11] *The Abbot* (1820), chap. 3.
[12] *Rob Roy*, chap. 28.

Scott. In court at Edinburgh they easily got the better of him. 'I heartily wish', Scott ended, 'he could have prevailed on himself to swagger a little.'[13]

It was no joking matter with Sir Walter when, in London in 1821, John Scott was killed by Christie, for Lockhart was closely and discreditably involved in it. He was then a young writer making his way, and very much at home in the field of scurrilous lampoon and abuse, the staple of Tory journalism; he was an active scribbler in *Blackwood's Magazine,* started in 1817 to swell the clamour of reaction. John Scott complained in the *London Magazine* which he edited of personal attacks in *Blackwood's,* ascribing them to Lockhart. Lockhart went to London to demand, through his barrister friend Christie, an apology or 'satisfaction'. A son of the manse, he might feel a need his father-in-law never felt of establishing his gentlemanliness by force of arms. Getting nothing out of John Scott, he 'posted' him as a coward, and returned to Edinburgh, leaving Christie embroiled with his enemy, and before long faced with the challenge that led to the moonlight at Chalk Farm and Scott's death. Sir Walter over-hastily took Christie's side, supposing him to have had 'no honourable mode of avoiding the sleeveless quarrel fixed upon him'. He did however write to Lockhart urging him in very strong terms to give up his connection with *Blackwood's,* and warning him that if anything like this should happen again 'You will not have public feeling nor the regard of your friends with you.'[14]

Another author may have had something to do with this case. In an early work, a sketch of legislative principles, that sturdy radical Hazlitt defended the duel as part of the rights of the individual, on condition that the act was 'voluntary and fair on both sides'[15]—a proviso impossible to be sure of. Later, like many others he seems to have found it hard to make up his mind, and according to Thomas Campbell the poet his 'peculiar taunting humour', and sometimes ill-considered talk, helped to incite John Scott into the fatal meeting. Christie accused him to Campbell of telling Scott that although he personally disapproved of duelling, and made no pretence of having the courage it required, he thought that a man of conventional opinions, like Scott, was in a different situation.[16]

Ostensibly at least Lockhart turned over a new leaf, but his party continued its ink-spattering, one of whose consequences was the death in March 1822 of Sir Alexander Boswell. Again Tory partisanship and

[13] *Journal,* i. 466, Editor's note.
[14] *Letters,* ii. 111–12. Editor's note; ii. 114 (24 Feb. 1821). Cf. ii. 31–2, on Lockhart's pen-skirmishings.
[15] Hazlitt, 'Civil and Criminal Legislation', in *Winterslow* (1839), 150.
[16] Cyrus Ridding, *Literary Reminiscences and Memoirs of Thomas Campbell* (London, 1860), ii. 145–7.

private sympathies put Sir Walter on the wrong side. Boswell had dined with him at his house in Castle Street just after completing—though his host knew nothing of this—his arrangements for the fight. Writing to Lockhart while Boswell lay dying he put the blame on Stuart, as a Whig 'desperado', but he rose above this narrowness when he added: 'I sincerely hope that this catastrophe will end the species of personal satire and abuse which has crept into our political discussions', at the cost of 'the lives of brave and good citizens'. Lockhart unctuously echoed this sentiment, and expressed his gratitude and that of his confederate John Wilson, of *Blackwood's*, for the sage advice which had preserved them 'from having any hand in all these newspaper skirmishes'.[17]

Scott himself, an enthusiastic Volunteer during the wars, twice came close to a whiff of the gunpowder of honour. The first episode, at Christmas 1813, was a travesty, but not sillier than many full-blown duels, and as dangerous as any. A poor German scholar whom he gave employment to, and who was a worshipper of Bacchus, suddenly one evening in the library announced that he could submit to insults no longer: 'I have brought a pair of pistols with me, and must insist on your taking one of them instantly.' Scott humoured him and got the pistols safely locked up; poor Henry Weber ended his days in an asylum at York, Scott bearing the expenses.[18]

Much later, in 1827 at the age of 56, he was threatened with a challenge from a very different foreigner, General Gourgaud, who had been an aide-de-camp of Napoleon's at St Helena and complained of being libelled by Scott in his biography of the emperor. Luckily the affair fizzled out, but Scott faced the prospect with complete seriousness and resolution. In such a case it would be very hard to say where inner honour, or self-respect, and outward honour, or regard to reputation, began or ended. It was rather late in life for adventures, he wrote in his journal, 'and as a reasonable man I would avoid such an arbitrament, but ... The country shall not be disgraced in my person.' A week later, after having chosen a second, he noted in another diary entry: 'It is clear to me that what is least forgiven in a man of any mark or likelihood is want of that article blackguardly called *pluck*. All the fine qualities of genius cannot make amends for it.'[19] Seemingly he had little fault to find with this judgement of the world.

Some of Scott's novelistic themes had a trying out in the narrative poems which first won him fame, and the duel appears in heroic garb in canto 5 of *The Lady of the Lake* with the hand-to-hand combat between

[17] *Letters*, ii. 137–8, 138 n.
[18] *Life*, iv. 129–31.
[19] *Journal*, i. 452 (27 Aug. 1827), i. 456 (4 Sept. 1827).

the disguised King James and Roderick Dhu. The Highland chief's men have surrounded James, alone in the wilds, but he chivalrously leaves them and fights him on equal terms. James, less powerful but better versed in fencing, wounds and disarms him, but then has him taken care of. Each thus displays the magnanimity that in Scott's view men of noble temper should possess; and there is a moment of true poetry before the swords clash when, as so many duellists must have done,

> Each look'd to sun, and stream, and plain,
> As what they ne'er might see again.

Duelling plays a prominent part, or at least comes in for discussion, in most of the novels. No doubt Scott like many others found it a convenient piece of a story-teller's stock in trade, useful for example for disposing of characters whose time has come to quit the stage. In the final paragraph of *The Bride of Lammermoor* he polishes off Sir William Ashton, and rounds off his ill-starred family's calamities, by killing him in a duel in Flanders. But usually the subject has its own weight. It recurs frequently in the early novels, Scott's best by far, about Scotland in times not long before his own. Several of their youthful heroes are from England, precipitated into a less orderly environment and uncertain what they should do, or whether to do anything. In this they reflect their creator's always divided mind, and the duelling issues they are apt to be drawn into are a fitting analogue of his state of being pulled in two directions at once.

He was convinced that both Scotsmen and Irishmen were more ill-tempered, though in different ways, than the English; and he looked upon Highlanders—Roderick Dhu leading the procession—as pre-eminently fiery. Captain MacTurk in *St Ronan's Well* is a Caledonian O'Trigger. He is 'that sort of person who is ready to fight with any one',[20] and although really estimable he delights in setting his friends by the ears, so as to play umpire in the combat he deems indispensable to restore good relations. Scott's portraits must have done much to make a stereotype of Highland irascibility. One of Marryat's ship's companies numbers a M'Foy, so bellicose that he has to be put ashore: he joins the army, and within three months, 'resenting some fancied affront', gets himself snuffed out.[21]

The novels of 1822 and 1823, *The Fortunes of Nigel* and *St Ronan's Well*, show very clearly the shadow of the events that had so lately impressed Scott so painfully. One, reversing the pattern of the first group, is about a young Scotsman (and an old Scottish king) in England. In the other we are back in Scotland, but on the Tweed,

---

[20] *St Ronan's Well*, chap. 3.
[21] *Peter Simple*, chap. 8.

close to the border and to Scott's country house; the characters and atmosphere are largely English, and it is the most 'contemporary' of all Scott's stories. This adds to the significance of its wealth of discussion of duelling, and of the concluding duel towards which it moves, where several details of Boswell's death, Lockhart tells us, are '*exactly* reproduced'.[22] A miscellaneous flock of visitors have collected for the season at the then fashionable spa at Innerleithen, with not much to do except for the ladies to form cliques and manœuvre for the leading position, and the gentlemen to collide more directly. They are 'a claret-drinking set', one lady complains, 'quarrelling and alarming our nerves every evening with presenting their pistols perpetually at each other'.[23]

Scott was always keenly alive to the incongruity between the duel in its ideal abstraction, and in the jostlings of ordinary life. He was well aware of how often a dispute emerged, like a malignant jinn, from the bottle. Drinking was another subject of perennial interest to him; he had grown up in days when it was reckoned effeminate for a man ever to taste water unmixed with alcohol. In the novels he preached against drunken quarrelling. In the first of them all Waverley is drawn into a vinous after-dinner session, abruptly turning into a Whig-and-Tory row, with rapiers coming out; next morning he wakes up with an alarming sensation of being committed to a fight with a local laird. Fortunately for him his good-natured host the Baron of Bradwardine feels it his duty to take the affair on himself, goes out before breakfast to deal with the laird, and brings him back lowering, with a damaged arm, to apologize.[24] Francis Osbaldistone in *Rob Roy* is another youth unaccustomed to potations; in 'the tumult of wine and passion' at his uncle's table, where a pint of claret is a mere sip, he strikes his cousin Rashleigh. Next morning he is prepared to express regret, feeling that 'true honour consisted not in defending, but in apologising for', a wrong deed. But an encounter is only postponed, and they come to blows in the college grounds at Glasgow, Rashleigh lunging 'more like a fiend than a man', the hero only saved by the intervention of the disguised Rob Roy.[25]

Scott might smile at the 'harmless enthusiasm' of his countrymen's sentimental feeling about the rivers of their native districts, and 'duels occasioned by any word of disparagement' of them;[26] but in his graver mood youthful petulance, or any clashes without solid cause, always came under his censure. Nigel has good reason for disliking the villain,

---

[22] *Life*, vii. 29 n.
[23] St Ronan's Well (1824), chap. 7.
[24] *Waverley* (1814), chap. 57.
[25] *Rob Roy* (1817), chaps. 12, 25.
[26] Ibid., chap. 28.

Lord Dalgarno, but foolishly loses his temper and goes for him in a royal park, where all brawling is taboo; as a result he has to go into hiding in a criminal quarter of London.[27] Young Bucklaw fastens a pointless quarrel on the Master of Ravenswood out of sheer thoughtless bravado, in the end threatening to strike him. He is soon stretched on the ground, at his opponent's mercy, but when allowed up recovers his good humour and shakes hands.[28] On the Jacobite march into England the mettlesome chief Fergus Mac-Ivor is indignant with Waverley for no longer wanting to marry his sister, who has refused him; he would like to draw his sword on the spot, but cannot help realizing that in modern times 'there must be some decent pretext for a mortal duel', something better than an Italian point of honour. 'For instance', Scott goes on ironically, 'you may challenge a man for treading on your corn in a crowd, or for pushing you up to the wall, or for taking your seat in the theatre'—but not, in 'the modern code', for a pure nothing.[29]

Youth is not alone at fault. In one of the last novels we see two seasoned military men, of Norman times, getting into an altercation and approaching a rift. They have no reason for it, except professional rivalry; each really esteems the other.[30] Scott draws a comparison with army men of his own day, of whom he knew many. Duelling can be defended, but only when there is serious warrant for an appeal to arms. Guy Mannering while serving in India fought a duel whose memory preyed on his mind. His friend Mervyn reassured him, in a long letter in somewhat prosy style but clearly meant by Scott to place duelling in its best light. Mervyn's contention was that every man is entitled to defend himself when the law cannot defend him; it cannot protect his 'honour' from insult, an injury which 'however trifling in itself is one of much deeper consequence to all views in life' than any wrong a highwayman can do: submission to it will tarnish a character for ever. As to religion, Mervyn makes the telling point that it has nothing to say against forcible defence of life or property; why not then of honour?[31] When Hogg read this novel he declared that 'Colonel Mannering is just Walter Scott, painted by himself'; his comment was repeated to the author, who smiled in assent.[32]

Scott was, needless to say, averse to anything like the bullying practised by the kind of man known as a 'professed duellist'. A good deal of what he felt about this can be learned from the Fair Maid of Perth's remonstrances to her lover, the honest smith Gow, a born fighter

[27] *The Fortunes of Nigel* (1822), chap. 12.
[28] *The Bride of Lammermoor* (1819).
[29] *Waverley*, chap. 57.
[30] *Castle Dangerous* (1832), chap. 8.
[31] *Guy Mannering* (1815), chap. 16.
[32] Lockhart, vi. 340.

who is always getting into frays or letting his admirers push him into them. He is no coarse ruffian, but a man of imagination, stirred by old ballads about Wallace and his feats. Scott may be suspected of some rueful feeling that later bards and minstrels, like himself, devoted too much of their art to celebrating strife and bloodshed.

Yet the opposite failing, cowardice, is if possible even more shocking. There are many scoundrels in the novels, but very few faint-hearts, except of the stock type of braggart-poltroon, like the noisy captain in *Nigel* who is worsted by a patriotic Londoner, no swordsman but a man of spirit.[33] To show the white feather is to invite social obloquy of a very disagreeable kind. Sir Bingo Binks at St Ronan's has lately married beneath him, under threat of having to fight the brother of a woman scheming for his money and title. A sluggard at bottom rather than a coward in grain, after failing to resent some rude treatment he becomes unpleasantly aware that he is 'on the road towards the ancient city of Coventry', as one guilty of 'that most unpardonable offence in modern morality, a solecism in the code of honour'. His credit rises with a jump when he lets MacTurk prod him into a challenge, and his opponent fails to turn up at the promised hour.[34] But in a far more important way, cowardice was to Scott, as to Shakespeare, one of his great teachers, a moral blight, not simply a frailty of nerves, and one that nothing else can atone for.

A true man, for Scott, must be ready to risk life when something of weight is at stake, and the reckless boldness of Gow, ready to fight for mere vainglory, stands out favourably by contrast with Conacher's besetting weakness, which finally, in the mass duel between chosen men of the clans, drives him to panic flight, desertion of followers who have sacrificed everything for him.[35] Bravery on the other hand is only in a very slight degree a redeeming virtue of Scott's villains, most of whom share it. No sympathy is invited for the reprobate Lord Etherington at St Ronan's, when we see him shot down by Mowbray, whose sister he has wronged.[36] Lord Dalgarno seems to be considered by Scott too worthless even to deserve this happy dispatch. Denounced by king and father for his conduct towards a lady, he is retreating to Scotland, with a citizen's wife he has seduced, to take possession of Nigel's estate by trickery, when he stops to await Nigel and fight it out. His challenge has not been delivered by the servitor; instead Dalgarno is ignobly shot by lurking bandits, and falls lifeless on his mistress's lap. Scott points the moral by misquoting *Lear*, on how our vices rebound on us.[37]

[33] *The Fortunes of Nigel*, chap. 12.
[34] *St Ronan's Well*, chaps. 12–13.
[35] *The Fair Maid of Perth* (1828), chap. 34.
[36] *St Ronan's Well*, chap. 39.
[37] *The Fortunes of Nigel*, chap. 36.

Anyone trying to make sense of the duel, as Scott with his strong vein of rationality could not help doing, had to equate it more or less with the old trial by combat, and assume that the right man would win. In *The Talisman* we have tournament and trial by battle thrown together. Ivanhoe is an embodiment, if a somewhat wooden-headed one, of the chivalric ideal of honour, and the quest for the holy grail of martial fame. Scott has to resort to a far-fetched expedient when his Saxon hero, weak from wounds and exhaustion, enters the lists to save Rebecca from execution, and his adversary the Templar falls dead, from 'the violence of his own contending passions'.[38] A story-teller might feel that he had a free hand to act for Providence. But in a short story, *The Mirror*, Scott faces the difficulty frankly, and virtually admits that there was no rhyme or reason in the duellist's 'satisfaction'. Captain Falconer happens to be in Holland in time to prevent his brother-in-law Sir Philip Forester, who has settled there, from bigamously marrying another woman. Quixotically he accepts a challenge which Sir Philip has no moral right to thrust on him, and is mortally wounded. 'Such are the ways of Heaven', comments Scott's pious narrator, 'mysterious in our eyes.' The words sum up what was haphazard and incalculable in all duelling. Old Sir Henry the Cavalier, in the bitterness of defeat, has to confess to himself at last 'the folly of thinking that a good cause can strengthen a weak arm'.[39]

As though weary of the dilemma, or of the whole creaking machinery of his cherished world of honour, Scott is quite ready at times to subject the duel to ridicule. It is a striking part of his paradox that he was oftener than not more successful with the plebeians who throng his Scottish novels than with high life; and in his early, most confident years of novel-writing his prevailing mood was one of humour, which allowed him to relish the oddities of social diversity, instead of being alarmed, as he was later, by the spectre of social collision. Mrs Dods the St Ronan's innkeeper, hearing of a duel hatched under her roof, is torn between fears for the safety of her amiable young lodger Tyrrel, and disgust at his having apparently backed out of his engagement with Sir Bingo: the credit of her establishment is compromised—'and what for should the honour of a substantial, four-nooked, sclated house of three stories, no be foughten for as weel as the credit of ony of these feckless callants that make such a fray about their reputation?'[40] Peveril after a street brawl is lodged in the same cell with Sir Geoffrey Hudson, Charles I's court dwarf, who relishes a chance to talk about his services

---

[38] *Ivanhoe* (1820), chap. 43.

[39] *Woodstock*, chap. 2. A true story curiously similar to the plot of Scott's 'The Mirror' concerns Anne Halkett and the Civil Wars; see Stone, 204–5.

[40] *St Ronan's Well*, chap. 14.

in the civil war, and above all to boast of having fought a duel and killed a man who sneered at his shape.[41]

But duelling had outlived much satire already, and could not be simply laughed away. The moment of horror at the end of a fatal encounter haunted Scott's mind. As he saw Etherington fall 'Mowbray stood fixed like a pillar of stone, his hand still clenched on the weapon of death, reeking at the touch-hole and muzzle.'[42] To Colonel Mannering it was 'torture' to look back on his Indian duel, ending he mistakenly believed in the other man's death, and caused by a mistaken suspicion that the youth had been paying court to his wife, whose death was an indirect consequence of the fight. He could never bear to read *Othello* again, he told his friend Mervyn.[43] That duels might easily come about through misunderstanding or deception was undeniable. In *Kenilworth* the Earl of Leicester's secretly married and fugitive wife Amy is protected by Tressilian; suspecting the worst, Leicester forces a fight on him. Tressilian offers a calm explanation, but his attacker is wild with fury, and has him down and is about to stab him to death when he is interrupted by the arrival of a boy, carrying a letter that proves the truth of Tressilian's words.[44]

One of Scott's weightiest pronouncements is to be found in another short story, *The Two Drovers,* in the judge's summing up at the trial of Robin Oig, who has stabbed an English yeoman to death in revenge for an affront. The judge can sympathize with a Highlander's alien concept of honour; his action arose 'less from any idea of committing wrong than from an unhappily perverted notion of that which is right'. Yet the act was murder, because premeditated, during an interval of two hours, and Robin must die for it. What more or what less could be Scott's honest verdict on any duellist with blood on his hands?

A long file of his characters protest, eloquently or trenchantly, to intending combatants against their folly or wickedness. In *The Antiquary* the old beggar, once a soldier, pleads with the two young men in language 'as bold and unceremonious as his erect and dignified demeanour'. Both seconds are impressed, and attempt a reconciliation; the obdurate M'Intyre's brother officer confesses himself 'unable to discover any rational ground of quarrel'.[45] Many a second must have wished at the last moment that he could decently withdraw. Age reproves froward youth again through the mouth of the worthy goldsmith Heriot, only to be rebuffed by Nigel—'Old men and young

---

[41] *Peveril of the Peak*, chap. 34.
[42] *St Ronan's Well*, chap. 39.
[43] *Guy Mannering*, chap. 16.
[44] *Kenilworth* (1821), chaps. 38–9.
[45] *The Antiquary*, chap. 20.

men, men of the sword and men of peaceful occupations, always have thought, always will think differently on such subjects.'[46] In *Peveril* the dyed-in-the-wool pastor Solsgrace delivers one of Scott's most impassioned homilies.[47] In *The Heart of Midlothian* too religion is invoked, when Reuben Butler, son of a Covenanter, walking in Holyrood Park meets with a youth who he guesses must be there to fight, and warns him that he will be violating one of his country's 'wisest laws', and, still more, 'a law, which God Himself has implanted within our nature'. On the stranger asking what law is this, 'with a deep and solemn voice' Butler answers: ' "Thou shalt do no MURDER" '.[48]

In *Anne of Geierstein* a young Englishman travelling in Switzerland has to get up at dawn to face the champion of Berne and his huge two-handed sword; a challenge was a 'sacred engagement', overriding all others. The 'magic dawn' of the hills makes a dramatic contrast with the two men's business, such as descriptions of duels often evoked. Their contest is cut short by the appearance of their host the Landamann, who sternly reprimands them for their resort to senseless, unchristian violence. Rudolph of Berne, though slightly wounded, is good-humoured, and they part friends; but later on jealousy gets the better of him, they meet in single fight on the battlefield, and he falls.[49]

On his own soil it is noticeable how Scott finds his spokesmen in these situations not in the ranks of the established Kirk or the episcopalian Church, but among dissenters of one kind or another. Mr Geddes the Quaker in *Redgauntlet* can be looked on as another embodiment, like Monksbarn, of the more sober, self-controlled side of Scott's nature. He is firm on his rights, but also on the duty to uphold them peacefully; he expatiates to his friend Latimer, the youthful hero, on the folly of considering 'the lightest insult as a sufficient cause for the spilling of blood'.[50] Not many of Scott's duels or quarrels arise from romantic love-affairs; but there is an admonition for the fair sex when the pious Lady Lochleven takes Queen Mary's attendant Catherine to task, in the royal captive's presence, as a girl of the kind 'who make giddy-fashioned revellers and deadly brawlers'.[51]

In *St Ronan's Well*, by contrast with Scott's grave moralizers, Touchwood treats all duelling with derision, both as one old enough to have left behind any such freaks and as a sturdy self-made man impatient of elegant affectations. 'Never tell me of your points of honour; all humbug, Captain MacTurk—mere hair-traps to springe woodcocks:

[46] *The Fortunes of Nigel*, chap. 29.
[47] *Peveril of the Peak*, chap. 9.
[48] *The Heart of Midlothian* (1818), chap. 11.
[49] *Anne of Geierstein*, chaps. 6, 35.
[50] *Redgauntlet* (1824), chap. 3 of narrator's journal, following Letter xiii.
[51] *The Abbot*, chap. 34.

men of sense break through them.' Duelling, he goes on to his scan-
dalized listener, besides being a crime is 'an idiotical and totally absurd
practice ... An honest savage has more sense than to practise it; he
takes his bow or his gun, as the thing may be, and shoots his enemy
from behind a bush.' Later on he harangues Mowbray in the same
strain. 'None of your G—damme doings, sir—your duels or your drub-
bings.' 'Sir, I must feel as a gentleman', Mowbray retorts. 'Feel as a
fool', returns Touchwood, 'for that is the true case.'[52]

It is not the whole case, as Scott sees it, and Touchwood is a
meddlesome, self-opinionated old fellow. But all the more thoughtful
characters have to wrestle painfully with themselves before they take
the fateful step, like Lovel in *The Antiquary*; or in *The Monastery* (chapter
20) as the fight between Halbert and Shafton draws near—a pointless
one between two men neither of whom is a bad man, and which will
finish by turning them both into fugitives. Even among the more
headstrong or frivolous, prudence may beget hesitations. Charles
Stuart, in hiding at Woodstock, undertakes a challenge, but then thinks
of his duty to his followers, before giving way to the irritated feeling
that he is a gentleman as well as a prince, 'obliged to give or claim the
satisfaction expected on occasion of differences among gentlemen'; all
true Englishmen will applaud him, he tells himself. Dr Rocheclife,
soldier turned parson, pleads with him in vain.[53] He is one of Scott's
many spokesmen who are no weaklings, but have given proofs of
courage and are thereby entitled to condemn its abuse.

Late in life, in *Count Robert of Paris*, when Scott's genius had burned
down close to the socket, but his anxious ponderings of men's dealings
with one another persisted, we see him still wrestling with this problem
so central to the fabric of his social being. As always he found it natural
to deprecate the kind of duelling inspired by mere animal energy.
Robert, at Byzantium, boasts to the emperor of how he spent a month
at an old forest chapel in France, where knights were wont to meet,
challenging all comers; accidents will happen, and one or two were
killed, but all enjoyed the exercise. The emperor replies that it is boyish
folly for men 'to cast away their lives in a senseless quarrel among
themselves'.[54] But such an argument could not free Scott from his
nagging doubts. Opposite philosophies, the two poles of his divided
personality, are upheld by Achilles, the polished commander, and
Hereward, the plain Saxon soldier of fortune. Someone has spoken ill
of their corps, the Varangian Guard; Hereward is aflame at the thought
of a duel, Achilles pooh-poohs the idea as barbarous, out of place 'in

[52] *St Ronan's Well*, chaps. 34. 36.
[53] *Woodstock* (1826), chaps. 27–8.
[54] *Count Robert of Paris* (1832), chap. 9.

any country of civilization and common sense'. He goes on to draw an ironical picture of a man killed, another puffed up and lauded, though if he had his deserts 'the victor, as he is termed, would have been sent to the gallows'. This may be logic, Hereward rejoins, but for a man to be called a liar is 'the same as a blow, and a blow degrades him into a slave and a beast of burden, if endured without retaliation'.[55]

Hereward's words are the more telling because he is a plain-dealing English commoner instead of a courtier, and because they express spontaneous feeling instead of artificial culture. Looked at the other way round, it was honour that was artificial, common sense natural. Later in the novel Anna Comnena, the emperor's daughter, is brusquely contemptuous of her husband Alexius's talk of his honour obliging him to fight Count Robert, and (not much to his regret) forbids it. The 'honour' of these Frankish knights, she says, is 'a species of Moloch, a flesh-devouring, blood-quaffing demon'.[56] When Alexius, none the less, is compelled to face trial by battle with Robert, to his great relief Hereward volunteers to take his place: Robert gallantly waives the disparity of rank, and they fight on foot with axes. Their 'duel' ends with two brave men making friends, and the Saxon taking service under the crusader count.[57]

Scott's dilemma was insoluble. The influence of his writings is hard to estimate, as with other much-read authors who treated the subject. In Britain, where the current was beginning to turn against duelling, he may well have helped to bring it to an end. Where it was still firmly rooted, he may have helped to prolong its life, as Mark Twain blamed him for doing in the American south. But whatever his ambivalences, he was not the slavish worshipper of the past that critics like George Borrow thought him. For Scott a duel was, at best, a sombre mandate of destiny, an irretrievable step in the dark. Yet as a story-teller he could never shake off its spell. At the end, in southern Italy in vain search of lost health, he was visibly struck at Malta by the sight of the street in Valletta where the knights fought their duels, and had an idea of working it into the final novel he was feebly struggling to write.[58]

[55] Ibid., chap. 2.
[56] Ibid., chap. 26.
[57] *Count Robert of Paris*, chap. 33.
[58] D. E. Sultana, '*The Siege of Malta' Rediscovered* (Edinburgh, 1977), 50.

14

Later British Writers

It has a strange quick jar upon the ear,
    That cocking of a pistol, when you know
A moment more will bring the sight to bear
    Upon your person, twelve yards off or so,
A gentlemanly distance, not too near,
    If you have got a former friend for foe,
But after being fired at once or twice
The ear becomes more Irish, and less nice.

Byron, *Don Juan*, canto 4.

SCOTT's neighbour Hogg might have no taste for duelling, but he made good use of it in his macabre novel about a man beguiled by predestinarian theology into a conviction that he can commit any sin without sinning. The tempter coaxes him to challenge his own brother; he demurs, but before long is inveigled into fighting and killing him, and stepping into the family estate.[1] Another Scot, born two years before Sir Walter, felt some of his perplexities about duelling, though as beseemed a Glasgow merchant's son he outgrew them less painfully. Thomas Campbell confessed to having been 'very irascible when young', and was glad to be able to recall that he had kept out of duels, 'though he confessed he had been several times nearly sending challenges'.[2] At dinner with some military acquaintances who were talking of occasions they had known when both parties were reduced to corpses, he told a less gloomy story of how he outfaced an aggressive French officer at Rouen in 1814 by pretending to be a fencing-master.[3]

But among the Romantic poets it was Byron, himself a semi-Scot, and as proud of his lineage as Sir Walter, who came closest to sharing his preoccupation with the duel. He shared Scott's uneasy footing, between Enlightened and feudal ideas, to say nothing of the pressure of Scottish religion. Brought up in un-aristocratic style, he might feel obliged to assert his rank by fighting rather than risk any appearance of hanging back. He took an interest tinged with superstition in the notorious duel fought by his predecessor in the title. This great-uncle,

[1] James Hogg, *The Private Memoirs and Confessions of a Justified Sinner* (1824; London, 1924), 193 ff.
[2] W. Beattie (ed.), *Life and Letters of Thomas Campbell* (London, 1849), iii. 255.
[3] Ibid. iii. 392–4.

he once told someone, had no notion of retiring from the world after it; he got an appointment as Master of the Staghounds, and always kept the death-dealing sword in his bedroom.[4] One of the tales the poet regaled his publisher Murray with was about the youthful frolics at his mansion of Newstead when his friends dressed up as monks, and he was the abbot. Some joke led to Matthews threatening to throw Hobhouse out of a window, on which the latter left the house, after solemnly telling Byron that only respect for his host kept him from claiming satisfaction.[5]

Byron could always see the ludicrous side of duelling, but he was ready for action, though never it seems actually obliged to stand fire. On his youthful travels, over-sensitive about the respect due to him, he challenged a general's aide-de-camp at Malta, 'a rude fellow, who grinned at something—I never rightly knew what', but who explained and apologized.[6] Oddly, Byron's erratic father, 'Mad Jack', had been the cause of a duel at Malta. When Moore had a grievance about Byron making game of the fiasco of his duel with Jeffrey, Byron wrote to him that he would welcome conciliation so long as his honour was not compromised, but otherwise was ready 'to make the atonement you deem it necessary to require'.[7] This was quite conciliatory enough to be the starting-point of a close friendship, and soon Byron was giving Moore a humorous report of how he had been 'called *in* the other day to mediate between two gentlemen bent on carnage', and had patched things up for them, 'after a long struggle between the natural desire of destroying one's fellow-creatures, and the dislike of seeing men play the fool for nothing'.[8]

Byron was in a less jocular mood when he wrote to Murray from Venice complaining of being slandered, together with Shelley, by that 'dirty, lying rascal' Southey, and talked of proving it 'in ink—or in his blood, if I did not believe him to be too much of a poet to risk it'.[9] He took care, when telling his publisher to print *Don Juan* without any bowdlerizing omissions, to add that the lines on Castlereagh must be left out, 'as I am not on the spot to meet him':[10] Byron had by then made England too hot to hold him. It must seem surprising that in *Don Juan* he did not tap more of the rich vein that duelling offered to the satirist. It had a place in his own experience very near the end, when he was at Missolonghi with the scratch force he had collected to aid

[4] Byron, *Letters*, 353.
[5] Ibid. 274.
[6] Ibid. 31 (2 May 1810).
[7] *Letters*, 59–60 (27 Oct. 1811); cf. D. L. Moore, 152.
[8] *Letters*, 77–8.
[9] Ibid. 195 (24 Nov. 1818); cf. D. L. Moore, 278.
[10] Ibid. 197 (25 Jan. 1819).

the Greek struggle for independence from Turkey. One of his officers wanted to fight two others, he wrote to his friend Kinnaird: he put all three under arrest until they came to terms, and 'if there is any more challenging, I will call them all out and wafer one half of them'.[11] Twenty days later he was dead.

In one of Peacock's conversation-novels the medievalizing Mr Chainmail laments the waning of 'the high impassioned love' of chivalric days. Men no longer break lances for ladies, or even rushes. 'We jingle purses for them, flourish paper-money banners, and tilt with scrolls of parchment.'[12] Tennyson's *Maud*, in 1855, showed Cupid still with a finger on the trigger, but victory followed by excruciating remorse. In the graphic, impressionistic narrative, hero and sweetheart were broken in on by her brother and the foolish 'babe-face lord', his preferred choice. The brother struck the hero in the face: an hour later the horrid echoes of their pistols

> thunder'd up into Heaven the Christless code
> That must have life for a blow.

Dying, the brother confessed that the fault was his, but the lover felt the brand of Cain, and could only seek relief by going off to serve his country in the Crimean War then raging, and shed Russian blood to banish the memory of British blood. Ruskin's thinking was—sometimes—less confused; he had much, far too much, to say in favour of war, as the source of all civilization and its arts, but he argued eloquently that if rulers and knights wanted to indulge in glorious strife they should do the fighting themselves, not drive masses of peasants into the arena.[13] War in other words ought to be a magnified tournament, or duel between rival élites.

Tennyson's friend Carlyle was a descendant of Scottish peasants, not lairds, but as he grew into a celebrity and oracle he cultivated contacts with aristocracy, and was sufficiently impressed by it, or its potentialities, to pin his chimerical hopes for England on its leadership. Duelling was one of its hallmarks that both fascinated and repelled, above all bewildered, him. He belonged to the religious revival, except in having no faith in creeds. In an early essay, in 1829, he deplored the drying up of morality into nothing better than the ambition of winning men's approval. Nowadays it would be 'a fool's trick to die for conscience. Only for "character", by duel, or in case of extremity, by suicide, is the wise man bound to die.'[14] In other words a duellist's

---

[11] *Letters*, 386 (30 Mar. 1824).
[12] *Crotchet Castle* (1831), chaps. 12, 16.
[13] *The Crown of Wild Olive* (1866), lecture 3.
[14] 'Signs of the Times', in *Scottish Miscellanies*, 243.

death was a kind of martyrdom, but of a very unworthy sort, in obedience to rules destitute of real meaning.

Carlyle's aim was to convert the upper classes to a higher allegiance, so that they might wisely guide the lower orders and avert social upheaval and chaos. This was the message especially of his *French Revolution*. In some passages there we can fancy him a Dumfriesshire yokel again, staring through a hedge at the petrified gestures of a strange world. Insulted in the Assembly, challenged by the young Duc de Castries, Charles Lameth met him that same evening in the Bois de Boulogne—'two men with lion-look, with alert attitude, side foremost, right foot advanced; flourishing and thrusting, stoccado and passado, tierce and quart; intent to skewer one another'.[15] Yet one may be left feeling that Carlyle had to caricature the duel in his inimitable way in order to smother a reluctant admiration for it. He could not help acknowledging something noble in an ordeal that men, not all of them feather-brained, had for so long been willing to submit to. Any defiance of death 'is one of the sincerities of Human Life, which bursts through the thickest-quilted formulas; and in ... all manner of ages, will, one way or the other, contrive to show itself'.[16]

For novelists it was a theme hard to eschew. Even for Jane Austen, with her single off-stage duel, it was part of the life around her, and she had two brothers in the navy. Still more was duelling part and parcel of genteel life in Ireland, as Scott's friend Maria Edgeworth well knew. She looked back from 1800, when she started to write, with comic extravagance, on Sir Kit Rackrent, who kept his wife locked up and was asked no impertinent questions about her because 'he was a famous shot, had killed his man before he came of age, and nobody scarce dared look at him'. When the lady was understood to be dying, however, and three others were jostling for her place, he had to fight their brothers one after the other; the third put an end to him. He was 'greatly lamented', and his adversary had to leave the country.[17]

More realistic is the story of Harry Ormond. It came out in 1817, the same year as *Rob Roy*: the events are supposed to take place a little earlier. Harry has a family resemblance to Scott's early heroes, young men turned out in an unfamiliar world and trying to keep their footing. He has no difficulty in getting into more quarrels than he has any desire for, beginning when the owner of a fighting-cock blames him for a mishap to a few of its feathers. A combat is arranged, but luckily the malcontent, on being told that Harry is an excellent shot, thinks better

[15] Carlyle, *French Revolution*, Pt. 2: 'The Constitution', Bk. 3, chap. 3.
[16] 'Two Hundred and Fifty Years Ago', 127.
[17] *Castle Rackrent* (1801), 19–22.

of it.[18] Much mischief is blamed by this woman writer on women. During a ball Harry is briefly in danger of having to take up a quarrel on behalf of his partner, the Hon. Miss Eliza Darrell, who is indignant at a lady of lesser rank presuming to usurp her place. 'Seeing how little his safety was in the eye of the gentle Eliza', Harry resolves to steer clear of such entanglements in future.[19]

But another female gets him into a worse scrape. There was a vogue in Dublin of stinging poetical squibs and pasquinades, all the more admired because they advertised 'a double portion of that personal promptitude to give the satisfaction of a gentleman, on which the Irish pride themselves'. One day at the tea-table a woman, heedless of the trouble she may be causing, recites some uncomplimentary lines that have caught her fancy, at the expense of Harry's guardian, Sir Ulick. They are warmly applauded by one of the men listening; Harry feels in duty bound to resent this. He comes off in the end with a slight wound, which raises him in the esteem of society: 'it was essential, not only to the character of a hero, but of a gentleman at that time in Ireland, to fight a duel'.[20]

In *Jane Eyre* a later authoress seems to take a less unfriendly view of the subject, when Mr Rochester tells the young governess he has engaged about his youthful infatuation with a Paris opera-dancer, and how, out of sight on the balcony, he heard her come in one evening with another lover, 'a young roué of a vicomte—a brainless and vicious youth'. He listened to her witticisms on his 'personal defects', before breaking in on the pair and cashiering his mistress in spite of screams and hysterics. Next morning he met the viscount in the Bois de Boulogne, and 'left a bullet in one of his poor, etiolated arms, feeble as the wing of a chicken'.[21] Jane is not at all shocked, we perceive, either by the liaison or by the duel; we may suppose if we like that the tale gives Mr Rochester an added glamour.

Irish novelists continued to find duelling one of the most serviceable items in their professional baggage. In that old favourite *Handy Andy*, Samuel Lover introduces us to the slang phrases of the time; pistols were 'flutes', an invitation to 'grass before breakfast' was a challenge. Lower-grade lawyers were barely eligible for the compliment. 'I wish he was more of a gentleman, for your sake', Dick the Devil remarks to Squire Egan, who has undertaken to fight one of them, after horse-whipping him. 'It's dirty work, shooting attorneys.'[22] Election-time

[18] *Harry Ormond*, chap. 12.
[19] Ibid.,chap. 19.
[20] Ibid.,chap. 21.
[21] Charlotte Bronte, *Jane Eyre* (1847), chap. 15.
[22] *Handy Andy*, chap. 3.

duels are more serious, and Edward's self-reproaches after the death of the brutal O'Grady, from a wound he has given him, are as impressive as Lover's limited talent can rise to. 'We make for ourselves laws of *honour*, and forget the laws of God!'[23]

Marx's keen interest in Ireland helped to make Charles Lever one of his best-liked novelists.[24] He judged him a realist, and some of Lever's own experiences might certainly have helped to make him one. Once, he told a friend, an officer's son came to Brussels, where he was then staying, 'for the express purpose of shooting me, in duello of course', because of an erroneous impression of his father having been misrepresented 'on a variety of delicate subjects'.[25] In a novel like *Jack Hinton* bullets are always flying about, while the law appears indifferent and even the Catholic church not bigotedly hostile. On the night before the young hero is to fight Ulick Burke, beaten by him in a steeplechase, two friends keep him company until the decanter is empty and they fall asleep in their chairs. One is the Revd Tom Loftus; Hinton notices that 'as the punch made more inroads upon him ... his holy horror of duelling was gradually melting away before the warmth of his Hibernian propensities'.[26]

A novel where Lever exchanges his Irish backcloth for a continental setting, *A Rent in the Cloud*, has for central character a man named Calvert, an officer on leave from India, cynically clever, unscrupulous, self-seeking, who likes to talk about 'the immeasurable difference' in every respect between a gentleman and a plebeian, however wealthy.[27] Much attention to detail, and sidelights on various aspects of duelling, lend the story a more convincing flavour than most of its kind. Events work up complicatedly to a duel in the Swiss Alps, between Calvert and an Englishman whose fiancée he has libelled. Having to look round for a second, he feels sure of finding 'some one who will like the cheap heroism of seeing another man shot at'.[28] When the duel is about to take place Calvert is careful that his second shall be the one to give the word, and instructs him before giving it to cough. He shoots his opponent dead, and, Swiss law in some cantons being strict, and worst in Basle, drives off at full speed for the frontier, leaving his second to face complaints of unfairness, and to be drawn into another duel and wounded.[29]

Among novelists who found the Peninsular War a happy hunting-

[23] Ibid., chap. 35.
[24] *Reminiscences of Marx and Engels*, 74.
[25] Fitzpatrick, ii. 11.
[26] *Jack Hinton*, chap. 28.
[27] *A Rent in the Cloud*, chap. 8.
[28] Ibid., chap. 7.
[29] Ibid., chaps. 10, 11.

ground was the Scotsman James Grant. Duelling finds mention on the first page of *The Romance of War*, and crops up again frequently, not without some genuine feeling for its darker shades, as well as those of battle. In Spain the young Highland hero Ronald Stuart and his comrades find murder more prevalent—"'tis not decently on the hillside that disputes are settled here', one of them observes.[30] Ronald is soon called out, however, by Count Balthazzar de Truxillo, who 'never visits Merida without fighting a duel with some one', and is displeased with the Scot's flirtation with his *inamorata*. Announcing himself as 'the most deadly shot in all Castille', he offers to spare him in return for a promise never to see Doña Catalina again. This is of course declined; they draw for first shot, and Ronald loses a feather from his bonnet; he then fires in the air, unable to shoot a defenceless man[31]—a predicament that many duellists must have found themselves in. Later on he again fires wide when he has to fight his old friend and fellow-officer Louis Lisle, who is under a mistaken notion that Ronald has jilted his sister, while Ronald mistakenly believes she has jilted him.[32]

Captain Marryat, after leaving the navy, was for some time an editor as well as novelist, and had a bloodless duel with an author ruffled by a review of his book. He too harked back in some of his tales to the great days of the Napoleonic wars, when he himself was afloat. It may have come more easily to a seaman than to an army officer to detect the absurdities of duelling. His Peter Simple, starting (like himself) as a midshipman at the age of fourteen, was instructed by his father, a clergyman, to avoid duelling, 'as it was flying in the face of my Creator; but aware that I must uphold my character as an officer, he left me to my own discretion'[33]—advice truly Anglican and discreet. Peter has no sooner entered the service than he gets into a row with a fellow-midshipman, and is assured by the other juvenile experts that he must fight. Each fires twice; it proves to have been a joke, with no bullets.

Things are not always so innocent, especially with an Irish friend of Peter's on the scene, eager to revenge him on a Captain Hawkins who has got Peter court-martialled and dismissed on false charges. O'Brien, now a general, forces Hawkins to challenge him, by publicly calling him a liar. 'Upon which', O'Brien reports with gusto to his friend, 'I shot him, with all the good-will in the world, and could he have jumped up again twenty times, like jack in the box, I would have shot him every time.'[34] But we only hear of this from his letter, and Marryat

---

[30] *The Romance of War*, chap. 7.
[31] Ibid., chap. 13: 'The Duel'.
[32] Ibid., chap. 34.
[33] *Peter Simple*, chap. 3.
[34] Ibid., chap. 64.

prefers the lighter side. In the same novel an eccentric Captain Kearney's collection of trophies includes a sword with which he once ran a Sicilian prince through in a duel, when it stuck so fast that they had to bring a pair of coach-horses to pull it out.[35]

In *Midshipman Easy* the comic highlight is reached when Jack Easy agrees to fight Mr Biggs the bos'n, and Easthupp the purser's steward, a Cockney and former pickpocket now anxious to be regarded as a gentleman. They go ashore at Malta, and Tallboys the gunner after much mathematical puzzling proposes a triangular exchange of fire. Easthupp objects, but Jack's friend Gascoigne silences him: 'you must know that your honour is in the hands of your second, and that no gentleman appeals'. Easthupp screws himself up and tremblingly points his pistol: Biggs's bullet hits him in the rear, Jack's goes through the bos'n's cheeks, knocking out two teeth and a quid of tobacco.[36] Here is an ever-running fount of humour, the theme of underlings aping the ways of their betters.

Charles Apperley, or 'Nimrod', in his fictional sketches of fox-hunting life in Yorkshire, though an enthusiastic chronicler reveals an incongruous dislike of duelling. After 'a brilliant run in the morning, which, in those days, was too often celebrated with Bacchanalian rites in the evening', a convivial party is fluttered by 'an unguarded expression' from the ubiquitous Irishman. An apology being refused by the offender, 'for the honour of Tipperary', he and Frank Raby, the hero, have to take the field. Both fire in the air, and the Irishman, 'a first-rate shot', then feels able to tender a handsome apology. That this tame conclusion is judged adequate points to the duel being by this time on the wane. When Frank is reproached by an acquaintance with letting the other man off too lightly, he exclaims that he wants no man's blood on his conscience, and when his critic talks of 'honour' he pokes fun at this 'darling attribute of the present age', and asks why in an era boasting of its refinement men should be 'unable to live correctly in society unless under fear of being shot, or compelled to shoot others'.[37]

For Dickens, the duel was so to speak jam: he was a middle-class moralist-novelist revelling in ridicule of a foppish, effete aristocracy, and a comedian revelling in human oddities and absurdities. How richly amusing he could make it he showed early on in *Pickwick*, with Mr Winkle, after a fancy-dress ball he has not been at, aroused next morning by an officer conveying a challenge. Compelled by his bogus reputation as a sportsman to accept it, he is taken aback by the

---

[35] Ibid., chap. 37.

[36] Pt. 2, chap. 2. Marryat's understudy Howard gives a similar picture of naval life and its frictions; see e.g. 183–4.

[37] 'Nimrod', 348–50.

equanimity with which Mr Snodgrass undertakes to be his second. 'It is extraordinary', Dickens remarks aside, 'how cool any party but the principal can be in such cases.'[38] In another episode Pott and Slurk, editors of the rival Eatanswill papers, retire after a brawl in an inn kitchen 'making vague appointments for mortal duel next day', but next day decide that 'they could do it much better in print'.[39]

In *The Old Curiosity Shop* we have another well-tried peg for hanging jokes on, plebeian inquisitiveness about the doings of the great. Mr Chuckster the young clerk and man of the world, 'justly considered by his friends to shine prodigiously' in his knowledge of current scandal, is about to relate 'the exact circumstances of the difference between the Marquis of Mizzler and Lord Bobby, which it appeared originated in a disputed bottle of champagne'.[40] As often, this was no more childish a *casus belli* than many that led to real hostilities; truth could be sillier than fiction. In *Dombey and Son* more emotional chords are touched, expertly if not altogether convincingly. Dombey's treacherous manager Carker absconds; so does his wife Edith, apparently with Carker, really seeking revenge against both men. It is not very easy to think of Mr Dombey, that cast-iron pillar of the City, contemplating a duel, but he has Major Bagstock to steer him. 'A shot is to be taken at this man. You have J.B. at your elbow. He claims the name of friend.' They pursue the runaways to their rendezvous, Dijon, where Edith alarms Carker by telling him she has seen her husband in the street. He sets off in panic flight back to England; why, can be explained only by improbable pangs of conscience, but the tension Dickens is piling up mounts steadily. In a final melodramatic but effective scene at a railway station in England, Carker waiting to board a train is shaken by suddenly seeing his pursuer close at hand, stumbles into the track of another train, and in his last moment sees the hated face 'change from its vindictive passion to a faint sickness and terror'.[41]

Thackeray went to Ireland, as described in his 1843 travel-book, ready like everyone else, if less gravely than some, to call up the picture, which by this time must have owed much of its high colouring to the novelists, of the sabre-rattling Irishman. At his Galway hotel, entrusted with the carving of the turkey, he was nervous he says of offending anybody by not giving him the choicest portion, having heard much of these 'dashing, daring, duelling, desperate, rollicking, whisky-drinking people'.[42] In many ways Thackeray was a parallel to Dickens; he too

[38] *The Pickwick Papers* (1837), chap. 2.
[39] Ibid., chap. 51.
[40] *The Old Curiosity Shop*, chap. 40.
[41] *Dombey and Son* (1847–8), chaps. 51, 54, 55.
[42] *The Irish Sketch Book* (1843), chap. 15.

loved to guy a decadent upper class, and invent comic low-life emulation of its customs, while condemning in earnest the type of gentleman who made duelling odious. Visiting Paris to write about the ceremony of Napoleon's body being brought back from St Helena to a new resting-place, he took occasion to laugh at the French for their stooping to copy the old moth-eaten nobility they had not long since kicked out of their country, and to go in for coats of arms and the rest of the 'wretched imitations of old, exploded aristocratic gewgaws'.[43]

John Bull was drifting the same way. It was the weakness of middle-class spokesmen like Thackeray, and of ill omen for the future of liberalism and social progress, that while they saw through the shams and impostures of the old order, they were much further removed from the mass of the people, whom they could only think of as servants, street vagrants, shop assistants. Stranded between old and new, the middle classes they wrote for would gravitate very largely towards the old, and lose any sense of direction of their own. The poor seem always to have loved tales of princes and palaces; Victorian novelists gave their readers enough noblemen to stock a dozen peerages. Their many low characters fancying themselves transformed overnight into gentlemen might be called a speeded-up version, half-intendedly satiric, of the bourgeois day-dream of gradual ripening into aristocracy. We laugh our own foibles off by foisting them on to others.

In one of Thackeray's stories, aptly entitled 'Shabby Genteel', George Brandon is intruded on by Mr Fitch, a Cockney painter, jealous of his attentions to a young lady who has 'read a vast number of novels'. Next morning Brandon wakes up with a headache and the gloomy reflection that 'If I shoot this crack-brained painter, all the world will cry out, "Murder!" If he shoots me, all the world will laugh at me!' Fitch too feels not very warlike, but he had somehow imbibed a notion that 'it was part of a gentleman's duty to fight duels, and had long been seeking for an opportunity'. Brandon's second, the dissipated Lord Cinqbars, is sensible enough to give them unloaded pistols; Fitch, having steeled himself to heroism, bursts into tears when he learns of the deception. 'What, do you gents call that a joke?'[44]

There is pathos here, but pure farce in the memoirs of C. Jeames de la Pluche, Esq., a footman enriched by railway speculation—except that if we look through charade to social reality, we can see the solid merchant or manufacturer turning himself into a gentleman. Jeames has a sort of fistic duel with his valet, whom he catches courting his Mary Hann: a heavier man, 'and knows the use of his ands as well as most men; but in a fite, *blood's everythink* ... I punish the raskle

[43] 'The Second Funeral of Napoleon' (1841).
[44] 'A Shabby Genteel Story' (1840), chap. 9.

tremenjusly.'[45] In another sketch we have a hilarious description of a modern tournament, no doubt suggested by the preposterous one organized by Lord Eglinton in 1839.[46] A more lifelike snapshot, of Lieutenant-General Sir George Granby Tufto, makes him look very much like the cantankerous Lord Cardigan. 'Selfish, brutal, passionate, and a glutton', he was sent young into the army, being unfit for anything else, and has made 'a good and gallant officer', devoting his free time to 'riding races, drinking port, fighting duels, and seducing women'.[47]

Vanity Fair, written in 1848 about life a generation before, might have been expected to make more of the subject. A duel threatens at one point between Colonel Rawdon Crawley, with the Allied forces in Paris, and an Irish colonel who has found fault with his mode of living by billiards and cards at the expense of greenhorns lured to his house by the blandishments of his wife, Becky Sharp; but the commander-in-chief nips it in the bud by sending for Crawley and giving him a stern warning.[48] Thackeray was inclined to keep his duels for historical novels with older settings. There too they are sometimes comic invention, though draped in much authentic detail. In *Catherine*, whose heroine is an understudy of Becky Sharp, a duel is prevented at the last moment by one party recognizing the other as a former corporal and thief. Count Galgenstein, a foreign envoy in London, tells his friend the abbé he is 'dying for want of excitement'; the last time he had any relief from ennui was when he was riding escort with his grand-duke's mistress's coach, and another nobleman pushed in front: in the ensuing encounter he ran this impertinent through, and was rewarded with his snug post in London.[49]

For weightier matter Thackeray found it easier to borrow from history and embroider, as in the three-a-side battle in Leicester Field which forms a central episode in *Henry Esmond*, with Lord Mohun its evil genius. The whole evening is vividly narrated with all its sordid ruffianism and crazy courage.[50] Barry Lyndon begins his retrospect of his eighteenth-century life with the tale of how, a mere boy in Ireland, fired with thoughts of his fighting ancestors, he forced a quarrel on Captain Quin, in spite of his family's efforts to hold him back—'it was my first affair, and I was as proud of it as of a suit of laced velvet'.[51] His pistol was Quin's extinguisher, and he had to go abroad and make his way in a wicked world. Amid the horrors and brutalities of war he

[45] 'The Diary of C. Jeames de la Pluche, Esq.', in *The Book of Snobs* (1847).
[46] 'Cox's Diary' (1840), for August.
[47] *The Book of Snobs*, chap. 9.
[48] *Vanity Fair* (1847–8), chap. 36.
[49] *Catherine* (1839–40), chaps. 6, 9.
[50] Bk. 1, chap. 14. On the importance of duelling in this novel, cf. Gilmour, 29–30.
[51] *Barry Lyndon* (1844), chap. 2.

learned to survive. He 'played at the bullet game' often, but with increasing caution: 'I may say, proudly for myself, that I never engaged in a duel unless I had a real, available, and prudent reason for it.'[52] Eventually he returned to Ireland in search of an heiress, and began by calling out a rival and wounding him.

His pious mother was delighted; she was indeed a woman of the grand old school, Barry reflected as he looked back in old age over his rise and fall; she 'would as lief have seen any one of her kindred hanged as shirking from the field of honour. What has become of those gallant feelings nowadays?'[53] Thackeray himself, looking back, not without a touch of nostalgia, over the thirty years since the death of George III, thought of the vanishing of the duel in England as part of 'a silent revolution'. He gazed at old gentlemen in clubs, and thought what dogs they must have been in their prime, in days when if 'in the petulance of play or drink' a man 'spoke a sharp word to his neighbour, he and the other would infallibly go out and try to shoot each other next morning'.[54] It was a valediction to a ghostly but still near past.

A minor but diverting writer had a novel out in 1856 where duelling can be seen sinking to the level of buffoonery. Wyndham Flitter, an engagingly artful dodger, manœuvres two acquaintances, neither of them 'gentlemen', into a quarrel and a meeting on Hampstead Heath— taking care to see that their weapons contain nothing but powder—in order to earn the gratitude of two frightened men.[55] It gets about that he himself has been fighting, and on the strength of this he is invited to dinner in the Tower with the officers. He enlarges on his duel all through dinner, with additions more and more exuberant, while the younger men listen admiringly; only one of them has been out, and 'that was in Ireland'. On his way home Flitter has to make a getaway from a gaming-house by way of the roof, and descends through a skylight into a hosiery store where a birthday is being celebrated. A young salesman, wanting to impress the girls, asks resolutely who he is. Flitter overawes him by pretending to be a Guards officer, and fiercely pronouncing the time-honoured formula: 'You have a card, sir . . .'[56]

Individuals born on the edge of a class they aspire to membership of may be the most inclined and best qualified to spin ideas about it and what it ought to be, just as frontiersmen make the keenest patriots. Trollope began life on the fringes of gentility, and his autobiography reveals how much he suffered from humiliation and the sense of

[52] Ibid., chap. 14.
[53] Ibid., chap. 2.
[54] *The Four Georges*, 115.
[55] Albert Smith, *The Pottleton Legacy* (London, 1856), chaps. 17, 19.
[56] Ibid., chaps. 23, 24.

exclusion. He learned in childhood some truths of class relations. 'It seemed to me that there would be an Elysium in the intimacy of those very boys whom I was bound to hate because they hated me.'[57] Such memories helped to give him his later, sometimes very acute, insights into the nature of class,[58] one of the subjects that most obsessed Victorians. It may be that Marx acquired some part of his conviction of the all-importance of class from living in class-ridden England.

Trollope set up his stall when duelling was entering its eclipse. A late novel shows him looking back on it like Thackeray, as something not long gone by. Jilted by the heir of a noble family, after her friends have all been bursting with envy, Augusta Mildmay can only bear her bad luck and try again. 'A few years since all the Mildmays in England, one after another, would have had a shot at the young nobleman.' Not much later, angry at Captain Jack de Baron's wanting to drop her, she longs for a return of 'the old days thirty years since—and for some old-fashioned brother, so that Jack might be shot at, and have a pistol-bullet in his heart'—though she also feels that she cannot live without him.[59]

Even in the good old days a Church dignitary (unlike a rank-and-file clergyman) could scarcely take the field, but the Dean of Brotherton, in the same novel, calls on the Marquis of Brotherton at his hotel and hurls him into the fireplace; the dean is of humble origin, and the peer has talked insultingly of his daughter.[60] This, we may guess, is how Trollope considered a foul-mouthed aristocrat ought to be treated, instead of being asked for polite 'satisfaction'. The unpleasant marquis, physically no match for his assailant, is left smouldering furiously, wishing he could have the dean in a room with him and 'a couple of loaded revolvers', or 'a pair of foils with the buttons off'.[61]

Meredith was learning to write in the later 1850s, when the duel was still a lively memory, especially for a Welsh-Irishman, even if a son-in-law of the sturdy iconoclast Peacock. In one of his first novels Richard Feverel is reconciled with his deserving wife Lucy, after an estrangement, but he has just been told that Lord Mountfalcon has been pursuing her, and feels it his duty to tear himself away from her in order to bring him to book. Mountfalcon thinks him off his head, but they meet, on the French coast: Richard is only lightly wounded, but his wife dies of the shock.[62] The note thus sounded was to vibrate through a great part of Meredith's writing. He thought intuitively of

[57] Trollope, *Autobiography* (1883), 15.
[58] Ibid., esp. 104–5.
[59] *Is he Popenjoy?* (1878), chaps 12, 15.
[60] Ibid., chap. 41.
[61] Ibid., chaps. 48, 50.
[62] *The Ordeal of Richard Feverel* (1859), chaps. 45, 46.

human relationships in terms of the duel; he could speak of an 'eternal duel' between man and woman.[63] Indeed a study of theme and symbol in his novels has revealed the duel as his archetypal image, his 'most central and complex metaphor for society's negative commitments', and his characters' struggles 'to dissociate themselves from destructive social attitudes'; as in *Vittoria*, where Italians fighting duels with Austrians may epitomize 'the tendency of primitive savagery, parading as patriotic idealism, to imperil the progress of true revolution'.[64]

Beauchamp's Career is an Anglo-French story in the time of the Second Empire. The well-born Nevil Beauchamp, who is to end as a socialist, begins, as a young midshipman outraged by French chauvinism, by inditing a general challenge to the whole Imperial Guard.[65] It is too late for duelling in England; when his uncle Mr Romfrey has a grievance against his neighbour Dr Shrapnel, Nevil's political mentor, instead of calling him out he comes to his house and thrashes him with a gold-headed riding-whip.[66] Meredith was readier than most British novelists to turn to the continent for settings; freedom of action for duellists was clearly one of its attractions. In *The Tragic Comedians* he made use of the death of Lassalle, the German socialist leader. One chapter in *Vittoria* is called 'The Duel in the Pass'. The heroine is trying to make her way over the mountains, when she is intercepted by Captain Weisspriess, a poor but ambitious soldier and 'the keenest swordsman in the Austrian army'. Angelo comes to the rescue, armed with nothing but a stiletto, and the two men seek a patch of level ground to fight on, in due form, with only the heroine for spectator. Angelo suddenly throws himself on the officer's sword, gets under his guard, and stabs him. Both are badly wounded, Angelo left master of the field.[67]

A late novel, though Meredith's first popular success, *Diana of the Crossways*, with a sparklingly Irish novel-writing heroine, shows Meredith turning back to the late years of duelling in England. No contest actually takes place, but threats, frivolous or serious, are bandied about, and there is a long dinner-table discussion, garnished with anecdotes, about the merits or demerits of the duel.[68] Irishmen are once more the great pistoleers, but Diana is sure that their temper can be turned to good ends; she, or Meredith, can hardly have failed to remember Beatrice and Benedick, and the slandered bride. When her friend Miss Paynham, who has no father or brother, is ill used, Diana tells a

---

[63] *Diana of the Crossways*, chap. 28; cf. chap. 10.
[64] M. Masterson, 'A Study of the Duel in Meredith', unpub. Ph.D. thesis (Toronto, 1976); see *Dissertation Abstracts International* (Ann Arbor, 1979).
[65] *Beauchamp's Career*, chaps. 1, 3.
[66] Ibid., chaps. 31, 32.
[67] *Vittoria* (1866), chap. 26.
[68] *Diana of the Crossways*, chap. 28.

confidante: 'With two words in his ear, I could arm an Irishman to do some work of chastisement:—he would select the rascal's necktie for a cause of quarrel.'[69] When her own reputation is breathed on, Mr Redworth, the solid English man of business, reports to the landowner Sir Lukin Dunstane that he has interviewed Lord Wroxeter and got an assurance that he has uttered no scandal. 'He professed his readiness to fight, if either of us was not contented.' Sir Lukin in company with an Irish officer friend visits editorial offices and leaves his card with a warning to print no gossip about Diana, on pain of 'personal and condign' punishment.[70]

What would have followed if an editor had shown fight, we are not told; but a terse dialogue in another novel, a fine flourish of aristocratic insolence, throws light on the dubious status of newspapermen, and the right way to deal with them. Miss Penrhys, out riding, meets Mr Richmond:

'You have read the paper?' he asked.
'You have horsewhipped the writer?' she rejoined ...
'Could we condescend to offer him satisfaction?'
'Would he dare to demand it?'[71]

Wilkie Collins started to write about the same time as Meredith, and he too could be fired by memories of the duel. In a long story reminiscent of Poe a young man of good family has been debarred from marrying a lady because her guardian knows of a taint of madness in his blood. He becomes obsessed with the aim of recovering the body of a rascally uncle, killed in a duel in Italy. With an emblazoned coffin ready for its reception he goes to Naples to hunt for it, with the help of an old document drawn up in advance by the two seconds. This specified the exact conditions for the fight, which had to be kept secret because the pope had lately urged all Italian governments to enforce the ban. The macabre tale ends with the unfortunate's mental collapse and death.[72]

In the prologue to a Collins novel, *The Black Heart*, a wealthy English country gentleman, Romayne, on a visit to Boulogne, is drawn into a card game in a shady gambling establishment, and accuses a general of cheating. Next day a pair of officers come to demand satisfaction on their commander's behalf. Romayne's companion wants him to refuse, on the ground that duelling has been abolished in England; the Frenchmen insist that anyone travelling abroad must respect 'the social laws of the country'. Romayne consents to fight, but early next morning has unwillingly to confront not the general, who is reported ill, but his

[69] *Diana of the Crossways*, chap. 18.
[70] Ibid., chaps. 13, 42.
[71] *Harry Richmond* (1871), chap. 26.
[72] Wilkie Collins, 'Mad Monkton'.

son. The pistols go off, the challenger falls dead, and the last the two Englishmen see, through a gathering mist, is his brother, a boy of thirteen, kneeling by the corpse. They return at once to England, Romayne a broken man, a prey to remorse and dark forebodings, feeling the mark of Cain on his brow.

Robert Louis Stevenson was a Scot indebted, inevitably, to Sir Walter, but drawn to the duel by echoes still heavy in the air of his native land, and by a certain fascination—in spite of or because of his being an invalid—with violence, the nerve-tingling exhilaration of combat. Not all the creatures of fancy in his *boutique fantasque* come alive, the more exotic of them less often than others. His story *The Suicide Club* ends with Prince Florizel of Bohemia confronting the wicked president; magnanimously willing to fight him, but insisting on swords—'this is more an execution than a duel', and 'a pistol-bullet travels so often on the wings of chance, and skill and courage may fall by the most trembling marksman'. The scoundrel recovers his nerve; danger stirs the manhood even in such a criminal. When it is over Florizel feels an immediate disenchantment. What use has it been? 'The existence of a man is so small a thing to take, so mighty a thing to employ!'[73]

Prince Otto of Grünewald takes umbrage at critical notes about him and his consort that an English traveller, Sir John Crabtree, has been compiling, and wants to fight him. Impossible, Sir John replies firmly: 'I cannot draw upon a reigning sovereign.' Reconciliation follows.[74] Less grand, but less stagy, is the episode in *Treasure Island* when Long John Silver threatens to 'call down' and fight one of his fellow mutineers, or 'gentlemen of fortune' as the pirates like to dub themselves.[75] But Stevenson's imagination, like Scott's, is most vital when his foot, as a writer, is on his native Scottish heath and its past. It is noticeable that his duels tend to be cut short. David Balfour, sick and exhausted by long trudging over the heather, is more and more irritated by his fellow fugitive Alan Breck, who has all the 'childish propensity to take offence' of the Highlander of fiction. At last David stings him into drawing his sword—but he at once throws it down. 'At this the last of my anger oozed all out of me', and they go on good friends once more.[76] They lodge for a night in the Braes of Balquhidder, where Rob Roy's grave is still shown; one of the famous marauder's sons, an outlaw like him, enters: he and Alan look at each other 'like strange dogs', or a pair of fighting-cocks, and trouble is about to break out when their

[73] *The New Arabian Nights* (1882), end of first story.
[74] *Prince Otto: A Romance* (1885), chap. 4.
[75] *Treasure Island* (1883), chap. 29.
[76] *Kidnapped* (1886), chap. 24.

quick-witted host averts it by producing his treasured bagpipes and inviting them to have a musical instead of martial competition.[77]

Later in his adventures David falls in with 'a gawky, leering Highland boy', Lieutenant Hector Duncansby, who has been set on by enemies to pick a quarrel and get him out of their way. Forgetting prudence, David lets himself be vexed, and soon—they are at Edinburgh—they are treading the familiar walk into Holyrood Park, 'that rough rocky desert', until they come to Hunter's Bog and 'a piece of fair turf'. They have no witnesses, and on the way David is sorely tempted to take to his heels. His adversary twice disarms him with ease, realizes that he knows nothing of swordsmanship, and is touched by his courage in fighting in spite of certain defeat. 'I am fery prave myself, and pold as a lions.' He admits that he has been instigated, and they make friends.[78] Many unexpected traits of character and conduct must have been struck out by the clash of swords.

It is in two late Stevenson novels that we have duels fought out, ferociously, to the end. In *The Master of Ballantrae*, set in mid-eighteenth-century Scotland, a duel forms the most realistic event in a painstakingly written but somehow not perfectly lifelike work. At cards one night with his brother, the Master drops hints about his liaison with Henry's wife. Henry strikes him in the face, and they go out forthwith into the cold shrubbery, the Master compelling the timid secretary Mackellar, who hates him, to carry two candles for them, instead of giving the alarm. Mackellar reproaches himself, but reflects glumly that 'a coward is a slave at the best'. Henry attacks, until his enemy too begins to feel 'the cold agony of fear'. He resorts to foul play, catching Henry's point with his free hand, but stumbles and is run through. He is left for dead, though he subsequently recovers and disappears. Henry is plunged into remorse, as they go indoors, and the old father and the guilty wife have to be told.[79] In all this Stevenson is at his best.

In the unfinished *St Ives* physical courage is shown as something that can lodge in the same frame with qualities more animal than human, and lend them a redeeming touch. The aristocratic St Ives, a prisoner in Edinburgh castle during the French wars, is smitten with the charms of a young lady who shows sympathy to the unfortunates; his fellow-captive Goguelot sees this, and talks about her in ruffian language. He is a brute who has risen from the ranks 'by an extreme heroism of bravery'. All the others are delighted by the excitement of a quarrel; a committee of honour is set up, and they make two weapons by unscrew-

[77] *Kidnapped*, chap. 25.
[78] *Catriona* (1893), chap. 8.
[79] *The Master of Ballantrae* (1889), chap. 5. D. Gifford debates the credibility of this duel in *Stevenson and Victorian Scotland*, ed. J. Calder (Edinburgh, 1981), 75.

ing a pair of scissors. The fight has to take place in the dark. Goguelot receives a mortal thrust, and meets death 'with something of the spirit of a Bayard'.[80] Whether or not Stevenson had read of it, a duel with scissor-blades actually took place, about the time his story belonged to, in India. An Irishman and a German, attached to a mercenary force of Germans employed there, fell out late at night, when no better weapons were to hand, and fought till both were badly damaged.[81]

A dream near the end of his life, on the other side of the world, may reveal better than any of Stevenson's writings how potent a spell the thought of duelling had laid on his mind, and how intimately it was associated with some of the emotions that he brought into *Ballantrae*. He described in a letter from his home in Samoa how overwork had given him a bad night: after long insomnia he 'dreamed a large, handsome man (a New Orleans planter) had insulted my wife, and, do what I pleased, I could not make him fight me; and woke to find it was the eleventh anniversary of my marriage'.[82]

By that time a British author's duels had to take place far away or long ago. Crusading against first philistinism and then capitalism, William Morris gathered strength by roaming in fancy among the stark realities, good or evil, of the Viking north. One of his prose romances, laid in a nameless mountainous land, contains an episode in the style of the sagas. A ruffian named Hardcastle forces his way into a peaceful homestead, proposing to stay there and make the women and other occupants his thralls. He is challenged by young Osberne, and generously enough agrees to fight with sword alone, Osberne having no other weapon, though unknown to Hardcastle it is a magic one. They go out to the 'hazelled' meadow, a space marked off with posts of hazelwood in true Nordic fashion. Hardcastle perishes, and Osberne gives him decent burial, 'since he died in manly wise, though belike he has lived as a beast'.[83]

One of Conan Doyle's sons sent a challenge to his biographer, Hesketh Pearson, on some trumpery ground, the more malapropos because Doyle had written a disapproving article in 1882 on duelling in France.[84] His dislike is visible also in one of his medical stories, *The Third Generation*, about a young baronet who has inherited a fatal taint from his grandfather, a 'notorious buck', one who 'gambled and duelled and steeped himself in drink and debauchery until even the

[80] *St Ives*, chap. 11.

[81] Stuart, i. 25–6.

[82] *Vailima Letters*, ed. S. Colvin (London, 1895), letter of 19 May 1891.

[83] William Morris, *The Sundering Flood* (London, 1897), chaps. 15–17.

[84] Information from Mr O. D. Edwards, of Edinburgh University, whose biography of Conan Doyle is in progress.

vile set with whom he consorted had shrunk away from him in horror'; a constellation of aristocratic vices well-known to readers by that time. In one of Doyle's novels an anecdote is recalled of an affair at Gibraltar when, the other party failing to arrive, the principal and his second fell out, and the latter was shot through the leg. An amiable old German remembers how he called out the skilled fencer who made off with his fiancée, only to be run through by his sword. ' "That is vat they call satisfaction", Baumser added, pulling his long red beard reflectively.'[85]

As the duel receded into the past, it might take on opposite shapes, Tennysonian fable or Gilbertian extravaganza. Knightly combats in the *Idylls*, like Gareth's with Sir Kay in *Gareth and Lynette*, look very much like duels. Lewis Carroll must be making fun both of them and of duelling when his Tweedledum and Tweedledee suddenly fly into a passion over a broken rattle, and the former vociferates 'Of course you agree to have a battle?' Alice has to help them don their armour of hearthrugs and coal-skuttles, and they are about to set to, one with a sword and the other with an umbrella, when a big crow scares them into running away. Later on the Red Knight and White Knight gallop up, and prepare to fight over whose prisoner Alice should be. 'You will observe the Rules of Battle, of course?' the White Knight enquires, to which his rival retorts 'I always do.' They bang away at each other until both fall off their horses, when they get up and shake hands.[86] It was a brilliant suggestion of Shane Leslie that *Alice* was the most scintillating of a shower of parodies or squibs loosed off at the Oxford Movement, and that Tweedledum and Tweedledee stand for High and Low Church, the two cavaliers for Thomas Huxley and Bishop Wilberforce.[87] Alternatively Carroll might be supposed to have known of the traditional battle between Carnival and Lent, sometimes depicted as fought with spoons and forks, and saucepan helmets: clearly ridicule of knights and their clatterings was implied.[88]

Various scenes in the Savoy Operas might be called a predestined epilogue to the duel, like the satyr-play following the tragedy. In *Princess Ida* bluestockings are laughed at, but lumbering dull-witted feudalists still more. Gilbert always enjoyed lampooning long pedigrees like Pooh-Bah's, or the British peerage. One of his happiest flashes is the dialogue between Lord Mountararat and Lord Tolloller, in friendly altercation about which of them is to have Phyllis, and the duel that must decide. Each feels that having to kill an old friend will burden the survivor

[85] *The Firm of Girdlestone* (1890), chap. 27.
[86] Lewis Carroll, *Through the Looking-Glass* (London, 1872), chaps. 4, 8.
[87] Shane Leslie, 'Lewis Carroll and the Oxford Movement' (1933).
[88] Burke, 124.

with lifelong regret—each charitably urges the other to escape this by being the one killed.[89]

Sadly Gilbert's chief duelling gambol came at the end of his collaboration with Sullivan, in *The Grand Duke; or, the Statutory Duel,* when—in 1896—both were past their zenith. It presents a mixture of high and low life, but, in contrast with the understrappers in Dickens or Thackeray who want to fight like their betters, here in the duchy of Pfennig Halbpfennig nobody wants to fight. A ruler a century ago resolved to suppress the duel, because it was bringing too many to the gallows, and ordained that quarrels were to be settled instead by drawing cards, the drawer of the lower card to be declared legally dead. Ernest, the theatrical manager, much prefers this. 'I hate a duel with swords. It's not the blade I mind—it's the blood.' Ludwig, his comedian, feels the same. 'I hate a duel with pistols. It's not the ball I mind—it's the bang.'

Appropriately, the last British man of letters who wanted to fight was the Anglo-Irishman George Moore. He had been living for ten years in Paris, where the field of honour was still well cultivated, and was trying to set up in London as a writer; he was badly in need, as he says in his *Confessions,* of something to puff him into celebrity or notoriety. A political wrangle one evening, in a Bohemian circle, with a handsome young nobleman, gave him a chance for a challenge. He counted on appreciation in the Liberal press, and 'a duel with a lord would be nuts and apples for the journalists'. He found it hard to enlist a second, and advisers on both sides thought the affair too meaningless for a fight, which would have to take place abroad.[90] It fell through; but it may well be that a good many duels really were fought for no better motive than to get into the news, to cut a dash. By the time Whistler sent Moore a challenge, on account of his taking sides with Sir William Eden in a dispute over payment for a portrait, the novelist had grown sensible enough to ignore it.[91]

[89] W. S. Gilbert, *Iolanthe* (1882), Act II.
[90] G. Moore, *Confessions of a Young Man* (1886), sect. xvi.
[91] E. F. Benson, *As We Were* (London, 1930), 225.

15

Western Europe: The Hundred Last Years

Nous avons déjà perdu beaucoup d'amis dont la mémoire vit entre nous; vous vous les rappelez, ô mes chers compagnons d'armes! Les uns sont morts par la guerre, les autres par le duel, d'autres par le suicide; tous hommes d'honneur et de ferme caractère, de passions fortes, et cependant d'apparence simple, froide et réservée.

Alfred de Vigny, *Servitude et Grandeur Militaires* (1835), Bk 3, chap. 2.

NORTHERN countries, though not Scotland, led the way in shaking off the duel, as an incubus from the past. It was early abolished in Iceland; in Sweden it was fading by the eighteenth century; in Norway, always a socially democratic country, it was not much more in the nineteenth than a peg for fantasy. Peer Gynt boasted of how, during his world-vaulting career, after breaking off an engagement to a girl of high rank he had to deal with seven young men of her family at once:

> I emerged from it the victor.
> Some blood was spilt; but still that blood
> Sealed my certificate of valour.[1]

Early in the century duelling was not uncommon in Belgium, partly because of Frenchmen crossing the border to fight with less fear of interference or publicity. A crop of fights arose from the struggle for independence from Holland, which was followed in 1841 by a strict ban.

Travelling in Portugal early in the nineteenth century, Lord Carnarvon observed that noblemen directed their pride and hauteur chiefly against one another; families of the longest and most unbroken descent were known as 'the Pure', and did not intermarry with others.[2] These rifts would hinder the aristocracy from playing a collective part in politics; they may also have been a stumbling-block in the way of duelling, which required recognition of equal rights within an élite. In Spain duelling lingered, with many other things, for want of a strong modernizing current to sweep it away, an industrial middle class in other words strong enough to have views of its own. Blanco White, the

---

[1] Ibsen, *Peer Gynt* (1867), Act IV, sc. i.
[2] Earl of Carnarvon, *Portugal and Galicia* (3rd edn., London, 1848), 46–6.

Spanish priest who despaired of his country and settled in England, wrote that only the lower classes of Spaniards fought about women now[3]. Officers may have been an exception. Stendhal relates that a Spanish half-pay officer at Narbonne, who had a young and pretty wife, 'was obliged to slap the face of a certain coxcomb'. Next day she was at the spot where they were to fight. The coxcomb thought she had come to restrain them; she replied 'I have come to bury you.'[4]

Politics, often sanguinary and further envenomed by the Church's alliance with reaction, supplied a frequent cause. It was an era of revolutions, civil wars, and counter-coups, and of ambitious new social strata, crowded with professional politicians and journalists. The fact that the officer corps, mainly career men of middle-class origin, though covetous of titles and estates, was always in the thick of politics, and was split between the jarring factions, helped to give political life its acrimony. In April 1836, at the height of the Carlist war, there was a duel between Mendizábal—the premier interviewed by the bible-selling Borrow—and Istúriz, another prominent figure on the Liberal side, but representing an earlier and less radical generation. They were placed at twenty paces, a safe range for most civilians, and their seconds forbade a second shot, but they were never fully reconciled.[5] Soon after the defeat of Carlism a new Cortes session opened, in February 1840, with the *Moderado* or conservative wing of Liberalism dominant. Abusive speeches resounded, and the atmosphere grew so heated that younger deputies got in the habit of bringing bludgeons or knives with them. Several duels were the predictable outcome, one between Mendizábal and Alejandro Mon, the right-wing economist.[6]

In two notable political duels fought in Spain, three out of the four combatants were French. In 1853 Pierre Soulé was appointed American minister at Madrid. He was a Frenchman by birth, a diehard republican exiled by the rise to power of Napoleon III; not in other respects a progressive, for after becoming an American he threw himself into the long-drawn efforts of the USA to filch Cuba and its rich slave-plantations from Spain. His private rancour against the French government embroiled him almost at once with its ambassador, the Marquis de Turgot, whom he shot through the knee in a duel on the Prado.[7] France's previous monarch, Louis Philippe, had gone to great pains before his fall in 1848 to marry his youngest son, the

---

[3] Joseph Blanco White, *Letters from Spain by Don Leucadio Do blado* (London, 1822), 268.

[4] Stendhal, *Love*, 243.

[5] P. Janke, *Mendizábal y la … monarquía constitucional en España* (Madrid, 1974), 212–13.

[6] Ibid. 305.

[7] See A. A. Ettinger, *The Mission to Spain of Pierre Soulé* (New Haven, 1932), chap. 7. The seconds tried vainly, the British minister reported, to avert a fight, and then to prevent more than a single shot (Lord Howden to Lord Clarendon, no. 146, 17 Dec. 1853, FO 72.726, Public Record Office).

Duc de Montpensier, to the younger sister of Queen Isabel, in the hope of adding Spain to the possessions of his own branch of the Bourbon dynasty. When Isabel was overthrown in 1868 Montpensier thought, not for the first time, that his chance had at last come. Unluckily for him, in March 1870 he was drawn into a duel with Isabel's erratic cousin and brother-in-law the demagogic Duke of Seville, whose death destroyed any prospect he may have had of ascending the throne.

Italy was, as always, a corner of Europe by itself, neither properly 'western' nor anything else; a country for more than half the century with no unity, no national army, and combining much culture with deep marks of the despotic rule denounced by Alfieri in 1777 in his study *Tyranny*. Its chapters on Honour and Nobility are full of suggestion as regards the social setting of the duel as a European institution; but there was little of an authentic aristocracy in Italy. Fear of those petty tyrants the Italian princes and their spies had degraded men, Stendhal believed; 'there is no such thing as foolish *honour*, which is replaced by a kind of petty social hatred'.[8] His novel-hero Fabrice could only compel the reluctant Count M. to fight by carrying him off to the hills near Bologna, where by distributing money he gathered some rustics as witnesses. Cornered, the count resisted with energy, but a sword-thrust sent him to his bed, where he was threatened with death if he informed the police.[9]

In 1820 Byron wrote from Ravenna to Moore about the attempt of his Teresa's husband to get a legal separation, for which, he explained, a great deal more evidence was required in Italy than for a divorce in England. 'All her relations are furious against him. The father has challenged him—a superfluous valour, for he don't fight, though suspected of two assassinations.' Byron himself was being warned of the need for precautions, 'so I take my stiletto and a pair of pistols in my pocket during my daily rides'.[10] He was careful also to be well guarded. A couple of years later he wrote to Walter Scott from Pisa that he and some other British visitors, out riding, had been rudely jostled by a mounted man in uniform whom they took for an officer. Byron challenged him, but he proved to be a mere sergeant-major, and rode off, only to be stabbed at a short distance by one of Byron's retinue. 'I have some rough-handed fellows about me.'[11]

A play like Torelli's *I Mariti* (1867) is full of duelling talk. Probably for most Italians it was on the stage that the duel had its strongest attraction now. Still, in the decade 1879–89, according to a table

[8] Stendhal, *Love*, 160.
[9] Id., *La Chartreuse de Parme* (1839), chap. 13.
[10] Byron, *Letters*, 257.
[11] Ibid. 325–6; cf. D. L. Moore, 280 ff.

someone compiled, a total of 2,759 duels were fought in Italy, nearly all with sword or sabre, which inflicted a good many wounds and fifty deaths.[12] Italy was now united, and ambitious of great-power status and a place in the colonial sun; nationalism may have been giving the duel new vigour.

France was the country of western Europe where it was most energetically alive. In Paris one had to be prepared to defend every word, Stendhal wrote, by a stroke of wit if possible—if not, sword in hand.[13] Duelling had its firmest adherents among the old nobility. After the Restoration, when they were recovering as much of their former status as they could, it helped to advertise their claim to be once more the nation's élite. They, as well as Allied officers, might have to defend themselves against Bonapartists smarting under their defeat. A case that gained wide celebrity, at home and abroad, was that of the Comte de St.-Morys, an officer of the Guard, formerly a royalist émigré in England. He was insulted by an ex-officer of the Revolution and the Empire, one Barbier, who at first refused to fight except on condition that they should stand with their pistols, only one of them loaded, *à bout portant* at each other's stomachs. St.-Morys was forbidden by his superior, the Duc de Mouchy, to agree to this, but was then humiliatingly suspended from service when he showed reluctance to cane his enemy in public. Eventually, after the Marshals of France had been consulted, they met and exchanged two shots in more normal fashion, and then fought with swords until St.-Morys fell: he was confused by his adversary unexpectedly proving to be left-handed.[14]

His anguished widow appealed to the army, and the magistrates, but got no response. She had no fault to find with ordinary affairs of honour, she declared, but Barbier had virtually plotted to murder her husband. She then put the matter into the hands of three lawyers, who drew up a lengthy 'consultation'. They felt unable to endorse the charge of murder; but they reviewed the history of French legislation against duelling, which had never been abrogated, and pronounced that it was illegal as well as uncivilized. They concluded by hoping that the publicity attached to this case would do something to discredit it and 'strike some fear into the many slaves of this barbarous habit'.[15]

After the revolution of 1830 the habit could underline an obstinate adherence to the 'legitimate' Bourbon branch. It was kept up far longer than in England, because in France aristocracy now had far less place in the national life, and more need of adventitious props. Frenchmen

[12] Baldick, 144.
[13] Stendhal, *Love*, 144.
[14] Comtesse de St.-Morys, 91, 232 ff.
[15] Ibid., 'Consultation'.

went on turning out treatises on the history and principles of duelling, partly to feed nostalgia, partly for instruction, and to initiate impressionable sections of other classes into the mysteries. In 1836 the Comte de Chateauvillard's *Essai sur le duel* was published. It included a complete code, to whose wide acceptance the signatures of eighty individuals high in the army or society testified. A good deal of the old cosmopolitanism still clung to the European upper classes, with French its chief carrier; it was the language of the drawing-room in Madrid and in Moscow. The essential sections of the *Essai* were translated, moreover, into German in 1839, and the next year into English. They supplied a minute classification of grievances, and a long list of ingenious variants of the usual routine, some of them, horseback fights for instance, calling for written agreements beforehand. 'Most horrible', to an English commentator's mind, was 'the duel with one loaded pistol'. He was writing thirty years after the book's appearance, and found it hard to believe that duelling, still rampant in France, was flourishing so few years ago in England too, where nowadays the bare thought of a duel was laughable.[16]

Old French legislation could in practice be disregarded, since the new penal code was silent. In the 1860s it began to be held by the supreme court that duelling was subject to ordinary criminal law, but little came of this; it was treated with even more lenity than the *crimes passionels* among which it could be classed by French sentimentality. For the benefit of officers, Justice could wink hard. Pugnacity had been refreshed by the long conflict with Europe, and near the end of the century Bernard Shaw could still think of the Frenchman as an anachronism, a human fighting-cock. Boys in the 1890s were playing a tournament game in the schoolyard, the bigger ones charging from opposite sides with small boys on their shoulders to do battle.[17] A national passion for shooting rabbits and other wild animals spread familiarity with firearms far wider than in Britain, where hunting was a preserve of the rich. Conscription, during the periods when it was enforced, deepened this. France suffered from recurrent domestic bloodshed, as well as foreign wars, two spells above all of violent reaction and massacre, after the crushing of the Paris workers' insurrection of June 1848 and that of the Paris Commune in 1871. The smell of blood was in the air too often for the deaths of a few duellists to be deplored.

Political upheavals were themselves productive of disputes and challenges, as 1789 had been. The revolution of 1848, which gave birth to the short-lived Second Republic, was soon followed by discords among its sponsors. Encounters between deputies to the newly elected Assembly

[16] Anon., 'The Code of Duelling'.
[17] H. A. Alain-Fornier, *Le Grand Meaulnes* (1913; English edn., Harmondsworth, 1966), 89–90.

were frequent. One unlikely duellist, after an altercation leading to fisticuffs in the lobby of the Palais Bourbon, was the philosopher Proudhon, who, however, declined a second invitation. Ledru-Rollin the republican and the conservative Denjoy met on 13 April 1849, at 5 p.m. near the Pont de Neuilly. Ledru-Rollin missed, Denjoy's pistol missed fire: invited to try again, he declined the chivalrous offer, and they shook hands.[18] It was pouring with rain, weather calculated to damp the ardour of any but the most combustible. A comedy of 1850 made use of the duelling theme to ridicule the old order. Two courtiers of Louis XV's time, Folleville and Manicamp, out shooting, quarrel about a duck; Manicamp pushes Folleville into a pond, just as the royal cortège comes riding by, and the next day, to escape a challenge, presses his daughter on Folleville, an engagement the latter is soon trying to back out of.[19]

Political émigrés have been known for their quickness to fall out with one another or with their new neighbours. There were fights among royalist émigrés in England in the post-1789 years, as Fanny Burney, alias Mme d'Arblay, observed with regret.[20] In 1835 Carlyle's wife, who took a romantic interest in refugees, got to know a French exile named Garnier, 'big, bull-like, black-eyed', with sabre-scars across his face. Early in 1844 he reappeared on the scene abruptly, unkempt and in dirty clothes, and boiling with fury at an English nation he said had insulted him—full of 'the *bloodiest* talk' about the twenty-five duels in which he had defended his honour, and the chastisement he had in store for the English.[21] Left-wing Frenchmen of the mid-century used to meet at a house in Rathbone Place and practise fencing and shooting. Marx went there now and then, 'and had some strenuous fights'. One good swordsman was Barthélemy, an enigmatic person who had fought at the barricades in 1848 but came to be suspected by other refugees of having turned spy for the French government. What may have been the last duel on English soil was fought between him and Cournet, a former French naval officer, insatiably busy with plots and schemes, who had to leave home when Napoleon III came to power. Cournet was killed, Barthélemy and the two seconds, as foreigners, got off with a short term in jail, but two years later he was hanged for murder.

Cataloguing the accomplishments of a young man of good family, Balzac says he was a good pistol-shot, rode well, and had fought a duel over some nothing, without killing his adversary. In a conversation in the same story someone explains to his companions the origin of the

[18] A. R. Calman, *Ledru-Rollin and the Second French Republic* (New York, 1922), 245, 288.
[19] Eugène Labiche, *Embrassons-nous, Folleville!* (Paris, 1850).
[20] *Diary and Letters* (1842–6), letters of 20 Dec. 1792.
[21] Hanson, 201, 301–2.

phrase *coup de Jarnac*: one of them, impressed by hearing how old it is, feels that it must be a 'noble' expression.[22] A mid-century play by two leading authors, Augier and Sandeau, which contrasts the noble with the bourgeois philosophy of life, takes duelling as one of the distinguishing marks. M. Poirier has made a fortune in business, but cherishes hopes of a title, and to further them marries his daughter and heiress to the profligate and bankrupt but blue-blooded Gaston, Marquis de Presles. Gaston is treated sympathetically by the writers, but it is hard to see him today as anything but a young wastrel who marries for money, keeps up an affair with another woman, lives by sponging on his father-in-law, and likes to talk about his honour.

His sole virtue, if it is one, is readiness to fight, not for his country, since it is no longer under legitimate monarchy, but for this mystic honour. His friend the Duc de Montmeyran, in other ways less harebrained, supports him. 'Our rights are abolished, but not our duties . . . we shall remain for ever subject to a code sterner than the law, this mysterious code that we call honour.'[23] Gaston has a duel on his hands, a result of gambling and his liaison; his wife Antoinette is in despair; Gaston is persuaded to humiliate himself by abandoning the duel; she pardons him for everything, and then, carried away by admiration for aristocratic values, as her father is by desire for a peerage, exclaims: 'Now, go and fight!' 'Oh, dear wife,' he responds, 'you have my mother's heart!'[24] An apology from the enemy sets all right. He is a M. Grimaud who has promoted himself to Vicomte de Pontgrimaud and expects a duel with a real marquis to do him good socially, but at the last moment thinks better of it.

A good part of the bourgeoisie was as willing as the Poirier family (not their friend M. Verdelet, an epitome of uncompromising bourgeois good sense) to adopt aristocratic modes. Manufactures were sluggish; by comparison with the moneyed classes in Britain, the French were still very much of the old mould, easily drawn to the magnet of land-investment, and with it to the *ignis fatuus* of gentility. Zola commented on its appeal to the provincial bourgeoisie of Aix, consumed with desire to be invited to the noble houses whose doors were closed to them.[25] Proust's upper-middle-class narrator, exquisitely aesthetical, can mention casually to his Albertine a duel he has been in.[26] By fighting (or sometimes pretending to fight) duels, men of the nineteenth century could identify themselves with a French chivalry stretching back to

[22] H. de Balzac, *La Maison Nucingen* (1838); *Œuvres complètes* (Paris, 1865), xxiii. 7, 14.

[23] Augier and Sandeau, Act II, sc. ii.

[24] Ibid., Act IV, sc. iv.

[25] Jack Lindsay, *Cézanne, his Life and Work* (London, 1969), 7.

[26] *The Guermantes Way*, trans. C. K. Scott Moncrieff (London, 1930), ii. 62.

Charlemagne, and so gain emancipation, at least in fantasy, from the narrow limits of the counting-house. As in England the taste for duelling could spread lower down, and also wider, infecting some of France's always numerous foreign settlers. In 1821 a wealthy Polish Jew called out a Geneva stockbroker who had seduced his wife, and got killed for his pains, but the victor incurred much opprobrium,[27] probably in his walk of life more than if he had refused to fight. By the 1830s ordinary tradesmen were fighting, sometimes with similar fatal consequences.

Altogether the French bourgeoisie, compared with the English, was absorbing more of the worse attributes of nobility, whose better potential (as well as its worst habits) had been cramped or suffocated in France by the monarchy. As usual, the example set by the army was important. Its general view was that duelling was necessary to protect offended honour, and acceptance of a challenge was virtually compulsory, though a man giving offence without rhyme or reason might be censured. De Vigny's description of his post-1815 generation is of men at least as likely as their British compeers to find duels a welcome relief from boredom; he speaks of 'the fatuous conceit, idle and ignorant, of the young officers of that time, perpetual smokers and gamblers.'[28] In the officer corps down to 1914 there was always a considerable aristocratic residue, which could lay claim to special innate gifts for leadership. The calamitous faith in the offensive, accepted by the army planners before 1914, may be traceable in part to it. To fight duels, and in war to attack, without counting the cost, can be seen as cognate expressions of the aristocratic spirit.

In the time of the Second Empire the army rank and file came to be mainly composed of professional, long-term soldiers, thought politically more reliable. Among them, especially the NCO's, readiness to emulate their superiors could gain ground. 'There is hardly a regiment in the garrison of Paris', Steinmetz wrote in 1868, 'which has not its professed duellist, officer or private.'[29] With the Third Republic a mass conscript army came into being, and in a country socially far more democratic than England a conscript serving in the ranks might be more a gentleman than many of his officers.

Bonapartism, that ancestral form of fascism, revived the militaristic spirit of the First Empire, and carried its voracious colonial campaigning much further. Service in Mexico or China, or the protracted conquest of Algeria that was now being completed, nurtured a brutalized type of officer who might relish duelling, as well as repression, for its own sake. One such was the Marquis de Gallifet, prominent in

---

[27] Steinmetz, ii. 115.
[28] *Servitude et grandeur militaires*, Bk 1, chap. 3.
[29] Steinmetz, i. vii.

1871 in the butchery of the Communards. At the opera one night in 1858 he accused the Comte de Lauriston of staring at his wife through a pair of opera-glasses, and was vindictive enough, after being put out of action by a slight wound, to insist on a second meeting, something atavistic by that time even in France.

When army men with itching sword-hands were content to slash one another, it might be felt that no great harm was done; but as in other military countries there was always a risk of their wanting to bully and browbeat civilians, and of the duel being put at the service of corporate interests or spites. In 1831 General Bugeaud, who was to be the most successful 'pacifier' of Algeria, fought and killed a member of the Assembly. In 1858 there was loud public protest over an incident in which a journalist was called out because he had written something critical of the officer corps. In a sword fight he further inflamed the military temper by defeating and wounding his challenger; this man's second, another junior officer, immediately forced him to fight again, and nearly killed him. A large crowd watched another contest in which an officer met his death at the hands of the brother of a woman he had seduced.[30] It may be supposed that duels concerned with women were the likeliest to arouse interest, and when bruited in advance to draw the most spectators.

Politics and journalism, more and more inextricable, were prolific of quarrels in which 'honour' could be held at stake. In France, the English reviewer of Chateauvillard remarked, 'the journalist must make up his mind to a duel as one of the incidents of his profession'. A striking number of prominent politicians took the field at one time or another, though politics might not always be the cause. Thiers had to meet an angry father. He fired in the air; such a confrontation must often have been one-sided, because even if the man called out was really blameless, sympathy was not likely to be with him if he injured the lady's protector. But Bonapartism did much to envenom political feeling. Early in 1870 Marx's daughter Laura, married to the French socialist Paul Lafargue, wrote from Paris to a sister about excitement there over the arrest of Henri de Rochefort, editor of *La Marseillaise*, and some unrest in the workers' quarters. One of the editorial staff, Grousset, had accused Prince Pierre Bonaparte, the emperor's disreputable cousin, of slandering him, and challenged him to fight. His colleague Victor Noir, calling at the prince's house as his second, was fired on and killed; Pierre must have fallen into a panic. Rochefort wrote an article denouncing this as murder, and was given a six-months' sentence.[31] He

[30] Steinmetz, ii. 146–7, 167 ff.

[31] *The Daughters of Karl Marx: Family Correspondence 1866–1898*, trans. F. Evans (London, 1982), 62–4.

was a marquis turned journalist, and a leftist whose chequered career lobbed him back in later days to the right.

Napoleon III's fall, and the Commune, again intensified political bitternesses, and the republic was for long unstable; while the catastrophic defeat by Prussia may have left patriots feeling that they must heal national honour or self-respect by blazing away at one another, and showing the world that French courage had outlasted French supremacy. At any rate, amid a spate of crises and scandals, duelling flourished on a scale that has led to its survival being called 'one of the stranger aspects of Republican manners'.[32] In 1877 Gambetta, the trumpeter of resistance to Prussia in 1870, had a fight with Bardy de Fourtou, then minister of the Interior. In the hot August of 1887, when rumours of plottings by the demagogue General Boulanger filled the air, Engels was writing to Laura Lafargue from his holiday place, Eastbourne, and commented on two abortive quarrels: one between Francis Laur and Paul de Cassagnac, the other between General Boulanger and Jules Ferry, a recent premier with much responsibility for the French seizure of Vietnam. 'French, like all other politics', are under the influence of the hot weather. 'Tout rate, même les duels'— everything hangs fire, even the duels.[33] Cassagnac edited a right-wing paper with the well-chosen name *Autorité*, and like his father before him was a blatant bully. Lafargue conjured up in a pamphlet a fantasy picture of politicians, generals, and so on transformed into popular entertainers, among them Cassagnac, 'in full duellist costume, rolling his eyes and twisting his mustache, spitting out burning tow', and threatening everyone with his father's pistol.[34]

Next year Boulanger drew his sword, in the most ineptly momentous duel of the era. His popularity was swelling, a successful coup seemed within his reach, when his heated language in an Assembly debate on revision of the constitution compelled the prime minister, Floquet, to challenge him. Floquet was an elderly, near-sighted lawyer, no match for a fire-eating warrior, but to the astonishment of all it was Boulanger who came off second-best, with a wound. The affair took place with great publicity, at the back of a fashionable house, young ladies offering cool beverages to pressmen in the front garden.[35] To the French public Boulanger's misadventure had a fatal flavour of the absurd, and it was one reason for the collapse of his ambitions in the following year, and flight abroad followed by suicide.

Writers found in duelling a profitable part of their wares. Dumas

[32] R. D. Anderson, *France 1870–1914* (London, 1977), 87.
[33] *Frederick Engels–Paul and Laura Lafargue Correspondence* (Moscow, 1960), ii. 55–6.
[34] Paul Lafargue, *Le droit à la paresse* (1880; English edn., 1907, repr. Chicago, 1975), 64–5.
[35] Edgar Holt, *The Life of Georges Clemenceau 1841–1929* (London, 1976), 71–2.

senior was inspired by the memoirs of the seventeenth-century soldier of fortune D'Artagnan to set his Three Musketeers going; the Church put them on the Index, as too likely to spread romantic ideas about the duel. He displays an interest in the detail of fencing, as in the fight in *The Forty-Five Guardsmen* where Chicot anticipates the modern mode of standing firm-footed and depending on wrist strength instead of leaping to and fro; he banters his opponent with a running commentary on the passes he is executing, before finally pinning him to the wall like a huge insect. With *La Dame aux camélias* his son furnished Verdi with the plot where jealousy between Alfred and the baron results in the fight, and the latter's wound, of which 'la traviata' learns on her deathbed.

Men of letters and of the arts could be as irritable as any politicians, though not all were eager to emulate their own fighting heroes or villains. Berlioz when baulked in love set off in a fury from Florence to Paris with loaded pistols and a bottle of strychnine, not to face his rival but, in his own words, to shoot 'two guilty women and one innocent man', and then take poison. Fortunately his temper cooled before he reached Nice.[36] Literary duels were frequent. Most of these ended harmlessly, like Sainte-Beuve's; but one pair of novelists fired no fewer than four shots each on behalf of their views about the merits of classical as against romantic literature, and could only be separated when too badly hurt to go on.[37] Englishmen might fall out over women, or horses, but scarcely over so insignificant a question as this; the stormy battle of words in Paris in 1830 over Victor Hugo's romantic drama *Hernani* makes it less incredible that Frenchmen should be willing to fight about stylistic principles.

To Maupassant the duel was both a stimulating theme and an experience. He made free with too many women to escape molestation, though his renown as a marksman is said to have deterred some husbands from making themselves a nuisance. He paid the penalty in a different way, by dying of syphilis. But the psychology of fear interested him. His story of a coward (*Un lâche*, 1884) tells of a man lying awake all night and then shooting himself, unable to face the duel he is committed to. In a longer story, *L'Héritage*, there is a graphic study of the feelings of a man for whom the prospect of a duel was an earthquake, just as that of war is for a nation. Such sensations must have been frequent among the widening circles of those who were 'gentlemen', and could be called on for satisfaction, by social assent and usage rather than ancestral warrant. In the course of a dispute Lesable throws an inkpot at another man, who talks to his friends, all

[36] *The Life of Hector Berlioz, Mémoires* (1870; English edn., London, 1912), 102 ff.
[37] Steinmetz, ii. 119.

awkwardly ignorant of duelling niceties, and sends a challenge. Lesable refuses an apology, but then realizes with a shock what he is in for. 'Un duel! Il allait avoir un duel!'—a peaceable fellow who had never dreamed of the possibility, never fortified himself by thinking about it beforehand. Mutual explanations, instead of a fight, end the matter, to the disappointment of their acquaintances, and the indignation of Lesable's wife, who taxes him with timidity.

Another story, *Un duel*, shows us an individual to whom duelling is equally foreign but who, under sufficient provocation, can rise to the occasion. He is a wealthy businessman, has served in Paris in the National Guard during the Franco-Prussian war, and is now leaving the stricken city to join his family in Switzerland. An improbably brutish Prussian officer in the same railway carriage persists in harassing him; a pair of inscrutable Englishmen look on in silence. At last M. Dubois is goaded into jumping on his tormentor and beating him. The boor demands satisfaction. They get out at Strasburg and walk to the ramparts, with the Englishmen and a pair of Germans as witnesses. By a fluke (more frequent it may be in fiction than in history) Dubois, who has never held a pistol, shoots his opponent dead. The Englishmen, suddenly jubilant, shake his hand, give three cheers, and hurry him back with them to the train.

Maupassant's novel *Bel Ami* (1885) was to receive the accolade of being made into a film, whose success must have owed much to a concluding scene invented for it, a dramatic duel in which the good-looking cad who has lived by preying on women finally meets with his deserts.

As late as 1900 a municipal councillor perished in a duel in Paris with a member of the Assembly, and as late as 1920 a bill to outlaw duelling was proposed. But the mortality rate in recent years had not been heavy, and what had been a secret ceremony was turning into a theatrical stunt to attract notice. Given the prevalent corruption of French political life, which erupted in 1892 in the great Panama Canal scandal, duels with their parade of nice concern for honour could supply a cosmetic disguise for the profession as a whole. Clemenceau is credited with twenty-two affairs, and, as befitted the name he earned of 'the Tiger', he was proficient with both sword and pistol. 'Yet his duels were singularly bloodless; only one of his opponents seems to have been wounded at all seriously.'[38] He often fired wide, he told an acquaintance; others may have done the same, on the principle of one good turn deserving another. In the wake of the Panama scandal he was attacked in the Chamber by his enemy Paul Déroulède, the

[38] Holt, 18 n. 1.

nationalist author and agitator banished in 1900 as a plotter against the republic. A crowd of three hundred watched their meeting on the racecourse; *Le Petit Journal* published a picture of the gathering.[39] Three shots were to be exchanged, at twenty-five metres. Neither was hit, which left room for suspicion of some arrangement; the outcome may have been just as well for Clemenceau, since the crowd was not on his side.

This kind of token or symbolic duel was little more than playing to the gallery; or, to resort to a less dignified image, the duellist was coming to resemble a dog perfunctorily scratching a street pavement with its hind paws. What must be regretted is that the fire-eaters of 1914 could not have found an equally economical way of fighting their duel. The 'phoney war' on the western front in 1939–40, indeed, was not without some resemblance to a duel preceded by an agreement to fire in the air.

[39] Reproduced in Wilkinson, 35.

16

Under the Old Monarchies

> The Christian scheme ... forbids all enmity or even resistance. The result is that with the moderns Courage is no longer a virtue. Nevertheless it must be admitted that cowardice does not seem to be very compatible with any nobility of character ... cowardice seems contemptible, and personal Courage a noble and sublime thing.
>
> Schopenhauer, *On Human Nature* (trans. T. B. Saunders (London, 1897), p. 9).

HESSE in the 1820s was misgoverned by the electoral prince William I and his mistress; when his unsavoury favourite Heyer von Rosenfeld was called to account by an officer the ruler sheltered him by promptly proclaiming duelling a capital crime. But this ban was exceptional. Germany was still semi-feudal, and the young Engels could write of 'Barons from head to toe, in every drop of blood the fruit of sixty-four equal marriages, and in every glance a challenge!'[1] Whitman, an English resident familiar with the country gentry of Silesia, described their mostly dull, monotonous life, more vacuous even than that of their English counterparts. Pride of family was its backbone, game-shooting and cards its recreations. Duels brought a welcome occasional animation. 'There was something barbaric, almost Russian, about these people ... They were argumentative, truculent, and quarrelsome, with a code of honour of the army paramount among them.'[2]

As in the west, duelling spread to sections of the bourgeoisie, one symptom of how this class, in what by 1900 was Europe's strongest industrial nation, was succumbing to atavistic 'neo-feudalism' and strident militarism. The patriotic and liberal-reforming movement paved the way for the unification of 1871, but it was Bismarck and the Prussian army that took the lead, while liberalism fell by the wayside. German industrialization was a far more headlong process than British or French; it brought a more sudden and urgent threat of socialism, and a recoil from change and disappearance of old landmarks, a vertigo like that of a traveller transported to a distant time zone. In a world of machines a reassurance was needed that the human being was still

[1] E. Stepanova, *Frederick Engels* (Moscow, 1970), 16.
[2] Whitman, 77.

supreme, even if he could only be so in the guise of a Nietzschean superman working himself into Wagnerian rages.

Germans as a nation, so long disunited and timidly subservient to princelings and prelates, were well fitted for a double life of reality and fantasy. Among the higher classes this had its rehearsal in student life, where the banning of progressive societies in 1819 and the revival of the reactionary *corps* were a foreshadowing of the liberal débâcle of 1849. College fraternities devoted much of their time to what they called 'renowning' (*renommieren*)—swaggering, bragging, brawling, anything to give themselves airs and out-strut their rivals.[3] When the great philologist Max Müller was a student at Leipzig in 1841–3, four hundred duels took place there in a single year, though only two deaths resulted. He himself carried away from the duelling place, a romantic woodland outside the town, the scars of three fights. Theology students, he found, preferred pistols to swords, because they could not afford to be seen with scarred faces, but their encounters were 'generally the most harmless, except perhaps for the seconds'.[4] Wars for national unification popularized all warlike fashions, duelling among them; though there were also student controversies on the subject during the 1860s, Liberalism fighting a rearguard action.

Duelling evolved a form unique to the student corps, the *Mensur*.[5] It was a display of stoic courage before a watchful audience; vital parts were protected, and opponents hacked at each other with sabres and acquired scars as though winning medals. The *Mensur* was stamped with the humourless heaviness peculiar to the Germany of that epoch. It was a herd activity: two men fought, but among a queue of others waiting for their turn. All the elements of the duel were there, reduced to the crudest terms, while the absence of any meaningful motive apart from self-display and obedience to an artificial class code exposed the duel's essential absurdity. The same students gathered to drink beer together, each glass swallowed in unison at the leader's command.

An anecdote survives of a Polish student at Heidelberg in 1883 who was jeered at when he turned out on a new-model English bicycle, and on replying in kind found two youths wanting to fight him. On an American friend's advice, he insisted on his right to choose a revolver instead of swords; at which he heard no more of them.[6] But German influences percolated into Poland, part of which had long been under Prussian rule, and some students there had similar clubs, cultivating a species of duelling.

[3] J. Russell, *Tour in Germany* (1828), i. 109, 120–2.

[4] F. Max-Müller, *My Autobiography: A Fragment* (London, 1901), 16, 124–6. Lever witnessed a duel at Göttingen when a student there (Fitzpatrick, i. 70).

[5] There is a classic description in Jerome K. Jerome, *Three Men on the Bummel* (1900), chap. 13.

[6] 'Alpha of the Plough', 144–6.

After 1815 there were too many duels in the Prussian army, which had been tasting blood in the wars; in 1821 the functions of the courts of honour were extended, in an attempt to arouse a higher collective sense of honour among officers. Little came of this, and 1827 began with a memorandum to the king from General von Borstell, surprising for its insight into the class character and psychology of the duel, and arguing that it had degenerated, and was 'quite unsuitable to modern times'.[7] A royal order next year deplored its spread. In 1843 the war minister, General Boyen, wanted to make resort to the honour courts compulsory, but this was soon watered down, because officers thought it a sneaking way of getting out of a challenge.[8] Frederick William IV's unbalanced mind dwelt fondly on flights of medieval fancy. In 1846 at Münster there was a solemn public spectacle, like an old trial by combat, when a pair of officers were licensed by a court of honour and the magistrates to fight with sabres, over a matter arising from a game of billiards. One was wounded; a virtuous embrace followed.[9]

Outside Prussia military attitudes were various. In Bavaria there was no real bar to duelling. In Saxony, an enquiry in 1858 found, 'an officer who refuses to fight may expect automatic dismissal'. In Austria on the other hand duelling had long been illegal, and the new military code of 1855 prescribed the same penalties as the ordinary penal code.[10] It may be that in the multinational Habsburg empire, only just recovering from the Hungarian, Italian, and other national risings of 1848–9, duelling was deemed too likely to disrupt the officer corps. But as time went on it came to be considered, here too, a necessary spur. In 1900 Lieutenant the Marquis Tacoli was degraded to the ranks for failing to resent an insult.[11]

In 1874, following the triumphant wars of 1864–70, Prussian regulations, now applied to the whole of Germany, were revised again. Practically, duelling had a free licence. There was an accompanying admonition from the emperor, William I, that his officers' mode of living should be honourable, free from the vices of drunkenness, gambling, and stock-market dabbling. They were often hard up, as the hunt for dowries indicated. British officers, in 'good' regiments at least, had private incomes; the cream of the German officer corps was drawn from the proud but poor squirearchy of the lands beyond the Elbe. Junkers were also businessmen of a sort, trying to run their estates for profit, and having to stand firmly on their dignity to mark themselves off from

[7] Demeter, App. 13.
[8] Ibid. 130–5.
[9] Steinmetz, ii. 286–7.
[10] Demeter, 319, 322–3.
[11] Prokowsky, 161–2.

ordinary money-makers. Their younger sons went into the army or higher civil service, as Engels wrote, and aristocratic connections were thereby extended, but the whole class was economically shaky, and in need of State subsidies.[12]

In western Germany manufacturing wealth threatened to submerge old claims of family and birth; the theme of the *nouveau riche*, like the one in *Rosenkavalier*, was becoming a favourite of fiction. Here again 'honour' was a necessary bulwark. Meticulous rules covered every detail of an officer's deportment; Prussian bureaucratic minuteness was applied to this task of propping up the phantom virtue of a bygone age. Duel and *Mensur* may no doubt have helped to keep the German army keyed up for action, in the years between 1871 and 1914 when German officers saw scarcely any active service, and had to fall back on other ways of manifesting courage. A soldier who never fights comes to border on the ridiculous, or must feel that he does. Meanwhile French, Russian, and above all British officers had continual opportunities to distinguish themselves in colonial wars, and pile up ribbons.

An officer who baulked at fighting, when there was deemed sufficient cause by his regiment, was compelled to resign. By a two-thirds majority its officers could get rid of any member they disliked.[13] This would usually mean anyone suspected of unorthodox opinions on any subject. Many commanders seem to have disliked courts of honour, as a shackle on the free-born gentleman's right, and did not always regard themselves as bound by the regulations. Men of means but not of noble blood were proud to hold rank as reserve officers; to be admitted to this dignity they had to subscribe to the code. How wide a deviation it represented from the natural bent of bourgeois thinking and behaviour may be gauged by the fact that duelling had far less place in the navy, a late creation whose officers came mostly from the professional middle classes of the seaports. Imperfect statistics available for 1870 to 1895 show only ten naval duels, while more than two hundred and fifty army officers were disciplined for duelling in breach of the rules.[14]

Men high up in the army were sufficiently wide awake to learn how to push their ambitions by backstairs links with the press. But when William II came under criticism in some newspapers he threatened to have the editors called out by his aides-de-camp. Prudence prevailed, and they were made to smart by quieter methods. But all armies resented press criticisms, and in his polemic against militarism the German socialist leader Karl Liebknecht wrote that a uniform, an NCO's as well as an officer's, 'in many fields really seems to be *legibus*

[12] F. Engels, *The Role of Force in History*, trans. J. Cohen (London, 1968), 90–1.
[13] Vagts, 178.
[14] J. Steinberg, 'The Kaiser's Navy and German Society', *Past and Present*, 28 (1964), p. 107.

solutus and sacrosanct'; duelling was one of the many malpractices he found fault with in both German and foreign armies.[15] In 1914 the hitherto Germanophil author of *Three Men in a Boat* recalled memories of 'German *offizieren* swaggering three and four abreast along the pavements, sweeping men, women and children into the gutter.'[16] It should be added that by Whitman's account it was sometimes a civilian who was guilty, under festive influences, of molesting an officer, and lawyers, doctors, etc., brought up on student duelling, might be 'ready to "give satisfaction" on the slightest preparation'. He instanced an affair in a garrison town, ending with a wounded civilian and a dead officer, which nearly caused a riot between army and public.[17]

Many German writers had something to say about duelling, from one angle or another. Goethe's memoirs tell how in youth he helped to avert a fight that would have resembled a great many others in its silliness. A choleric captain drinking too much in a café talked rudely enough to a young man to goad him into a challenge. Goethe reasoned with him, he grew hysterically contrite, and next morning was quite ready for an apology to the youth, who on his side had 'small liking for quarrelling' and was happy to accept it.[18] In *Werther*, where a challenge or two might be looked for, nothing of the sort turns up; the ruffled husband is a staid businessman, not a gentleman with a frail eggshell of honour to brood on. He has a pair of pistols, which his wife's admirer borrows, ostensibly for a journey, really to shoot himself with. This romantic novel, which Goethe always thought highly of but took care not to reread, looks today distressingly mawkish and lachrymose; but there is force in a remark of his disciple Eckermann, when they were discussing it, that there would always be emotions like Werther's, because in every epoch there is 'so much secret discontent and disgust with life, and in single individuals there are so many disagreements with the world'.[19] It has a bearing on duelling as much as on suicide. A high point in the long stage history of the duel comes in *Faust*, when Gretchen's brother Valentine, just home from the wars, challenges the seducer, is mortally wounded by Faust with Mephistopheles' help, and dies cursing her.

In another colloquy with Eckermann the aged poet said he was struck by 'how large a portion of the life of a rich Englishman of rank is passed in duels and elopements'. This was a somewhat over-coloured impression of high life in England; likewise his notion that Byron's

---

[15] Karl Liebknecht, *Militarism and Anti-Militarism* (1907; trans. G. Lock, Cambridge, 1973), 34, 143–4 n. 56.
[16] Jerome, *My Life*, 12.
[17] Whitman, 79.
[18] Goethe, *Poetry and Truth* (English edn, London, 1913), i. 340–1.
[19] Ibid. 90.

amorous intrigues compelled him to be always practising pistol-shooting. 'Every moment he expected to be called out.'[20]

All Europe's old nobilities were stragglers from an epoch whose three score years and ten were long over, and could only be spun out by more or less black arts. Of hardly any can this be said more exactly than of the Prussian military élite, in whose more gifted and sensitive members the morbidities of the class were sometimes painfully incarnated. One such was Heinrich von Kleist, the soldier, poet, playwright, and story-teller who in 1811, at the age of thirty-four, shot a married woman dying of cancer, and then himself, in a suicide pact. He was 'a rationalist tormented by his loss of faith in Reason and desperately searching for certainty'.[21] His long story *The Duel* is one version of this search, in a medieval setting of a kind dear to nostalgic Romanticism.

Count Rotbart, on trial for a murder he has instigated, declares that at the time he was closeted with the lady Littegarde. Appearances are against her, and she is disgraced. Her admirer Friedrich von Trota undertakes to fight Rotbart, and a ceremonial contest is held in the castle square of Basle, before the emperor himself. Friedrich is defeated and gravely wounded, but still refuses to believe that God's 'mysterious verdict' proves Littegarde's guilt, whereas she is confounded and numbed by it. His faith in heaven is justified: Rotbart, from a scratch in the fight, contracts a fatal infection, and just as hero and heroine are at the stake awaiting execution, confesses his crime. Divine justice is thus manifested, but in a very roundabout way. Kleist's verdict on the trial by combat, and by implication on its heir the modern duel, remains ambiguous. Wagner in 1848 could be more sanguine, with his Lohengrin's victory as champion of the lady Elsa.

By that date the duel was under frequent debate, largely critical. Schopenhauer could not help paying tribute to courage, but honour seemed to him an attribute that by itself does nothing to lift man above the animal level: 'it is as dark a delusion as any other aim that springs from self'. Civic honour is good, because it means good conduct; 'knightly honour' means only 'the path of violence', the desire to strike fear into others, as the robber-barons of old did.[22]

Schopenhauer had for parents a banker and a novelist. Nietzsche was the son of a pastor. In an early essay on education he tells how he and a fellow-student at Bonn once retired to a secluded upland to practise their favourite pistol-shooting, and were interrupted by an old

[20] J. P. Eckermann, *Conversations with Goethe* (1836, 1848; Everyman edn., London, 1930), 90 (24 Feb. 1825).

[21] Kleist, Introd., 48.

[22] Schopenhauer, *On Human Nature*, trans. T. B. Saunders (London, 1897), 116–17. Cf. Prokowsky, 144–6, 153.

philosopher who supposed them to be fighting a duel, and launched into a long tirade against 'the insane code of honour', as in reality 'the code of folly and brutality', unworthy above all of students, 'the intelligence of the future, the seed of our hopes'. In reply to 'this rough, though admittedly just, flood of eloquence', the two young men answered irritably that they had their own views, and needed no instruction. What these views were, Nietzsche leaves us to guess, but they were obviously not very favourable to duelling.[23]

Later he made room for some palliations, like the stock argument that the code limited bloodshed, and taught men to be cautious of how they comported themselves with others. It could be urged, he thought, that if a man is so susceptible to what others think of him that he wants to make it a life-or-death issue, he is entitled to do so. 'We are the heirs of the past, of its greatness as well as of its exaggerations, without which no greatness ever existed.'[24] This dictum at least has a ring of truth. But Nietzsche was developing an admiration, antithetical to Schopenhauer's viewpoint, for everything aristocratic, and liked to fancy himself a scion of Polish nobility. His concept of war as man's natural occupation, testing and exalting his will to live and will to power, had much in common with the ideology of the duel. Nietzsche himself was not cut out to be a duellist, though once, while he was in the midst of *Zarathustra*, disappointment with Lou Salomé made him clash with his friend the psychologist Paul Rée, to the point of writing vitriolic letters and telling Rée he would have pleasure in giving him 'a lesson in practical morals with a few bullets'.[25]

After the defeat of the German revolutionary movement of 1848–9 a split took place among Communist League exiles in London, and dissensions went so far that one evening Marx received a challenge from Willich. 'Marx treated that Prussian officer trick for what it was worth', Wilhelm Liebknecht recorded, but the young hotspur Conrad Schramm took the affair on himself, and he and Willich (whose second was Barthélemy) met on the Belgian coast. Schramm had never held a pistol, while his opponent, an ex-officer, was a crack shot, and he was lucky to be only knocked senseless by a bullet that grazed his head. In the Marx household there was great anxiety until he turned up, bandaged but cheerful.[26] What he thought he had accomplished is hard to guess.

Less fortunate, a few years later, was Ferdinand Lassalle, whose fate

[23] Nietzsche, *On the Future of our Educational Institutions* (1872); *Works*, ed. O. Levy, iii (London, 1910), 21 ff.

[24] *Human, All-too-human* (1878); Pt. 1, *Works*, vol. vi, 1909), 284–45.

[25] See H. A. Reyburn *et al.*, *Nietzsche* (London, 1948), 293 ff.

[26] W. Liebknecht, in *Reminiscences of Marx and Engels*, 113; F. J. Raddatz, *Karl Marx* (1975; English edn., London, 1975), 159.

had a precocious prelude when at the age of twelve he wanted to fight a duel with another schoolboy, over a girl, and had to be laughed out of the idea by his teacher.[27] Son of a well-to-do Jewish merchant, he wrote on philosophy, was jailed for some months for his part in the 1848 upheaval, and picked up law in the course of a long-drawn suit which he won for the Countess Hatzfeldt against her husband. In 1862 he plunged again into politics; in 1863 he was able to organize the first workers' party in Germany; next year he perished, at the age of thirty-nine. He had become infatuated with a girl named Helene von Dönniges, and succeeded in winning her affections away from a Romanian, Yanko von Rakowitza, to whom she was more or less engaged. Her family put its foot down; Yanko was of better birth, and Lassalle was no suitable relative for Helene's father, a Bavarian diplomat, or her army brother. Lassalle wrote an offensive letter to the father, with a challenge which was brushed aside; Lassalle was then challenged by Yanko. He died three days after their duel; Countess Hatzfeldt had his body embalmed and arranged a suitable theatrical progress for it down the Rhine.[28] Nine years later, when Good Friday fell on his birthday, a socialist paper published an article called 'Death and Resurrection', extolling him as another Messiah. Staid Marxists disapproved.[29]

Helene married Yanko, who was suffering from an incurable illness; she had two other marriages, and was for some time on the stage. Towards the close of this colourful life, Jerome K. Jerome made the acquaintance at Munich of 'a grand-looking, red-haired dame', a baroness living in 'a sombre, silent street', pouring tea for guests in a dismal parlour with shabby furniture, and found it hard to realize that this woman, in her 'flaming youth, when she made havoc in the world', had been Lassalle's love and the Clotilde of Meredith's novel.[30] He did not foresee that her last adventure would be suicide.

Clearly the liberal movement had, even in Germany, some democratizing influence, or a man of Lassalle's origin would scarcely have been eligible as a duellist in such company. He may have been desirous of asserting his claim to the status of gentleman. In 1858 he had refused on principle a challenge from a petty official named Fabriz, who then, with a friend, set on him in the street; Lassalle retaliated with his stick. This got about, and he wrote to Marx for advice, saying that if he persisted in declining the challenge he would be exposed to damaging

[27] A. Schirouauer, *Lassalle*, trans. E. and C. Paul (London, 1931), 31.
[28] Footman, 148 ff.
[29] O. Chadwick, *The Secularization of the European Mind in the Nineteenth Century* (Cambridge, 1975), 79–80.
[30] Jerome, *My Life*, 161.

charges of pusillanimity. Marx thought it worth while to consult Engels and Wolff, in Manchester, before he composed a long answer, with their joint recommendation. They agreed that the attack in the street put Fabriz beyond the pale, so that there could be no question of his being entitled to satisfaction. Intrinsically, Marx went on, the duel could not be called simply either good or bad. 'There is no doubt that the duel in itself is irrational and the relic of a past stage of culture.' On the other hand, because of the one-sidedness of bourgeois life (he must have meant its prostration before what could be measured in pounds, shillings, and pence) 'certain individualistic feudal forms assert their rights in opposition to it'. Thus the duel 'as an exceptional *emergency resort* may be adopted in exceptional circumstances'. But a fight with Fabriz would be mere compliance with outworn convention. 'Our party must set its face resolutely against these ceremonials of rank ... The times are far too serious now to allow one to become involved in such childishness.'[31]

Lassalle would have done well to read this verdict again six years later. Marx both regretted his death and thought it laughable, part of an aristocratic pose. 'If he had taken his mission seriously he would not have exposed his life for a farce ... It was typical of him to dream of marching into Berlin with red-haired Hélène at the head of battalions of workers.'[32] The event must have hardened socialist feeling against the duel, and helped to close the small loophole left by Marx and Engels and their generation. In 1872 at the Hague congress of the First International, where the long struggle between Marx and Bakunin ended in the latter's expulsion, Cuno rejected a challenge from Rudolph Schramm. 'I had renounced duelling', he recalled later, 'as a ridiculous remnant of the Dark Ages'; bearing the scars of eleven student duels, he could afford to ignore any aspersion on his courage.[33]

Socialist criticisms of the duel, as illegal or unconstitutional, found echoes among those liberals who had not, like the 'National Liberals', succumbed to Bismarck. Fights were reported and censured in the press, and it was known that not all officers approved of them. Some had a place in the more scandalous purlieus of high society and politics. Several abortive feuds there centred round Baron von Holstein, long the grey eminence of the foreign office. In 1892 complaints by the chief of staff Count Waldersee of a press campaign against him, probably inspired by Holstein, brought a challenge from the latter. In the same year press attacks on himself induced him to challenge Count Hencken.

[31] Letter of 10 June 1858, in *Karl Marx and Friedrich Engels; Correspondence 1846–1895: A Selection*, trans. Dona Torr (London, 1934).
[32] Franzisca Kugelmann, in *Reminiscences of Marx and Engels*, 283.
[33] T. Cuno, ibid. 211–12.

In both cases, redolent of Germany's bizarre hotchpotch of old and new, a veto by the Kaiser cut things short.[34] In 1906 Holstein was manœuvred into resigning at last; he blamed Prince Philipp zu Eulenburg, long a prime favourite of the Kaiser, and wrote him a letter alluding to his homosexuality, which brought a challenge in reply. This time the seconds patched up a peace.[35]

The moral philosopher Paulsen may have been typical of German liberalism in seeing that all logical argument went to condemn the duel, yet being unable to bring himself to reject it altogether. He considered it, in most cases, 'a wanton sport with one's own or another's life', often amounting to 'atrocious Murder'; and he found fault with its 'class morality', or 'Herrenmoral', and 'the law infected by it'. That 'two young fellows who, under the influence of liquor, happen to jolt each other, are compelled to face each other with pistols', was outrageous. Yet there must be certain cases where a man was unable or unwilling to appeal to the courts, and the duel might have to be kept as 'a possible expedient'.[36]

Paulsen found an excuse for the *Mensur* as a mode of settling petty disputes, as an exercise, and as fostering a rough manliness.[37] Max Müller condoned duelling among students at German universities on the ground that their social composition was very diverse, all considered themselves equals, and something drastic was needed to enforce good manners.[38] But there was indignation at Bonn university when the Kaiser made one of his ranting speeches there and praised the duelling fraternities. In the first years of this century the *Mensur* was being debated afresh, and objections were raised to the whole ethos surrounding it, as conditioning young men to unthinking acquiescence in the system they found.[39]

A similar current of opinion against the adult duel had religious reinforcement. Lutheranism had always been closely tied to state and monarchy, yet a new catechism for Prussian military schools in the 1890s denounced duelling sweepingly; a man's honour could be tarnished only by his own misconduct.[40] The Catholic church had always rejected it, but was now doing so in Germany more uncompromisingly. Catholics were a minority, only gradually reconciled to the incorporation of the southern states like Bavaria in the German union, and the Centre party representing Catholic interests drew most of its popular support from

[34] J. von Kürenberg, *The Life of Fritz von Holstein* (1932; English edn., London, 1933), 106–8.
[35] Ibid. 235–6.
[36] F. Paulsen, *The German Universities and University Study* (English edn., London, 1906), 375–6.
[37] Ibid. 376–7.
[38] Max Müller, *Autobiography*, 274–5.
[39] Samuel and Thomas, 120–1.
[40] Demeter, 142.

the middle and lower-middle classes there. A resolution of the Sacred Congregation in 1890 condemned both principals and seconds concerned in student duelling.[41] By 1900 duelling among Bavarian officers, not long since commoner than in Prussia, had almost vanished. They were more likely than in Prussia to belong to the middle classes. In 1897 a Catholic deputy in the Reichstag alleged that many families discouraged their sons from entering the army because it exposed them to the need to fight duels; he spoke of 'embarrassing inquisitions' into young candidates' views on the subject.[42]

Some unsavoury incidents helped to stir public opinion. In one of these Max Weber came forward. He had been a *Korpsstudent*, like his father before him, and acquired the obligatory scars, but Professor Mommsen can describe him as 'a merciless critic of all feudal pretensions'. In 1895 a Saarland manufacturer, Baron von Stumm, capped a noisy anti-socialist press campaign by challenging a moderate opponent, Adolf Wagner. The latter preferred to ask for a court of honour to arbitrate; Stumm accused him of cowardice. Weber intervened with a press article denouncing the bully's conduct. He was repelled by Stumm's 'parvenu mentality', and suspected him of angling for support from the Kaiser. To Weber all this was, as he said, 'loathsome public duel bravado', part of the feudalizing pose of a higher bourgeoisie trying to block all social policies and evolution in Germany.[43]

Under pressure of opinion, in 1897 additions were made to the army regulations. There was disgust among progressives at the duel being thereby in a sense endorsed, instead of being swept away. Anti-duelling societies were set up in 1902 in both Germany and Austria. But the changes were meant to enable the army to move with the times, and in the years before 1914 duelling was entering its twilight. Conservatism, with the Kaiser on its side, was still strong, however, and as late as 1906 its obstinacy brought the subject into the greatest political prominence it ever attained in Germany. Early in that year a deputy of the Centre put down a question in the Reichstag for the chancellor, Bülow, as to his government's attitude to duelling in the army. It was during the later stages of the Moroccan crisis, and Bülow was a much-harrassed man. He left it to a scratch committee, including members of the Kaiser's military cabinet, to draft a reply, which he approved without reading. Its key phrase was that 'the officer corps will be unable to tolerate in its ranks anyone who is not prepared to defend his honour

---

[41] Bouscaren, 856 (Canon 2351).

[42] J. Steinberg, 'The Kaiser's Navy and German Society', *Past and Present*, 28 (1964), p. 107.

[43] W. J. Mommsen, *Max Weber and German Politics 1890–1920* (1959, 1974; trans. M. S. Steinberg, Chicago, 1984), 99.

with weapon in hand'. In fact in the previous year there had only been a single army duel, but the bluntness of the wording upset some Protestants, and outraged many Catholics, for it could be taken to mean that no conscientious Catholic was admissible.[44]

In all his first five years as chancellor Bülow had been assisted by good relations with the Centre; now he had handed a weapon to a new generation in the party, from the south and south-west, who were soon heckling him over other issues too. Caught between this opposition and the impatient fumings of the Kaiser, Bülow was in deepening trouble. In 1907 he had to risk an election, two years later he fell from power. Such were the consequences that the duel could contribute to, in the twentieth century, in the most powerful state in Europe.

Duelling was always a strange blend of anarchic individualism with servile obedience to an unnatural rule. Its disregard of higher interests, so blatant in Germany in 1906, gave it its place in Mickiewicz's poem, as an epitome of the disunity that plagued all Poland's attempts to recover its freedom. Robak in *Pan Tadeusz* is striving to band the gentry together to profit by the opportunity held out by Napoleon's invasion of Russia, and the judge, who has been angrily insisting on an apology from the count, or else satisfaction, feels his patriotic blood stirring. But the dispute still rankles, and Thaddeus tells his uncle the judge that he is taking it on his shoulders; the count and his adherents attack and plunder their house, until they in turn are engaged by a Russian detachment, and the Poles are compelled to stand together. Thaddeus proposes to end the battle by a single combat; a Russian officer named Rykov, a decent fellow, agrees; the count comes forward to fight it out with him, after a courteous exchange of bows before they cross swords— 'it is the custom of men of honour, before proceeding to murder, first to exchange greetings'.[45] Mickiewicz's comment is ironic, but there is an illustration here of how the duel could in a way transcend divisions between nation and nation.

In Russia Alexander I favoured duelling; under his brother Nicholas I (1825–55) there was a reversion to stricter views, and it was one of the offences for which an officer might be reduced to the ranks—a penalty unknown to most armies where the officer corps was of more authentically thoroughbred origin. Dostoevsky speaks of a conservative type of officer who 'regarded duels as something unthinkable, atheistic, French', and remarks that points of honour were so outlandish that they could only be discussed in a literary kind of Russian meaningless

---

[44] See Terence Cole, 'Kaiser versus Chancellor', in R. Evans (ed.), *Society and Politics in Wilhelmine Germany* (New York, [1978]).

[45] Mickiewicz, Bks. 6, 8.

to the ordinary man.[46] None the less the duel continued to push its way in. It was part of the European culture imported by the upper classes, which entitled them to put themselves on a par with the English whose clothes and racehorses they admired, or the French whose language it was an indispensable qualification to be able to speak. A class of serf-owning landowners, an aristocracy exceptionally oppressive, useless, and morbid, had special need of artificial excitements. 'When there is no war they are bored', Chekhov wrote.[47] Duelling could be a welcome stopgap. In *The Varieties of Religious Experience* William James quoted some words of General Skobelev, conqueror of Central Asia, about his passionate love of danger, in all its forms, for instance the duel.[48]

In practice duelling was coming to be tolerated in the army, if the cause was not disreputable, but sometimes officers were not permitted to act as seconds. Forbes the British war correspondent discovered this in 1877 while covering the Russian campaign in the Balkans. Some officers were quartered in a house at Tirnova in Bulgaria where there was a pretty and coquettish daughter, Maritza. She won the love of a hussar named Andreiovich, who returned from a perilous expedition to find her on the sofa with dragoon captain Sablanoff. By striking his rival and pulling his nose the hussar made a duel inevitable, and Forbes was enlisted as his second. Sablanoff was badly hurt; Maritza nursed him patiently, but plighted her troth to Andreiovich, and Forbes ran across her later searching distractedly for him on a stricken field. He was believed dead, but survived, and the couple married.[49]

Shortly before the end of his reactionary reign in 1894 Alexander III formally established duelling in the army; it was 'only in keeping with the rest of his domestic policy'.[50] He was in most ways in sympathy with Slavic rather than Germanizing ideas, but the example of the Kaiser's army must have weighed with him here. He had been trying to modernize his forces in the light of lessons of the costly Balkan war, and must have wanted to instil a better tone into the officer corps, something a tsar could scarcely contemplate by any more civilized method. With the coming of universal conscription, about half the total number of officers were 'nobles', but a high proportion of these were ensconced in the Guards, the Staff, or the cavalry.[51] Ordinary line regiments were officered by socially very inferior material. There was a cleavage of this kind in other armies; it was well marked in the British, but was nowhere nearly so sharp as in Russia.

[46] *Notes from Underground*, 58.
[47] *The Notebooks of Anton Chekhov*, trans. S. S. Koteliansky and L. Woolf (London, 1921), 30.
[48] William James, 263 n.
[49] Archibald Forbes, *Memories and Studies of War and Peace* (1895; London edn., 1896), 189 ff.
[50] C. Lowe, *Alexander III of Russia* (London, 1895), 202.
[51] See my *European Empires from Conquest to Collapse* (London, 1982), 137–8.

The most graphic picture of garrison life comes from A. I. Kuprin's novel *The Duel*, based on his own experiences of service from 1890 to 1897. The officers he portrays, stationed in a dreary provincial town, are an ill-paid, uncultivated lot, who drink, get into debt, gamble, sometimes cheat at cards or embezzle funds, and treat their men with callous brutality. These dead souls find their most agreeable outlet, apart from boozing, in riding roughshod over civilians, 'obscure individuals to be thrashed and insulted without rhyme or reason'.[52] Some part of this mentality may be ascribed to the presence of numerous Germans in the officer corps, from the Baltic provinces conquered in bygone days by German land-grabbers.[53] In Kuprin's story suicides of both officers and men are frequent. Duelling is the favourite topic of talk, as a relief from the senseless daily round, and a theme with a gentlemanly flavour. After a disgraceful orgy of drinking and brothel-visiting joined in by most of the officers, two of them who came to blows are brought before a regimental court of honour and sentenced to resign their commissions or fight a duel.[54] This rite will somehow, like a human sacrifice, restore the regiment's profaned honour.

Pushkin's writings make copious use of the duel, apart from the famous incident in his long poem *Eugene Onegin* where Lensky fights and is killed by his friend and neighbour Onegin. They are firing at each other because Onegin, from sheer boredom at a country ball, has flirted with Lensky's young lady. She loses no time in marrying a smart officer, and Pushkin congratulates her dead lover on his redemption from a life of rural stupidity.[55] In one of the longest of Pushkin's short stories, *The Captain's Daughter*, set in the time of the great peasant and Cossack rebellion led by Pugachev in the 1770s, a young man entering the army and sent to a forlorn outpost is told by the commander's wife of another man of good family, Shvabrin, who has been expelled from the Guards and sent here because of having killed a lieutenant in a sword fight. He and the newcomer are soon deadly enemies, with the commander's daughter Maria as the apple of discord. An old lieutenant, risen from the ranks, refuses to act as second, and descants on the folly of such deadly feuds, much as Eddie Ochiltree remonstrates with the two young men in *The Antiquary*. The rivals are about to fight without any seconds when he appears on the scene with a file of soldiers and puts them under arrest. They soon find another opportunity to fly at each other.[56]

---

[52] *European Empires from Conquest to Collapse*, 14–15, 275.
[53] Cf. an episode in Turgenev, *On the Eve* (Harmondsworth, 1950), chap. 5.
[54] Kuprin, 308 ff.
[55] Chap. 6, stanza 39.
[56] Chaps. 3, 4 (in *Prose Tales*).

Pushkin is critical of the duel from another point of view in his story *Doubrovsky*, where a boorish squire of the old school amuses himself by having a young French tutor pushed into a room with a fettered but ferocious bear. The youth coolly puts a pistol to its ear and shoots it. He always carries one, he tells the squire's daughter, in case of any indignity for which his lowly status may not entitle him to satisfaction. This wins her heart, by letting her see that 'bravery and proud self-respect did not belong exclusively to one class'. In *The Shot*, duelling is the theme throughout. In another remote station, where drinking, gambling, and fighting or gossiping about duels are the younger officers' only recreation, a rather older man, a dead shot always practising with his pistol, allows a drunken insult to pass. This lowers him in the estimation of the rest. 'Want of courage is the last thing to be pardoned by young men, who usually look upon bravery as the chief of all human virtues, and the excuse for every possible fault.' He goes away, but before leaving reveals to a confidant the secret of a former duel that has left him unwilling ever to engage in another.

In the young poet Lermontov's novel *A Hero of Our Time* (1839) the story reaches its climax in the encounter between the well-bred dilettante 'hero' Pechorin, serving in the Caucasus, and Grushnitsky, a candidate-officer serving, according to the curiously democratical custom of the tsarist army, his preliminary spell in the ranks. The clash is elaborately prepared, and narrated in great detail. They have met at a fashionable spa, Grushnitsky has been supplanted by Pechorin in the regard of a young lady, and has revenged himself by calumniating her. His cronies, men of the same lack of breeding that Kuprin was to meet with half a century later, talk him into a plan to palm off on Pechorin, who has challenged him, an unloaded weapon. Further west in Europe such foul play was very rare, in history or literature; even in Russia it cannot have been common. Pechorin sees through the scheme. He insists on their standing on the edge of a rocky ledge, so that whichever is hit will roll down, and his death be attributed to accident. There could be no 'satisfaction' for honour in such an arrangement, only satisfied revenge. They toss for first shot, Grushnitsky wins, and a bad conscience makes him miss, though they are only six paces apart. Pechorin then loads his pistol, and gives him a last chance to withdraw his calumny. Irritated vanity and the shame of exposure force him into a kind of unintended nobility; he refuses, and pays with his life.[57]

Pushkin and Lermontov were progressives, men of European culture, but they were unable to reject the insidious venom that came with it in the form of the duel. It is probable that more writers were personally

---

[57] Mikhail Lermontov, *Selected Works* (Moscow, 1976), 276 ff.

involved in duelling matters than in any other country. On them more than anyone else pressed the weight of a heavy, mephitic air; many had brushes, if no worse, with authority. It was hardly possible that a genius like Pushkin should escape them. He got into hot water early with some of his writings, and was banished to southern Russia, which may have saved him from being drawn into the Decembrist rising of 1825. On the road to the eastern Turkish town of Erzerum, for some years in Russian hands, he passed the corpse of a writer named Griboedov, killed during a tribal rising while serving as a political officer with the troops then subjugating the Caucasus. His body had been dragged about the streets for three days, and was recognizable only by a duelling scar.[58]

When allowed to return Pushkin had the dubious benefit of being patronized by the autocrat Nicholas, who liked to pose as sponsor of native Russian letters. Pushkin's frivolous wife Natalya may have come in for an equal share of the imperial favour, and others may have had their share of hers. In 1836 an anonymous writer sent copies to him and others of a coarse lampoon informing him that he was a cuckold.[59] Natalya had been attracted lately to a young Frenchman, Georges Dantès or d'Antès. Pushkin's suspicion fell on him: a challenge followed, and early in 1837 a duel that ended a life of only thirty-seven years. His opponent fled abroad, and lived to be a successful financier and senator of France. He was a royalist of the right-wing legitimist faction. Pushkin had never ceased to be obnoxious to the more reactionary circles in the capital, and surmises were quickly afloat, and have never been laid to rest, that his death had been somehow brought about by their machinations.[60] It caused a sensation at the time, taking on 'the character of a national calamity'; the government was alarmed, and had the body removed hastily for burial.[61]

Lermontov's death in a duel, at the still earlier age of twenty-six, followed only four years later. This brilliant young man had been enrolled, as befitted his birth, in a Guards regiment, from which he was summarily packed off to the Caucasus for writing a poem, quickly famous, on the death of Pushkin as a disguised assassination. Allowed back before long to St Petersburg, he continued to gall court society with his epigrams and satires. His duel in 1840 with the French ambassador's son, a bloodless meeting, was only the pretext for his second banishment to the Caucasus. There a year later, at the Pyatigorsk spa,

[58] J. F. Baddeley, *The Russian Conquest of the Caucasus* (London, 1908), 202 ff.

[59] The affair is discussed in E. H. Carr, 317 ff.

[60] This is the theme of a Soviet novel, *Death of a Poet*, by Leonid Grossman (trans. E. Bone, London, n.d.). C. de Grunwald, *Tsar Nicholas I* (English edn., London, 1954), sums up impartially (pp. 241–3).

[61] Janko Lavrin, *Pushkin and Russian Literature* (London, 1947), 63.

he met his death at the hands of another officer. Pyatigorsk figures in his novel, and it has been conjectured that this quarrel had some connection with the story. Circumstances gave rise to suspicions similar to those surrounding Pushkin's death, and they are still current in Russia. It was 'a duel that looked very much like murder', said the writer of a recent tribute to his genius.[62]

These two deaths must have had a chastening effect on later Russian writers, at least on what they said if not always on what they did. A spell in the navy must have helped to open Ivan Goncharov's eyes. His first novel, in 1847, preached a regular homily against duelling. Young Alexander wants to fight Count Novinsky, for stealing his lady-love, and requests an uncle to be his second. The cynical senior tells him that he will be making a fool of himself; also that if the count agrees, 'according to the rule he would have the first shot' (this can only have been an occasional custom), and that if Alexander succeeds in killing him it will not get his Nadya back: instead he will be 'sent for a soldier'. Violence is not the way to win. 'We don't live in the Kirghiz steppe. The civilized world knows other weapons.' A lover should rely on patience and intelligence: 'that is the true duel in our age'.[63]

Dostoevsky's novelette *The Gambler*, on the other hand, presents a positive side of the duel, the right to take part in it as an assertion of an educated man's claim to equal status with persons of higher rank. The narrator is a humble tutor, like the Frenchman in Pushkin's story about the bear: a tutor was in the same indeterminate social position as a governess in England. A titled Frenchman calls on him on behalf of a baron whom he has offended, bringing not a challenge but an injunction to mend his manners. When the tutor says he will go and see the baron personally, his visitor warns him that he may find himself turned out of the house by a lackey. In that case, he retorts, he will get his English friend Mr Astley to act for him: he is 'the nephew of a real English lord, the Lord Piebroch', and if the baron refuses to see *him* he is likely to feel insulted, and call him out.[64] An English milord was not to be trifled with, in Russia or anywhere else, but the quaint name Dostoevsky invents does not suggest much familiarity with the species.

There is a similar but more morbid vein of feeling in *Notes from Underground* (1864), whose narrator is a failure, a nobody, cursed with the introverted consciousness nowhere more diseased than among intellectuals in tsarist Russia. He forces his unwelcome company on some prosperous acquaintances, gets drunk, is outraged by their contempt for him, and when they go off to a brothel follows them through the

[62] *Soviet Weekly* (London), 13 Oct. 1984.
[63] I. Goncharov, *The Same Old Story* (1847; English edn., Moscow, n.d.), 180 ff.
[64] *The Gambler* (1866; Everyman edn., London, n.d.), 193.

snow in a sleigh, determined to force one of them to fight him at dawn, by slapping his face, and yet all the time painfully aware of the stupidity of what he is doing.[65] One of his nagging memories is of being humiliated in a billiard-room by a tall officer, and longing to be able to fight him. Dostoevsky had served three years in the army after his arrest in 1849 and exile to Siberia. His later drift into religion and conservatism may be partly explainable as the result of an early spirit of revolt frittering itself away in futile self-tormenting about an intellectual's social position in a society fit only for abolition.

Alexander Herzen, the wealthy radical son of a landowner and a serf-girl, who spent most of his life in exile, remembered his father as an old man with only one welcome visitor, a retired general; as subalterns in a Guards regiment they had both been court-martialled, his father for acting as a second, the friend for fighting a duel.[66] A ghoulish anecdote in his memoirs came from an old jailer in a prison where Herzen spent some time, who had been a soldier and served in the Balkan campaign of 1805. His company commander there, a kindly man liked by his soldiers, fell in love with a Romanian woman, and was chagrined at her preferring another officer. He asked Herzen's informant and a comrade to wait for her on a bridge near the rival's house, and drown her. They duly caught her, put her in a sack, and threw her into the river. Next day their commander went to the other man, told him what had been done, and offered to fight. He expiated his crime by suffering a severe wound, from which he never recovered. 'I was horrified', Herzen writes, 'by the childlike indifference with which the old man told me this story.'[67]

In exile Herzen could not avoid entanglement in the rancours endemic among refugees. His wife Natalie became too fond of their young German acquaintance George Herwegh, a successful left-wing poet who had been in one of the 1848 risings. In 1852 the husband received a letter from him claiming Natalie as his lover and one of her children as his own, and demanding a fight: according to the surviving draft of his letter he proposed as weapons their teeth: 'Let us tear each other's throats like wild beasts—since we are no longer men.' Long snarlings followed this loud bark.[68] A feature of the case was the calling in of arbiters, one of them Mazzini, to form a court of honour: this mode of adjusting or regulating disputes was making its way from military circles to civilian.

Tolstoy in youth had a passion for gambling. Duelling added to the

---

[65] *Notes from Underground*, 94 ff.
[66] Alexander Herzen, *Childhood, Youth and Exile*, Memoirs, trans. J. D. Duff (London, 1980), 78.
[67] Ibid. 170–1.
[68] Carr, 124 ff.

thrill of risk the glory of risking life instead of only money. Tolstoy seems to have been lured towards it by an evil demon, his own or of his class; the ostensible grounds on which he was ready to fight look very feeble. In 1865, when he was 27 and the Crimean War, in which he had smelled powder, was still raging, someone sent the writer Nekrasov, as editor of a literary journal, a letter critical of Tolstoy's work. Nekrasov was distressed at Tolstoy's angry reaction, and told him that if he really meant to fight the letter-writer, he must fight him too.[69] The critic sensibly kept quiet, and Tolstoy soon repented of his folly; yet before long, on two distinct occasions—the first in Paris, early in 1857—he was at loggerheads with Turgenev. The ten years' older author may not, it has been suggested, have relished competition from the younger one. This may or may not have been what made him threaten to punch Tolstoy's face in reply to criticism of his way of educating his daughter.[70] An altercation which came close to inflicting irreparable loss on Russian literature had begun at the country house of their friend Fet, with Tolstoy falling asleep over Turgenev's masterpiece *Fathers and Sons*. Tolstoy went home and wrote to him demanding a duel, a real combat, not a merely formal one in the style of 'literary men who finish up with champagne'. Turgenev tendered an apology, expressing readiness to 'stand fire' if it was not accepted; the anxious Fet tried in vain to mediate—Tolstoy relented—meanwhile Turgenev took offence again. . . .[71] There are hints here and elsewhere that authors (Byron for one) were apt to be sensitive to an opinion they suspected others of having about them, that they were men of words only, incapable of deeds.

Tolstoy underwent a slow, painful conversion to Christian pacifism, rejection of all violence, and of nearly all that was valuable in western culture along with its evils, such as duelling. He was long perplexed by the injunction to turn the other cheek, which 'shocked all the prejudices of aristocratic, family, and personal 'honour', in which he had been brought up'.[72] Lamenting in old age acts that youth and a volcanic temperament had betrayed him into, he recalled how 'I killed men in war, and challenged men to duels in order to kill them . . . there was no crime I did not commit', yet people saw nothing amiss.[73] In the later 1860s while he was writing *War and Peace* he could still applaud a war of patriotic defence, but a changed attitude to the duel comes out in one that he weaves into the novel.

---

[69] Maude, i. 148–9.
[70] Ibid. i. 227–34.
[71] Ibid., and Tikhon Polner, *Tolstoy and his Wife* (English edn., London, 1946), 31–2 (and cf. 15).
[72] Maude, i. 33.
[73] Ibid. i. 181.

Peter, very much like Pushkin, receives an anonymous letter coarsely accusing his wife of infidelity with the handsome, arrogant Dologhow. That evening at a dinner Peter is stung into challenging him, and next morning they are in a small clearing in a pine-wood, covered with snow. Convinced after a sleepless night of his wife's guilt, Peter is outwardly cool, inwardly thinking 'this duel is sheer murder'; but he is too indifferent to life to listen to the remonstrances of his second, who 'like all men who get entangled in an affair of honour, had not taken this meeting seriously till the last moment'. Never having held a pistol, Peter has to ask how to fire it. Tension mounts unbearably. 'The quarrel, so trivial in its beginning, could not now be stopped. It was going its deadly way, irrespective of human volition.' There is visible here one facet of the gloomy predestinarianism that pervades the entire novel. The word is given; Peter fires first, and by a fluke hits Dologhow, who lies writhing on the ground, burning with hatred; he calls up his last energy to fire, and misses. Peter walks away, saying to himself 'What folly! What folly! Death! Falsehood!' His reward is to be told by his wife that the man has *not* been her lover, and to be bitterly re-proached for making her a laughing-stock. He leaves her, and goes abroad.[74]

At a house-party in one of Turgenev's novels a game of forfeit is being played after dinner, and Zinaida makes up a tale in Oriental style about her being passionately in love with a man. One of the men asks the others what they would do if they knew this to be true. She volunteers to tell them—'You, Byelozvorov, would have challenged him to a duel; you, Maidanov, would have perpetrated an epigram against him.'[75] In another work a disappointed lover solaces himself with furious threats of calling out his silver-tongued rival, and of how he will 'plant a bullet in his learned brains'; pointlessly, because in fact the rival has already given the young lady up.[76]

In *Fathers and Sons* a duel actually takes place. Bazarov, the earnest young devotee of science, is working at his microscope when the jealous Kisanov comes in and asks what he thinks about duelling. Bazarov's reply is that in principle it is an absurdity, from a practical point of view it may be a different matter. Kisanov says that in that case he wants a fight; why, he declines to say, except that he dislikes Bazarov. They arrange to meet next morning. Left alone, the man of science reflects on this jumble of high-mindedness and idiocy, all as artificial as a dog being trained to dance on its hind legs. Yet he feels that he had no choice. What nonsense! he keeps repeating to himself on his

[74] Tolstoy, *War and Peace* (1864–9; Everyman edn., London, 1911), Pt. 1, chaps. 73–4.

[75] Turgenev, *First Love* (1860; English edn., Harmondsworth, 1978), 80.

[76] *Rudin* (1855; English edn., Harmondsworth, 1975), 132.

way to the rendezvous. There are no seconds. They are very polite; Kisanov loads the pistols, Bazarov measures the distance. They move towards each other, and fire; Kisanov is hit, his opponent staunches the bleeding, and they sit waiting for a conveyance, each awkwardly self-conscious, the aggressor ashamed of his hectoring behaviour.[77]

Chekhov's novelette *The Duel* was written in the early 1890s, a time when he was having arguments with a Darwinian zoologist, an advocate of the survival of the fittest.[78] Von Koren in the story is another such zoologist, at a station on the Caucasian coast. He is intolerant of Layevsky, a minor civil servant who has run away with someone's wife, as a decadent idler, and they drift towards a clash. Each has a sense of being in the grip of destiny, an abstraction which we can translate into the force of social convention. Layevsky knows 'how stupid and senseless duels were . . . all the same, at times there was no other course of action'. Von Koren admits that it is easy to say a duel is in essence no better than a tavern brawl, but a power stronger than ourselves may force us into it, as into a patriotic war.[79] Each is risking arrest, and up to three years prison if the other is killed: civilians had less immunity than army men. A young deacon, thinking of his peasant background, feels that educated men ought to be attacking social evils, not each other.[80] When the moment comes, the whole thing seems to Layevsky 'mysterious, incomprehensible and terrifying'.[81] Yet, after it has passed off without damage, its effect proves beneficial. The shock of relief at being still alive makes the loafer turn over a new leaf and work hard; he wins Von Koren's respect, and they part good friends.

There is no such good from evil in Chekhov's play of 1901, *Three Sisters*. In the last Act we learn that Irina's fiancé, Lieut. Baron Tusenbach, is about to fight Captain Solyony, who writes verses, fancies himself a new Lermontov, and has already had two duels. They should be prevented, Masha exclaims; Tchebutykin the army doctor shrugs it off. 'The baron is a very good fellow, but one baron more or less in the world, what does it matter?' He may be supposed to embody the indifferentism or moral irresponsibility of a society where the individual has no civic being, hence little inclination to concern himself seriously with others, little sense even of the reality of anyone or anything. When someone argues that everything concerned with duelling, even a doctor's presence at the scene, is immoral, Tchebutykin merely rejoins: 'That only seems so . . . We are not real, nothing in the world is real,

[77] *Fathers and Sons* (1861), chap. 24.
[78] R. Wilks, Introd. to Chekhov, *The Duel and Other Stories*, 7.
[79] *The Duel*, 91–6.
[80] Ibid. 104 ff.
[81] Ibid. 112.

we don't exist.' Tusenbach is killed, and the sisters are left to ask themselves why there is so much evil, with only the thought for consolation that, in spite of everything, life must go on.

In Kuprin's novel when some of the officers are chatting about duelling before a regimental ball, one is sensible enough to say that its proper place is only among dandies in the Guards; an ordinary man throwing away his life leaves his family to starve. The opposite opinion is defended by a hulking ruffian who is convinced, besides, that a duel is nothing unless somebody is killed; his notions of war are equally bloodthirsty.[82] Kuprin's view of the duel as the hallmark of a vicious society comes out in full near the end, when Romashov's friend takes him out in a boat and vainly urges him in a long monologue to summon up his moral courage and refuse to take part in the fight that is being forced on him. War and church-religion are equally degenerate remnants of the past. A new age must come, bringing with it a Utopian society where 'men will be gods'.[83]

[82] Kuprin, 129 ff.
[83] Ibid. 321 ff. Kuprin's impoverished family put him into an army school at the age of eleven. On him and his novel see R. Luckett, 'Pre-Revolutionary Army Life in Russian Literature', in G. Best and A. Wheatcroft (ed.), *War, Economy, and the Military Mind* (London, 1976), 21 ff.

17

Europe Overseas

Sir Walter Scott ... sets the world in love with dreams and phan-
toms ... with the sillinesses and emptinesses, sham grandeurs, sham
gauds, and sham chivalries of a brainless and worthless long-
vanished society ... In our South ... the genuine and wholesome
civilisation of the nineteenth century is curiously confused and
commingled with the Walter Scott Middle-Age sham civilisation
... with the duel, the inflated speech, and the jejune romanticism
of an absurd past.

Mark Twain, *Life on the Mississippi* (1883), chap. 46.

AN adventurer in Balzac, home from the East with an ill-gotten fortune,
receives a creditor of his father 'with the impertinence of a young man
of fashion who, in the Indies, has killed four men in different duels'.[1]
Europe was inclined to think of its offspring dwelling or sojourning
anywhere in the colonial world as quick to hate and to kill. A prevalent
laxity of police must go far to justify the opinion. All Europe's familiar
discords reappeared there, even literary susceptibility. In Martinique
in 1836 a writer called out a journalist who ventured to find fault with
his novel, and lost his life in its defence.[2] One can only hope that the
work deserved this parental devotion.

Boredom must have caused more quarrels than anything else. Few
settlers, soldiers, or officials were capable of any intelligent interest in
the countries they went or were sent to. Officers in particular yawned
away a tedious existence with what few excitements they could make
for themselves, often thrown together in small groups in unwholesome,
pest-ridden environments. Professional jealousies were rife. Drinking
was the main recourse, and the fumes of liquor could be speedily
followed by the smoke of pistols. Ennui and frictions might be worst of
all among young men cooped up on board ship. In 1833 two midshipmen came ashore at Singapore from HMS *Curacoa* to relieve their
feelings. One died a few days later; the other, and the seconds, were sent
for trial to Bombay, where they were acquitted.[3] Even war could not
always put a stop to private grudges. A losing campaign far from home,

---

[1] *Eugénie Grandet* (1833; Nelson edn., Paris, 1945), 249.
[2] Steinmetz, ii. 325–6.
[3] C. B. Buckley, *An Anecdotal History of Old Times in Singapore* (Kuala Lumpur, 1965), 226.

like that of Napoleon III's army in Mexico, would fray men's nerves and temper. A Jewish corporal Berg of the Foreign Legion distinguished himself there. He had forfeited an army commission by falling foul of a superior; he was now promoted to second-lieutenant, but was soon embroiled again with a fellow-officer, and killed.[4]

It was in the West Indies that Europe's worst instincts found a natural habitat in the slave plantations. Ideas of superiority of class or of race have much in common. Duels were fought by classes which believed themselves exalted by Providence or Nature above the rest; slave-owners were lifted up higher still. In societies based on violence and inhumanity men might well be readier to hazard their lives in the heat of the moment. It was an atmosphere not unlike Ireland's, only far worse, and with yellow fever, that avenging angel, always at hand. In the memoirs of Colonel W. K. Stuart, which bristle with duels—he himself fought three in the course of his service years from 1829 to 1864—one character recalled was the proud son of a father guilty of 'the most horrid cruelty to his slaves', but not hanged until he actually had a woman boiled alive. This was on the Danish island of Tortola, where British troops were sent to help in forestalling a rising by the 'blackies'. A rambling, imbecile tale of drunken frolics and challenges leads to 'the beautiful little fighting ground', which 'was always kept in a state of preparation, for many a Tortolian had kissed the daisies on that emerald turf'.[5]

In the British West Indies of his earlier days, Stuart says, the number of duels 'would indeed make a man of the present day open his eyes'. Soldiers stationed there caught the local contagion; the 'quadrillions of hungry mosquitoes' referred to by an officer writing about his comrades' duellings in 1806[6] must have added to their irritability. In Guiana Stuart had to take the field with a young man who 'lived but to fight', had already chalked up half a dozen duels, and died mad.[7] In Barbados cock-fighting went on all day, sometimes all night; 'enormous sums were lost and won … duels and death were often the result'.[8] In Jamaica, the island's historian writes, 'Drunken quarrels happened continually between intimate friends, which generally ended in duelling.'[9]

One summer morning at Calcutta in 1783 William Hickey got up before daybreak, 'gently left Mrs. Hickey in a profound sleep', and set off in a post-chaise with his second on the three miles to Alipur,

[4] Mercer, 79–80.
[5] Stuart, i. 203 ff.
[6] Leask and McCance, 252.
[7] Ibid. i. 256 ff.
[8] Ibid. i. 105.
[9] Edward Long (1774), cited by Calder, 478.

reflecting very likely that he might soon be wrapped in even deeper slumber. His business was with Nathaniel Bateman, a close friend turned enemy, who accused him of scurrilous talk. Bateman won the toss, and missed; Hickey followed, and missed; a reconciliation came about. 'The seconds were much pleased with our respective conduct.'[10]

India was the grand centre-piece of Europe's world rule, and the principal base of British military power. Not surprisingly it had a good share of the duelling that went on outside Europe. The duel kept its place in spite of good resolutions by the authorities to put down a practice that sometimes seemed to be unsettling things too much. 'To show how trivial a matter in those days brought men pistol to pistol', Colonel Stuart related an anecdote told by his father, who was in the army and in India before him, about an officer, who rose to be a general, addressing another at mess as 'Mr Mac', and being instantly called out.[11] Stuart himself had his last affair on his way out to India, when he and an Irishman fell out in a French casino: as a prelude to their duel Stuart knocked the offender down and deprived him of several teeth. Enraged at this, he demanded a second shot, unusual by that time; the seconds allowed it, to Stuart's surprise, but as he learned from one of them years later they put no bullets in the pistols.[12]

In India as in Europe duelling was most active among the military. These were of mixed composition. There were the three armies of the East India Company, based on the 'presidencies' of Bengal, Madras, Bombay, and more than half made up of native regiments under British officers; there were also 'royal' regiments, like the cavalry corps commanded by Walter Scott's son, who gave themselves superior airs. Habits and conventions in India and in Britain could reinforce each other. Both Reynolds and Tuckett, the two officers who fell foul of Lord Cardigan in 1840, had spent years in India. In general, Britain's vast empire can be said to have helped to perpetuate various practices, duelling and apoplectic drinking among them, that would otherwise have faded at home more quickly.

Possession of empire had a vital part likewise in promoting intimacy in Britain between old aristocracy and new bourgeoisie by supplying them with common interests. In the colonies, and in India above all, it enabled middle-class Britons to see themselves as part of a nobility of race, a *Sahib-log* or—a later term with the same meaning—*Herrenvolk*. In earlier days the Company officers came from mixed origins, with numerous foreigners, and they were much less well rewarded than civil officials except when war booty came their way. Hence they were

[10] Hickey, iii. 40, 149–53.
[11] Stuart, i. 17.
[12] Ibid. ii. 100 ff.

sensitive about questions of status, and observance of the code of honour, sometimes clumsily exaggerated, was an assertion of their claim to gentility. They were resentful of commissions being given to NCOs, as had to be done sometimes to make up for shortages.[13] A soldier from the ranks, turned editor, J. H. Stocqueler, left an amusing account of how he was called out by a staff captain for criticizing in his paper the management of the army's orphan school at Calcutta. They crossed the Hooghly river that same evening, in two boats; 'it might have been the Styx for one of us'. Stocqueler fired at the moon, while the captain's bullet hit the ground. 'The good little man made me a graceful bow; he was quite satisfied—so was I—and we were always better friends afterwards.'[14]

Cadets under training at the Calcutta institute applied themselves chiefly to 'the carefree pursuits of the prevailing image of a gentleman officer—one who drank hard, used foul language, gambled and duelled'. For this last recreation they framed a code of their own, and acted on it so zealously that in 1807 it was felt necessary to ban duelling among them.[15] Coming out so young, Anglo-Indians, as an observer said, too often 'carried the moods of schoolboys into the work of men'.[16] By the army duelling was not in itself regarded as illicit, but if it led to deaths or serious injuries notice had to be taken, especially if the proceedings had been in any way irregular. There was an awkward inconsistency of ideas here, which emboldened many to disregard official opinion altogether. Captain Middlemas in Scott's Indian novel came to grief by so doing, though he could plead that the man who agreed to fight him was the commanding officer of the regiment, 'an old cross-tempered martinet'. It was Middlemas, however, who stood out for a second shot, against the advice of the seconds, and with it killed his commander. 'Being universally blamed for having pushed the quarrel to extremity', he had to take to flight.[17] Scott hob-nobbed with neighbours home from India, and picked up a stock of information about British (not Indian) life there, so that details like these can be taken as true to life.

A man known to Stuart in the West Indies, as a friendly frolicsome chap, when a subaltern in Ceylon had been forced into a combat by a 'professed duellist', and killed him at the first shot. He was exonerated by a court-martial, but the memory preyed on him, and drove him to

[13] G. J. Bryant, 'The East India Company and its Army 1600–1778', unpub. Ph.D. thesis (London, 1975), 273–4.

[14] H. Hobbes, *John Barleycorn Bahadur* (Calcutta, 1944), 404–5.

[15] Amiya Barat, *The Bengal Native Infantry* (Calcutta, 1962), 75–6, citing W. Carey.

[16] H. G. Keene, *A Servant of 'John Company'* (London, 1897), 133.

[17] Scott, *The Surgeon's Daughter* (Edinburgh, 1827), chap. 9.

drink, until he lost his life by a falling out of a high window.[18] Some seniors did their best to discourage or veto duelling. One such was Major-General Hay Macdowall, commanding in the first Ceylon war in 1803–5, where reverses could be ascribed to poor officering. After Ensign Barry had been reprimanded for inciting a fellow-officer to challenge a superior, which was forbidden, Macdowall castigated them publicly for 'insubordination and want of discipline', and roundly denounced duelling as 'barbarous, unmilitary and immoral'.[19]

A stern view was sometimes taken by the civil courts, in serious cases and perhaps especially when the sufferer was a civilian and his opponent an army man. This was so at Bombay in 1802 when a man was shot dead. Both the lieutenant responsible and his second were tried for murder and sent to Botany Bay, one for fourteen years, the other for seven.[20] In those days, according to tales that went on being told for many years, some old hands made money by luring newly arrived greenhorns into drinking and gambling; if they complained about 'the ungentlemanly manner in which they had been swindled', they would be called out and taught a lesson not lost, it may be assumed, on others. A sadder tale is of a raw cadet at Madras who got into an argument at an evening festivity with 'a noted duellist', and foolishly called him a liar. They met on the beach next morning; the captain refused to accept an apology, as he was urged to do, and shot him through the head.[21]

A similar death might be an echo of old unhappy far-off things. At Poona in 1842 an Irish regiment was joined by an Ensign Sarsfield, a boy of 19 from an old Catholic family. His presence was obnoxious to the other officers, all Protestants. A pretext was soon found for sending him to Coventry, and his life was made miserable until at last, at the mess table, he threw his wineglass in the face of one of his persecutors. A duel took place at once, by moonlight. His death was reported as due to cholera.[22] Sudden mortality from disease was always common, and in the hot climate burial had to be hastened, so that it was not hard to hush up deaths from other causes, and a great many must have gone unrecorded.

In 1841 the 47th Native Infantry were sent to the unwholesome Arakan coast of Burma, and posted for eight months at Kyook-Phoo.

---

[18] Stuart, i. 186–7.

[19] G. Powell, *The Kandyan Wars* (London, 1973), 117. A story told of Outram as a youngster betokens a more indulgent attitude on the part of some men high up; see L. J. Trotter, *The Bayard of India* (Everyman edn., London, 1909), 115.

[20] Steinmetz, ii. 183.

[21] Hobbes, op. cit., 77–8.

[22] R. Bond, 'A Duel at Poona', *Mirror*, Calcutta (Feb. 1984). I am indebted to Dr Premen Addy for a copy.

An officer came to know, through someone else's unauthorized reading of private letters, that another officer had called him 'an unmitigated beast'. The two faced each other that evening on the beach. The aggrieved one was in too bad a temper to hit his mark; after two failures, and being denied a third shot by the other man's second, he threw his pistol at his opponent, shouting 'Then, Sir, you are a damned coward.' Word of the encounter got out, the two were placed under arrest, and a court of enquiry was set up. It sent the two offenders, the tattler and the too pertinacious challenger, to Calcutta to face a court-martial in Fort William. Both were cashiered, for 'ungentlemanly conduct'. The tell-tale at least was no loss to the regiment, 'as he was generally half-sodden with drink'.[23]

The officer, later Major-General Pughe, who recorded this event in a manuscript autobiography, also recalled an affair a few years afterwards at Benares. Two men came to blows at dinner in the mess. 'After personal assaults there was no other alternative but a duel.' He had to act as a second. They went off to the firing-range at once; it was a bright moonlit night—as so often on these occasions. No doubt the bottle had been circulating, and thanks perhaps to this, in alliance with the inconstant moon, two shots were exchanged ineffectively; one was 'much nearer hitting me', Pughe remarks, 'than the man for whom it was intended'. Next day the general, who had somehow heard all about it, summoned Pughe, and sitting in his carriage while the band played gave him a fatherly admonition. Had any accident occurred, he pointed out, the seconds would have been in 'a very unpleasant predicament'. An interval ought always to be allowed; they should have waited till morning, to see if some 'accommodation' might be possible.[24] It was a more flagrant breach of decorum that, Pughe says, virtually ended duelling in India. An officer sent a challenge, by his second, to 'a man whom they had wantonly insulted'. They were arrested, broke out from detention, and repeated their challenge. 'This of course was a very serious military offence. They were brought to a Court Martial and cashiered.'[25]

As in Britain almost at the same time, once the army packed up its duelling pistols civilians were quick to follow suit. Another factor must have been the shattering blow of the Indian Mutiny in 1857, quite enough to make Britons feel they could not afford to waste powder and shot on one another. Perhaps the presence of increasing numbers of British wives and daughters was a deterrent; women might be more averse to being left widowed or fatherless out in India than at home.

---

[23] Pughe, 79–81.
[24] Ibid. 81–2.
[25] Pughe, 84. On duels in India see also H. J. Wale, *Sword and Surplice* (London, 1880), 22, 110.

Early in this century when Kitchener as commander-in-chief was engaged in heated polemics with the viceroy over military policy, he was heard to mutter fiercely that he would enjoy calling Lord Curzon out.[26] He had Anglo-Irish blood. But the time for such self-indulgence had passed away. Anglo-India made up for the loss by a devotion to Sport, i.e. the killing of birds and animals, fanatical even by British or French standards. Galloping after wild boar, or stalking tigers, men could work off rankling grievances, exhibit their nerve and courage, and compete without hurting each other.

There were no Indian commissioned officers until long after duelling ended. We have little record of how Indians thought about it. Some may have seen it as proof of a British pugnacity which it would be rash to provoke; others may have felt that masters so apt to shoot one another would not be hard to get the better of, and the early stages of the Mutiny could be called confirmation. The commonest reaction may have been the bewilderment felt by the sepoy NCO Sita Ram, when he saw a new captain calling on the eccentric major in charge of his regiment, and being kept standing until he sat down unbidden. The major broke into a torrent of abuse, and the captain knocked him down. Next morning he saw them at the rifle butts, with two other officers, and the major carried to his house dead. 'How curious are the customs of these foreigners!' Sita Ram noticed the same thing among British privates, who fought with their fists, sometimes until one man was killed; they too 'lose face if they refuse to fight'.[27] Emulation of their officers must have helped to inspire this rude chivalry.

Occasionally a combat in the old heroic style might take place between a European and a native champion. During the punitive expedition of 1860 against the Mahsud Waziri tribe in Afghanistan, Captain Keyes of a Gurkha unit, when a fight was going badly, engaged the enemy leader in a 'sword battle': all the other combatants paused to watch, until the Waziri chief fell, and his men took to flight.[28] One of the exploits credited to Buffalo Bill was a 'tomahawk duel' with a Sioux chieftain. To the same family of adventures belongs the epic fight between Sir Henry and King Twala in Rider Haggard's novel of unknown Africa.[29] Hand-to-hand trials like these concentrated into moments the long era of Europe's rise to supremacy.

To stop other people from fighting was a prime item in what Europe, the fighting continent, saw as its duty to the world. An ingenious official

---

[26] D. Dilks, *Curzon in India* (London, 1970), ii. 240.

[27] Sita Ram, *From Sepoy to Subedar* (1873; London, 1970), 62–3. Cf. Anon, 'Duelling in our Indian Army', 240, on NCOs and even privates emulating their officers; and, on the French colonial army, 'Pierre Loti', *Le Roman d'un Spahi* (Paris, 1881), chap. 15.

[28] E. Bishop, *Better to Die: The Story of the Gurkhas* (London, 1977), 44.

[29] *King Solomon's Mines* (1886), chap. 14.

in Somaliland in the 1880s devised a kind of duel as a mitigation of bloodshed. Nomad tribesmen coming to Berbera had to leave their weapons at the police station; if two fell out and caused a disturbance they were made to dig a grave, then given their weapons and told to fight; the winner would have to bury the other. This cooled even the most inflammable tempers.[30]

It is hard to imagine the duel being adopted by many Asians or Africans, even among those most in contact with European life. When General Gordon was in Egypt he was angered by disparaging remarks about another Englishman by the chief minister, Nubar Pasha, and wanted to call him out, on the freakish ground that Vivian and himself both belonged to the Order of the Bath. 'Nubar Pasha must apologize or fight.' The bemused dignitary condescended to an apology.[31] Another Pasha showed more spirit. The last duel fought by a British officer— with love having the last word—is said to have taken place at Paris in 1910, between a nephew of Winston Churchill's mother and an Egyptian functionary who challenged him because of indiscreet letters to his consort. The culprit took an intensive course in fencing, and emerged from an hour-long contest with no more than a slight wound.[32] As he was killed early in the War, he had won only a brief respite.

Sidney Smith's joke about a coming species of South American duellists armed with blowpipes[33] suggests that Europeans took Latin America, as a nursery of honour, not too seriously. A study of patrician politics in nineteenth-century Chile brings out the importance of the 'great game' as the chief mode of competition with the élite. 'Suave drawing-room contests' were its staple, 'between magnates of the same rank, divided neither by ideas not by interests', but willing to spend huge sums on senatorial seats, as a distraction from the idleness of wealth.[34] No need seems to have been felt, as in Britain, of an accompaniment of duels. Cabinet came and vanished, the public remained profoundly indifferent.

At any rate, divergences between the duelling histories of northern and southern Europe had a continuation beyond the Atlantic; Anglo-Saxon America showed a much heartier appetite than the Latin countries. Stendhal was far out in his belief that high-flown notions of honour could have little place 'where actions are habitually judged by their degree of usefulness', as in the USA.[35] He associated 'honour' with

[30] I. M. Lewis, *The Modern History of Somaliland* (London, 1965), 47–8.
[31] C. Chevenix Trench, *Charley Gordon* (London, 1978), 154.
[32] Leslie, 285–6.
[33] Review of C. Waterton, *Wanderings in South America*, in *Edinburgh Review* (1826).
[34] A. Edwards Vives, *La Fronda aristocrática: Historia política de Chile*, 6th edn. (Santiago, 1966), 161, 178.
[35] Stendhal, *Love*, 119.

monarchies, and Brazil had an emperor until 1889; but its Portuguese ancestors had not been eager duellists. Racial mixing, there or in Mexico for instance, must have made the practice less congenial.

Canada as a French colony was a land mostly of peasants, with some gentry of the same feudal breed as in France, and army men. There was duelling on a limited scale, always with swords. British duelling soon had a sturdy offshoot in the new province of Upper Canada, or Ontario, incorporated in 1792 and peopled by Loyalists who left the American colonies when they broke away, and new settlers from Britain. An artificial aristocracy quickly formed, with office-holders from England setting the tone, and much squabbling and jostling for places. For those eager to claim membership of the élite, willingness to fight was a useful certificate. There is a decided contrast here with Australia. Emigration to the antipodes came later, when duelling in Britain was petering out, and brought with it fewer of the genteel or would-be genteel. Australia was too remote, as well as democratically unruly.[36] From across the ocean Canadian society might look not much better, a beargarden where opportunities for fighting would never be hard to find. An Edinburgh writer in 1828 fixed on bad relations between British and French as one cause. 'Their reciprocal abuse is most un-measured', replete with insults that in England 'would exclude the utterer from company ever afterwards'. Among the English-speakers in Upper Canada, 'adventurers from home, or American back woodsmen', polish and culture were scanty, the press reflected 'the general ardour of young societies', and furious personal attacks were habitual.[37] 'Social slights', a modern writer says, 'were magnified beyond all significance; gossip was virulent.'[38]

British criminal law was in force from the outset, but where duelling was in question with the same elasticity as at home. How little it told against a man's character to have 'been out' may be seen from the fact of a Sheriff Macdonell being succeeded in office by a man whom he stopped in mid-fight four years previously. A trial judge would faithfully expound the law, but after a 'fair' duel the prosecution would not press its case, and juries did not expect it to.[39] So it was for instance after a fight on a winter's day in 1800, arising from a Mrs Small's rudeness to

[36] Officers posted in Australia might fight, as they did everywhere; a duel of 1801 is recorded by R. Hughes, *The Fatal Shore* (London, 1987), 327. For a more freakish case, in 1830, see 577. A fatal affray in 1802 between naval officers at the Cape, which was about to be retroceded to Holland, necessitated a special Commission of Oyer and Terminer in London: see calendar of the *Baga de Secretis* file, in the Public Record Office, Bundle lxxxv.

[37] *Constable's Miscellany* (Edinburgh, 1828), 327, 334.

[38] *The Town of York 1793–1815*, ed. E.G. Firth (Toronto, 1962), pp. lxxviii–ix. 'York' was Toronto's early name.

[39] Riddell, 'The Duel', 166; cf. E.C. Guillet, *Early Life in Upper Canada* (Toronto, 1933), 111.

a Mrs White, and Mr White, 'exceedingly exasperated', hinting that Mrs Small was no better than she should be; to which Mr Small retorted as could be expected. They were both Englishmen, John White the province's first attorney-general, Major John Small clerk of the executive council. White died in the evening after their meeting, a friend wrote to inform his brother-in-law at Lincoln's Inn, but 'under the most excruciating Torture' he 'submitted to his fate with a most pious and Christian Resignation to the divine will and forgiveness of all his Enemies'. Small surrendered to justice, and was acquitted, but his wife's reputation suffered, and she was left 'a social pariah'.[40]

Of all early cases the one that made most stir was between John Ridout, a young student, and S. P. Jarvis, fought in July 1817 near what is today the corner of Yonge Street and College Street in Toronto.[41] There had been bad blood between the families, and the duel it led to went off with less than the neat precision of a well-conducted affair. Ridout was nervous, fired too soon, and then had to stand still waiting to be shot down by his vindictive enemy. A coroner's jury found that Jarvis killed him, 'not having the fear of God before his eyes but moved and seduced by the instigation of the Devil'. He was tried for manslaughter, and this time the prosecution was in earnest, but as the court was assured that no irregularity had occurred he was acquitted. In 1828 further recriminations led to the two seconds being prosecuted, as they had not been at the time; one was a son of the then attorney-general, the other of John Small. They too left the court without a stain on their names.

A pathetic instance of how men could be dragooned into fighting by social opinion comes from the town that is now Ottawa, in 1833. John Wilson, a law student born in Scotland, was knocked down by a fellow-student, Robert Lyon, who complained of his retailing rash aspersions made by Lyon on a young lady. Wilson had no taste for duelling, and only challenged him under persuasion of friends. Son of a poor farmer, he was said to be sensitive about his social position, and to have felt compelled to be 'tenacious of his character', whereas if he had been of higher rank he could have overlooked the incident. Lyon was killed; Wilson and his second were both acquitted, on a broad hint from judge to jury.[42]

Far away in Halifax, in 1819, the first criminal trial held in the court-house which is today the seat of the Nova Scotia legislature was that of R. J. Uniacke, son (one begins to expect this) of the attorney-general,

[40] Firth, lxxx, 231.
[41] Ibid. 261–2; Riddell, 'The Duel', 168–70; J. Lownsbrough, *The Privileged Few* (Toronto, 1980), 47–8, 64–5.
[42] Riddell, 'The Duel', 172–6.

for killing a man in a duel. This province had been another place of settlement of Loyalists from New England, some bringing aristocratic notions with them; and Uniacke soon went free. Various prominent figures in Canadian history have places in the duelling roll, like Sir Charles de Salabarry, a stalwart of the war of 1812 with the USA— William Weekes, an immigrant Irishman—Sir W. C. Meredith—Sir G. E. Cartier, Quebec rebel of 1837 and later co-founder with Sir J. A. Macdonald of the Federation. British officers stationed in Canada might be involved. In 1838 Major H. J. Warde of the Royal Scots was killed on the racecourse at Montreal by a citizen, Robert Sweeney. His funeral was attended by the entire battalion and garrison.[43]

There was no shortage of religion in Canada, but its influence in such matters was limited. In 1838 the Revd W. Taylor, pastor of the United Secession Church at Montreal, was moved by a recent occurrence there to preach and publish a sermon against duelling in very strong language. It rehearsed most of the arguments that divines could bring to bear. Duelling was a sin 'contrary to the will of God', one that 'excludes from salvation'. Esteemed though it might be as genteel, it was in truth 'a savage remnant of the times of ignorance and feudal barbarity', and a death resulting from it was 'murder of the most aggravated kind'. A duellist was worse than an assassin, who at least did not affect noble sentiments. He might, as Cowper had written, be hurrying an unprepared soul into eternity, raising his hand 'against soul and body at once'. Taylor made a shrewd point when he said there are always men who 'imagine they will attain some consequence, if they can involve themselves in a quarrel with a great man'.[44] Here was one more penalty of greatness.

By mid-century opinion was turning against the duel. Papineau the French Canadian separatist rejected a challenge in 1836, and Sir Francis Hincks in 1844. In 1849, when W. H. Blake, an incomer brimming with Irish eloquence, was attacking the so-called 'Family Compact' that kept the Tories in power, he received two challenges, one of them from J. A. Macdonald, then a headstrong youth; intervention by friends kept this from taking effect. A late incident was one at Quebec in 1854, beginning with a lengthy exchange of letters between George Irvine and Thomas Pope, over words used by them in court, the former requiring and the latter refusing an apology. At last the two, having bowed to each other in due form, found themselves standing back to back, and on the word being given moving to the specified distance of fourteen paces apart before turning and firing. They fired together,

[43] Leask and McCance, 425. Richardson the Canadian novelist had a bad time with Guards officers at Montreal: see Riddell, *Richardson*, 118 ff.; Beasley, 112–14.

[44] Taylor, 'A Testimony'.

Irvine into the air; this touched Pope, and they exchanged amicable words and shook hands. 'I suppose,' Pope was moved to remark, 'that the usages of society require this sort of thing, but I think it a most absurd way of settling a difficulty.'[45] It is indeed hard to comprehend why a man with a grievance should risk his life and deliberately forgo the chance of scoring off his enemy. By the end of the 1850s the duel was extinct. Denison's memoirs of his career as a militia cavalry officer[46] overflow with hard feelings and hard words, but no question of a duel ever arises. British example was, of course, a prime factor.

Early colonial America was decidedly unfavourable to duels. Its first was a scuffle between two indentured servants, who were tied together neck and heels and left to think things over.[47] In the 1680s the nephew of a governor of New York was convicted of manslaughter. In Penn's Quaker colony duelling was punishable with 'hard labour in the house of correction'. Puritan feeling was still stirring in Benjamin Franklin's condemnation of the duel as a trial in which a man sets himself up as his own judge and 'undertakes himself to be the executioner'. He tells, us in his autobiography that as a newspaper editor he eschewed any scandalous material, unlike many others who had no scruples about 'gratifying the malice of individuals by false accusations ... augmenting animosity even to the producing of duels'.[48]

By that time the colonies were moving towards independence from Europe, but at the same time imbibing various of Europe's worse attributes, for whose reception widening class division opened the way. A bourgeoisie, or mercantile aristocracy, was growing in the bigger towns, southern slavery was spreading its blight, and many younger, impressionable Americans were going to Britain for holidays, business, or study of law or medicine. A 'snobbish importation' was going on of fashions like cards, dancing, and the wearing of the 'small-sword'; along with this, duels were 'seriously infecting the Colonies', whereas formerly fists and cudgels had sufficed even southern planters. The presence of British troops during the French and Indian wars aroused 'the sophomoric admiration of young American Quality for the fire-eating ways of Captain Spontoon and Ensign Spatterdash'.[49]

In Winston Churchill's juvenile novel about a young man from Maryland who visited London and had a nocturnal duel with a malignant Duke of Chartersea, the hero was back at home when the War of Independence was approaching and party strife intensifying. 'Bitter

[45] J. Young, *Correspondence*.

[46] Lt. Col. G. T. Denison, *Soldiering in Canada* (London, 1900).

[47] J. C. Furnas, *The Americans ... 1587–1914* (New York, 1969), 192.

[48] Benjamin Franklin, *The Autobiography and Other Writings*, ed. L. J. Lemisch (New York, 1961), 108–9.

[49] Furnas, 192–3.

controversies were waging in the *Gazette*, and names were called and duels fought weekly.'[50] When hostilities broke out they became still commoner. Americans were fighting the British, but also continuing to ape them; when a French army arrived to aid the rebellion European influence was reinforced. In Washington's 'Continental army' challenges were nominally forbidden, but accepting them was not. General Charles Lee, who like his second was on Washington's staff, was wounded by Colonel John Laurens; Colonel John Cadwallader fought General Thomas Conway, General Robert Howe fought Christopher Gadsden. A duel with fatal results took place in May 1777, when Button Gwinnett, a signatory of the Declaration of Independence, was killed by the fiery Lachlan McIntosh. Celtic names, it will be noticed, recur among these combustible characters, as in Canada.

In the springtime of freedom both Tom Paine and Jefferson were among progressives who wanted the death penalty for duelling, and opposition to it on religious or other grounds was outspoken. A late eighteenth-century print, 'The Way of Good and Evil', shows men and women on two paths, conducting to 'Eternal Life' and 'Destruction'. The latter, beset with temptations, winds past brothel, saloon, jail, till it reaches the waiting flames where sinners, top hat and frock coat and all, are swallowed up. In a small inset picture close by the route a pair of duellists stand, pistol-hands outstretched.[51]

In 1804 Dr Timothy Dwight, president of Yale college, preached a powerful sermon in the chapel. It was extraordinary, he said, that killing was universally punished with death, except in Christian countries when committed by persons of 'superiority and distinction'. In medieval times it was at least believed that the issue of single combat was determined by God. 'Modern duellists neither believe, nor wish, God to interfere in their concerns.' Civilized men fight, like savages, for no better reason than 'because it is glorious'. How Christ would have blackened his name, the preacher went on, rising to a startling height, if he had sent someone a challenge, or fought a duel! A thrilling peroration painted a wife left widowed with her children—'See her eyes rolling with phrenzy, and her frame quivering with terror.'

A few months later the sermon was repeated at New York, and published there. The reason for this, and the genesis of the sermon itself, is likely to have been an event of not many weeks before its first delivery. This was the most eye-catching contest in American history, and the most resounding in American politics, in which Alexander Hamilton was killed by Aaron Burr. America has chosen some very odd pilots, but none more freakish than Burr, then vice-president under Jefferson.

[50] *Richard Carvel* (1899; London, 1928), 356–7, 397.
[51] R. Cavendish, *Visions of Heaven and Hell* (New York, 1977), 25 (reprod.).

He was a man of irrepressible ambition who saw Hamilton as an obstacle in his path. Hamilton agreed to the fight reluctantly, and against his principles. Burr was tried for murder, with the usual negative outcome; his next throw of the dice, an attempt apparently to conquer Texas for himself from Mexico, brought on him charges of treason, and he had to remove for some years to Europe.

Many were shocked by the 1804 fatality, but habits of violence persisted. There was drastic legislation in Pennsylvania and several New England states. New York followed; but Fenimore Cooper ironically included duelling among the refinements of civilization making their way at the beginning of the century into settlements among the 'wild hills' of upper New York state.[52] In 1819 the new state of Illinois hanged a man for killing a neighbour in a rifle duel at the murderous range of twenty-five paces.[53] But many other states had no legislation, and combatants could dodge laws by crossing boundaries. It was an ex-governor of South Carolina, J. L. Wilson, who in 1838 edited the Irish Code so as to bring it into line with American predilections; he added a pious wish that gentlemen should be educated into respect for other men's feelings.[54] Tocqueville's impression was that social conditions accustomed men 'not to take offense in small matters'[55], but causes of strife seem often to have been quite as minimal as they often were in Europe. Being more openly licensed by law or custom than in most of Europe, the duel had no need to be kept under a veil, but frequently invited publicity shunned for social as well as legal reasons in England. The presence of spectators may have made combatants more desirous of a resounding victory. There was, besides, a more practical approach than in the refined ceremonial of the Old World. Men sought revenge, rather than 'satisfaction', and shot to kill. The duel was regressing to what it had been in Europe long before.

Europeans found these proceedings distasteful, as an uncouth parody of their own. Soon after tempers had been soured by the war of 1812–14, a Captain Johnson at Gibraltar was compelled to take on two Americans in succession; Steinmetz contrasted 'the irregular and unfair mode of fighting adopted by the Yankees, and the strictly honourable, spirited, and manly conduct of the Englishman'.[56] John Bull was for long unreconciled to the American rebels who, as he saw things, stabbed him in the back at the height of his duel with Napoleon. They were often considered to have degenerated, in the wild air of democratic

[52] *The Pioneers* (1823; Everyman edn., London, 1907), 77.
[53] Furnas, 529.
[54] J. H. Franklin, 45–6, 61.
[55] A. de Tocqueville, *Democracy in America*, Pt. 2 (1840; World's Classics edn., London, 1946), chap. 29.
[56] Steinmetz, ii. 249.

licence, into a race of savages, always ready to fly at one another's throats. Gambling for high stakes inflamed their tempers, they snatched up any weapons that came to hand. 'A Yankee will fight with muskets and buck shot', Scott's veteran declares, 'rather than sit still with an affront.'[57]

To Europeans the bowie knife was the trade mark of a Hobbesian state of nature. Its reputed progenitor, Colonel James Bowie, was a southerner mixed up in faction-fights over land speculation at Natchez in Mississippi. A contest on a sandbank there in 1827, swelling into a mêlée with pistols and knives both hard at work, stuck in men's memories. Every man is capable of 'murderous infernal' anger, Carlyle wrote, but it matters much how this finds vent—from drawing of 'Arkansas Bowie-knives, up to a deliberate Norse *Holmgamg*, to any civilised Wager of Battle.'[58] Aytoun the Scottish writer's satire on Americans, those 'thin-skinned sons of freedom', asks

> Why an independent patriot freely spits upon the floor,
> Why he gouges when he pleases, why he whittles at the chairs,
> Why for swift and deadly combat still the bowie-knife he bears ...[59]

Englishmen, 'Nimrod' boasted, learned boxing; they did not use stilettos, or 'gouge and maim their antagonists with the savage barbarism of North America'.[60]

Referring, more temperately, to the survival of some feudal traits within bourgeois society, Marx found the most striking case of it in 'the civil right of duelling' in the USA.[61] This proved to have deep roots in the progressive North, as well as deeper ones in the doubly enslaved South whose chains fettered white minds as well as black limbs. America had an élite of men who could claim, by birth or education (especially as lawyers, Tocqueville noticed), a status like that of the gentleman in England. They wanted to preserve their eminence, and duelling could be one means. Americans of British descent wanted to maintain their leading position in a country whose population was fast becoming a European hotchpotch; and it is noticeable that most of the names that stand out in its duelling annals hail from the British Isles.

A memoirist in 1861 looked back on a college rumpus leading to fisticuffs and a black eye; in the northern states, he thought, after the Burr–Hamilton duel there was no danger of such a thing being carried

[57] *St Ronan's Well*, chap. 34.
[58] 'Two Hundred and Fifty Years Ago', 127.
[59] W. E. Aytoun, *Stories and Verse*, anthology (Edinburgh, 1964), 309 ff.
[60] 'Nimrod', 229–30.
[61] Letter to Lassalle, 10 June 1858.

further.[62] Student duelling was left to the Germans. Yet for many more years politicians continued to settle scores in the old style, with gentlemen of the press following in their tracks. In 1826 Henry Clay, secretary of state and one of the most distinguished public men who failed to become president, fought a senator from Virginia dissatisfied with his handling of relations with Latin America. In 1838 two congressmen, Jonathan Cilley of Maine and William Graves of Kentucky, after a dispute as puerile as ever set a pair of children squabbling, faced each other with rifles at eighty yards. Cilley fell at the third discharge, dying. Half a dozen other congressmen were watching, and no protest was felt to be called for, though the shock to public opinion was considerable.[63] Despite New York law, the editor J. W. Webb was 'as notorious a duelist as any Creole dandy in Louisiana'; another fighting 'Manhattanite' was an internationally known banker. In 1831 William Cullen Bryant, the New England poet, editor, and journalist, was seen after a dinner-table row emphasizing his views with a whip. 'A certain incidence of horsewhipping and duels was normal among the upper strata in America.'[64] A sturdy individual ready with a humorous evasion when challenged (the details of the story vary) was Abraham Lincoln.

Men in uniform were prominent, as everywhere. In the USA with its Indian and Mexican wars they had more of a foot in the political door than in Britain, whose wars after 1815 were fought far away. American officers had the same kind of incentive as Russians for trying to put themselves on a level with western Europe, and alacrity at bandying bullets was the simplest way. Walt Whitman described the officer corps as 'a monstrous exotic' in his democratic clime, 'trebly-aristocratic' in its conventions.[65] A disproportionate number of southerners sought careers in the army, like 'that everlasting Virginny duellist, General Cuffy', as Sam Slick called him.[66] Others combined rank in the militia with political activity, like the Tennessee congressman and duellist General Samuel Houston, a fact that inflated the number of duels attributed to the army.[67]

Among regular soldiers General Andrew Jackson, also of Tennessee, stands out. 'Old Hickory' as his men called him carried a duelling bullet scar close to his heart. His most talked-of fight was with Charles Dickinson, over a racing debt, in 1806; his opponent's death did nothing to tarnish his warlike fame among his admirers. One of these was

[62] C. Benson, 'Reminiscences of American College Life', *Macmillan's Magazine*, 3 (Nov. 1860–Apr. 1861), 273.

[63] Andrew, 34–5; J. R. Franklin, 52–3.

[64] Furnas, 528, 530.

[65] Walt Whitman, *Democratic Vistas* (London, 1888), 36 n.

[66] T. C. Haliburton, *The Clockmaker* (Halifax, Nova Scotia, 1836; Toronto, 1958), 29.

[67] Webb, 70.

Herman Melville, equally an admirer of the tsar Nicholas I, 'the policeman of Europe'. There is a sidelight here on a deep-seated discord in the American mentality, today more prominent than ever, between ostentatious respect for freedom and admiration for power, however despotic, when exerted in accord with American interests or prejudices. In 1829 Jackson was elected president. He was one of many army men on whom Indian wars must have had a coarsening influence. On Indian frontiers trouble about women was common; still, 'there were occasional romances like that of the Fort Snelling lieutenant who fought a duel with a brother officer over his Sioux sweetheart whom he later married'.[68]

By mid-century duelling was on the wane in the north, as in Canada; a sign of this was that more care was taken for secrecy, whereas in the south contests were still proudly paraded. Ownership of slaves enabled planters and their wives to feel very superior, like Russian landowners with their serfs. When the civil war came Marx was sardonic about sentimental Tory sympathy for 'ladies from New Orleans, yellow beauties, tastelessly adorned with jewels' purchased by Negro toil.[69] New Orleans was the metropolis of southern 'chivalry'. Only the south had regular meeting-places, like London or Paris, and New Orleans boasted the most celebrated, the 'Dueling Oaks', which had its own well-starched etiquette and regularly drew a concourse of onlookers: pistoleers could preen themselves to their hearts' content. A traveller in the 1830s reported a 'rage for duelling' so feverish that 'a jest or smart repartee is sufficient excuse for a challenge'.[70] The best training in fencing and shooting was to be had there, each establishment 'little more than a school for duelists'.[71]

Critics of southern life often reckoned this proclivity among its vices. Underlying it was an instinctive desire to impress the black man with the warlike fire and fury of the white man, a hypertrophied version of the desire in Europe to impress the lower orders. But here too we may see a brutal ruling class inflicting on itself the punishment that its victims were seldom able to inflict. The wealthy R. D. Spaight who entered Congress in 1798 as a pro-slavery man perished four years later at the hands of his successor. A dozen years later a traveller described the arrogant masters of the slave states as quarrelsome because unused to any restraint, and added: 'Duelling is not only in general vogue and fashion, but is practised with circumstances of peculiar vindictiveness.'[72] Mark Twain as a boy in Hannibal, Missouri, saw two doctors fight in

---

[68] F. Downey, *Indian Wars of the US Army* (Derby, Conn., 1964), 128.
[69] Article of 20 June 1862, in Karl Marx and Friedrich Engels, *The Civil War in the United States, Collected Works*, English edn., vol. xix (London, 1984).
[70] J. R. Franklin, 41.
[71] Ibid. 45.
[72] Francis Hall, *Travels in Canada and the United States in 1816 and 1817* (London, 1818), 460.

the street with 'sword-canes'. At Richmond, capital of Virginia and during the civil war of the Confederation, in 1846 two editors set about each other with pistols and 'went on into a freestyle hacking match with bowie knives, tomahawks and broadswords. One died shockingly mangled.' The other was acquitted by 'a right-thinking jury'.[73] The south was poorly policed, and duelling was echoed by outbreaks of violence against Germans, Irish, and other newcomers, as well as blacks.

Even here there were objectors, who must often have felt that they were spitting against the wind. Even Georgia, reckoned the worst state of all, with an estimated total of over a thousand duels before 1807, had laws, though they were taken little notice of. Fresh impetus to opposition came from a fight in 1828 between G. W. Crawford and T. E. Burnside. This had its roots in local politics, the former representing the big-planter faction and his adversary the small farmers. Both were lawyers, and Crawford, son of a senator under attack in the other side's newspapers, was attorney-general of the state. They met in Creek Indian territory, so as to be out of reach of any laws, before a throng of white and Indian spectators. Burnside, steadily refusing an apology for the press articles, was killed at the third shot. Crawford's performance helped to ensure a bright political future. But an Anti-dueling Association took the matter up, and next year a fresh state law was passed.[74]

As the slavery controversy sharpened, conservatives tried to silence their critics by dint of challenges, much as royalists did when the French Revolution got under way. When northerners were not prepared to fight, methods still more rough and ready were sometimes resorted to. After an anti-slavery speech in Congress in 1856 Charles Sumner was brutally assaulted and half-killed by another congressman, a southern gentleman named Preston Brooks, whose feat earned him much southern applause. In 1859 D. C. Broderick, a United States senator from California, was mortally wounded in a duel with D. S. Terry, chief justice of the same state. It was partly a dispute over patronage, but Terry was a slavery man, and Broderick was escorted to the grave by a large gathering, as a martyr of the abolitionist cause. In such a case a duel might, for once in a way, be worth while.

William Howard Russell, the famous war correspondent, was in the USA to watch the coming of the civil war. On 5 April 1861 he dined at a French restaurant in Washington with the Southern Commissioners, and learned something of their philosophy. They were convinced that all northerners were so deeply sunk in materialism

[73] Furnas, 529. On duelling in the South see also F. W. Dawson, *Reminiscences of Confederate Service 1861–1865* (1882; Baton Rouge Louisiana State Univ., 1980), pp. xiii–iv, 102–3, 155–7, 164–6.

[74] See Cleveland.

and money-grubbing that they would never be ready to draw the sword. These sabre-rattlers exhibited 'a degree of something like ferocity ... towards New England which exceeds belief', and an equal contempt for old England as a nation cankered with peace, lost to the 'highly wholesome and meritorious' practice of duelling, and preferring sordid acceptance of money as compensation for a stolen wife. In the south there was only one way. 'The man who dares tamper with the honour of a white woman, knows what he has to expect. We shoot him down like a dog.' Russell ventured to wonder whether female virtue which had to be safeguarded with a pistol could be worth much, but his query was not understood. They added an argument too gross for him to do more than hint at in his book—that there could be no excuse for making love to white women in a society where a man with physical needs had only to buy himself a black girl.[75]

One white woman from New Orleans was Adah Menken, who was playing her 'Naked Lady' part in *Mazeppa* at New York, during the Civil War, when doubts were cast on her loyalty. She met them by inviting any man in the audience to fight her on the stage, with sword or pistol, and followed this up with a public display of skill at fencing and shooting.[76]

Among the flood of new immigrants the vast majority belonged to Europe's poorest classes. Many brought with them old habits including primitive modes of fighting, sometimes jumbled up with duelling of a sort, which they could practise now by way of a declaration of new-found independence. Blood feuds sprouted in some hill regions. There, as in one of O'Henry's stories, men were 'shot at the plough, through their lamp-lit cabin windows, coming from camp-meetings, asleep, in duello, sober and otherwise'.[77] Americans were a turbulent democracy, in some ways ready to defy their ruling élites, but in as many ways wanting to imitate them, as they have continued to do more and more whole-heartedly. Engels commented on the paradox of Americans 'clothing the most modern tendencies in the most mediaeval mummeries', a working-class movement calling itself the 'Knights of Labour'.[78] There was always free access to weapons, legitimated in earlier days by the need for the common man to be ready to defend home or country; a right to use them for settling private disagreements could be claimed in the name of equality.

Duelling on European lines belonged to the cities, there being no landed gentry except the southern planters; more unpretentious

---

[75] W. H. Russell, *My Diary North and South* (London, 1863), i. 92–4.
[76] Edwards, chap. 15.
[77] O'Henry, 'Squaring the Circle', in *The Voice of the City* (1908).
[78] Pref. to American edn. of *The Condition of the Working Class in England* (1886).

versions were a frontier growth. The 'Wild West' was to some extent
a legend; it seems that even when it was at its worst there were worse
species of violence, from duelling to lynching, in the south. Still, as
Paxon observed in his interesting study of frontier psychology, 'The
duelling code survived longest in the parts of the United States in which
frontier roughness lasted longest'; he ascribed this in part to 'the intense
sensitiveness bred by loneliness and equality', and noted that pioneers
were the readiest to admire fighters like Burr and Jackson.[79] In 1835 at
the River Laramie trading-fort Kit Carson, later renowned as pathfinder, Indian Agent, finally brigadier-general, first emerged to fame,
when he accepted 'the boastful challenge of the French bully Shúnar',
and came out of the duel victorious.[80] The Californian gold-rush set off
a demand for six-shooters, a lightweight naval .36 model proving
particularly well adapted either to single combat or to straightforward
homicide.[81] At San Francisco newspapers were in the habit of 'advertising duels as if they were stage performances'.[82]

If some of America's men of letters were also men of the pistol,
Benjamin Franklin was not the only one who tried to turn his countrymen's minds away from it. In the *Ingoldsby Legends* there is a long
comic poem called 'The Black Mousquetaire', a skit on the Dumas type
of dashing duelling rake; its hero amuses himself of an evening by
sallying forth, well primed with liquor, to 'pink' a citizen in the street,
and the author alludes to goings-on nearer home:

> similar pranks
> Amongst young men who move in the very first ranks.[83]

Marryat's burlesque duel in *Midshipman Easy* was taken up and given
further extravagance by Bret Harte in one of his parodies of European
novelists: his purser is accused of insulting the whole cockpit and invited
to fight six men at once.[84]

It was fitting that the writer fondest of deriding and denouncing all
such Old World fustian should be a southerner, 'Mark Twain'. His
charge against Scott, his complaint of 'the Sir Walter disease' infecting
the south with pseudo-chivalrics, has been repeated in more recent
times.[85] Whatever truth it may have must be taken as sad evidence of
how the dross of a novelist of genius can be valued, in the wrong

[79] F. L. Paxon, *History of the American Frontier 1763–1893* (Boston, 1924), 251.

[80] L. R. Hafen, *Broken Hand: The Life of Thomas Fitzpatrick* (1931; Lincoln, Nebraska, 1973), 148.

[81] W. E. Hollon, *Frontier Violence: Another Look* (New York, 1974), 25–6.

[82] Baldick, 134.

[83] R. H. Barham, *The Ingoldsby Legends* (1840).

[84] Bret Harte, 'Mr. Midshipman Breezy', in *Sensation Novels Compressed*, Everyman edn. of Harte's *Tales and Poems* (London, n.d.), 175.

[85] 'Mark Twain', *Life on the Mississippi* (1883; World's Classics edn., London, 1962), p. xiv; cf. Webb, 66.

environment, higher than his gold; though Scott was not read by southerners only. Colonel T. W. Higginson, who commanded a Black regiment on the Federal side in the Civil War, was one appreciative reader.[86] Twain quoted the prospectus of a 'Female College' in Kentucky which imparted to young ladies the virtues of southern life, 'the highest type of civilisation this continent has seen', and sardonically appended press reports of disgusting southern murders, blood-feuds, a duel on the highroad between a youth with a club (who was killed) and another with an axe, a well-connected pair in Virginia quarrelling too late at night to find pistols, and fighting with butcher's knives instead. New Orleans was a centre of cock-fighting as well as duelling; he described a beak and claw tournament, with an audience 'in frenzies of delight'.[87]

A few years later he conjured up a tournament in ancient Britain, before King Arthur and his court, with Sir Sagramour le Desirous confronting Hank Morgan the Yankee, one a tower of steel on his war-horse, the other unarmoured, on a nimble pony on which he dodges the knight's spear round and round the lists, and finally jerks him out of the saddle with a lasso. Others, and in the end Sir Lancelot, are dealt with in the same unceremonious fashion, before Hank has another round with Sagramour and shoots him with a revolver. 'The day was mine', he is left to reflect gleefully. 'Knight-errantry was a doomed institution. The march of civilisation was begun.'[88] After another century it is clearer than it could be to Mark Twain that getting rid of feudal relics is not a complete passport to a true civilization.

Besides being a comic masterpiece, *A Yankee at the Court of King Arthur* was an onslaught on the Old World's archaic class system, and the militarism and everything else that went with it. Its author was a firm anti-imperialist, as he showed when the American conquest of the Philippines took place a decade later. Thorstein Veblen, the Norwegian-American sociologist, was then writing *The Theory of the Leisure Class*. He touched on the duel as an institution of the idle rich, or one shared by it with army officers and 'lower-class delinquents', who he thought had much the same temperament. 'It is only the high-bred gentleman and the rowdy that normally resort to blows' for settling their differences.[89]

In the Civil War disputes over appointments or tactics were acrimonious in both armies, but seldom led to duels except on the Confederate side. After the defeat of the south duelling withered away even

[86] T. W. Higginson, *Army Life in a Black Regiment* (1870; New York, 1962), 176, 187.

[87] Ibid. 271–3, 296–7.

[88] *A Yankee at the Court of King Arthur* (1889), chap. 39.

[89] Thorstein Veblen, *The Theory of the Leisure Class* (1889; New York, 1953), 166.

there; the last formal duel in America is said to have happened in 1877, and any repetition would be a crime under Federal law. In the 1880s a satirist lamented that it was no longer considered nice:

> To split a rival like a fish, or slice
> A husband like a spud, or with a shot
> Bring down a debtor doubled in a knot.[90]

Today we hear a leading American political philosopher declare quite seriously that 'Culture is inherently feudal ... It is both good and necessary that culture should be feudal in character.'[91] If so, conceivably duelling has a future as well as a past. Its disappearance, a pessimist might urge, has only made room for worse things, and every American city is now a Wild West.

[90] Ambrose Bierce, *The Enlarged Devil's Dictionary*, ed. E. J. Hopkins (London, 1967): see 'Duel'.
[91] R. Nisbet, *Twilight of Authority* (London, 1976), 119–20.

18

Epilogue and Retrospect

Honour ... that enigmatic mixture of conscience and egoism ...
compatible with much selfishness and great vices and ... astonishing illusions ... has become, in a far wider sense than is commonly believed, a decisive test of conduct in the minds of the
cultivated Europeans of our own day.

Burckhardt, *The Civilization of the Renaissance* (1860), Pt. 6, chap. 1.

IN a novel by Kingsley about social problems a sensible doctor gets rid
of a young squireen who comes bearing a challenge, in the style he has
read of in fiction, by saying he will fight his principal only across a
handkerchief, and will then fight *him* likewise.[1] To Kingsley in 1857
sanitary reform loomed larger than 'honour'. One may wonder whether
it was fact or fantasy when P. G. H. Fender, one-time captain of Surrey
and the man who scored a century in thirty-five minutes, told an
interviewer a few weeks before his death in 1985 at the age of 92, that
shortly before 1914 he won a sword duel, concerned with a girl, and
still owned a sword-stick presented to him by his gallant opponent.[2]

Across the Channel, when Flaubert's Frederick in 1869 had to face
a duel, with a viscount, 'a terrible agony gripped him at the thought
that he might show fear on the duelling-ground'. But the encounter
was to prove a somewhat ridiculous affair, and Rosanette's vanity-
tickling notion of its being fought on her account was a delusion.[3]
Edmond Rostand had a vast success in 1905 with his play about Cyrano
de Bergerac, who is shown fighting a duel with another viscount in
1640, and making up a ballade about the contest while thrusting and
parrying. This might be good theatre, but its artificiality marks it
as belonging to a time when an archaic institution was running to
seed, or growing freakish. Bicycles and balloons were sometimes
employed as mounts; at Paris in 1908 a balloon was shot down, and
both the combatant and his second lost their lives.[4] Such fatalities were

---

[1] Charles Kingsley, *Two Years Ago* (1857), chap. 14.
[2] T. Coleman, *Guardian* (6 May 1985).
[3] G. Flaubert, *Sentimental Education* (1869; English edn., Everyman edn., London, 1941), 211,
241.
[4] Baldick, 161–2.

exceptional; the duel in France, nearing its end, was returning to the limited, usually harmless, style so often found among primitive peoples.

Anti-duelling associations were sprouting in many lands, even for instance in 1902 in Hungary, which could be denominated 'a duelling country *par excellence*':[5] feudal survivals were stronger there than anywhere else in the Habsburg empire. East of the Rhine, however, duelling was not nearly so much on its last legs as in western Europe. In 1901 Somerset Maugham reflected in his notebook that 'public opinion and law are sometimes antagonistic—as in duelling on the continent'.[6] In his diatribes against the idiocy of war, as 1914 approached, Norman Angell was very conscious of how closely akin were dogmas about the impossibility of abolishing the duel, or abolishing war. Educated Europeans he wrote could still be heard declaiming that to abandon duelling was ' "not in human nature" ... the notion that honourable people should ever so place their honour at the mercy of whoever may care to insult them is, they assure you, both childish and sordid'—despite the abandonment of the duel by the whole Anglo-Saxon world.[7]

This abandonment had accompanied freedom from conscription, which on the continent had now become a universal instead of a selective obligation. But everywhere concepts of war were being democratized, aristocratic honour blown up into 'national honour'. Angell heard 'the standards of the *code duello* ... daily brought before us by the rhetoric of the patriots'.[8] A country must fight when its honour or prestige was compromised, General von Bernhardi maintained, because they formed 'an essential part of its power'.[9] In like manner they had always buttressed that of the aristocracies. What the duel had been for gentlemen—an *ultima ratio*, as an objector had written long since, resorted to indiscriminately on any occasion, grave or frivolous[10]—war now was for rulers who were infecting their peoples with the belief that it would be shameful to surrender 'national honour' to international laws or courts.

Highwaymen, the same objector had remarked, are agreed on all hands to be wicked, but ' "gentlemen" it seems may claim the exclusive privilege of pistolling one another whenever they please'.[11] Again, just as the duellist claimed exemption in his chosen sphere from ordinary law, monarchs whose hands were increasingly tied in home affairs, and almost equally the small cliques in control of foreign policy in the

[5] *Enciclopedia Universal Ilustrada* (Madrid, n.d.), article on 'Duelo'.
[6] Somerset Maugham, *A Writer's Notebook* (Harmondsworth, 1967), 69 (1901).
[7] Norman Angell, *The Great Illusion* (1909; enlarged edn., London, 1933), 311.
[8] Ibid.
[9] *Germany and the Next War* (English edn., London, 1914), 49–50.
[10] C. Moore, 259.
[11] Ibid. 255.

'Western democracies', set their 'honour' above the common welfare of mankind. For a government to declare war, or a gentleman to offer a challenge, was a 'noble' action; and *nobilis* (originally *gnobilis*) meant 'notable', or 'noteworthy', as applied to someone in the public eye, obliged therefore to sustain the reputation he is credited with. What is implied is a neurotic sense of being always under observation, by a man's peers and by an alien humankind staring from a distance, ready to jeer or mutiny at any hint of weakness. A gentleman's standing with his underlings, a government's with its subjects, would depend very much on their standing among their equals. None of the diplomats and generals of 1914 could risk appearing the first to give way, any more than duellists could resist the pressure of social opinion. The sword-bearers rushed at one another in a collective frenzy, a desperate effort to reassert themselves, something like the *Ragnarök*, the last, all-engulfing conflict of the old Norse gods.

Aristocracy and monarchy had always shared the same intertwining destinies, and did so to the bitter end. Duelling had helped to bolster an atavistic class, by stiffening its self-respect and extorting the admiration of many below it. War had the same function on a grander scale. But willingness to hazard life or limb for a straw can be recognized as a symptom of a lurking insecurity, a shadow of impermanence. Nietzsche's injunction to 'live dangerously' summed up the existence that Europe's upper classes had condemned themselves to. The mystique of war generated by it took vivid shape in the rhapsodic welcome given to the call to arms in 1914 by young French officers who, Edmund Gosse the ex-Plymouth Brother rhapsodized, 'sought their death in a spirit of delirious chivalry'. ' "La vie est bonne et belle" ', he quoted from a letter written by one of them shortly before his death, ' "et la guerre est une chose bien amusante." This is the type of Frenchman who fights for the love of fighting.'[12] Only a class like the French aristocracy, for which duelling had for so long been a memento of former greatness, or its imitators, could have attitudinized about war in this mystico-dilettante fashion.

For the last time, war could be looked to for God's arbitrament, as ordeal by combat had once been. The folly of the men of old who 'blindly and absurdly' expected Providence to sway single combat in favour of the more deserving had long since been discarded.[13] But the same faith was transferred, with all the more conviction, to collective, national clashes. In each belligerent country men believed Heaven to be, very properly, on their side. Whoever won or lost, it could be sure

[12] Edmund Gosse, 'The Gallantry of France', in *Three French Moralists* (London, 1918), 138, 165.
[13] Bosquett, 35.

of its Te Deums—until 1914–18, when it was too slow to make up its mind.

The Great War may not have been a war to end war, but it might be called a duel that virtually ended duelling. A few Germans were still calling each other out during the war years;[14] but part of the reaction against everything 'Prussian' after 1918 was that duelling became illegal in the Germany of the Weimar Republic. It persisted in some corners, the *Mensur* under the euphemistic title of 'Landwehr' or militia fencing. Adam von Trott zu Solz, executed in 1944 for complicity in the plot against Hitler, as a student at Göttingen could write with gusto about a session when 'blood flowed in streams', and laud its lessons in self-control.[15] Catholic attention was drawn to what was going on, and in 1923 it was made clear that the condemnation published in 1890 was still in force. Two years later the Church was called upon to determine whether this applied only to 'contests which involve some danger of grievous wounding'; a consultor's view that student fights were outside 'the common, ancient, and accepted definition' of the duel was dismissed.[16]

In the army too duelling was not extinct, and one of the *faux pas* that led to the dismissal of General von Seeckt as chief of staff of the new Reichswehr in 1926 was his circulating an order to regulate duelling between officers without consulting the responsible minister. Fascism resurrected duelling, along with so much other debris from the past. Mussolini smiled on it, and three years after Hitler came to power it was legalized in Germany, under the supervision of special tribunals, with the caveat that it was not to be resorted to except as 'the ultimate means for the defence of honour'.[17] Brownshirts as well as regular officers were eligible; indeed, the privilege now became open in principle to all, since every German, as a member of the *Herrenvolk*, was 'noble'. Fascism artificially speeded up the process by which scraps of culture or habit descend from high to low, and the heroics of bygone days were greedily swallowed by a petty-bourgeoisie with no standing-ground of its own. This class, or agglomeration rather than true class, has collectively at most times had less than any other to contribute to human progress, though individually some of its members—partly because more truly 'individual' than those of any solider classes—have contributed most of all. Wilhelmine Germany had seen much aristocratizing of the bourgeoisie, Nazi Germany carried neo-feudalism

---

[14] Prokowski, 165.
[15] C. Sykes, *Troubled Loyalty: A Biography of Adam von Trott zu Solz* (London, 1968), 27.
[16] Bouscaren, 856–7 (Canon 2351).
[17] Demeter, App. 18.

further, with 'courts of honour' for factory workers and entailed 'peasant estates' for farmers.

But no revival could be more than a galvanic spasm. The Second World War completed the work of the First in transforming European society and sentiment, by uprooting aristocracy at last from most of its strongholds. Formerly, Karl Barth could write, it was usual for Christian moralists to discuss duelling side by side with war, but this would now be redundant: the duel had come to be 'tacitly accepted as so much veritable nonsense', and could be dismissed as obsolete. 'If only we had made the same progress in respect of war!'[18] Student duelling survived 1945 for a few years in both Germany and Austria; there has been a duel or two in France. At Nottingham quarter-sessions on 17 June 1968, a 'duel of honour' was reported between two Hungarian immigrants; it took place late one evening in a secluded lane, and caused some injuries.

Some of the conventional preoccupations of the honour code had been fading, and had now faded out. One was the 'reputation' formerly so important to ladies and their guardians. With partners changing even more frequently than in the eighteenth century, fighting about such a matter was scarcely to be thought of; a cynical Iago might say of his fair one, as well as his purse, ' 'tis something, nothing; 'twas mine, 'tis his.' A fire-eating general in a Wodehouse story might horsewhip a young man on the steps of his club for trifling with a niece's affections, but even this was pure farce.

'There was a time', a Japanese scholar wrote of the character assassination of the Cold War years, 'when it would have been cause for a duel.'[19] McCarthyism was indeed a case where, if ever, the passing of the duel might be regretted. But ordinary political vituperation was becoming a matter of hard words breaking no bones. Most men do not much mind being insulted, a pacifist answered when Hilaire Belloc tried to convince him that the suppression of duelling had given more licence to 'injustice and oppression and unredeemed insult'.[20] During the Irish elections of 1982 the opposition leader Dr Fitzgerald was reported on 20 November to have stated that the premier, Mr Haughey, who accused him of collusion with London over Ulster, was lying, and knew he was lying. In the golden days of 'Old Corruption'—rotten boroughs, bribes, sinecures, and 'honour'—a duel would have been inescapable. Today the public is only too apt to take for granted that all politicians, on occasions at least, are liars.

Fading out of reality, the duel has lived on as a cherished theme of

---

[18] Karl Barth, *Church Dogmatics*, vol. 3, pt. 4 (English edn., Edinburgh, 1961), 450.

[19] Maruyama Masao, in *E. H. Norman*, ed. R. W. Bowen (Toronto, 1984), 86.

[20] H. Belloc, *The Cruise of the 'Nona'* (London, 1928), 107.

fantasy, grave or gay. Music has been as much indebted to it as ever, if sometimes less romantically. In Prokofiev's unfinished opera *Madalena*, set in old Venice, the leading lady is discovered by her husband and his friend to have been the latter's lover, without his knowing her identity. The two men resolve to kill her; she persuades them that honour requires the husband to punish the lover first. They fight, both fall and she coolly departs to start a new life. In an early Puccini opera Edgar fights and defeats Frank, and goes off with his mistress, but there is a happy sequel. When they meet later on Frank is grateful for having been relieved of her, and Edgar, tired of her by now, joins him in the army, much to her indignation. She ends by murdering the heroine. A later comer to duelling is the ballet, most effectively in Prokofiev's *Romeo and Juliet*. From the same original came the remarkable dance drama, with Leonard Bernstein's music, *West Side Story*, about slum life in New York, where an aristocratic practice has drifted down to the lowest social level, with knife in place of rapier. A hero wounded in a duel dies pathetically in the last scene of Granados's *Goyescas*, like Don Juan at the end of Strauss's tone-poem. One of Honegger's first ambitious orchestral works, *Horace Victorieux*, was inspired by the well-worn theme of the 'duel' between the Horatii and Curiatii, with the love interest prominent.

In the nostalgic vogue of the historical novel duelling has had a cherished corner; as a stock subject it corresponds with the 'moving accident' of Jane Austen's time, or the *obbligato* car chase in a Hollywood crime story. Generations of novelists have worked over the past, or its more sensational features, until the colours have dimmed like those of an old garment too often washed. From a work like *The Tower of London* by Harrison Ainsworth, in 1840, with its chapter 'Of the Duel between Courtenay and Simon Renard', a long decline may be traced towards one like *Sir John Dering* in 1924, by Jeffery Farnol, in whose opening pages we learn that Sir John during five years' residence in Paris has had twenty-three duels forced on him. He rescues a country girl from Lord Sayle, 'an inveterate duellist', and they have an impromptu fight, won of course by Sir John, who dazzles a crowd, gathered for the purpose of lynching a witch, with what he airily calls 'a few gasconading flourishes'.[21] The cinema has made much similar use of the duel in its excursions into past times. In one of the latest of these, a tale of the Jesuits in Paraguay, a mercenary soldier performs penance for killing his brother in a duel.[22] Conrad's pair of officers of the First Empire, Thackeray's Barry Lyndon, have had new incarnations on the screen.

[21] J. Farnol, *Sir John Dering* (London, 1924?), chaps. 1, 41. In this category might be placed John Buchan, *The Isle of Sheep* (chap. 12); A. E. W. Mason, *Lawrence Clavering* (chap. 8); M. Denuzière, *Louisiana* (trans. J. P. Wilson).

[22] *The Mission* (1986), directed by Joffé. Cf. the film version of Dumas's *The Corsican Brothers*.

Occasional serious use has been made of the duel in fiction concerned with twentieth-century life. In a Hungarian story written in 1926 a colonel is told off by the panjandrums of an aristocratic club to deal with a journalist they consider to have insulted it. There is to be a duel in the afternoon at the barracks. The colonel is unwontedly uneasy, feels a craving for food, cannot help telling the waiter at lunch 'I am going to shoot a man today whom I have never seen ... who will be stood up in front of me like a dummy on a drill-yard.' In the end his nerves play him false, and it is he who is killed.[23] A Second World War film, *The Life and Death of Colonel Blimp*, contrasted a guileless English gentleman with ruthless German cunning; it contained effective scenes about a duel with a German officer before 1914 and the frightening convolutions of the Prussian code of honour. More typical is a post-1918 tale by 'Sapper' whose hero encounters in a hotel bar in Egypt a German, 'a huge gorilla dressed in clothes', who of course is soon pouring out a torrent of abuse against England. An unconventional combat is arranged, the two men stalking each other in rough country with rifles, as though out hunting. Baron Stockmar, as might be expected, loads his with dumdum bullets, only legitimately used against natives; an honest English bullet through the brain terminates his vile career.[24]

From this level the duel, which had long since made its way from Europe to the Americas, was well prepared for its further leap into outer space. On Edgar Rice Burroughs's planet Mars a green warrior (with four arms) can challenge his ruler to single fight and, if he wins, take the throne. In the popular film *Star Wars* there was a combat with laser-beam swords between the villain and another former member of a knightly order drawing its strength from a half mystical, half pseudo-scientific, 'Force'. An episode of that much-enjoyed television serial *Star Trek* showed Mr Spock, the half alien first officer, returning to his native planet under the spell of a periodical mating fever, to fight a ritual duel for a mate who, luckily, turned out not to want him. An Isaac Asimov hero is subjected to a bizarre duel in empty space.[25]

But the duel has lent itself most successfully in our century to burlesque. Having early shaken off bondage to 'honour', Britain could lead the way here. A Scot of humble birth, J. M. Barrie, followed close on W. S. Gilbert with his adventures of Peter Pan. There is parody of both the Wardour Street style of the historical novel, and the public-school version of Honour, in the duel between Peter and Captain Hook.

---

[23] Gyula Krudy, 'The Last Cigar at the Grey Arab' (Budapest, 1928), in *Forty-four Hungarian Short Stories*, ed. Lajos Illes (Unesco, 1979).

[24] 'Sapper' (H. C. McNeile), *Jim Maitland* (London, 1923), chap. 2.

[25] *Pirates of the Asteroids* (New York, 1953), chap. 4.

Both splendid swordsmen, after a 'Proud and insolent youth!' and a 'Have at thee!' they go at it until Peter disarms Hook; 'with a magnificent gesture' he invites him to resume his weapon. As his strength fails, Hook's last wish is to display 'good form' to the end; memories of games at his old school flit through his brain. Finally, when Peter gives him the *coup de grâce* by kicking him overboard, instead of with cold steel, Hook can call out mockingly 'Bad form', as he goes content to the waiting crocodile.[26]

More rough and ready examples of burlesque are easy to find. One of Burroughs's Martian tales has a chapter entitled 'Duel to the Death', a laboriously facetious narrative (humour was not his forte) about the hero having to confront the champion warrior of a tribe of savages, who delivers a long fierce tirade and then runs away.[27] A recent television take-off of *The Scarlet Pimpernel* includes a duel between an English rescuer of victims of the French Revolution and a French police chief in England on a secret mission: the two stood back to back, and at the signal the Frenchman walked too far, into a muddy horsepond.[28] One of the Irish comedian Dave Allen's inimitable television sketches showed two decrepit old gentlemen fighting a duel from their wheelchairs by each bringing a young woman to unrobe, in the hope of the other collapsing at the spectacle; the outcome was that both succumbed. But no making fun could be more hilarious than a duel pictured in a Japanese film, with a Scotsman in kilts capering ridiculously as he drove his opponent back;[29] a long-esteemed European institution was being shown as the outside world has been likely to see it.

All the same, if duelling were to come back it could be expected to find appreciative spectators, attuned by the entertainers to its charms and thrills, and some imitators. Already, under this tutoring, life as well as art has sometimes mimicked it. In 1979 a fourteen-year-old girl in Yorkshire arranged a fight for her favour between two youths, though apparently with nothing worse than their fists.[30] Three years later, in the course of a tipsy family revel, a soldier and his stepfather challenged each other to a 'duel' with shotguns; they only meant to settle who was quicker on the draw, but one gun went off, fatally. Early in 1985 a veterinary surgeon summoned to a Scottish farm to treat an injured horse found a gate shut to prevent him from leaving, and was challenged by the short-tempered owner to a fight, with either firearms or knives and forks.[31] The same year saw a prosecution in England for

[26] J. M. Barrie, *Peter and Wendy* (London, 1911; based on the play *Peter Pan*, 1904), chap. 15.
[27] E. R. Burroughs, *Synthetic Men of Mars* (1941; London, 1951), chap. 21.
[28] An episode in the 1985 series 'Carry On'.
[29] BBC programme, 'Can They Mean Us?' (18 Sept. 1985).
[30] *Guardian* (11 Oct. 1979).
[31] *Scotsman* (30 Mar. 1985).

THE MORE YOU'VE GOT ...

... THE BETTER YOUR CHANCES OF WINNING

Reproduced by permission of the Department of National Savings

cock-fighting, which the RSPCA believed to have been reviving, along with dog-fights, for some years, and in other countries as well.

Oddest of all, at Edinburgh in 1985 two brothers, John and Paul Burnside, charged with armed robbery, took their stand on a right, never formally abolished in Scotland, to have their case decided by battle instead of by jury. This caused a flutter in legal quarters, especially as the queen's champion who would have to appear against them in Parliament Square was the Lord Advocate for Scotland. Hasty researches led to the conclusion that the right was no longer valid; in any case, the Edinburgh professor of law held, the applicants had forfeited it by failing to throw down a white glove in the presence of their accusers.[32]

More revealing than any such mimicry, of how deep an impression the duel has left on the European mind, is its metaphorical extension,

[32] *Guardian* (20 Apr. 1985); *Scotsman* (23 Apr. 1985).

UPON LOSING
A DUEL.

Assuming these will be your last moments on earth, make the most of them.

Do not lurch around clutching your mortal wound like some third-rate ham in a melodrama.

Have your second bring you your *Falstaff* cigars.

Immediately the rich tobaccos, firm packed in best Connecticut leaf, will have you feeling at peace.

Offer your victorious opponent a pre-selected *Falstaff*.

As the thing detonates upon lighting, relax in the knowledge that you'll look a damn sight better at your funeral than he will at his.

This extract taken from the Falstaff Guide for Gentlemen.

Reproduced by permission of Collett, Dickinson and Pearce

begun long since by writers like Donne and Milton, or Crashaw with his poem on a 'duel' between lute-player and nightingale, and still throwing out fresh shoots. We speak of the 'musical duel' between Mozart and Clementi as pianists, in the imperial presence. 'It was like a duel', Pushkin wrote, when the gambler Hermann in *The Queen of Spades* played his final card against Chekalinsky. Tolstoy compared the Russian people's guerrilla resistance to Napoleon to a wounded duellist snatching up a cudgel to defend himself with.[33] 'It has been a duel between you and me, Mr Holmes', said Professor Moriarty, visiting him in a last effort to induce a foeman worthy of his steel to withdraw; and their hand-to-hand fight above the Reichenbach Falls was a true duel *à outrance*, with a prelude of knightly courtesy.[34]

A novelette of our own day by a multitudinously read authoress is entitled *Duel with Destiny*. A journalist described the television debate

[33] G. Best, *Humanity in Warfare* (London, 1980), 120–1.

[34] Conan Doyle, 'The Final Problem' in *The Memoirs of Sherlock Holmes* (London, 1894).

of 1981 between President Giscard and his successor Mitterrand as taking place 'in the atmosphere of an eighteenth century duel'; the Socialist challenger, in a letter setting out his conditions, invoked 'the long tradition of French honour'.[35] On firing ranges, shooting at a turning target has come to be known as 'duelling'.[36] A racehorse named 'Duelling' was running in 1985. Advertisers have not neglected the motif. How much better it is to have many savings-bonds instead of a few has been illustrated by a cartoon of two men ready for a duel. Expiring duellists have been recommended to solace their last moments with a fragrant cigar.

One of Dr Johnson's arguments in defence of duelling was that if international warfare was consistent with morality—as no good Christian doubted—private war must be equally so. Boswell agreed, and went further: duelling clearly had 'better reasons for its barbarous violence' that the massacre of thousands in battle.[37] One may think this less a justification of the duel than a sidelight on the hypocrisy of the modern State in banning it while making war its favourite business. Most of its anti-duelling laws were left to gather dust on the shelf, partly it may be from a sense of its own false position, more deliberately in earlier times from a calculation hinted at by Voet. Kings and governments might feel safer if they left their nobles free to work off discontents by fighting one another.[38] Thanks to the duel, impulses of private violence could in a remarkable way be made conducive to social stability, instead of disruptive.

At any rate it had a very long life, and there were probably some in every era who were convinced that it had never been so rampant as in their own lifetime. In the Spain of early modern times it was thought of as 'a natural and recurrent episode in a nobleman's life'.[39] In Pascal's France the duelling code appeared to him 'the dominant passion' of the aristocracy, 'ce point d'honneur qui les engage à toute heure à des violences bien contraires à la piété chrétienne'.[40] In the Netherlands Voet was writing gloomily of the duel as one facet of the universal strife, the *bellum immortale*, reigning ever since the fall of man. He wanted duellists packed off to expend their fury on Turks or pagans.[41] Defending an anti-duelling thesis at Erfurt university in 1741 a candidate presented his subject as a highly topical one—'quid enim hodie Duellis frequentius occurrit?' Man's nature was perpetually quarrelsome, but it was 'the foolish conviction of the children of this epoch that honour and

---

[35] *Guardian* (3 May 1981).

[36] Wilkinson, 53.

[37] Boswell, *Johnson*, ii. 47 (19 Apr. 1773).

[38] Voet, 230, in chap. 30: 'Utrum duellorum ulla sit utilitas?'

[39] Leguina, 15.   [40] Pascal, Letter 7.   [41] Voet, 221, 234.

reputation were injured by a single offensive word', and could only be restored by fighting, 'at the highest peril of both bodily and eternal life'.[42]

Later in that century the Metropolitan of Spain, replying to a query from a confessor, observed that even if in their enlightened age there might be no Quixotes charging windmills, there was still need of writers like Cervantes to expose the madness of the duel, that remnant of Gothic barbarism, which had no proper place even in the army, but was fit only for savages, or for 'atheists and materialists'.[43] About the same time the Anglican clergyman Moore lamented that duelling was 'a custom of such fashionable and honourable report', though, as became his station, he acknowledged the 'respectful deference ... due to the sentiments and manners of those, who move in the superior walks of life'.[44] In France amid the political rancours of the Bourbon Restoration it seemed to the widowed Comtesse de St.-Morys that 'today, in our laws as in our customs, the duel is no longer a capital crime, but a title to glory'.[45] A generation later an officer serving in India deplored its prevalence among his brethren: it was 'pretty nearly as much a matter of recurrence with them, as a dish of curry at the mess-table'.[46] In every successive era fresh recruits from outside were waiting to enter Carlyle's 'fate-circle'. In attenuated forms the old aristocratic lure has still not lost all its charm. On 17 January 1984, the Duke of Norfolk announced on behalf of the College of Heralds, in a radio interview, that it was prepared to bestow a coat of arms on practically anyone who might want it, for a modest fee of under a thousand pounds.

Humanism teaches, Walter Pater held, that nothing that has stirred men deeply can ever altogether lose its meaning for us; nothing especially, it may be added, that men have been ready to wager their lives on. The duel could be pondered by sober thinkers because it distilled an essential part of the moral life of a class, a civilization, a long span of history. In modern times it broke out first, like an epidemic, among the lower nobility of France, roistering Gascon cutters and thrusters, and the like; its spread to social strata so remote from this origin is a salient instance of how standards of conduct—like religious beliefs—adopted in one milieu can be taken up in others, historically far apart from it. National temperament made for greater or less receptivity; social systems were still more decisive. In Ireland they can

---

[42] Strecker, 4–5.
[43] Lorenzana, 1.
[44] C. Moore, 218.
[45] Comtesse de St.-Morys, 44.
[46] Anon., 'Duelling in our Indian Army', 237.

be seen working together. Arthur Young observed that the class most addicted to duelling there was made up of the smaller country gentry or squireens, 'who hunt in the day, get drunk in the evening, and fight the next morning'.[47] Sir Jonah Barrington admitted his countrymen's foible, but palliated it by calling to mind 'the romantic but honourable spirit of Milesian chivalry', and asserted that 'the strongest friendships were sometimes formed, and frequently regenerated, on the field of battle'.[48]

The duel became a unique point of convergence of political, social, artistic, and many other currents. It may be thought of as one of those compulsive dreams that mankind only gradually awakens from, nightmares engendered by an unwholesome collective life. Irrational as it might be, it was no more so than a great deal that is inexplicable in the human condition itself, that strange medley of the fascinating and the hideous, tragedy and obscenity and romance. It was because of this heterogeneity lying behind the formal logic or neat insanity of the duel that it could find analogies or stir echoes in so many other provinces of human life. Imaginatively presented in drama or fiction it could become an emblem of man's struggle with fate, or with heaven or hell, or with his fellow-men, or with himself, an epitome of his whole destiny.

Duelling was a male institution, emphasizing the gulf between the sexes, as well as the classes. Affrays very often concerned women, and so constituted a link, but far oftener than not of an unedifying kind. Physical strength gave the man his superiority, physical courage was its justification; the duel, still more than the massed battlefield, was the acid test of fear or bravery, and its record sheds much light on their psychology. We may guess if we like at a suppressed wish in men for women some day to intervene and rescue them from their own folly. They may have done so oftener in fiction than in fact. Rousseau's heroine Julie implores her lover not to fight that hardened English duellist 'mylord Édouard'; in spite of her military connections, she thinks of duels as 'the lowest degree of brutalism that men can descend to'.[49] She appeals to the milord also, and brings the two men together. Susan Ferrier makes one of her most deserving characters, when abused and threatened, answer coolly: 'I am no duellist. I wish you good morning.'[50] In one of Charles Reade's novels the actress Peg Woffington, both ravishing and good-hearted, stops a fight by suddenly emerging from an inner room and throwing off the disguise which has led to the

[47] A. Young, 205.
[48] Sir Jonah Barrington, *Rise and Fall of the Irish Nation* (Paris, 1833), 33–4.
[49] *La Nouvelle Héloïse* (1765), Pt. 1, Letter 57.
[50] Susan Ferrier, *Destiny* (1831), vol. 1, chap. 12.

quarrel.[51] A Spanish painter depicted two agitated women throwing themselves between their men's sword-points.[52]

Like its remote ancestor the ritualized tribal combat, the duel showed angry men wanting to fight, but also to have social sanction for their doings. Need of public approval could often mean submission to the dictates of others, in place of spontaneous action. A sensible pair might agree to go through the motions of fighting, to satisfy opinion, without doing each other any harm; the Erfurt candidate thought this legitimate,[53] forgetting the bad example a realistic pretence of duelling would set. Far oftener a duellist was caught between two pressures, an external one fixed and unwavering, an inner one shifting and uncertain.

Many must have experienced something akin to the sensations of Brutus

> Between the acting of a dreadful thing
> And the first motion.

In an early novel of Henry James, with a background of European politics unusual for him, the young craftsman Hyacinth has rashly pledged himself to carry out an act of terrorism when summoned to do so; he has no relish for the prospect, but cannot bring himself to back out, partly we may assume because the aristocratic parentage this foundling likes to credit himself with pricks him on. His patroness enquires from his old friend whether he has talked to the young man about it. 'He would tell me nothing', is the reply. 'It would be like a man giving notice when he is going to fight a duel.'[54] Whether by the author's intention or not, the parallel is a telling one; Hyacinth's emotions are very close to those of a man committed against the grain to a duel. When after a long interval of painful waiting the call comes, he uses the pistol he is given to shoot himself instead. He and Maupassant's coward were born under the same star.

To make game of duelling was always easy, as John Cockburn said: 'nothing is more inconsiderate, foolish and ridiculous'. Yet he had to acknowledge that it was reckoned 'so proper to Birth and Quality, and so suitable to the Character of a Gentleman', that those who kept out of it were 'censured as Mean-spirited and Cowardly Persons'.[55] Well might his fellow clergyman Moore find in duelling annals 'astonishing proofs of the force and prevalence of wayward fashion over sound judgment and reason; of the despotic tyranny and usurpation of the

[51] Charles Reade, *Peg Woffington* (1853), chap. 13 (near end of novel).
[52] Garnelo; photograph in *Enciclopedia Universal*, 'Duelo'.
[53] Strecker, 24.
[54] Henry James, *The Princess Casamassima* (1886), chap. 37. A duel figures in *The American* (1877).
[55] John Cockburn, v. 132.

flitting phantom "honour" '.[56] Throughout history societies have lived within the walls and under the roof of ideas and conventions slowly drying up into things they could only half or fitfully believe in, but could not break away from, for fear of a disruption of the social fabric. Men are always dying, a Great War essayist wrote, 'for other people's opinions, prejudices they have inherited from someone else, ideas they have borrowed second-hand'.[57] Modern man, more than his ancestors, has an overblown false consciousness, a brain stuffed not mainly with lessons from life, but with the thinking of whole generations and centuries, heavy enough to weigh down the feeble carrier; and today ghostly voices find sponsors to supply them with megaphones.

For the same shabby reasons men have always been killing, as well as being killed. Many novices of the duel who survived the death or mangling of their adversaries must have been haunted for the rest of their days by remorse like Macbeth's. 'Wake Duncan with thy knocking!' A man would feel this all the more if he had been the aggressor, or if his enemy had been an old friend, as was not seldom the case. The winner of the Wexford election duel in 1807 suffered so much later on that his mind gave way. On the day after the Chalk Farm duel in 1820 Christie wrote to Lockhart that he had fired his first shot in the air, and only aimed the fatal second bullet at his opponent because his second urged on him the duty of self-preservation. 'This has been to me the most heart-rending transaction that has happened in my life, and I would most willingly have changed places with him.'[58] And Lovel in *The Antiquary*, hurrying away into hiding, suffered a similar revulsion of feeling; 'what would he now have given to regain the sense of innocence which alone can counterbalance a thousand evils!'[59]

Such heart-searchings fitted the fundamental irrationality of the duel, as an ordeal proving nothing more than—to borrow the title of John Drinkwater's play about the Trojan war, and war in general—'X equals O'. Duelling stories over the ages leave an impression, above all, of freakishness, an unbalance of individual mentality reflecting a collective outlook distorted by social division. 'Functionalists' have supposed that all established social rules must be useful, and hence willingly submitted to. Duelling did indeed have a social function, but for the benefit only of a class, and at the expense of its individual members; it was certainly not always voluntary. Here and there a man might be defending a genuine principle, but such exceptions were lost in the welter of meaningless scrimmages; and the wrongdoer had as

---

[56] C. Moore, 275.
[57] 'Alpha of the Plough', 111–12.
[58] Scott, *Letters*, ii. 112 n.
[59] Chap. 28.

much chance of adding to his sins as of meeting with punishment. Any élite guilty of elevating itself above the level of common humanity is liable to inflict unnatural penalties on itself. On the field of honour the dominant class sought, in effect to expiate its collective sins.

For the individual or class lacking any valid ties with the community, life must take on an insubstantial quality; it may then be most effectively ballasted by death, or the fear of it and the effort to defy it, which can lend substance to the emptiest existence. This counter-reality could be elevated into the sentiment of Honour, the one firm footing, De Vigny wrote in his dithyramb about it, that he had found in the 'dark sea' of life: 'a proud, inflexible sentiment, an instinct of incomparable beauty', reigning as sovereign over all armies—a masculine religion.[60] Its devo- tees could not be always at war, but 'the bubble reputation' could always be looked for on the duelling-ground. Renaissance Europe suffered from a thirst for fame and remembrance, a kind of dizziness or light-headedness accompanying the rediscovery of history, antiquity, literature, the enlargement of all horizons. 'À belle vie, belle mort': Brantôme's salute to the duellist has the accent of an infantile inability to peer beyond the momentary burst of applause into the long silence of nothingness. There was indeed, joined to strong group consciousness, a childlike something in the cult of honour peculiar to a class like an aristocracy, which never truly grows up.

Impulses that made men feel their 'honour' to be at stake were never 'exclusively aristocratic', it has been pointed out: they were 'a silent presence' in life at every level and in every era of European history.[61] Duelling stood, like war, in total contradiction to the religion professed by Europe, helping thereby to illumine the contradictions at the heart of European civilization, as of no other. Parsons and bishops, says a speaker in Mandeville's dialogue, could be heard laughing disdainfully at anyone who put up with an affront instead of retaliating like a gentleman.[62] Yet the imperatives of the duel had an affinity with the Christian recognition of an individual duty to obey a higher law, when this conflicted with the law of the land. Honour could expand well beyond the cramping limits of any artificial cradle; it must have had some equivalent in every human society worth the name.

Physical courage was the essence of the cult in its most imposing European guise. It was the quality without which a man was unworthy of membership of an élite, but, more broadly, of membership of the human race. Coustard de Massi in 1768 looked down on the decadent Spaniard and 'the present race of perfumed fops' in his own country,

[60] De Vigny, Bk. 3, end of chap. 10.
[61] Bossy, 288, in Bossy (ed).
[62] Mandeville, 79.

and claimed for duelling the gift of the celebrated French *politesse*, and 'the origin and hereditary succession of French valour', found so irresistible by all the nation's foes; to suppress it would undermine warlike courage, along with men's love of glory, 'the darling passion of their souls'.[63]

Certainly a man schooled to behave politely to someone about to try and shoot him might well be capable of civility in any circumstances. As to courage, with the widening of conscription in Europe, the coming of the nation in arms, it became every man's duty to possess this sovereign virtue, and to face a firing-squad if he lacked it, even though the officer caste still claimed it in a fuller measure. With this democratizing, the spirit of the tribe, where every man was born to be a warrior, was reawakening. It was no doubt a primitive spirit, an elementary self-assertiveness. Children dare each other to run across roads in front of moving vehicles. Marooned on a Brazilian plateau among prehistoric monsters, Conan Doyle's young Irishman could feel able, despite a too vivid imagination, to bring himself to do anything he was 'dared' to do; like Flaubert's duellist he suffered from an 'overpowering fear of seeming afraid'.[64]

Modern man's freightage of ancestral thoughts and beliefs has deepened his acute sensitiveness to the idea of death, of the extinction of his inflated, half-fictitious self. Medieval Europe was haunted by the *timor mortis*, with one side of its mind, while the other was sheltered by the cult of arms and heroic defiance of death: another expression of the yawning gap between its contradictory ideologies, roughly superimposed on social cleavage between high and low. Death's shadow lies perpetually across mankind's sundial; to see others willingly exposing their lives, in accord with socially approved principles, offers a kind of relief, as well as sanctifying the social order. A duellist's death had a dignity not shared by death from disease or accident; the onlooker could admire it, while feeling a comfortable glow at the fact that *he* was still alive, and the reassurance that his own existence, which must end one day, was after all not so very important.

'Life is nothing in itself: only death can fix upon it the proper value'— so a duellist might feel in the exaltation of the moment, and so a European serving with the Turkish army in 1877 says that he and all the garrison of Plevna felt as the long-drawn siege neared its desperate end, and they prepared to march out and break through the Russian lines or perish.[65] This was only a war, meaning as little as most wars beyond sound and fury. But in many or most parts of the world, though

[63] Massi, 92 ff.
[64] Conan Doyle, *The Lost World* (London, 1912), 86, 207–8.
[65] F. W. von Herbert, *The Defence of Plevna, 1877* (rev. edn., London, 1911), 257.

in more comfortable countries and eras the fact is easily forgotten, physical courage has been and is demanded, too often in its extremest degree, by higher duties also, political or religious or intellectual; and without the willingness of some men to face perils voluntarily, not under compulsion or mass hypnosis, there would be no progress for mankind. Ruminating in Germany on the duels going on all round him, Crabb Robinson found himself, very likely to his surprise, agreeing with Schelling's dictum that a man not prepared to play boldly with his life on occasion, as though with a toy, cannot be possessed of life in its highest human vigour.[66]

[66] Robinson, 128.

WORKS CITED

This is not a bibliography of duelling, but a list of works cited in the text, of two kinds: (*a*) those relating specifically or largely to the duel; (*b*) those cited in more than one chapter. Those of the first kind are marked with an asterisk. A work by F. Billacois, *Le Duel dans la société française, 16ᵉ–17ᵉ siècles* (Paris, 1986), appeared too late for me to be able to make use of it.

Here and in the notes, the date given is that of the edition quoted; the date of first publication is only given in the case of earlier works.

* 'ALPHA OF THE PLOUGH', *Leaves in the Wind* (London, 1920).

* ANDREW, D.T., 'The Code of Honour and its Critics ... in England, 1700–1850', *Social History*, 5, no. 3 (1980).

* ANDREWS, R.H., 'Politics at Pistol Point', *Mankind* (Jan. 1971).

* Anon., 'The Code of Duelling', *Chambers' Journal* (18 May 1867).

* Anon., 'Duelling in our Indian Army', *Coeburn's United Service Magazine* (1844), Pt. 3.

ASHMOLE, ELIAS, *Autobiographical and Historical Notes*, ed. C. H. Josten (Oxford, 1966).

ASPINALL, A. (ed.), *The Correspondence of George, Prince of Wales 1770–1812* (London, 1963–71).

* AUGIER, ÉMILE, and JULES SANDEAU, *Le Gendre de Monsieur Poirier* (Paris, 1854).

AULNOY, Mme D', *Travels into Spain* (1690: English edn., London, 1930).

* BALDICK, R., *The Duel: A History of Duelling* (London, 1965).

* BARBER, C.L., *The Idea of Honour in the English Drama 1591–1700* (Göteborg, 1957).

* BARBER, R., *The Knight and Chivalry* (London, 1974).

* BARRINGTON, Sir JONAH, *Personal Sketches of his Own Times* (London, 1827–32).

* B[ASNAGE], Monsieur, *Dissertation historique sur les duels et les ordres de chevalerie* (Amsterdam, 1720).

BASSERMANN, L., *The Oldest Profession* (London, 1967).

BATES, DAISY, *The Passing of the Aborigines* (London, 1972).

BAYNE-POWELL, R., *Eighteenth-century London Life* (London, 1937).

* BEASLEY, D.R., *The Canadian Don Quixote ... Major John Richardson* (Erin, Ont. 1977).

* BENNETTON, N.A., *Social Significance of the Duel in Seventeeth-century French Drama* (Baltimore, 1938).

BLOCH, MARC, *Feudal Society* (London, 1965).

* BOHANNAN, P. (ed.), *Law and Warfare: Studies in the Anthropology of Conflict* (New York, 1967).

BOLTON, G.C., *The Passing of the Irish Act of Union* (London, 1916).

Border Ballads, ed. W. Beattie (Harmondsworth, 1952).

*BOSQUETT, ABRAHAM, *The Young Man of Honour's 'Vade Mecum'* (London, [1817]).

BOSSY, JOHN (ed.), *Disputes and Settlements: Law and Human Relations in the West* (Cambridge, 1983).

BOSWELL, JAMES, *Corsica* (Glasgow, 1768).

—— *The Journal of a Tour to the Hebrides with Samuel Johnson* (1785; Nelson edn., n.p., n.d.).

—— *The Life of Samuel Johnson* (1791; 3 vols., London, 1926).

—— *The Ominous Years*, Journal, 1774–1776; ed. C. Ryskamp and F. A. Pottle (London, 1963).

BOTTOMORE, T. B., *Élites and Society* (Harmondsworth, 1966).

BOUSCAREN, T. L., *The Canon Law Digest* (Milwaukee, 1934).

*BOVA, B., *The Duelling Machine* (London, 1977).

*BRANTÔME, PIERRE DE BOURDEILLE, Seigneur de, *Mémoires contenans les anecdotes de la cour de France ... touschant les duels* (*Œuvres Complètes*, new edn., Paris, 1823), vol. 6.

BRATHWAIT, RICHARD, *The English Gentleman* (London, 1630; fac. edn., Amsterdam, 1975).

BRINTON, CRANE, *A History of Western Morals* (London, 1959).

*BRYSON, F. R., *The Point of Honor in Sixteenth-century Italy* (New York, 1935).

BURCKHARDT, JACOB, *The Civilization of the Renaissance in Italy* (1860; London, 1878).

BURKE, PETER, *Popular Culture in Early Modern Europe* (London, 1979).

Byron, The Letters of Lord, ed. R. G. Howarth (Everyman edn., London, 1936).

CALDER, ANGUS, *Revolutionary Empire* (London, 1981).

CARLYLE, THOMAS, *The French Revolution* (1837).

*—— *Historical Sketches of Notable Persons and Events in the Reign of James I and Charles I*, ed. A. Carlyle (London, 1902).

—— *Scottish and Other Critical Miscellanies* (Everyman edn., London, 1915).

*—— 'Two Hundred and Fifty Years Ago: Duelling', in *English and Other Critical Essays* (Everyman edn., London, 1915).

CARR, E. H., *The Romantic Exiles* (1933; Harmondsworth, 1949).

CASTIGLIONE, BALDESAR, *The Book of the Courtier* (Venice, 1528; English edn., Harmondsworth, 1967).

CELLINI, BENVENUTO, *Autobiography* (Naples, 1728; English edn., Harmondsworth, 1956).

CHAPMAN, GEORGE, *Bussy d'Ambois* (1607).

*CHATEAUVILLARD, Comte de, *Essai sur le duel* (Paris, 1836).

*CHEKHOV, ANTON, *'The Duel' and Other Stories* (1891–5; English edn., Harmondsworth, 1984).

*—— *Three Sisters* (1901); English edn. trans. C. Garnett (London, 1923).

CHOLMONDELEY, R. H., *The Heber Letters 1783–1832* (London, 1950).

*CLARK, Sir G., *War and Society in the Seventeenth Century* (Cambridge, 1958).

*CLEVELAND, L. G., 'The Crawford–Burnside Affair and the Movement to Abolish Dueling in Georgia', *Research Studies* (Dec. 1976).

*COCKBURN, Revd JOHN, *The History and Examination of Duels* (London, 1720).

COLE, G. D. H., *Studies in Class Structure* (London, 1955).

*COLLIER, JEREMY, 'Of Duelling', in *Essays upon Several Subjects* (2nd edn., London, 1698).

*COLLINS, WILKIE, 'Mad Monkton', in *The Queen of Hearts* (London, 1859).

*CONRAD, JOSEPH, 'The Duel', in *A Set of Six* (New York, 1925).

COON, C. S., *The Hunting Peoples* (Harmondsworth, 1976).

*COUNCIL, N., *When Honour's at the Stake: Ideas of Honour in Shakespeare's Plays* (London, 1973).

DAVIDSON, H. R. ELLIS, *Gods and Myths of Northern Europe* (Harmondsworth, 1964).

*DEMETER, KARL, *The German Officer-Corps in State and Society 1650–1945* (English edn., London, 1965).

DICKENS, CHARLES, *Nicholas Nickleby* (1838–9).

—— *The Old Curiosity Shop* (1841).

*DOSTOEVSKY, FYODOR, *Notes from Underground* (1864; English edn., London, 1981).

DURKHEIM, ÉMILE, *Suicide: A Study in Sociology* (English edn., London, 1952).

*DWIGHT, Revd TIMOTHY, 'A Sermon on Duelling' (New York, 1805).

EDGEWORTH, MARIA, *Castle Rackrent* (Dublin, 1800).

*—— *Harry Ormond* (1817; Shannon, 1972).

EDWARDS, S., *Queen of the Plaza. The Provocative Story of Adah Isaacs Menken* (London, 1969).

*ETHEREGE, Sir G., *The Comical Revenge* (London, 1664).

EVELYN, JOHN, *Diary* (1st. edn., ed. Wm. Bray, London, 1818).

*FEEST, C., *The Art of War* (London, 1980).

FIELDING, HENRY, *Joseph Andrews* (1742).

FITZGERALD, E. (trans.), *The Rubáiyát of Omar Khayyám and Six Plays of Calderón* (London, 1853; Everyman edn., London, 1928).

FITZPATRICK, W. J., *The Life of Charles Lever* (London, 1879).

*FOOTMAN, D., *The Primrose Path: A Life of Ferdinand Lassalle* (London, 1946).

*FRANKLIN, J. H., *The Militant South 1800–1861* (Cambridge, Mass., 1956).

FROUDE, J. A., *The English in Ireland in the Eighteenth Century* (London, 1874).

GADE, J. A., *Christian IV, King of Denmark and Norway* (London [1927]).

*GAILEY, ALAN, *Irish Folk Drama* (Cork, 1969).

*[GEDDES, Bp. JOHN], 'Reflections on Duelling, and on the Most Effectual Means for Preventing It' (Edinburgh, 1790).

*GILBERT, W. S., *The Grand Duke; or, The Statutory Duel* (1896).

GILMOUR, R., *The Idea of the Gentleman in the Victorian Novel* (London, 1981).

GILPIN, W., Diary, ed. P. Benson as: *My Dearest Betsy. A Self-portrait of William Gilpin 1757–1848* (London, 1981).

*GOLDSMITH, OLIVER, *The Vicar of Wakefield* (London, 1766).

GRAMONT, Comte de, *Memoirs,* compiled by A. Hamilton 1713 (English edn., London, 1902).

GRANT, JAMES, *Old and New Edinburgh* (3 vols., London, n.d.).

*—— *The Romance of War* (new edn., London and Glasgow, 1889).

*GREENE, ROBERT, *Friar Bacon and Friar Bungay* (London, 1594).

GUTTSMAN, W. L., *The British Political Élite* (London, 1963).

HALL, JOSEPH, *Works*, ed. P. Hall (Oxford, 1937–9).

HANSON, L. and E., *The Life of Jane Welsh Carlyle* (London, 1952).

HARRIS, MARVIN, *Cannibals and Kings* (London, 1978).

*HERBERT OF CHERBURY, Lord, *Autobiography*, ed. Sidney Lee (2nd edn., London [1906]).

HIBBERT, C., *Wolfe at Quebec* (London, 1959).

*HICKEY, WILLIAM, *Memoirs*, ed. A. Spencer (London, [1913]).

HOBHOUSE, L. T., *Morals in Evolution* (London, 1915).

*HOWARD, EDWARD, *Rattlin the Reefer* (London, 1836).

HUIZINGA, J., *The Waning of the Middle Ages* (Harmondsworth, 1955).

HUME, DAVID, *The History of England*, abr. R. W. Kilcup (Chicago, 1975).

*HUTTON, A., *The Sword and the Centuries* (London, 1901).

JACKSON, W. T. H., *Medieval Literature* (New York, 1966).

*JAMES, MERVYN, 'English Politics and the Concept of Honour 1485–1642', Past and Present, Suppl. no. 3 (1978).

JAMES, WILLIAM, *The Varieties of Religious Experience* (New York, 1902).

JEROME, JEROME K., *My Life and Times* (London, 1984).

JOHNSON, SAMUEL, *Journey to the Western Islands of Scotland* (London, 1775); ed. R. W. Chapman (Oxford, 1924).

JONE, Revd HERIBERT (ed.), *Moral Theology* (2nd edn., Westminster, Md., 1946).

JONSON, BEN, *The Alchemist* (London, 1610).

—— *The Magnetic Lady* (London, 1632).

KEEN, M., *Chivalry* (New Haven, Conn., 1984).

*KELLY, G. A., 'Duelling in Eighteenth-century France', in *The Eighteenth Century: Theory and Interpretation*, 21/3 (1980).

*KLEIST, HEINRICH VON, '*The Marquise of O.*' and Other Stories (1810–11; English edn., Harmondsworth, 1978).

KUNENE, MAZISI (trans.), *Emperor Shaka the Great: A Zulu Epic* (London, 1979).

*KUPRIN, A., *The Duel* (English edn., London, 1916).

LACLOS, P. A. F. CHODERLOS DE, *Les liaisons dangereuses* (Paris, 1782; English edn., Harmondsworth, 1961).

LEASK, J. C. and McCANCE, H. M., *The Regimental Records of the Royal Scots* (Dublin, 1915).

*LEGUINA, E. DE, Barón de la Vega de Hoz, *Bibliografía é Historia de la Esgrima Española* (Madrid, 1904).

*LERMONTOV, MIKHAIL, *A Hero of Our Time* (1839).

LESLIE, ANITA, *Jennie: The Life of Lady Randolph Churchill* (London, 1969).

*LEVER, CHARLES, *Jack Hinton the Guardsman* (Dublin, 1843).

*—— *A Rent in the Cloud* (London, 1869).

LEWIS, I. M., *Social Anthropology in Perspective* (Harmondsworth, 1976).

LOCKHART, J. G., *The Life of Sir Walter Scott* (Edinburgh, 1837–8; 10 vols., Edinburgh, 1902).

*LORENZANA, F. A., Archbishop of Toledo, 'Sobre si era lícito aceptar el desafío', in *Pastorales y Cartas* (Madrid, 1779).

*LOVER, SAMUEL, *Handy Andy* (1842).

MACAULAY, T. B., Lord, *Miscellaneous Essays* (Collins edn., 2 vols., London, n.d.).

McMANNERS, J., *Death and the Enlightenment* (Oxford, 1981).

*MANDEVILLE, BERNARD DE, *An Enquiry into the Origin of Honour and the Usefulness of Christianity in War* (London, 1732).

MARRYAT, Capt. F., *Mr. Midshipman Easy* (London, 1836).

*—— *Peter Simple* (London, 1834).

*MARTORELL, JOANOT, *Tirant lo Blanc* (Valencia, 1490; English edn., London, 1985).

Marx and Engels, Reminiscences of, Institute of Marxism–Leninism (Moscow, n.d.).

*MASSI, A. P. COUSTARD DE, *The History of Duelling* (English edn., London, 1770).

MAUDE, AYLMER, *The Life of Tolstoy* (1908–10; rev. edn., World's Classics, London, 1930).

*MAUPASSANT, GUY DE, *Contes et nouvelles* (Paris, 1974); see 'Un lâche'; 'L'héritage'; 'Un duel'.

*MAXWELL, CONSTANTIA, *Country and Town in Ireland under the Georges* (London, 1940).

MEISEL, J. H. (ed.), *Pareto and Mosca* (Englewood Cliffs, New Jersey, 1965).

MERCER, C., *The Foreign Legion* (London, 1966).

MEREDITH, GEORGE, *Beauchamp's Career* (London, 1876).

—— *Diana of the Crossways* (London, 1885).

MOLMENTI, P., *Venice*, trans. H. F. Brown, Pt. III, Vol. 2 (London, 1908).

MONTAGU, ASHLEY, *The Nature of Human Aggression* (London, 1978).

MONTAIGNE, MICHEL DE, *Essays*, trans. J. Florio (London, 1603; World's Classics edn., London, 1904–6).

MONTESQUIEU, Baron de, *Lettres Persanes* (Paris, 1721).

*MOORE, Revd CHARLES, *A Treatise on Duelling* (London, 1790).

MOORE, D. L., *Lord Byron, Accounts Rendered* (London, 1974).

Moore, Sir John, The Diary of, ed. Sir J. F. Maurice (London, 1904).

MOSCA, GAETANO, *The Ruling Class, Elementi di Scienza Politica*, trans. H. D. Kahn (New York, 1939).

NEVILL, R. (ed.), *Leaves from the Note-books of Lady Dorothy Nevill* (London, 1910).

NEVILLE, SYLAS, *Diary (1767–1788)*, ed. B. Cozens-Hardy (London, 1950).

*'NIMROD' (Charles Apperley), *The Life of a Sportsman* (London, 1832; London, 1948).

*O'CONNELL, DANIEL, *Correspondence*, ed. W. J. Fitzpatrick (London, 1888).

OMAN, C. W. C., *Wellington's Army 1809–1814* (London, 1912).

PALMERSTON, Lord, *Letters to Laurence and Elizabeth Sulivan 1804–1863*, ed. K. Bourne (London, 1979).

PARETO, V., *Sociological Writings*, ed. S. E. Finer (New York, 1966).

PARRY, G., *Political Élites* (London, 1969).

PASCAL, BLAISE, *Lettres provinciales* (Paris 1656–7).

PEACHAM, HENRY, *The Compleat Gentleman* (London, 1662; fac. edn., Amsterdam, 1968).

PEPYS, SAMUEL, *Diary*, ed. H. B. Wheatley (London, 1949).

PHILLPOTTS, B. S., *Edda and Saga* (London, 1931).

PIRENNE, H., *A History of Europe from the Invasions to the Sixteenth Century* (English edn., London, 1939).

POTTLE, F. A., *James Boswell: The Earlier Years 1740–1769* (London, 1966).

POWIS, JONATHAN, *Aristocracy* (Oxford, 1984).

*PROKOWSKY, D., *Die Geschichte der Duellbekämpfung* (Bonn, 1965).

*PUGHE, Maj-Gen. J. R., 'Autobiography', ed. Lt.-Gen. Sir A. A. Bingley, unpub. MS (National Army Museum, London).

*PUSHKIN, ALEXANDER, *Prose Tales*, trans. E. Keane (London, 1914).

RADDATZ, F. J., *Karl Marx* (London, 1979).

RAMSAY, DEAN, *Reminiscences of Scottish Life and Character* (repr. of 22nd edn., Edinburgh, 1947).

RICHARDSON, SAMUEL, *Clarissa, or the History of a Young Lady* (London, 1747–8; 4th edn., London, 1751).

*RIDDELL, W. R., 'The Duel in Early Upper Canada', *Journal of the American Institute of Criminal Law and Criminology* (May 1915).

—— *John Richardson* (Toronto, 1923).

ROBINSON, HENRY CRABB, Letters, ed. E. J. Morley, in *Crabb Robinson in Germany 1800–1805* (London, 1929).

ROWSE, A. L., *The Elizabethan Renaissance* (2nd edn., London, 1974).

*ST.-MORYS, Comtesse de, *Mémoire et consultation* (Paris, 1818).

SAINT-SIMON, Duc de, *Historical Memoirs* (abbrev. English edn., London, 1972).

SAMUEL, R. H. and R. H. THOMAS, *Education and Society in Modern Germany* (London, 1949).

*SCOTT, WALTER, *The Antiquary* (Edinburgh, 1816).

—— *Count Robert of Paris* (Edinburgh, 1831).

—— *Familiar Letters*, ed. D. Douglas (Edinburgh, 1894).

—— *Journal, 1825–32* (Nelson edn., London [1926]).

SÉGUR, Comte PHILIPPE DE, *Un Aide-de-camp de Napoléon* (Nelson edn., Paris, n.d.).

—— *La Campagne de Russie* (Nelson edn., Paris, n.d.).

*SELDEN, JOHN, *The Duello, or Single Combat* (London, 1610); in *Works* (London, 1726), vol. 3.

—— *Table Talk*, ed. R. Milward (London, 1689; London, 1887).

SHARPE, J. A., *Crime in Seventeenth-century England: A County Study* (Cambridge, 1983).

*SHERIDAN, RICHARD, *The Rivals* (1775).

*SIEVEKING, A. F., 'Fencing and Duelling', in *Shakespeare's England*, ed. Sidney Lee *et al.* (Oxford, 1916).

*SMOLLETT, TOBIAS, *The Expedition of Humphry Clinker* (1771; Everyman edn., London, 1943).

*—— *Travels through France and Italy* (1766; London, 1907).

Spectator, The, 1711–14, ed. G.G. Smith, for Everyman's Library, London, 1907.

STADEN, HEINRICH VON, *The Land and Government of Muscovy 1578–1579,* trans. T. Esper (Stanford, 1967).

STEINMETZ, A., *The Romance of Duelling in All Times and Countries* (London, 1868).

STENDHAL, Love (De l'amour) (English edn., Harmondsworth, 1975).

STONE, LAWRENCE, *The Family, Sex, and Marriage in England 1500–1800* (rev. edn., Harmondsworth, 1979).

*STRECKER, E.W., *Dissertatio Ethica 'Utrum Duellum sit Licitum'* (Erfurt, 1741).

*STUART, Col. W.K., *Reminiscences of a Soldier* (London, 1874).

SULLY, Duc de, *Memoirs* (new English edn., London, 1856).

SUTHERLAND, J. (ed.), *The Oxford Book of Literary Anecdotes* (Oxford, 1975).

*TAYLOR, Revd W., 'A Testimony Against Duelling' (Montreal, 1838) (Acknowledgements are due to the Metropolitan Toronto Library Board).

TENNANT, C., *The Radical Laird: A Biography of George Kinloch 1775–1833* (Kineton, 1970).

TEX, J. DEN, *Oldenbarnevelt* (Cambridge, 1973).

THACKERAY, W.M., *The Four Georges* (London, 1855; London, 1909).

*—— *The History of Henry Esmond* (London, 1852).

THOMAS, KEITH, 'The Social Origins of Hobbes' Political Thought' (repr. in *Seventeenth-century England,* ed. W.R. Owens, Open University, Milton Keynes, 1980), ii. 186 ff.

TREITSCHKE, H. VON, *History of Germany in the Nineteenth Century* (abbrev. English edn., Chicago, 1975).

TURGENEV, I.S., *Fathers and Sons* (English edn. 1861; trans. R. Hare, London, 1947).

*VAGTS, ALFRED, *A History of Militarism* (rev. edn., New York, 1959).

*VIDAL, GORE, *Burr* (London, 1974).

*VOET, PAULUS, *De Duellis licitis et illicitis* (Waesberg, 1658).

VOLTAIRE, *The Age of Louis XIV* (Paris, 1751; Everyman edn., London, n.d.).

WALPOLE, HORACE, *Correspondence,* ed. W.S. Lewis 48 vols. (London, 1937–).

WARNER, MARINA, *Joan of Arc* (London, 1981).

*WEBB, J.R., 'Pistols for Two ...', *American Heritage* (Feb. 1975).

WEBER, MAX, *The Interpretation of Social Reality,* anthology, ed. J.E.T. Eldridge (London, 1971).

—— *The Theory of Social and Economic Organization* (Pt. I of *Wirtschaft und Gesellschaft*), ed. T. Parsons (Edinburgh, 1947).

WEST, Sir ALGERNON, *Recollections, 1832 to 1886* (London, 1899).

WILBERFORCE, WILLIAM, *A Practical View of the Prevailing Religious System of Professed Christians* (London 1797: London, 1834).

*WILKINSON, F., *The Illustrated Book of Pistols* (London, 1979).

WILSON, J.D., *Life in Shakespeare's England* (Harmondsworth, 1944).

*WOODHAM-SMITH, C., *The Reason Why* (Harmondsworth, 1958).

*WORMALD, JENNY, 'Bloodfeud: Kindred and Government in Early Modern Scotland', *Past and Present*, 87 (1980).

YOUNG, ARTHUR, *A Tour in Ireland: With General Observations on the Present State of that Kingdom: Made in the Years 1776, 1777, and 1778, and Brought Down to the End of 1779*, ed. C. Maxwell (Cambridge, 1925).

*YOUNG, JOHN (ed.), 'Correspondence ... between Messrs Irvine and Pope' (Quebec, 1854) (Acknowledgements are due to the Metropolitan Toronto Library Board).

Index

OXFORD

MORE OXFORD PAPERBACKS

Details of a selection of other books follow. A complete list of Oxford Paperbacks, including The World's Classics, Twentieth-Century Classics, OPUS, Past Masters, Oxford Authors, Oxford Shakespeare, and Oxford Paperback Reference, is available in the UK from the General Publicity Department, Oxford University Press (JN), Walton Street, Oxford OX2 6DP.

In the USA, complete lists are available from the Paperbacks Marketing Manager, Oxford University Press, 200 Madison Avenue, New York, NY 10016.

Oxford Paperbacks are available from all good bookshops. In case of difficulty, customers in the UK can order direct from Oxford University Press Bookshop, 116 High Street, Oxford, Freepost, OX1 4BR, enclosing full payment. Please add 10 per cent of published price for postage and packing.

LIFE IN THE THIRD REICH

Edited by Richard Bessel

This volume offers a series of short articles, originally published in *History Today*, which present some new approaches to the study of Nazi Germany. Some of the subjects may be familiar, but their treatment is not.

THE AGE OF ILLUSION

Ronald Blythe

'*The Age of Illusion* accomplishes more than any orthodox history . . . a moving and stimulating study.' *Sunday Times*

In this brilliant reconstruction of Britain between the wars Ronald Blythe highlights a number of key episodes and personalities which characterize those two extraordinary decades. The period abounds in astonishing figures: the Home Secretary, Joynson-Hicks, cleaning up London's morals while defending General Dyer for the massacre of 379 Indians at Amritsar; Mrs Meyrick, the night-club queen, being regularly raided at the '43'; John Reith putting the BBC on its feet and the public in its place; headline stealers such as Amy Johnson, T. E. Lawrence and the body-line bowling controversy. And behind this garnish façade we are shown the new writers emerging from their embarrassingly middle-class backgrounds, and the birth of Britain's first radical intelligentsia.

Ronald Blythe writes with perception, humour and conviction and provides a vivid and compelling portrait of Britain over twenty turbulent years.

THE STRUGGLE FOR STABILITY IN EARLY MODERN EUROPE

Theodore K. Rabb

Theodore K. Rabb's contemplative book offers a new interpretation of seventeenth-century Europe, focusing on a crucial transition from turmoil to relative tranquility. The book shows, in splendid illustrations, how painters, writers, and scientists reflected the change that is his main theme—the shift from belligerence to restraint, from upheaval to calm.

HEART OF EUROPE

A Short History of Poland

Norman Davies

In this book Norman Davies provides a key to understanding the social and political inheritance of modern Poland. By delving through the historical strata of Poland's past he demonstrates that the present conflict is but the latest round in a series of Russo-Polish struggles stretching back for nearly three centuries.

'Another masterpiece; *Heart of Europe* has sweep, a rare analytical depth and a courageous display of the author's personal convictions. The book begins and ends with Solidarity; the unique labour movement thus serves as a frame for the nation's history.' *New York Times Book Review*

'should never be out of reach of anyone . . . who wishes to keep track of the infinitely complex interplay of forces in Poland today and tomorrow' *Catholic Herald*

'A deep, heartfelt analysis which sets Poland's poignant, but currently stalemate, situation in its historical context.' Linda O'Callaghan, *Sunday Telegraph*

THE FRENCH REVOLUTION

J. M. Roberts

Dr Roberts studies the puzzling nature of what came to be called the French Revolution, with its Janus-like aspect, looking to past and future at the same time. The five main sections of the book deal with the beginnings of the Revolution; the Revolution in France seen as a great disruption; the Revolution in France as the vehicle of continuity; the Revolution abroad; and the Revolution as history and as myth. There is also a review of recent scholarship in the field.

This lively and authoritative book, which will appeal to the general reader and the student of history alike, makes a significant original contribution to our understanding of the French Revolution.

'Dr Roberts has packed a great deal into a short space and his great knowledge and lucid style make this into an excellent introduction to a complex subject.' *British Book News*

'deserves to become a classic' *Journal of European Studies*

An OPUS book

PSYCHOTHERAPY IN THE THIRD REICH

The Göring Institute

Geoffrey Cocks

At the zenith of Nazi persecution, the profession of psychotherapy achieved an institutional status and capacity for practice unrivalled in Germany before or since. This controversial study of the growth of interest in psychotherapy under the Nazis is essential reading for anyone interested in Nazi Germany or psychotherapy.

'A remarkably interesting book, distinguished by solid research and sound judgement.' *The New York Times*

THE IMPACT OF ENGLISH TOWNS,
1700–1800

P. J. Corfield

English towns in the eighteenth century displayed great vitality and diversity. While elegant social life was in its heyday in Bath, Hogarth was painting the horrors of London's Gin Lane, and the first Liverpool Docks were opened in an atmosphere of confidence. The book examines both the impact of English towns and their collective influence on the wider economy and society. The towns were a powerful force for change, but urban growth is not presented as the 'first cause' of industrialization. Drawing upon much new material, what Dr Corfield's synthesis reveals is the complexity of the transformation that eighteenth-century towns were themselves undergoing.

'Penelope Corfield looks back on eighteenth-century England from a refreshingly new vantage point . . . All in all, the work succeeds admirably in fulfilling its primary objective of providing an account for the "general reader as well as for students". Among professional historians it is certain to stimulate a new appreciation of that hitherto neglected urban terrain that lies between the early modern town and the Victorian city.' *Journal of Economic History*

An Opus book

GERMANY 1866–1945

Gordon A. Craig

This is the history of the rise and fall of united Germany, which lasted only 75 years from its establishment by Bismarck in 1870. It is a history of greed, fear, cruelty, and the corruption of power on the one hand; of courage, struggle for liberty, and resistance to tyranny on the other; and Gordon Craig, Professor of History at Stanford University, tells it brilliantly.

Professor Craig's study has become standard reading for students of modern German history.

'the best account so far available of Germany from Bismarck to Hitler' *Times Literary Supplement*

MAFIA BUSINESS

Pino Arlacchi

On 25 April 1982, Pio La Torra, a member of the Italian Parliament responsible for the proposed anti-Mafia laws, was gunned down in Palermo. General Carlo Dalla Chiesa was immediately sent to replace him, but four months later he and his wife were murdered. A week later, anti-Mafia legislation was approved, and in February 1986 the largest ever Mafia trial began in Naples.

These murders and their aftermath result from the emergence of a new Mafia; international entrepreneurs combining large-scale business and banking activity with drug-dealing, political corruption, and widespread violence. Vastly wealthy, they move in fashionable societies all over the world.

'The classic text on "*La Nouva Mafia*" . . . Arlacchi's powerful book is a timely reminder of what could happen should the "honoured society" expand its society even further.' *Listener*

BUKHARIN AND THE BOLSHEVIK REVOLUTION

Stephen F. Cohen

For more than two decades Bukharin's career was central to the turbulent history of Soviet Russia and the communist move-ment: he made important contributions to Lenin's original leadership, and after 1917 was a Politburo member, editor of *Pravda*, head of the Comintern, chief theoretician, and, for three years, co-leader with Stalin of the Communist Party. He was tried as an 'enemy of the people' and executed by Stalin in 1938.

'Professor Cohen, in this brilliantly written, meticulously documented monograph, has not only reconstructed the tragedy of a fascinating man . . . he has also produced a classic study of the intellectual development of the foremost Bolshevik theoretician . . . He has, in a word, achieved a breakthrough in Soviet studies.' *Observer*

THE INDUSTRIAL REVOLUTION
1760–1830

T. S. Ashton

The Industrial Revolution has sometimes been regarded as a catastrophe which desecrated the English landscape and brought social oppression and appalling physical hardship to the workers. In this book, however, it is presented as an important and beneficial mark of progress. In spite of destructive wars and a rapid growth of population, the material living standards of most of the British people improved, and the technical innovations not only brought economic rewards but also provoked greater intellectual ingenuity. Lucidly argued and authoritative, this book places the phenomenon of the Industrial Revolution in a stimulating perspective.

An OPUS book

REBELLION OR REVOLUTION?

G. E. Aylmer

'This is an ideal book, either to give an initial report of the state of the field, or to sum it all up . . . The conciseness and the accuracy are formidable, and so is the unfailing intellectual fairness.' Conrad Russell, *London Review of Books*

Civil war, regicide, republic, the Cromwellian protectorate, the restoration of the monarchy: some of the most exciting and dramatic events in English history took place between 1640 and 1660. Gerald Aylmer conveys the massive and continuing psychological and emotional impact of those times, and offers an up-to-date analysis of the causes, significance, and consequences of what happened.

The period was dominated by such powerful personalities as Charles I, John Hampden, John Pym, Oliver Cromwell, and John Lilburne; but Dr Alymer also attempts to discover the views of the anonymous mass of the population who lived through the political and religious upheavals of the mid-seventeenth century.

An OPUS book

WAR IN EUROPEAN HISTORY

Michael Howard

This book offers a fascinating study of warfare as it has developed in Western Europe from the warring knights of the Dark Ages to the nuclear weapons of the present day, illustrating how war has changed society and how society in turn has shaped the pattern of warfare.

'Wars have often determined the character of society. Society in exchange has determined the character of wars. This is the theme of Michael Howard's stimulating book. It is written with all his usual skill and in its small compass is perhaps the most original book he has written. Though he surveys a thousand years of history, he does so without sinking in a slough of facts and draws a broad outline of developments which will delight the general reader.' A. J. P. Taylor, *Observer*

'It is, at one and the same time, the plain man's guide to the subject, an essential introduction for serious students, and in its later stages a thought-provoking contribution.' Michael Mallet, *Sunday Times*

An OPUS book

EARLY MODERN FRANCE
1560–1715

Robin Briggs

This book provides an overall interpretation of a decisive period in French history, from the chaos of the Wars of Religion to the death of Louis XIV. A clear but economical narrative of the major political events is combined with an analysis of the long-term factors which decisively moulded the evolution of both state and society.

'A very fine, thorough and conscientious study of a formative period of French History . . . his account of the French provinces in the age of Richelieu and Louis XIV . . . is one of the best things of its kind in English.' *Sunday Telegraph*

'This vigorously-written book deserves wide use as an introduction to absolutist France.' *History*

An OPUS book